PRIVATE LIBRARIES IN RENAISSANCE ENGLAND

A Collection and Catalogue of Tudor and Early Stuart Book-Lists

Volume VII
PLRE 151–166

Medieval and Renaissance Texts and Studies

Volume 370

PRIVATE LIBRARIES IN RENAISSANCE ENGLAND

A Collection and Catalogue of Tudor and Early Stuart Book-Lists

Volume VII
PLRE 151–166

R. J. Fehrenbach
General Editor

Joseph L. Black
Editor

ACMRS
(Arizona Center for Medieval and Renaissance Studies)
Tempe, Arizona
2009

The publication of this volume has been supported by a grant from the National Endowment for the Humanities, an independent federal agency.

© Copyright 2009
Arizona Board of Regents for Arizona State University.

Library of Congress Cataloging-in-Publication Data

Private libraries in Renaissance England : a collection and catalogue of Tudor and early Stuart book-lists / R. J. Fehrenbach, general editor, E. S. Leedham-Green, editor in the United Kingdom.

v. 1--(Medieval & renaissance texts & studies : v. 87, 105, 117, 148, 189, 271, 370)

Includes bibliographical references and index.

Contents: v. 1. PLRE 1-4.--v. 2. PLRE 5-66.--v. 3. PLRE 67-86.--v. 4 PLRE 87-112.--v. 5 PLRE 113-137.--v. 6. PLRE 138-150.--v. 7. PLRE 151-166.

ISBN 0-86698-099-7, v. 1; ISBN 0-86698-151-9, v. 2; ISBN 0-86698-170-5, v. 3; ISBN 0-86698-188-8, v. 4; ISBN 0-86698-231-0, v. 5; ISBN 0-86698-314-7, v. 6; ISBN 978-0-86698-418-8, v. 7.

1. Private libraries--England--History--1400-1600--Sources. 2. Private libraries--England--History--17th-18th centuries--Sources. 3. Books and Reading--England--History--16th century--Sources. 4. Books and reading--England--History--17th century--Sources. 5. Private libraries--England--Catalogs--Bibliography. 6. Book collecting--England--History--Sources. 7. Library catalogs--England--Bibliography. I. Series.

Z997.2.G7P75 2004
017'.1'0942--dc20

91-18418

∞
This book is made to last.
It is set in Adobe Caslon,
smyth-sewn and printed on acid-free paper
to library specifications.
Printed in the United States of America

To Elisabeth Leedham-Green

who laid the foundation

Table of Contents

Table of Annotated Book-lists by PLRE Number — ix
Table of Annotated Book-lists by Owner — xi
Contributing Editors — xii
Advisory Editors — xiii
Acknowledgments — xv

Common Abbreviations
   Sources — xvii
   Degrees — xxiii

Introduction — xxv

ANNOTATED BOOK-LISTS — 1

APPENDICES
   PLRE Cumulative Catalogue — 287
   Additions and Corrections, PLRE Addresses — 311

INDICES
   Authors and Works — 319
   Editors and Compilers — 343
   Translators — 345
   Stationers — 349
   Places of Publication — 357
   Dates of Publication — 363

Table of Annotated Book-lists by PLRE Number

PLRE 151: Richard Lewis (d. c.1590) *Manciple*
STUART GILLESPIE

PLRE 152: Richard Payne (d.1597) *Scholar (B.C.L.)*
MARC L. SCHWARZ

PLRE 153: Christopher Tillyard (d.1598) *Scholar (B.A.)*
MARC L. SCHWARZ

PLRE 154: William Mitchell (d.1599) *Scholar (B.Th.)*
D. V. N. BAGCHI & JOCELYN SHEPPARD

PLRE 155: George Barton (d.1602) *Scholar (B.Th.)*
RIVES NICHOLSON

PLRE 156: Richard Fisher (d.1602) *Scholar (M.A.)*
JOSEPH L. BLACK & JULIETTE M. CUNICO

PLRE 157: William Gearing (d.1607) *Cleric (chaplain), Scholar (M.A.)*
R. J. FEHRENBACH

PLRE 158: Abel Trefry (d.1610) *Scholar*
JOSEPH L. BLACK & JULIETTE M. CUNICO

PLRE 159: Walter Brown (d.1613) *Cleric, Scholar (B.Th.)*
JOSEPH L. BLACK

PLRE 160: Edward Homer (d.1614) *Scholar (M.A.)*
STUART GILLESPIE

PLRE 161: Thomas Hudson (d.1618) *Scholar (B.A.)*
RIVES NICHOLSON

PLRE 162: Richard Kilby (d.1620) *Scholar (D.Th.)*
JOSEPH L. BLACK & R. J. FEHRENBACH

PLRE 163: John Read (d.1623) *Manciple*
RIVES NICHOLSON

PLRE 164: Anonymous (inventory, c.1650) *Scholar (probable)*
WILLIAM M. ABBOTT

PLRE 165: John Hutton (d.1652) *Scholar (B.A.)*
JOHN A. BUTLER

PLRE 166: Henry Jacob (d.1652) *Scholar (M.A., B.M.)*
RIVES NICHOLSON

Table of Annotated Book-lists by Owner

Anonymous (inventory, c.1650)	PLRE 164
George Barton (d.1602)	PLRE 155
Walter Brown (d.1613)	PLRE 159
Richard Fisher (d.1602)	PLRE 156
William Gearing (d.1607)	PLRE 157
Edward Homer (d.1614)	PLRE 160
Thomas Hudson (d.1618)	PLRE 161
John Hutton (d.1652)	PLRE 165
Richard Kilby (d.1620)	PLRE 162
Richard Lewis (d. c.1590)	PLRE 151
William Mitchell (d.1599)	PLRE 154
Richard Payne (d.1597)	PLRE 152
John Read (d.1623)	PLRE 163
Christopher Tillyard (d.1598)	PLRE 153
Abel Trefry (d.1610)	PLRE 158
Henry Jacob (d.1652)	PLRE 166

Contributing Editors

WILLIAM M. ABBOTT
Associate Professor of History, Fairfield University

D. V. N. BAGCHI
Senior Lecturer in History, University of Hull

JOSEPH L. BLACK
Associate Professor of English, University of Massachusetts Amherst

JOHN A. BUTLER
Former Professor of British Studies, Chiba University, Japan

JULIETTE M. CUNICO
Adjunct Faculty, Department of English and University Honors Program, University of New Mexico

R. J. FEHRENBACH
Professor of English, Emeritus, College of William and Mary

STUART GILLESPIE
Reader in English Literature, University of Glasgow

RIVES NICHOLSON
Assistant Librarian, Louisiana State University Libraries

JOCELYN SHEPPARD
Principal Consultant, Red House Consulting

Advisory Editors

Peter W. M. Blayney
Mark H. Curtis † 1994
W. Speed Hill
Arthur F. Kinney
Nati H. Krivatsy † 2009
F. J. Levy
James K. McConica
David McKitterick
W. B. Stephens
Laetitia Yeandle
Heather Wolfe
Georgianna Ziegler

Assistant Editors
Sandra Burr
Rives Nicholson

Consulting Editor
E.S. Leedham-Green

Consulting Editor for the Oxford Project
Simon Bailey

Acknowledgments

I remain greatly indebted to the following for financial support: the National Endowment for the Humanities, an independent federal agency; the Gladys Krieble Delmas Foundation; Katherine K. Curtis for her gift from the estate of her husband, Mark H. Curtis, one of PLRE's original Advisory Editors; Gillian T. Cell, past Provost of the College of William and Mary; and P. Geoffrey Feiss, current Provost of the College of William and Mary.

Support, however, is not limited to financial assistance. As I wrote in the first volume of this series, PLRE is a "highly collaborative and complex project," and support and collaboration have reflected that complexity. I am pleased to have the opportunity to recognize the many people who, in such different ways, have advanced this volume in particular and PLRE in general.

The Information Technology staff at the College of William and Mary repeatedly addressed technical problems invariably arising with a project so dependent on computers, providing assistance without which this project simply could not have proceeded. I am grateful to all in that department for their generous help, but I am particularly indebted to Tracey Encarnacion, Jennifer Harrison, Patty Herrera, Julie Martin, Sean Pada, Lance Richardson, and Kitty Smith. For an entirely different kind of assistance, I thank Fiona Piddock, Librarian of Lincoln College, Oxford, who provided information about Richard Kilby's gift of books to Lincoln in 1620 (see PLRE 162). Simon Bailey, Archivist of the University of Oxford, continued to provide valuable help by answering questions about the manuscript inventories at the Bodleian. I wish, however, to recognize with special thanks Heather Wolfe, Curator of Manuscripts at the Folger Shakespeare Library, for her idea to make the PLRE database available to scholars via the Folger's website, and I am deeply indebted to Michael Poston, Database Applications Associate at the Folger, for managing to turn that idea into a reality by magically transforming the original database, woefully antiquated by current computer standards, into a useful scholarly tool, *PLRE.Folger*. As a result, PLRE has been able to fulfill its originally-stated aim of being available to scholars both in print and in a searchable database.

Finally, with this volume I am pleased to welcome Joseph L. Black as Volume Editor for PLRE; he succeeds Elisabeth Leedham-Green who remains with the project as Consulting Editor. I am profoundly grateful to both for their invaluable contributions in bringing to a conclusion not only the present volume but also the editing of the Oxford book-lists, a task of nearly two decades. Conclusions, however, do not arrive without beginnings, and with the dedication of this volume I seek to recognize not only the uncommon contribution that my good friend has made to PLRE but also, in a province larger than this or any particular project, her groundbreaking work in the history of the book in early modern England.

R.J.F.
Williamsburg, Virginia
2008

Common Abbreviations

Sources

A&R A. F. Allison and D. M. Rogers. *A Catalogue of Catholic Books in English Printed Abroad or Secretly in England 1558–1640*. Bognor Regis, 1956 [Reprints 1964 and 1968].

ARCR A. F. Allison and D. M. Rogers. *The Contemporary Printed Literature of the English Counter-Reformation between 1558 and 1640*. 2 volumes. Aldershot, 1989–1994.

Adams H. M. Adams. *Catalogue of Books Printed on the Continent of Europe, 1501–1600, in Cambridge Libraries*. 2 volumes. Cambridge, 1967.

Alumni Cantabrigienses — John Venn and John Archibald Venn. *Alumni Cantabrigienses: A Biographical List of All Known Students, Graduates and Holders of Office at the University of Cambridge from the Earliest Times to 1751, Part I*. 4 volumes. Cambridge, 1922–1927 [Reprint 1974].

Alumni Oxonienses — Joseph Foster, compiler. *Alumni Oxonienses: The Members of the University of Oxford, 1500–1714, Their Parentage, Birthplace, and Year of Birth* . . . 4 volumes. Oxford, 1891–1892.

Arber *A Transcript of the Registers of the Company of Stationers of London*, edited by Edward Arber. 5 volumes. London/Birmingham, 1875–1894 [Reprint 1967].

Athenae Cantabrigienses — C. H. Cooper and T. Cooper. *Athenae Cantabrigienses*. 3 volumes. Cambridge and London, 1858–1913 [Reprint 1967].

Athenae Oxonienses — Anthony à Wood, with additions by Philip Bliss. *Athenae Oxonienses: An Exact History of All the Writers and Bishops Who Have Had Their Education in the University of Oxford. To Which Are Added the Fasti, or Annals of the Said University*. 5 volumes. London, 1813–1820.

Aureliensis *Index Aureliensis: Catalogus librorum sedecimo saeculo impressorum*. Volumes 1–15. Baden-Baden, 1965–2005 [incomplete].

Benzing	Josef Benzing. *Lutherbibliographie. Verzeichnis der gedruckten Schriften Martin Luthers bis zu dessen Tod.* Baden-Baden, 1966.
Bezzel	Irmgard Bezzel. *Erasmusdrucke des 16. Jahrhunderts in Bayerischen Bibliotheken.* Stuttgart, 1979.
BCI	E. S. Leedham-Green. *Books in Cambridge Inventories: Booklists from Vice-Chancellor's Court Probate Inventories in the Tudor and Stuart Periods.* 2 volumes. Cambridge, 1986.
BL	*General Catalogue of Books Printed to 1955* [in the British Library].
BN	*Catalogue Général des Livres Imprimés de la Bibliothèque Nationale* [Paris].
Boase	C. W. Boase, ed. *Register of the University of Oxford. Volume 1 (1449–1463; 1505–1571).* Oxford, 1885.
Bodleian	*Catalogus librorum impressorum Bibliothecae Bodleianae in Academia Oxoniensi.* 4 volumes. Oxford, 1843–1851.
BRUC	A. B. Emden. *A Biographical Register of the University of Cambridge to 1500.* Cambridge, 1963.
Brunet	Jacques-Charles Brunet. *Manuel du libraire et de l'amateur de livres.* 6 volumes. Paris, 1860–1865 [Reprint 1922] (Supplements, 2 volumes, 1878–1880).
BRUO	A. B. Emden. *A Biographical Register of the University of Oxford to AD 1500.* 3 volumes. Oxford, 1957–1959.
BRUO2	A. B. Emden. *A Biographical Register of the University of Oxford AD 1501 to 1540.* Oxford, 1974.
BSB	*Bayerische Staatsbibliothek alphabetische Katalog 1501–1840.* 60 volumes. Munich, New York, London, Paris, 1987–1990.
BT	Elly Cockx-Indestege and Geneviève Glorieux. *Belgica Typographica 1541–1600. Catalogus librorum impressorum ab anno MDXLI ad annum MDC in regionibus quae nunc Regni Belgarum partes sunt.* Nieuwkoop, 1968.
CBEL	George Watson, editor. *The New Cambridge Bibliography of English Literature [600–1660].* Volume 1. Cambridge, 1974.
CLC	David J. Shaw. *The Cathedral Libraries Catalogue: Books Printed on the Continent of Europe before 1701 in the Libraries of the Anglican Cathedrals of England and Wales.* Volume 2. 2 parts. London, 1998.
Clark	Andrew Clark, ed. *Register of the University of Oxford. Volume 2.* 4 parts (1571–1622). Oxford, 1887–1889.

Clessius	Joannes Clessius. *Unius seculi eiusque virorum literatorum monumentis tum florentissimi, tum fertilissimi, ab anno Dom. 1500 ad 1602. Nundinarum autumnalium inclusive elenchus consummatissimus librorum.* Frankfurt am Main, 1602.
Cockle	Maurice J. D. Cockle. *A Bibliography of Military Books up to 1642.* Second edition. London, 1957 [Reprint 1978].
Copinger	W. A. Copinger. *Supplement to Hain's Repertorium Bibliographicum [with supplements].* London, 1895 [–1914] [Reprints 1926 and 1950].
Cranz	F. Edward Cranz. *A Bibliography of Aristotle Editions, 1501–1600.* Second edition, with addenda and revisions by Charles B. Schmitt. Baden-Baden, 1984.
CSPD	*Calendar of State Papers: Domestic Series.*
CSPD, *Addenda*	— *Calendar of State Papers: Domestic Series, Addenda, 1580–1625.*
CTC	*Catalogus Translationum et Commentariorum: Medieval and Renaissance Latin Translations and Commentaries.* Eds. Paul Oskar Kristeller, F. Edward Cranz, and Virginia Brown. Volumes 1–8. Washington, D.C., 1960–2003 [incomplete].
DM	T. H. Darlow and H. F. Moule. *Historical Catalogue of the Printed Editions of the Holy Scripture in the Library of the British and Foreign Bible Society.* [English and Non-English] 2 volumes. London, 1903–1911. [See DMH following.]
DMH	T. H. Darlow and H. F. Moule (with revisions by A. S. Herbert). *Historical Catalogue of the Printed Editions of the Holy Scripture in the Library of the British and Foreign Bible Society.* [English; Volume 1 of DM revised] London, 1968.
DNB	*Dictionary of National Biography.*
Durling	Richard J. Durling. "A Chronological Census of Renaissance Editions and Translations of Galen." *Journal of the Warburg and Courtauld Institutes* (1961), 24:230–305.
EUL	*Catalogue of the Printed Books in the Library of the University of Edinburgh.* 3 volumes. Edinburgh, 1918–1923.
Erichson	Alfredus Erichson, ed. *Bibliographia Calviniana.* Berlin, 1900 [Reprints Nieuwkoop, 1960, 1965, and 1979].
Gardy	Frédéric Gardy. *Bibliographie des oeuvres théologiques, littéraires, historiques et juridiques de Théodore de Bèze.* Geneva, 1960.
Goff	F. R. Goff. *Incunabula in American Libraries: A Third Census* [with supplements]. New York, 1973 [Revised 1964 edition].

Greg	W. W. Greg. *A Bibliography of the English Printed Drama to the Restoration*. 4 volumes. London, 1939–1959 [Reprint 1970].
Griffiths	John Griffiths. *An Index to Wills Proved in the Court of the Chancellor of the University of Oxford, and to Such of the Records and Other Instruments and Papers of that Court as Relate to Matters of Causes Testamentary*. Oxford, 1862.
GW	*Gesamtkatalog der Wiegendrucke*. 9 volumes. Leipzig/Stuttgart, 1925–1938, 1968–1991 [incomplete].
Hain	L. Hain. *Repertorium Bibliographicum*. 2 volumes. Stuttgart, 1826–1838, 1891 [Reprints 1948 and 1966].
HC *1509–1558*	S. T. Bindoff, editor. *The House of Commons 1509–1558 (The History of Parliament)*. 3 volumes. London, 1982.
HC *1558–1603*	P. W. Hasler, editor. *The House of Commons 1558–1603 (The History of Parliament)*. 3 volumes. London, 1981.
HMC	*Historical Manuscripts Commission*.
Harris	C. R. S. Harris. *Duns Scotus*. Volume 1. Oxford, 1927.
IGI	*Indice generale degli incunaboli delle biblioteche d'Italia*. 6 volumes. Rome, 1943–1981 [incomplete].
Jayne	Sears Jayne. *Library Catalogues of the English Renaissance*. Reissue with new preface and notes. Godalming, 1983.
Keen	Ralph Keen. *A Checklist of Melanchthon Imprints Through 1560*. Sixteenth Century Bibliography 27. St. Louis, 1988.
Ker	N. R. Ker. "The Provision of Books," in *The Collegiate University*, edited by James McConica. Volume 3 of *The History of the University of Oxford*, General Editor, T. H. Aston. Oxford, 1986.
Klaiber	Wilbirgis Klaiber. *Katholische Kontroverstheologen und Reformer des 16. Jahrhunderts*. Münster, 1978.
Köhler	W. Köhler. *Bibliographia Brentiana*. Berlin, 1904 [Reprint 1963].
Labarre	Albert Labarre. *Bibliographie du Dictionarium d'Ambrogio Calepino (1502–1779)*. Baden-Baden, 1975.
Lohr II	Charles H. Lohr. *Latin Aristotle Commentaries, II. Renaissance Authors*. Florence, 1988.
Madan	Falconer Madan. *Oxford Books: A Bibliography of Printed Works Relating to the University and City of Oxford or Printed or Published There*. 3 volumes. Oxford, 1895–1931 [Reprint 1964].

McConica	James McConica. "Elizabethan Oxford: The Collegiate Society," in *The Collegiate University*, edited by James McConica. Volume 3 of *The History of the University of Oxford*, General Editor, T. H. Aston. Oxford, 1986.
NK	Wouter Nijhoff and M. E. Kronenberg. *Nederlandsche Bibliographie van 1500 tot 1540*. The Hague, 1923–1966.
NLM6	Richard J. Durling. *A Catalogue of Sixteenth Century Printed Books in the National Library of Medicine*. Bethesda, Maryland, 1967.
NLM7	Peter Krivatsy. *A Catalogue of Seventeenth Century Printed Books in the National Library of Medicine*. Bethesda, Maryland, 1989.
NUC	*National Union Catalogue. Pre-1956 Imprints.*
OED	*The Oxford English Dictionary.* 20 volumes. Second edition. Prepared by J. A. Simpson and E. S. C. Weiner. Oxford, 1989.
Oates	J. C. T. Oates. *A Catalogue of the Fifteenth-Century Printed Books in the University Library, Cambridge.* Cambridge, 1954.
ODNB	*Oxford Dictionary of National Biography* [online].
Ong	Walter J. Ong, S. J. *Ramus and Talon Inventory. A Short-Title Inventory of the Published Works of Peter Ramus (1515–1572) and of Omer Talon (ca. 1510–1562) in Their Original and in Their Variously Altered Forms.* Cambridge, Massachusetts, 1958.
PCC	*Prerogative Court of Canterbury.*
Pell	M. Pellechet and M. L. Polain. *Catalogue général des incunables des bibliothèques publiques de France.* 26 volumes. Liechtenstein, 1970 [Reprint].
Peter-Gilmont	Rodolphe Peter and Jean-Francois Gilmont. *Bibliotheca Calviniana.* 3 volumes. Geneva, 1991-2000.
Polain	Marie Louis Polain. *Catalogue de livres imprimés au XVe siècle des bibliothèques de Belgique.* 4 volumes [and supplements]. Brussels, 1931–1978.
Proctor	Robert Proctor. *An Index to the Early Printed Books in the British Museum: From the Invention of Printing to the Year MD.* 2 volumes [and supplements]. London, 1898–1906 [several reprints in the 1920s].
RRstc	James J. Murphy. *Renaissance Rhetoric: A Short-Title Catalogue of Works on Rhetorical Theory from the Beginning of Printing to A.D. 1700, with Special Attention to the Holdings of the Bodleian Library, Oxford.* New York and London, 1981.

RRstc2	Lawrence D. Green and James J. Murphy. *Renaissance Rhetoric: Short-Title Catalogue 1460-1700*. 2nd edition. Burlington, Vermont and Aldershot, UK, 2006.
Shaaber	M. A. Shaaber. *Check-list of Works of British Authors Printed Abroad, in Languages Other Than English, to 1641*. New York, 1975.
Staedtke	Joachim Staedtke. *Heinrich Bullinger Bibliographie*. Volume 1. Zürich, 1972.
Starnes	DeWitt T. Starnes. *Renaissance Dictionaries. English–Latin and Latin-English*. Austin, 1954.
STC	A. W. Pollard, G. R. Redgrave, W. A. Jackson, F. S. Ferguson, and Katherine F. Pantzer. *A Short-title Catalogue of Books Printed in England, Scotland, and Ireland and of English Books Printed Abroad, 1475–1640*. Second edition. 3 volumes. London, 1976–1991.
Stübler	Eberhard Stübler. *Leonhart Fuchs: Leben und Werk*. Munich, 1928.
VD16	*Verzeichnis der im deutschen Sprachbereich erschienenen Drucke des XVI. Jahrhunderts*. 22 volumes. Stuttgart, 1983–1995.
VHc	Ferdinand Vander Haeghen. *Bibliographie des oeuvres de Josse Clicthove*. Ghent, 1888.
VHe	Ferdinand Vander Haeghen. *Bibliotheca Erasmiana*. Ghent, 1893 [Reprints in 1961, 1972, and 1990].
Wellcome	*A Catalogue of Printed Books in the Wellcome Historical Medical Library*. Volumes 1–2. London, 1962.
Wing	Donald Wing. *Short-title Catalogue of Books Printed in England, Scotland, Ireland, Wales, and British America and of English Books Printed in Other Countries: 1641–1700*. Revised edition. 3 volumes. New York, 1972–1988.

Degrees

B.A.   Bachelor of Arts

M.A.   Master of Arts

B.C.L.   Bachelor of Civil Law

B.Cn.L. Bachelor of Canon Law

B.Gram. Bachelor of Grammar

B.M.   Bachelor of Medicine

B.Th.   Bachelor of Theology

D.C.L.   Doctor of Civil Law

D.Cn.L. Doctor of Canon Law

D.U.L.   Doctor of Civil and Canon Law (LL.D.)

D.M.   Doctor of Medicine

D.Th.   Doctor of Theology

O.P.   Ordinis Praedicatorum

Introduction

With this volume, PLRE completes publication of 162 book-lists[1] contained in the inventories taken between 1507 and 1653 under the jurisdiction of the Chancellor of Oxford University (exercised by the Vice-Chancellor), mostly for the purposes of probate. The lists are published in chronological order (see **Order** under *Methodology and Format* below); sixteen lists, dating from c. 1590 to 1653, appear in the present volume. Volume 2 of PLRE [1993] contains sixty-two lists, Volume 3 [1994] contains twenty, Volume 4 [1995] contains twenty-six, Volume 5 [1998] contains twenty-five, and Volume 6 [2004] contains thirteen lists. Like all book-lists in this Oxford series, the lists appearing in this volume are found in manuscripts in the Oxford University Archives housed in the Bodleian, specifically in the probate records and the Chancellors' Registers. These records have been made available on microfilm by Research Publications under the title *The Social History of Property and Possessions: Part I: Inventories and Wills, Including Renaissance Library Catalogues, from the Bodleian Library, Oxford, 1436–1814* (Reading, England, 1990).

Contributing Editors work from transcriptions of the manuscripts made by the late Walter Mitchell, M.A. (sometime Assistant to the Keeper of the University Archives). By granting PLRE permission to use his transcriptions, a labor of many years, Mr. Mitchell immeasurably reduced the time required to make this information available to the scholarly community. Mr. Mitchell's professional generosity placed the PLRE project and scholars working in the Tudor and early Stuart periods greatly in his debt. One list, the largest of all the Oxford book-lists, was, however, not transcribed by Mr. Mitchell and appears in this volume as PLRE 159. It was transcribed as well as edited by Joseph L. Black.

The purpose and three-part design of PLRE has been described in its first volume, to which the reader is referred for details (PLRE, Volume 1, pp. xvi–xviii). In brief, however, Part 1 of PLRE is the published form of annotated booklists associated with Tudor and early Stuart men and women; PLRE 151-166 are contained in this volume. Part 2 is in electronic form and is a cumula-

---

[1] This number differs from the total given in volume 1; in editing, several lists were identified as printer's stock or as books borrowed from colleges, not personally owned books.

tive and more detailed catalogue of those lists and others (Appended, or APND lists) previously published elsewhere. *PLRE.Folger*, the electronic form of the entire PLRE database, Volumes 1–7 and all the APND lists (as found under 2, APND LISTS in the Cumulative Catalogue at the end of PLRE volumes), can be accessed via the website of The Folger Shakespeare Library or directly at http://plre.folger.edu. Searches of the PLRE database will result in a variety of additional information about the book-lists. As it is made clear in the detailed descriptions of the published and electronic forms (PLRE, Volume 1, pp. xvi–xvii), the PLRE database and the PLRE volumes are different and complementary presentations of the material in PLRE. They are not substitutes one for the other. Part 3, the PLRE Cumulative Catalogue, is a series of indices and concordances to the complete PLRE database. This Cumulative Catalogue, which appears near the end of each volume of PLRE, is regularly enlarged and revised to incorporate newly edited book-lists.

Errors and Corrections

Anyone with even a passing acquaintance with early book-lists knows that their fragmentary and too often simply illegible entries make identifying books an extremely difficult task. Further, details of these early books resist uniformity, even when the works are identifiable; yet this information must be uniformly entered into a database to meet the categorical requirements of PLRE's design and purpose. However methodical and careful the labor, providing error-free information under such conditions is more to be wished than realized. Happily, however, the ease with which a database can be corrected promises that any misdirection PLRE may inadvertently provide will be temporary, and will encourage PLRE's users to become part of the scholarly collaboration that has always been central to the project. The editors of PLRE ask, therefore, that errors noted and corrections proposed be forwarded (with supporting evidence for the corrections) to either address following the *Additions and Corrections*.

Methodology and Format

Identification and Annotation. Identification of items, the annotations, and the bio-bibliographical introductions preceding the book-lists are the work of diverse scholars and reflect their individual research and study. But collaboration, intending to provide a reasonable uniformity, is routine at all editorial stages of the PLRE project. Consistency is necessary to avoid offering confusing information when the results of research conducted by individual scholars are combined; it is also required to meet the practical demands of a searchable database. For example, editorial consultation would discourage identifying a late sixteenth-century manuscript entry of *Elucidarius poeticus* as the school text written by Johann Gast and issued, apparently, in a single edition (1544) to the disregard of the widely published encyclopedic work of the same name by Hermann Torrentinus, appearing as it did in at least a dozen editions before 1600. If, however, a Contributing Editor has good reason to question whether such an entry represents the Torrentinus title, the Gast work, or Robert Estienne's book, another popular work of that same name, the Torrentinus identification would carry one of the standard PLRE qualifying terms, *probable* or *perhaps*. Understandably, annotations to such an item may also vary from one Contributing Editor to another.

Among the most troublesome entries to identify with consistency and uniformity are the appearances, by name only, of various widely published authors such as Virgil, Quintilian, Horace, Terence, Sallust, Lucian, and Homer. On occasion, context and supplementary information (e.g., *cum commento*) will help to identify these entries as *Works*, but generally editors choose to qualify such items with *probable* or *perhaps* if they do not list them as *Unidentified*. Similarly, when an entry consists of the name of an author popularly associated with one particular title, that work is assumed in the absence of a clear connection to one of his less well-known works, with a qualification often attached. Thus, an entry of "Agostino Dati" will usually result in an identification of *Elegantiolae*, and an entry of "Theodorus, *Gaza*" will normally result in an identification of *Institutiones grammaticae*, both usually qualified. Such differences as may appear in identifications and commentary, then, reflect the regard that PLRE has for reasonable disagreement among scholars, particularly in an area of research where the primary material is so often fragmentary and imprecise.

Order. Within each volume, the book-lists are presented in chronological order by year of the owner's death, or, if the date of death is unknown, by year of an owner's will if extant, and then alphabetically within each year. In some cases, however, the dates of death and a will are unknown; in others, documents and biographical sources disagree about the dates; and in still others, such dates are irrelevant (e.g., an inventory of books may have been compiled for purposes other than evaluating an owner's estate, with the owner dying years later). In these cases, other information, such as the date of the inventory, is used to determine the place of a booklist in PLRE order. An explanation of the determining date is parenthetically appended to each owner's name in the Table of Contents. For more complete information about the owners' dates of deaths, wills, and inventories, readers are directed to the individual introductions and to the PLRE database.

Introduction. Each book-list is preceded by an introductory essay treating biographical and bibliographical matters relating to the owner and the collection. The introduction is not intended to provide a complete analysis of the book-list, and even less a full study of the owner's life. Except where two dates are provided (e.g., 25 February 1587/88), all dates are given in new style.

Except when an owner is widely known by an early form of his name, names of owners have been regularized according to modern forms with, in many cases, variant spellings provided. Such alternate forms are derived from published sources such as BRUO, BRUO2, and *Alumni Oxonienses*; whenever the form given in BRUO or BRUO2 (the standard authorities on members of Oxford University to 1540) differs from the adopted PLRE form, it is listed first among the variants and identified. The name of the owner at the head of the introduction is followed by: the owner's profession and appropriate academic degrees (if any), the kind of source the list of books is taken from (inventory, receipt, will, etc.), and the date of that book-list.

For nearly all of these Oxford men happening to die in residence at whatever stage of their academic career, PLRE has chosen to use the generic term "scholar" to indicate their presumed avocations at the time of death and to distinguish graduates still at the University from those who had gone out into the world. Most of them would have been at least in minor orders, and a good many of them supported in their studies by the revenue of one or more benefices, but they are not here designated "clerics" except where there is some evidence that they were actively serving a cure. (Similarly, medical graduates are not designated "physician" in the absence of evidence for their actually having practiced as such.) Instead their status is indicated either by the term "student," for those who had not yet graduated, or by their degree or degrees. A Doctor of Theology who had pursued the conventional course would previously have graduated B.A., M.A., and B.Th. The dates, and any other details, of these earlier degrees will, when documented, be found in the introductions to each list, but in the headings the senior degree alone will usually be found. Two degrees are given where neither is significantly senior to the other (as in the case of a Doctor of both Civil and Canon Law), where more than one senior faculty is involved (as in the case of a theologian having also qualified in canon law), or when holding certain degrees together indicates the exercise of an option (it was, for example, possible to proceed to medical degrees either via the arts course or not: where a Bachelor of Medicine had previously graduated M.A., both degrees are shown).

Classmarks and Transcriptions. The Oxford University Archives classmark of the document containing the book-list and the source of any previously published transcriptions of the list are appended to the introduction.

Reference List. Placed between the introduction and the annotated entries and serving both, a reference list provides a bibliography of works cited in each (except for the sources found in the Common Abbreviations). The form used in the reference list is the Author-Date System of the *Chicago Manual of Style*, 13th ed., 1982, 399–435.

The List of Books. The book-list is presented, with clarifying emendations, as it appears in the manuscript. Each entry is preceded by its assigned PLRE Number.

Introduction   xxix

Entries. Each entry is composed of some or all of the following:[2]

> **PLRE Number Book-list entry**
> Name of author (alternative name of author). *Title of work*. Other contributors. Place of publication: stationer(s), date or range of dates.
> STC status. Annotations. Language(s) of book. Cost or appraised value and date of same. Current location of the book.[2]

PLRE Number. A PLRE Number is always composed of at least two numbers separated by a period. The number preceding the period identifies the place of the book-list within the PLRE catalogue, and the number following the period identifies the individual entries within that book-list. Thus, the forty-seventh item in the third book-list published in PLRE is assigned *3.47*. A PLRE Number that carries an extension (beginning with a colon) identifies an entry in the book-list that represents two or more works. If published separately, the works are assigned numeric extensions (e.g., *3.48:1* and *3.48:2*); if published together in one volume, they are assigned letters (e.g., *3.49:A* and *3.49:B*). Entries that contain unidentified multiple works are assigned an appropriate range extension (e.g., *3.50:1–4* would be used to identify "four bookes of verse"). If the number of works listed is unknown, the extension given is "multiple" (e.g., *3.51 multiple* would be used to identify "divers small bookes"). PLRE numbers in APND lists (see p. xxvi above) are preceded by *Ad*, as in *Ad4.36*.

Book-list entry. Within certain limits, book-lists are transcribed to reproduce as faithfully as possible the entries as they appear in the manuscript. The letters *u/v* and *i/j* are regularized and modernized, and thorn is transcribed *th*. Readily identifiable contractions and abbreviations are not altered (e.g., *agt*, *Mr*, and *wch*), but the less common ones, along with unusual or ambiguous spellings, are followed by an emendation placed in square brackets (e.g., *The trades inclease* is transcribed as *The trades inclease* [*increase*]). Damaged or otherwise illegible portions of the manuscript are treated similarly (e.g., *fil us* [to represent a hole between the *l* and the *u* in the manuscript] is transcribed as *fil*us* [*filius*]). Where an item is recorded as an object of bequest in a Latin will, its accusative form is retained.

Name of author (alternative name of author). Names are STC forms; for names not appearing in the STC, forms are taken from a list of Uniform Names developed by PLRE. Uniformity, as well as ease of recognition, is the goal of PLRE in establishing names. But 1) in cases where the established name differs from the form in the entry and may cause confusion for the user, and 2) in cases where two

---

[2] PLRE has attempted to avoid the use of signs and symbols; this design is most prominently seen in the use of *perhaps* and *probable* (or *probably*) to convey degrees of doubt, and of commonly employed abbreviations, such as *c.* and *et seq.*

different forms make virtually equal claims for recognition among scholars, parenthetical alternative forms are given. Examples: Nicolas Des Gallars is followed by (Nicolaus Salicetus), John Holywood by (Joannes Sacrobosco), and Nicolaus Tudeschis by (Panormitanus).

On occasion, the name of an editor will appear in this place, his role appropriately identified. *Unidentified* is used when the author cannot be identified from the entry (which is different from an identified work having been published anonymously).

Title of work. The title of a work (short title, usually terminating with the first full stop) is entered when known. Often, however, the precise title is impossible to determine from the truncated and abbreviated entries commonly found in early booklists. Further, the standard bibliographical sources (e.g., BL, Goff, Adams), on which Contributing Editors usually depend for determining titles, frequently modify the actual titles. The main principle here, then, must be to identify the *work* rather than a particular title, especially when a work has gone through several editions with varied titles. As with names, uniformity is essential if titles in the PLRE database are to be selected for analysis. Accordingly, a Uniform Titles list has been developed by PLRE along the following principles: 1) a work that exists in a single edition is identified by its short title; 2) a work that exists in two or more editions that bear only slightly varying titles is identified by one of these titles; 3) a work that exists in several editions with widely varied titles is identified by an artificial title, a) in a construction to reflect one or more of the existing titles, but b) often in a construction designed to describe the work without any attempt to simulate a title. Artificial titles are always enclosed in square brackets. Livy's [*Historiae Romanae decades*] is an example of the first kind of artificial title mentioned above (3a), and [*Aristotle—Ethica: commentary*] by Walter Burley is an example of the latter (3b). *Unidentified* is provided when the precise work represented by the entry cannot be determined.

Other contributors. The names of translators, editors, compilers, and illustrators (their contributions appropriately described) are found here. The forms used follow the same principles described in the section *Name of author* above.

Place of publication. If an entry is identified as a single edition of a single work, the city of publication is provided, regularized and modernized. If the entry represents a work of more than one edition printed in more than one city, one of three general locations is provided: *Britain* (if the identified printing houses were all in the British Isles), *Continent* (if the identified printing houses were all located on the Continent), and *Britain or Continent* (if editions were known to have been issued from different presses located in the British Isles and on the Continent). If a work is completely unidentified, the phrase *Place unknown* is used; where the place of publication of an identified book is unknown, the phrase *Place not given* is used.

For non-extant manuscripts, the phrase used is *Provenance unknown* in accordance with the generally less precise geographical origins of most surviving manuscripts. The phrase should not be interpreted as relating to previous ownership.

Stationer(s). When an entry represents a specific, identifiable edition, every stationer involved in the publication of the book (printer, publisher, bookseller) is supplied. But since Contributing Editors generally rely upon bibliographical sources rather than a copy of the identified book for this information, the forms of presentation differ. Accordingly, varied forms will be found, such as: "G. Eld for L. Lisle'" and "per Johannem Barbier, expensis Dionisii Roce," but also the nondistinguishing "George Bishop, Ralph Newberie, and Robert Barker"; the same stationer will appear in various constructions: "ap. J. Dayum," but elsewhere "John Day" and "J. Daye." All stationers, however, are accessible by uniform names in the database and in the index to stationers at the end of each volume.

When a work is identified as having been published in a single city, but the precise edition of several possibilities issued by different printing houses cannot be determined, the phrase *different houses* is given. If the place of publication is identified as *Britain*, *Continent*, or *Britain or Continent*—signifying the impossibility of determining a precise place of publication—the impossibility of determining the stationer obviously follows and this section is left blank. *Stationer unknown* is used when a work is completely unidentified or when the printer, publisher, or bookseller for a known book has not been identified by bibliographers.

Date or range of dates. If a precise date of publication is known, it is provided. If two or more editions of different dates are possibilities, either a range of dates (given as, for example, *1562–1573*) or the phrase *date not determined* is provided. NOTE: except for works listed in the STC and in Shaaber (which together offer for English authors a practical comprehensiveness if not absolute inclusiveness) date ranges must be understood to be at best a guide. The range represents the limit known to the Contributing Editor who has consulted a number of bibliographical sources, but the chance that at least one earlier or later edition exists unknown to the Contributing Editor remains a possibility. The same reservation also applies to works presented as a sole edition, and doubts, therefore, must be harbored even when a single date is given. A work, however, that is known to have gone through several editions over several years understandably invites questions about any attempt to assign a date range with certainty (excepting the few authors for whom comprehensive censuses exist). Such uncertainty is particularly a problem with authors who were widely published during this period (Aristotle, Saint Augustine, Cicero, Duns, *Scotus*, Peter Lombard, and Virgil, to name but a few). For works published in multiple editions over a great period of time even when the *editio princeps* and the latest possible edition are known, date ranges are generally not provided as not being helpful (e.g., 1485-1634) and are assigned instead the convention: *date not determined*.

STC status. A variety of self-explanatory phrases appear in this section, but the primary purpose of this information is to identify the work represented as an STC (or Wing) book. When a work is *known* to have been published both in England and on the Continent, and the edition cannot be identified, its STC (or Wing) number and its non-STC status are both cited. If, however, an entry is unidentified, nothing can be determined about its place of publication; therefore, the phrase *STC/non-STC status unknown* is used. When a work issued in more than one edition is identified as an STC (or Wing) book, but the precise edition cannot be determined, only the first possible STC (or Wing) number is given, and *et seq.* is appended.

Here also is indicated whether an entry is considered to be something other than a printed book, e.g., a manuscript or a book of blank leaves intended for use as a notebook. An entry is assumed to be a printed book unless clear evidence is provided to the contrary (the use of terms and phrases such as *scriptus, books of parchment, written sermons,* or *a book of clean paper*).

Annotations. Here Contributing Editors furnish whatever information they believe will be useful and instructive in connection with the entry. All citations are abbreviated according to the *Chicago Manual of Style*'s Author-Date System (Chapter 15); full bibliographical sources are found in the Common Abbreviations and in the Reference Lists appended to the individual introductions to book-lists.

Language(s). The language (or languages) of the book is given here. If multiple, the languages are listed, without punctuation, in alphabetical order and in the order of probability. Thus, *English Greek Latin* will be found if all are known to have been employed, but *Latin Greek (probable) English (perhaps)* when doubts of varying degrees exist. When two or more languages are of equal probability, even if the book is not likely to be in multiple languages, they are entered alphabetically with the same qualifying term as in *English* (*probable*) *Latin* (*probable*), not *English or Latin.*

Cost or appraised value and date of same. Either 1) the amount the owner paid for the book represented or 2) its appraised value as estimated by the compiler of the book-list is furnished here; the date when the amount was paid or when the appraisal was made is usually limited to a year, which always precedes the day and month when they are given.

Current location of the book. This information is restricted to the physical book cited in the booklist and should not be misunderstood to identify locations of other copies of the book. Whenever possible, the repositories are cited as they appear in the STC (1:xlix–liii), identified by name, not by symbol.

PRIVATE LIBRARIES IN RENAISSANCE ENGLAND

A Collection and Catalogue of Tudor and Early Stuart Book-Lists

Volume VII
PLRE 151–166

Richard Lewis. Manciple: Probate Inventory. c.1590

STUART GILLESPIE

Richard Lewis is identified as manciple of University College and "deceased" in the inventory of his goods dated 6 May, no year provided. Griffiths (39) dates the inventory "cir 1590," with which Jayne (129) concurs, and Ker (470n) supplies 1590 as the year of Lewis's death, which cannot be independently verified.

Lewis was on his decease manciple of University College, Oxford. PLRE 137 is a booklist for a John Lewis who was also manciple of University College, Oxford, 1556-79. There is no known connection between the two individuals, but the two lists show considerable contrasts between the libraries of two men of the same calling, time, and place. The only overlaps are the common authors Cicero, Terence, and Virgil. The collection of John Lewis is typical of what "might have been read by arts and theology graduates" (PLRE 137, Volume 5: 292) whereas his namesake Richard's is less pietistic, much more literary, and perhaps higher-brow. However, manciples were in a position to extend loans, for which books might be accepted as surety, and in Richard's case the last two listed items are noted by the scribe as being "in pawne." Hence we cannot be sure these libraries are true reflections of their owners' tastes and interests.

However, that two items were so annotated in Richard's list suggests the other forty items were not in pawn. If the rest were Lewis's own possessions, they bespeak a much more learned individual than would normally be expected of someone in the non-academic post of manciple. There is a Hebrew psalter and Greek grammars; there is theology, philosophy, rhetoric, grammar, history, and literature, among which the largely classical collection includes standard playwrights and poets. Multiple works of several authors are found (in some cases perhaps constituting a uniform set, or part of one): Cicero, Isocrates, Ovid, and Virgil. And Erasmus, represented in the earlier John Lewis inventory only by a Bible commentary, appears here as the author of the *Colloquies, Adagia,* and *De copia verborum.*

Oxford University Archives, Bodleian Library: Hyp.B.15.

§

151.1	Textoris epitheta
151.2	Plautus cum Commenta
151.3	Oswaldus in spheram
151.4	Erasm: copia verbo:
151.5	Codex Theodosiani
151.6	Codex Justiniani
151.7:1	2 Metamorphosis Ovidii
151.7:2	[See 151.7:1]
151.8	Cicero: duae oratio:
151.9	Erasmus de Copia verborum
151.10:1	Isocratis Oratio ad demonicum bis
151.10:2	[See 151.10:1]
151.11	Willichius in epistolas Pauli ad Timotheum
151.12	Organum Aristotelis
151.13	Luciani dialogi
151.14	Ceporini grammatica graeca
151.15	Salustius
151.16	Compendium Ethices per Foxium
151.17	Testamentum grece
151.18	Epistola Monlucii
151.19	Cicero: episto: familia:
151.20	Testamentum latin: Erasmi
151.21	Dialectica Caesarii
151.22	Catechismus Nowelli
151.23	Terentius
151.24	Virgilius
151.25	Sintaxis Poselli
151.26	Rudimenta grece grammatice
151.27	A boke of presidentes
151.28	Ludovicus de bello germanico
151.29:1	Ovidii Epistolae et Metamorphosis
151.29:2	[See 151.29:1]
151.30	Placo
151.31	Virgilii bucolica
151.32	Seton
151.33	Acolastus de filio prodigo
151.34:1	Oratio pro lege Manilia cum Marcello
151.34:2	[See 151.34:1]
151.35	Apthonius
151.36	Valentinius
151.37	Colloquium Erasmi

151.38   Pro Pub: sestio oratio
151.39   Cathecismus
151.40   Hebrue psalter
151.41   Tullie de oratore
151.42:1 Chiliades Erasmi and a greeke Lexicon
151.42:2 [See 151.42:1]

§

151.1   Textoris epitheta

Joannes Ravisius (Textor). [*Epitheta—Epitome*]. Britain or Continent: date not determined.

STC 20762.5 *et seq.* and non-STC. *Language(s)*: Latin. Appraised at 10d in c.1590

151.2   Plautus cum Commenta

Titus Maccius Plautus. *Comoediae*. Continent: date not determined. *Language(s)*: Latin. Appraised at 16d in c.1590

151.3   Oswaldus in spheram

Erasmus Oswald Schreckenfuchs. *Commentaria in Sphaeram Joannis de Sacrobusto*. Basle: ex officina Henricpetrina, 1569.

Contains the text of Holywood's *Sphaera mundi*. Adams S729. *Language(s)*: Latin. Appraised at 20d in c.1590

151.4   Erasm: copia verbo:

Desiderius Erasmus. *De duplici copia verborum ac rerum*. Britain or Continent: date not determined.

STC 10471.4 *et seq.* and non-STC. Another copy, perhaps two, at 151.9. *Language(s)*: Latin. Appraised at 2d in c.1590

151.5   Codex Theodosiani

Theodosius II, *Emperor of the East*. *Codex Theodosianus*. Continent: date not determined.

Language(s): Latin. Appraised at 16d in c.1590

151.6   Codex Justiniani

Justinian I. *Codex*. (*Corpus juris civilis*). Continent: date not determined. *Language(s)*: Latin Greek (perhaps). Appraised at 18d in c.1590

151.7:1   2 Metamorphosis Ovidii
Publius Ovidius Naso. *Metamorphoses*. Britain or Continent: date not determined.
STC 18951.5 *et seq.* and non-STC. See 151.29. *Language(s)*: Latin. Appraised with one other at 8d in c.1590

151.7:2   [See 151.7:1]
Publius Ovidius Naso. *Metamorphoses*. Britain or Continent: date not determined.
STC 18951.5 *et seq.* and non-STC. See 151.29. *Language(s)*: Latin. Appraised with one other at 8d in c.1590

151.8   Cicero: duae oratio:
Marcus Tullius Cicero. [*Selected works—Orations*]. Britain or Continent: date not determined.
STC 5308.3 *et seq.* and non-STC. See 151.34, 151.38. *Language(s)*: Latin. Appraised at 2d in c.1590

151.9   Erasmus de Copia verborum
Desiderius Erasmus. *De duplici copia verborum ac rerum*. Britain or Continent: date not determined.
STC 10471.4 *et seq.* and non-STC. Another copy at 151.4. Manuscript entry reads *bis*, perhaps deleted, following title, which may refer to the copy at 151.4, may indicate that two copies are represented here, or, it may have been a scribal error intended for the next item. *Language(s)*: Latin. Appraised at 2d in c.1590

151.10:1   Isocratis Oratio ad demonicum - bis
Isocrates. *Ad Demonicum*. Continent (probable): date not determined.
Probably not an STC book, but see STC 14276. With two copies, one may be English; see also STC 20054. See the next record. *Language(s)*: Latin (probable) English (perhaps). Appraised with one other at 4d in c.1590

151.10:2   [See 151.10:1]
Isocrates. *Ad Demonicum*. Continent (probable): date not determined.
Probably not an STC book, but see STC 14276. See the annotations to the preceding. *Language(s)*: Latin (probable) English (perhaps). Appraised with one other at 4d in c.1590

151.11   Willichius in epistolas Pauli ad Timotheum
Jodocus Willich. *Commentaria in utramque ad Timotheum Pauli epistolam*. Strassburg: apud Cratonem Mylium, 1542.
Language(s): Latin. Appraised at 4d in c.1590

151.12 Organum Aristotelis
Aristotle. *Organon*. Britain or Continent: date not determined.
STC 756 *et seq.* and non-STC. *Language(s)*: Latin (probable) Greek (perhaps). Appraised at 4d in c.1590

151.13 Luciani dialogi
Lucian, *of Samosata*. Unidentified. Place unknown: stationer unknown, date not determined.
STC/non-STC unknown. Whether a selected or collected edition of the *Dialogues* cannot be determined. *Language(s)*: Latin (probable) Greek (perhaps). Appraised at 4d in c.1590

151.14 Ceporini grammatica graeca
Jacobus Ceporinus. *Compendium grammaticae graecae*. Britain or Continent: date not determined.
STC 4913 *et seq.* and non-STC. *Language(s)*: Latin Greek. Appraised at 3d in c.1590

151.15 Salustius
Caius Sallustius Crispus. Unidentified. Place unknown: stationer unknown, date not determined.
STC/non-STC unknown. *Language(s)*: Latin. Appraised at 1d in c.1590

151.16 Compendium Ethices per Foxium
Sebastiano Fox Morzillo. *Ethices philosophiae compendium*. Continent: 1554–1561.
Treats Aristotle and Plato. *Language(s)*: Latin. Appraised at 4d in c.1590

151.17 Testamentum grece
[*Bible—N.T.*]. Britain or Continent: date not determined.
STC 2793 *et seq.* and non-STC. *Language(s)*: Greek. Appraised at 4d in c.1590

151.18 Epistola Monlucii
Jean de Montluc, *Bishop*. *Epistola de Andium Duce in regnum Polonicorum allegendo*. Lusignan: excudebat Ivo Durerius, 1573–1574.
See Adams M1725, where the work is mistakenly ascribed to Blaise de Monluc. *Language(s)*: Latin. Appraised at 2d in c.1590

151.19 Cicero: episto: familia:
Marcus Tullius Cicero. *Epistolae ad familiares*. Britain or Continent: date not determined.

STC 5295 *et seq.* and non-STC. *Language(s)*: Latin. Appraised at 2d in c.1590

151.20 Testamentum latin: Erasmi

[*Bible — N.T.*]. Translated by Desiderius Erasmus. Britain or Continent: date not determined.

STC 2800 *et seq.* and non-STC. *Language(s)*: Latin. Appraised at 3d in c.1590

151.21 Dialectica Caesarii

Joannes Caesarius, *Juliacensis. Dialectica.* Continent: date not determined. *Language(s)*: Latin. Appraised at 2d in c.1590

151.22 Catechismus Nowelli

Alexander Nowell. *Catechismus.* London: (different houses), 1570–1590.

STC 18701 *et seq.* Whether the larger, middle, or shorter version cannot be determined. *Language(s)*: Latin (probable) English (perhaps) Greek (perhaps). Appraised at 2d in c.1590

151.23 Terentius

Publius Terentius, *Afer.* Probably [*Works*]. Britain or Continent: date not determined.

STC 23885 *et seq.* and non-STC. *Language(s)*: Latin. Appraised at 2d in c.1590

151.24 Virgilius

Publius Virgilius Maro. Probably [*Works*]. Britain or Continent: date not determined.

STC 24787 *et seq.* and non-STC. *Language(s)*: Latin (probable) English (perhaps). Appraised at 2d in c.1590

151.25 Sintaxis Poselli

Joannes Posellius. *Syntaxis linguae graecae.* Continent: 1565–1589. *Language(s)*: Greek Latin. Appraised at 2d in c.1590

151.26 Rudimenta grece grammatice

Unidentified. Continent (probable): date not determined.

Probably not an STC book, but see STC 6044a. Aldus Manutius's Greek grammar, issued once under the title *Rudimenta grammatices*, is possible, but it was published in 1501 (Venice), almost certainly too early for this list. Also possible are Richard Croke, *Introductiones in rudimenta graeca* and Georgius Macropedius, *Graecarum institutionum rudimentum*, both published decades after Manutius's work. *Language(s)*: Greek Latin. Appraised at 1d in c.1590

151.27   A boke of presidentes
A book of precedents. London: (different houses), 1543–1588.

STC 3327 *et seq.* Several editions include a preface by Thomas Phaer, and the work as a whole is often attributed to him. *Language(s)*: English. Appraised at 3d in c.1590

151.28   Ludovicus de bello germanico
Luis de Avila. *Commentariorum de bello Germanico libri duo.* Translated by Gulielmus Malineus. Antwerp: in aed. Joan. Steelsii, 1550.

Aureliensis gives two editions, same place and publisher. *Language(s)*: Latin. Appraised at 4d in c.1590

151.29:1   Ovidii Epistolae et Metamorphosis
Publius Ovidius Naso. *Heroides.* Continent: date not determined.

See 151.7:12. Conceivably this entry represents two items from an edition of Ovid's *Works*, collected or selected. If two discrete books entered as one, the second could have been published in England. *Language(s)*: Latin. Appraised with one other at 3d in c.1590

151.29:2   [See 151.29:1]
Publius Ovidius Naso. *Metamorphoses.* Continent (probable): date not determined.

Probably not an STC book. See the annotations to the preceding. *Language(s)*: Latin. Appraised with one other at 3d in c.1590

151.30   Placo
Probably Plato. Unidentified. Continent: date not determined.

Joannes Plactomus, primarily a medical writer, is unlikely but should be considered. *Language(s)*: Greek (probable) Latin (probable). Appraised at 3d in c.1590

151.31   Virgilii bucolica
Publius Virgilius Maro. [*Bucolics*]. Britain or Continent: date not determined.

STC 24814 *et seq.* and non-STC. English translation possible but unlikely given the form of entry. *Language(s)*: Latin. Appraised at 2d in c.1590

151.32   Seton
John Seton. Probably *Dialectica.* London (probable): 1545–1584.

STC 22250 *et seq.* By far his most often published work. *Language(s)*: Latin (probable). Appraised at 3d in c.1590

151.33   Acolastus de filio prodigo

Gulielmus Fullonius (Gulielmus Gnapheus). *Acolastus de filio prodigo*. Britain or Continent: date not determined.

STC 11469.5 and non-STC. *Language(s)*: Latin. Appraised at 2d in c.1590

151.34:1   Oratio pro lege Manilia cum Marcello

Marcus Tullius Cicero. *Pro lege Manilia*. Continent: date not determined.

Conceivably a small collection rather than two separate items. *Language(s)*: Latin. Appraised with one other at 1d in c.1590

151.34:2   [See 151.34:1]

Marcus Tullius Cicero. *Pro Marcello*. Continent: date not determined.

See the annotation to the preceding. *Language(s)*: Latin. Appraised with one other at 1d in c.1590

151.35   Apthonius

Aphthonius, *Sophista*. *Progymnasmata*. Britain or Continent: date not determined.

STC 699 *et seq.* and non-STC. *Language(s)*: Latin. Appraised at 4d in c.1590

151.36   Valentinius

Unidentified. Continent (probable): date not determined.

Probably not an STC book. Gregorius de Valentia and Ascanius Valentinius are two possibilities. *Language(s)*: Latin (probable). Appraised at 3d in c.1590

151.37   Colloquium Erasmi

Desiderius Erasmus. *Colloquia*. Britain or Continent: date not determined.

STC 10450.6 *et seq.* and non-STC. *Language(s)*: Latin. Appraised at 1d in c.1590

151.38   Pro Pub: sestio oratio

Marcus Tullius Cicero. *Pro Sestio*. Continent: date not determined. *Language(s)*: Latin. Appraised at 1d in c.1590

151.39   Cathecismus

Unidentified [catechism]. Place unknown: stationer unknown, date not determined.

STC/non-STC status unknown. *Language(s)*: Latin (probable). Appraised at 1d in c.1590

151.40   Hebrue psalter

[*Bible — O.T. — Psalms*]. Continent: date not determined.

Perhaps a liturgical psalter. *Language(s)*: Hebrew. Appraised at 4d in c.1590

151.41   Tullie de oratore
Marcus Tullius Cicero. *De oratore*. Britain or Continent: date not determined.
STC 5290 *et seq*. and non-STC. *Language(s)*: Latin. Appraised at 3d in c.1590

151.42:1   Chiliades Erasmi and a greeke Lexicon
Desiderius Erasmus. *Adagia*. Continent: date not determined.
The compiler is not likely to have entered an English translation in this manner. This item is described with 151.42:2 as being *in pawne* in the inventory, presumably deposited by Lewis as sureties against a loan. *Language(s)*: Latin. Appraised with one other at 10s in c.1590

151.42:2   [See 151.42:1]
Unidentified [dictionary]. Continent: date not determined.
This item is described with 151.42:1 as being *in pawne* in the inventory, presumably deposited by Lewis as sureties against a loan. The first Greek dictionary printed in England was published in 1619; see STC 21805.9. *Language(s)*: Greek. Appraised with one other at 10s in c.1590

PRIVATE LIBRARIES IN RENAISSANCE ENGLAND 152

Richard Payne. Scholar (B.C.L.):
Probate Inventory. 1597

MARC L. SCHWARZ

Richard Payne (Paine, Payn) was a scholar at New College in 1568 and was admitted B.C.L. at that college on 27 June 1576 (Clark 2: iii, 63; *Alumni Oxonienses*, 3:1129). Foster in the *Alumni Oxonienses* entry notes that someone of this name was vicar of Bredon in Worcestershire in 1591–92. An inventory of Payne's goods was taken on 23 November 1597 following his death, and he is described in that manuscript inventory as "Richard Paine, bachiler of the civill law, of Hart Hall." His will was proved at Oxford on 9 November 1597, when he was also identified as being of Hart Hall (*Alumni Oxonienses* and Griffiths, 47).

More than half the identified books in Payne's collection are standard works of theology (including Calvin's *Institutes* in French) and most of the remainder are standard works of law. Rounding out the library are Plutarch in French, Du Bartas's *Sepmaine* in either French or English, and four groups of unidentified works: two bundles of pamphlets (one of works in French, the other probably works of theology), some "old Bookes" (possibly on canon law), and "a company of ould schole bookes and Pamphlitts."

Oxford University Archives, Bodleian Library: Hyp.B.17.

§

152.1:1   4 Bibles
152.1:2   [See 152.1:1]
152.1:3   [See 152.1:1]
152.1:4   [See 152.1:1]
152.2:1 multiple   Calvin uppon the greater and lesser prophitts
152.2:2   [See 152.2:1]
152.3:1–2 Bilson 2 volum: and D. Reinold:
152.3:3   [See 152.3:1–2]

152.4:1   Hadden contra Osorium, Beza in the 3 Chap. of Canticles uppon the epistles Jeuell liffe and Apologie
152.4:2   [See 152.4:1]
152.4:3   [See 152.4:1]
152.4:4   [See 152.4:1]
152.4:5   [See 152.4:1]
152.5   Concilii Tridentini Examen octavo
152.6 multiple   A parcell of pamphitts
152.7   Calvins sermon uppon his harmony of the evangelistes
152.8   Calvins Institucions in French
152.9:1   Statutes 3 volum: with Littleton's tenures
152.9:2   [See 152.9:1]
152.10:1 Vigelius uppon the Digestes and his Dialectica Juris
152.10:2 [See 152.10:1]
152.11   Corpus Juris civilis cum glossa
152.12   Institutes
152.13   Corpus cum glossa
152.14   Vocabularium
152.15 multiple   A number of old Bookes
152.16 multiple   A number of French pamphittes
152.17   Plutarkes workes in French, quarto
152.18   Haebrew gramer, psalter, lexicon
152.19   Cousins Apology
152.20   Bartas his Weekes
152.21 multiple   A company of ould schole bookes and Pamphlitts

§

152.1:1   4 Bibles
The Bible. Britain or Continent: date not determined.
STC 2055 *et seq.* and non-STC. A heading "Divinitie books" precedes the section containing 152.1–152.8. At least one of the four Bibles would doubtless be in Latin. Since several of Payne's books are described as being in French, one of the four might be in that language. *Language(s)*: English (probable) Latin (probable) French (perhaps). Appraised with three others at 26s 8d in 1597.

152.1:2   [See 152.1:1]
The Bible. Britain or Continent: date not determined.
STC 2055 *et seq.* and non-STC. See the annotations to 152.1:1. *Language(s)*: English (probable) Latin (probable) French (perhaps). Appraised with three others at 26s 8d in 1597.

152.1:3   [See 152.1:1]
The Bible. Britain or Continent: date not determined.
STC 2055 *et seq.* and non-STC. See the annotations to 152.1:1. *Language(s)*: English (probable) Latin (probable) French (perhaps). Appraised with three others at 26s 8d in 1597.

152.1:4   [See 152.1:1]
The Bible. Britain or Continent: date not determined.
STC 2055 *et seq.* and non-STC. See the annotations to 152.1:1. *Language(s)*: English (probable) Latin (probable) French (perhaps). Appraised with three others at 26s 8d in 1597.

152.2:1 multiple   Calvin uppon the greater and lesser prophitts
Jean Calvin. Unidentified. Place unknown: stationer unknown, date not determined.
STC/non-STC status unknown. The first part of this manuscript entry is taken to be two or more of Calvin's commentaries on the books of Isaiah, Jeremiah, and Ezekiel. The valuation suggests a large collection. *Language(s)*: English (probable) French (probable) Latin (probable). Appraised with others at 10s in 1597.

152.2:2   [See 152.2:1]
Jean Calvin. [*Minor prophets: commentary*]. Geneva: (different houses), 1559–1581.
Language(s): French (probable) Latin (probable). Appraised with others at 10s in 1597.

152.3:1–2   Bilson 2 volum: and D. Reinold:
Thomas Bilson, *Bishop*. Unidentified. Britain: date not determined.
Unidentifiable in the STC. *Language(s)*: English. Appraised with one other at 6s in 1597.

152.3:3   [See 152.3:1–2]
John Rainolds. Unidentified. Place unknown: stationer unknown, date not determined.
Unidentifiable in the STC. The "D." (Doctor) in the manuscript entry identifies the author as John Rainolds. *Language(s)*: English (probable) Latin (probable). Appraised with two others at 6s in 1597.

152.4:1   Hadden contra Osorium, Beza in the 3 Chap. of Canticles upon the epistles Jeuell liffe and Apologie
Walter Haddon. *Contra Hieron. Osorium, . . . responsio apologetica.* London: ex off. J. Daii, 1577.

STC 12593. The manuscript entry suggests the Latin version. An English translation was published in 1580. *Language(s)*: Latin. Appraised with four others at 6s in 1597.

152.4:2   [See 152.4:1]

Théodore de Bèze. *Sermons upon the three first chapters of the Canticle of Canticles.* Translated by John Harmar, *the Elder.* Britain: J. Barnes, sould [in London by T. Cooke], 1587.

STC 2025 and non-STC. Barnes was an Oxford printer. *Language(s)*: English. Appraised with four others at 6s in 1597.

152.4:3   [See 152.4:1]

Caspar Olevian. [*Galatians: commentary*]. Edited by Théodore de Bèze. Geneva: apud Eustathium Vignon, 1578–1581.

Bèze did not publish a commentary on the Epistles, and this work of Olevian's that he edited leads with *In Epistolam D. Pauli. . ..* Gardy (p. 174) cites two additional editions, 1579 and 1585 without providing a source or location. All other sources cite only the two represented by the date-range given here. *Language(s)*: Latin. Appraised with four others at 6s in 1597.

152.4:4   [See 152.4:1]

Laurence Humphrey. *Joannis Juelli Angli, episcopi Sarisburiensis vita et mors; verae doctrinae defensio.* London: apud J. Dayum, 1573.

STC 13963. The only biography of Jewel existing by the date of this inventory; the manuscript entry (*Jeuell liffe*), then, is descriptive, not an indication of language. See the notes to the following (152.4:5). *Language(s)*: Latin. Appraised with four others at 6s in 1597.

152.4:5   [See 152.4:1]

John Jewel, *Bishop. An apologie, or aunswer in defence of the Church of England.* London: R. Wolfe, 1562–1564.

STC 14590 *et seq.* Since the only "liffe" of Jewel that existed at this time was in Latin (see the preceding), this item could also be in Latin despite the manuscript entry that suggests English. If both in Latin, conceivably then Shaaber J168, a single volume, in which this work appears as well as the preceding along with Jewel's attack on Thomas Harding. *Language(s)*: English. Appraised with four others at 6s in 1597.

152.5   Concilii Tridentini Examen octavo

Martinus Chemnitius. *Examen concilii Tridentini.* (*Councils — Trent*). Continent: date not determined.

There was a single edition of a 1586 work with this title by Innocent Gentillet published in octavo, but Chemnitz's book was widely published, usually in folio, but sometimes in multi-volume octavo editions. The valuation suggests something more than an individual octavo book. *Language(s)*: Latin. Appraised at 4s in 1597.

152.6 multiple   A parcell of pamphitts
Unidentified. Places unknown: stationers unknown, dates not determined.
STC/non-STC status unknown. Assumed to be a collection of theological pamphlets. See the annotation to 152.1:1. *Language(s)*: Unknown. Appraised as a group at 6s in 1597.

152.7   Calvins sermon uppon his harmony of the evangelistes
Jean Calvin. *A harmonie upon the three evangelists, Matthew, Mark, and Luke.* (*Bible—N.T.*). Translated by Eusebius Pagit. London: (T. Dawson), imp. G. Bishop, 1584.
STC 2962. A commentary on the Gospel of John is also included, translated by Christopher Fetherstone. *Language(s)*: English. Appraised at 20d in 1597.

152.8   Calvins Institucions in French
Jean Calvin. *Institution de la religion chrestienne.* Continent: date not determined.
Language(s): French. Appraised at 20d in 1597.

152.9:1   Statutes 3 volum: with Littleton's tenures
Unidentified. [*England—Statutes*]. London: (different houses), date not determined.
STC 9347 *et seq*. A heading "Law common" precedes this entry. *Language(s)*: English Latin Law French. Appraised with one other at 13s 4d in 1597.

152.9:2   [See 152.9:1]
Sir Thomas Littleton. [*Tenures*]. Britain or Continent: date not determined.
STC 15719 *et seq*. *Language(s)*: English (probable) Law French (probable). Appraised with one other at 13s 4d in 1597.

152.10:1   Vigelius uppon the Digestes and his Dialectica Juris
Nicolaus Vigelius. *Digestorum pars prima (-septima).* (*Corpus juris civilis*). Basle: ex off. Oporiniana, 1567–1584.
The heading "Civill Lawe" precedes the group of books from 152.10:1 to 152.12. *Language(s)*: Latin. Appraised with one other at 13s 4d in 1597.

152.10:2   [See 152.10:1]
Nicolaus Vigelius. *Dialectices juris civilis libri III.* Basle: (different houses), 1573–1597.
Language(s): Latin. Appraised with one other at 13s 4d in 1597.

152.11   Corpus Juris civilis cum glossa

Justinian I. *Corpus juris civilis*. Continent: date not determined.
Language(s): Latin Greek (perhaps). Appraised at 13s 4d in 1597.

152.12   Institutes

Justinian I. *Institutiones*. (*Corpus juris civilis*). Continent: date not determined.
Language(s): Latin Greek (perhaps). Appraised at 12d in 1597.

152.13   Corpus cum glossa

Corpus juris canonici. Continent: date not determined.
This item is preceded by the heading "Canon lawe"; it can apply only to this item, the next, and perhaps the group of "old Bookes" that then follows. *Language(s)*: Latin. Appraised at 23s in 1597.

152.14   Vocabularium

Probably *Vocabularius juris utriusque*. Continent: date not determined.
Given the heading "Canon lawe," no other work is as likely. *Language(s)*: Latin. Appraised at 18d in 1597.

152.15 multiple   A number of old Bookes

Unidentified. Places unknown: stationers unknown, dates not determined.
STC/non-STC status unknown. Conceivably books on canon law; see the annotation to 152.13. *Language(s)*: Unknown. Appraised as a group at 3s 4d in 1597.

152.16 multiple   A number of French pamphittes

Unidentified. Places unknown: stationers unknown, dates not determined.
STC/non-STC status unknown. *Language(s)*: French. Appraised as a group at 2s in 1597.

152.17   Plutarkes workes in French, quarto

Plutarch. Perhaps [*Works*]. Translated by Jacques Amyot, *Bishop*. Paris: (different houses), date not determined.
Identifying the clear manuscript entry, "Plutarkes workes in French, quarto," as Plutarch's "Works" ironically poses problems. If the item is actually Plutarch's "workes in French," then it must be two or more independently published titles grouped together since Plutarch's collected *opera* was not published in French by the date of this inventory. Further, Amyot's translation of the *Moralia* bore the title: *Les oeuvres morales & meslees*, the lead words conceivably prompting the compiler to list the item as Plutarch's *Works*. The French editions of the *Moralia* that could possibly be in this collection, however, were printed in folio or octavo, and the compiler describes this book as quarto, a description that cannot

be totally ignored. Finally, it is also possible that the compiler casually described the French *Vitae parallelae*, Plutarch's most widely published collection, as the author's "workes." Initially appraised at 8*d*, then altered. *Language(s)*: French. Appraised at 8s in 1597.

152.18   Haebrew gramer, psalter, lexicon
Petrus Martinius. [*Mafteah leshon ha-kodesh*]. Translated by John Udall. Leyden: F. Raphelengius, 1593.
STC 17523. The title is transliterated from the Hebrew. The long title continues: ". . . wherein is conteineid, first the Hebrue grammar out of P. Martinius. Secondly, a practize upon the psalmes. Thirdly, a short dictionary." The possibility remains, however, that the compiler was describing three separate works. *Language(s)*: English Hebrew. Appraised at 3s in 1597.

152.19   Cousins Apology
Richard Cosin. *An apologie: of, and for sundrie proceedings*. London: Deputies of C. Barker, 1591–1593.
STC 5820 *et seq*. Only the 1593 edition includes Latin. *Language(s)*: English Latin (perhaps). Appraised at 20d in 1597.

152.20   Bartas his Weekes
Guillaume de Saluste du Bartas. [*Weekes*]. London: (stationer unknown), date not determined.
Unidentifiable in the STC. Most of du Bartas's works were not published in English until after the date of this inventory, and certainly the complete set of *Divine weeks* did not appear until the seventeenth century. This manuscript entry, however, strongly suggests a book or books in English. Which of the parts published in English represented here cannot be determined. See STC 21658 and 21662. Whether Payne's book is in English, especially given that his collection includes so many French works, cannot be determined for certain. *Language(s)*: English (probable). Appraised at 2s in 1597.

152.21 multiple   A company of ould schole bookes and Pamphlitts
Unidentified. Places unknown: stationers unknown, dates not determined.
STC/non-STC status unknown. *Language(s)*: Unknown. Appraised at 30s in 1597.

Christopher Tillyard. Scholar (B.A.): Probate Inventory. 1598

MARC L. SCHWARZ

Christopher Tillyard (Tilleard, Tilliard, Tilyard, Tillyarde, Tyllyarde) matriculated from Christ Church on 11 February 1592, "aged 17," and proceeded B.A. at Brasenose College on 22 February 1595 (*Alumni Oxonienses*, 4:1488). An inventory of his goods compiled after his decease was made sometime before 31 July 1598 (Griffiths, 61) and exhibited by his mother, Elizabeth Pory, who was the widow of William Tillyard according to an inscription in St. Mary's Church, Oxford, as recorded by Anthony Wood (Clark [Wood] 1899, 3:122). The owner of the books listed below is buried within that church with his family (Clark [Wood] 1899, 3:122).

Tillyard's library offers a small collection of standard works of theology, philosophy, rhetoric, logic, grammar, and classical literature; the collection of five "Singinge bookes" adds the lone more personal note.

Oxford University Archives, Bodleian Library: Hyp.B.19.

§

Clark, Andrew, ed. 1899. "*Survey of the Antiquities of the City of Oxford*," *Composed in 1661–6 by Anthony Wood*. Vol 3. Oxford: Printed for the Oxford Historical Society at the Clarendon Press.

§

153.1 natalis comitis
153.2 tullis orations
153.3 donet upon the Ethickes
153.4 Juels Apologie
153.5 vallerius maximus

153.6   parkins upon the Lordes prayer
153.7   Saundersons lodgike
153.8   a testament in lattin
153.9   Tullie de oratori
153.10   Ovedes metamorphoses
153.11   Osorius agaynst Haddon
153.12   Aristotles Ethickes
153.13:1   2 pallengenius
153.13:2   [See 153.13:1]
153.14   Aristotles lodgicke
153.15   Cammerarious upon tusculus questions
153.16   An answere of the bishop of winchester
153.17   Silva sinonimorum
153.18:1   Apthonius and Clares gramer
153.18:2   [See 153.18:1]
153.19:1   hiperius phisickes and gouldin Chayne
153.19:2   [See 153.19:1]
153.20   Horrace minutiosum epistols
153.21 multiple   Other ould bookes
153.22:1–5   5 Singinge bookes

§

153.1   natalis comitis

Natalis Comes. Unidentified. Continent: date not determined.
Language(s): Latin. Appraised at 2s 6d in 1598.

153.2   tullis orations

Marcus Tullius Cicero. [*Selected works—Orations*]. Britain or Continent: date not determined.
STC 5308 *et seq.* and non-STC. *Language(s)*: Latin. Appraised at 2s 6d in 1598.

153.3   donet upon the Ethickes

Donatus Acciaiolus. [*Aristotle—Ethica: commentary*]. Continent: date not determined.
Language(s): Latin. Appraised at 10d in 1598.

153.4   Juels Apologie

John Jewel, *Bishop. An apologie, or aunswer in defence of the Church of England.* London: R. Wolfe, 1562–1564.

STC 14590 *et seq.* The manuscript entry suggests the English, not the Latin, version. *Language(s)*: English. Appraised at 10d in 1598.

153.5 vallerius maximus

Valerius Maximus. *Facta et dicta memorabilia.* Continent: date not determined.
Language(s): Latin. Appraised at 8d in 1598.

153.6 parkins upon the Lordes prayer

William Perkins. *An exposition of the Lords prayer, in the way of catechising.* Britain: 1592–1597.

STC 19699.5 *et seq.* This may very well be the rare first and unauthorized edition (STC 19699.5), swiftly repudiated by Perkins (STC 16700), since that unauthorized edition was titled *Perkins upon the Lords praier*, a phrase that does not appear on the title pages of the authorized editions. *Language(s)*: English. Appraised at 8d in 1598.

153.7 Saundersons lodgike

John Sanderson. *Institutionum dialecticarum libri quatuor.* Antwerp: ex officina Christopheri Plantini, 1589.

No extant edition published in England exists by the date of this inventory, though two Oxford editions (1590 and 1594) have been cited (see DNB), and the Oxford, 1602, edition is identifed on the titlepage as *editio tertia*; see Shaaber S30. *Language(s)*: Latin. Appraised at 6d in 1598.

153.8 a testament in lattin

[*Bible—N.T.*]. Britain or Continent: date not determined.

STC 2799 *et seq.* and non-STC. *Language(s)*: Latin. Appraised at 6d in 1598.

153.9 Tullie de oratori

Marcus Tullius Cicero. *De oratore.* Britain or Continent: date not determined.

STC 5290 *et seq.* and non-STC. *Language(s)*: Latin. Appraised at 4d in 1598.

153.10 Ovedes metamorphoses

Publius Ovidius Naso. *Metamorphoses.* Britain or Continent: date not determined.

STC 18951 *et seq.* and non-STC. *Language(s)*: Latin (probable) English (perhaps). Appraised at 4d in 1598.

153.11   Osorius agaynst Haddon

Jeronimo Osorio da Fonseca, *Bishop*. *A learned and very eloquent treatie* [sic], *writen in Latin by H. Osorius, wherein he confuteth a certayne aunswere made by M. W. Haddon*. Translated by John Fen. Louvain: apud J. Foulerum, 1568.

STC 18889 and non-STC. The manuscript entry suggests an English edition, but a Latin version is possible. *Language(s)*: English. Appraised at 6d in 1598.

153.12   Aristotles Ethickes

Aristotle. *Ethica*. Britain or Continent: date not determined.

STC 752 *et seq.* and non-STC. The manuscript entry is in English, but a scholar was likely to have had a Latin, or even a Greek, version. See 153.14 and 153.15 where a definitely non-English text is entered in English titular form. *Language(s)*: Latin (probable) English (perhaps). Appraised at 10d in 1598.

153.13:1   2 pallengenius

Marcellus Palingenius (Pietro Angelo Manzolli [Stellatus]). *Zodiacus vitae*. Britain or Continent: date not determined.

STC 19138.5 *et seq.* and non-STC. For another copy, see the following (153.13:2). *Language(s)*: Latin (probable) English (perhaps). Appraised with one other at 6d in 1598.

153.13:2   [See 153.13:1]

Marcellus Palingenius (Pietro Angelo Manzolli [Stellatus]). *Zodiacus vitae*. Britain or Continent: date not determined.

STC 19138.5 *et seq.* and non-STC. With two editions, the chance increases that one is English. *Language(s)*: Latin (probable) English (probable). Appraised with one other at 6d in 1598.

153.14   Aristotles lodgicke

Aristotle. [*Selected works—Logica*]. Continent: date not determined. *Language(s)*: Latin. Appraised at 10d in 1598.

153.15   Cammerarious upon tusculus questions

Joachim Camerarius, *the Elder*. [*Cicero—Quaestiones Tusculanae: commentary*]. Continent: date not determined.

Language(s): Latin. Appraised at 8d in 1598.

153.16   An answere of the bishop of winchester

Probably Robert Horne, *Bishop*. *An answeare made by Rob. bishoppe of Wynchester, to a booke entituled, The declaration of suche scruples, touching the othe of supremacy, as J. Fekenham, by wrytinge did deliver*. London: H. Wykes, 1566.

STC 13818. Given the construction of the manuscript entry ("*of* the bishop of winchester"), the item is identifed as a work likely with "answer" in the title written by one who is Bishop of Winchester at the time of publication. This work by Horne fits better than any other, and the exchange between Horne and Feckenham, *Abbot of Westminster*, who refused to take the Oath of Supremacy, was widely distributed. The Feckenham work is included in this book. *Language(s)*: English. Appraised at 4d in 1598.

153.17   Silva sinonimorum

Simon Pelegromius. *Synonymorum sylva*. Britain or Continent: 1548–1598.

STC 19556 *et seq*. and non-STC. *Language(s)*: English Latin. Appraised at 4d in 1598.

153.18:1   Apthonius and Clares gramer

Aphthonius, *Sophista. Progymnasmata*. Britain or Continent: date not determined.

STC 699 *et seq*. and non-STC. *Language(s)*: Latin. Appraised with one other at 6d in 1598.

153.18:2   [See 153.18:1]

Perhaps Nicolaus Clenardus. [*Institutiones linguae graecae*]. Britain or Continent: date not determined.

STC 5400.5 *et seq*. *Language(s)*: Greek Latin. Appraised with one other at 6d in 1598.

153.19:1   hiperius phisickes and gouldin Chayne

Andreas Gerardus, *Hyperius*. [*Aristotle — Physica: paraphrase*]. Britain or Continent: 15741585.

STC 758 and non-STC. A peculiar coupling of works. Almost certainly not bound together. *Language(s)*: Latin. Appraised with one other at 8d in 1598.

153.19:2   [See 153.19:1]

Probably William Perkins. *A golden chaine, or the description of theologie, containing the order of the causes of salvation and damnation according to Gods woord*. Translated by Robert Hill. Britain: 1591–1597.

STC 19657 *et seq*. The less often published, *A golden chaine, taken out of the psalmes of King David* (STC 21235) by Thomas Rogers is another possibility. See the annotation to the preceding. *Language(s)*: English. Appraised with one other at 8d in 1598.

153.20   Horrace minutiosum epistols

Quintus Horatius Flaccus. *Epistolarum libri duo et in eas praelectiones methodicae per C. Minoem*. Commentary by Claude Mignault. Paris: apud Aegidium Beys (excud. Dionysius Duvallius), 1584.

A second issue in 1584 does not carry Beys's name. *Language(s)*: Latin. Appraised at 6d in 1598.

153.21 multiple   Other ould bookes

Unidentified. Places unknown: stationers unknown, dates not determined.

STC/non-STC status unknown. *Language(s)*: Unknown. Appraised at 2s 6d in 1598.

153.22:1–5   5 Singinge bookes

Unidentified. Places unknown: stationers unknown, dates not determined.

STC/non-STC status unknown. *Language(s)*: Unknown. Appraised at 12d in 1598.

PRIVATE LIBRARIES IN RENAISSANCE ENGLAND 154

William Mitchell, Scholar (B.Th.)
Probate inventory and bequest, 1599

D.V.N. BAGCHI AND JOCELYN SHEPPARD

Mitchell (Michell, Mytchell, Michel) was a fellow of the Queen's College, Oxford. The books listed at his death at the age of about forty point to a man of decidedly Protestant, and specifically Reformed, allegiance; but they also suggest accomplishments in the broad range of humane learning, including the classics, history, politics, mathematics, botany, and medicine, that were expected of a scholar and a gentleman in the late sixteenth century.

Mitchell went up to Oxford from Westmorland in 1581. His choice of the Queen's College was no doubt determined by its historic association with northwest England. He entered university life relatively late (his age at matriculation is recorded as 22), but his timing was fortunate. Archbishop Grindal was shortly to die and to bequeath not only a grammar school at St Bees for natives of Cumberland and Westmorland, but also scholarships for them at Queen's (Collinson 1979, 280). Mitchell was elected one of the college's first two Grindal Scholars in 1583/4 (Magrath 1921, 1:228). He graduated Bachelor of Arts in 1585, and Master of Arts in 1588 (being made fellow in December of that year), and proceeded to the Bachelor of Theology degree eight years later (*Alumni Oxonienses* 3:1009; Magrath 1921, 2:229).

Mitchell's probate inventory has attracted attention for a variety of reasons. It was one of the last substantial Oxford inventories in which the titles of books were individually listed, before the ownership of large private libraries became so widespread that it was more practical to appraise the entire collection *en bloc* (Ker, 471). The list also illustrates the "increasing stress on the later Calvinist writers and English authors" that characterized the Reformed camp by the end of the sixteenth century (Dent 1983, 98). It is generously stocked with, in descending order, the commentaries and controversial works of Bèze, Zanchius, Junius, Piscator, Daneau, Chemnitius, and Marlorat, along with a leavening of Lutheran authorities. The strong representation of homegrown authors includes

Bilson, Udall, and Travers. Among earlier authorities, Aquinas stands out; but the almost complete absence of early church fathers is remarkable. This fact may place Mitchell among the more advanced Protestants of his day, or it may simply reflect the readier availability of patristic editions in college libraries.

Mitchell's collection incorporated the largest library of works by classical historians among the wills proved at the vice-chancellor's court (Curtis 1959, 136). His interest in more recent history is indicated by the presence of Philippson (Sleidanus), Camden, and Stow. Bodin's *De republica* and Machiavelli's *De principe* and the *Discorsi* put Mitchell in the company of others in the Oxford of his day who took a more than common interest in current political theory (Curtis, 137). It has been written of Mitchell that "[a]mong the 245 books left among his effects, there are enough in Greek to suggest that a *theologus* of no particular reputation or distinction might be expected, by the 1590s, to have a practised command of the language" (Greenslade 1986, 315). The presence of several Greek grammars and a significant number of texts in both Greek and Latin may give a clue to how Mitchell picked up his Greek, while the Hebrew grammars and the Hebrew text of Genesis indicate that he was at least on his way to trilingualism at the time of his death.

Three of the Zanchius titles (the *Tractationum theologicarum volumen* [154.32], the *De operibus Dei* [154.35] and the commentary on Ephesians [154.34]) were donated to Queen's College Library from Mitchell's estate (Queen's College Ms 566). The relative meagerness of this gift should not be taken to suggest lack of gratitude to his alma mater on Mitchell's part so much as the fact that the library's holdings of Reformed theology were already so complete. Grindal's benefaction of 1583 had ensured that Queen's was, with Magdalen, the greatest Protestant library of Elizabethan Oxford (Dent 1983, 96–97). Although eighty of Grindal's books are still *in situ*, Mitchell's three Zanchius titles had passed out of the Library's possession by the time a guard book was compiled in the nineteenth century (*ex inf.* Amanda Saville, Librarian of the Queen's College).

Oxford University Archives, Bodleian Library: Hyp.B.16.

§

Collinson, Patrick. 1979. *Archbishop Grindal, 1519–1583*. London: Jonathan Cape.
Curtis, Mark. 1959. *Oxford and Cambridge in Transition, 1558–1642*. Oxford: Clarendon Press.
Dent, C.M. 1983. *Protestant Reformers in Elizabethan Oxford*. Oxford University Press.
Greenslade, S.L. 1986. "The Faculty of Theology," in *The Collegiate University*, ed. James McConica. Volume 3 in *The History of the University of Oxford*, gen. ed. T.H. Aston. Oxford: Clarendon Press, pp. 295–334.

Magrath, John R. 1921. *The Queen's College*, 2 vols. Oxford: Clarendon Press.

§

154.1	Eusebius fol.
154.2	Demosthenes fol.
154.3	T. Livius fol.
154.4	Biblia Junii fol.
154.5	Bellar. 3bus vol. fol.
154.6	Cemnitii Exa: fol
154.7	Sadielei opera fol.
154.8	Lexicon Bas: fol.
154.9	Dixtionarium Cal. fol.
154.10	Marlorat. in nov. test
154.11:1	Aretius in Evan. et Acta fol.
154.11:2	[See 154.11:1]
154.12	Aretius in Epist. fol.
154.13	Aquinatis Catena fol.
154.14	Idem [Aquinatis] in Epistol. fol.
154.15	The Rhemist testa fol.
154.16	Lavat. in proverbia et ecclesiasten fol.
154.17	Mollerus in psal: fol.
154.18	Pelican: in Evang et acta fol.
154.19	Zwinglius in Nov test. fol.
154.20	Whitgift and Cartw: fol.
154.21	Bezae nov. testa: fol.
154.22	P. Martyr in Judic. fol
154.23	English bible fol.
154.24	Calvini opera 10 vol. fol
154.25	Teleman Hesus: in psal fol.
154.26	Stapul: in Log: fol.
154.27	Idem [Stapulensis] in phys. fol.
154.28	Servius in virg. folio
154.29	Rossinus de antiq: Rom. fol
154.30	Plutarch: Vita Engl: fol.
154.31	Coperi dictionar.
154.32	Zanch: de redemp:
154.33	Idem [Zanchius] de trib: Eloem
154.34	Idem [Zanchius] in Epist.
154.35	Idem [Zanchius] de creat:
154.36	Cic opera 2bus vol.
154.37	Lambin in Horat.
154.38	plautus

154.39	Arist. phys. Grece
154.40	Britannia Camdeni
154.41	Stoe his Cronicle
154.42	Guliel. parisiensis
154.43	Baroes Method
154.44	antid. Wickeri
154.45	Organ. pacii
154.46	Clenard: gramm. greca.
154.47	Serm. disc. de tempore
154.48	Liber cartaceus
154.49	Udall upon the Lament.
154.50	Dering upon Heb.
154.51	Beza upon can.
154.52	Wilcocks in prov.
154.53	Idem [Wilcox] in psal.
154.54	Luther. in Gal. eng.
154.55	Cemnitii Har: 2bus vol.
154.56	Eiusdem [Chemnitii] loci communes 3bus vol.
154.57	Bells motives
154.58	Juel in Har: per Witak.
154.59	Synops: Willet
154.60	Text: Epith
154.61	Zanch: Cate.
154.62	Raynoldi Idol.
154.63	Idem [Raynoldi] in Hartum
154.64	The Remonst.
154.65	Bilson church gvt.
154.66	Beza et Sarav.
154.67	Beza de divers. grad. minist
154.68:1	Junius in Gen: et Danielem
154.68:2	[See 154.68:1]
154.69	Idem [Junius] in exodum
154.70	Anlys. Typ.
154.71	Offic Cic cum commentariis
154.72	Marlo: in Gen. 2bus vol
154.73	Daneus in minor. prophet.
154.74	Ecumenius in Epist.
154.75	Rolochus in Epist Rom.
154.76	Juel in Epist Thess.
154.77	Beza de resur.
154.78	Idem [Beza] de passione
154.79	Zanch. de sacra scrip
154.80	Zanch. de incarnat

154.81	Melanth. loci communes
154.82	Junius de Theologica
154.83	Arist. Eth. grecolat
154.84	Lawneus epitom. inst. Cal.
154.85	Mornaeus de virit chris. releg
154.86	Beza de controvers in caena domini
154.87	Aretius: examen theol.
154.88	Zanchii loci communes
154.89:1	Spicil. [spicilegium] in prov: et eccles
154.89:2	[See 154.89:1]
154.90	Bilson contra Alanum
154.91	Babington upon the commandments
154.92	Idem [Babington] upon the Lo: prayer
154.93	A Conferenc twixt Frailty and Faith
154.94	Calvini catech
154.95 multiple	divers catechis: bound together
154.96	Resolut. pars utraque
154.97	Basting. Catechis. Engl.
154.98	parei Catech. 2bus vol
154.99	English Bible.
154.100	Hieron. biblia
154.101	Marlorati loci communes
154.102	Danaeus in orat. dominicam
154.103	piscator in Matth.
154.104	piscator in reliquos evangelistas
154.105	piscator in Epist. Rom. et Corinth.
154.106	Piscat. in reliquas Epistolas
154.107	Serranus in Ecclesiastem
154.108	2ex translatio in psal.
154.109	Hyperius de rat. studii theol.
154.110	Zepperus
154.111	Amandus polan.
154.112	August. de Haeres.
154.113	fenneri loci communes
154.114	Trident. Catech.
154.115	petrus Lombardus
154.116	Melchioris Cani Loci communes
154.117	Wilcocks in cantic
154.118	Hemingii catech.
154.119	vocabularius utriusque Juris
154.120	Scaliger de subtil.
154.121	Fernel. 2bus vol.
154.122	Bodini de repub.

154.123	Isocr: grece et Lat.
154.124	Herodian gre. et Lat.
154.125	Suetonius
154.126	pomponis Mela
154.127	Valer. Ma.
154.128	Justin. Hist.
154.129	Sleiden. de 4or monarch.
154.130	Casar. Comment.
154.131	Thucid.
154.132	Curtius
154.133	Herodotus
154.134	pagnini thesaur.
154.135	Vigandi gramm. Heb.
154.136	Udalls gramm. Heb.
154.137	Martin: Gramm Heb.
154.138	Ceporin gramm. Grae.
154.139	Rami gram. Grae.
154.140:1	Horat. bis
154.140:2	[See 154.140:1]
154.141	Virgil
154.142	Terentius
154.143	Sabinus in ovid Metamorph
154.144	Ovidii Epist
154.145	Sophocles Latin
154.146	Homer Odyss: greco lat
154.147	Eiusdem. [Homer] Il. greco. lat
154.148	Licosthenis aphth.
154.149	A rth: ad Heren.
154.150	Quintillian
154.151	fonsecae Logica
154.152	Alexander ab Alexand.
154.153	Latina grammatica lillii
154.154	Danaeus in Bell 2bus vol.
154.155	Spangenbergius in Epist
154.156	Eobani Hessi psalterium
154.157	ferus in exodum et
154.158	Machiovel princeps
154.159	Eiusdem [Macchiavelli] discursus.
154.160	frigii logica et
154.161	Goclenius in Eth
154.162	Idem [Goclenius] in phys.
154.163	Mantuanus.
154.164	Manutii Epist.

154.165 Arist. Rhetorica
154.166 Arist. phys
154.167 Rodolphi dial.
154.168 Institut. Justin.
154.169 codex Juris civ
154.170 Ascami Epist
154.171 Purbachii Theor.
154.172 conputus astro. Skonbordii
154.173 proclus de sphera
154.174 Bakers Arith.
154.175 Erasmi Adagia
154.176 Summa conciliorum
154.177 Palingenius
154.178 Canitii Summa
154.179 Liber cartatius follio
154.180 Irvin, paraleisis
154.181 Cordius de pharmacis
154.182 Schola Salerni
154.183 Lemnius
154.184 Pindarus
154.185 Salust
154.186 Elianus var. Hist
154.187 Aesopi fab. graece et lat.
154.188 Enchirid. pro animabus regendis
154.189 Beza upon Job.
154.190 Aquinas in Job:
154.191 frig questiones geom
154.192 The reformed cathol
154.193 Muffett upon the prov
154.194 Concil: Trident
154.195 piscator in Acta
154.196 Concilii Trident gravamina
154.197 Sandersoni Logica
154.198 Juris quo utimur Epitome
154.199 An introduction to the Script
154.200 Gemma fabri
154.201 Ecclesiastica disciplina
154.202 Junii politia et
154.203 Enchirid catecheticon
154.204 first part of the key of phy
154.205 ferus in Job.
154.206 Reward of religion
154.207 Harmonia confessionum 4to

154.208	Perkins his Creed
154.209	Juells Lyfe
154.210	liber cartaceus
154.211	A table of the bible
154.212	Talaeus Rhetorick
154.213	Marclinus Rhet
154.214	Macropedius
154.215	Rami Logica
154.216	Scribonii Logica
154.217	Rami Logica
154.218	Busbequius
154.219	De esculentis et poculentis
154.220	Caninius grammar graec
154.221	De inferno tractatus
154.222	Antichoppinus
154.223	Sebastians phy.
154.224	Perkins de praedestinatione
154.225	De unica ratione concionandi
154.226	The government of the tonge
154.227	Treatise of repentance
154.228	Ramea rhetorica
154.229	Sanctuary of salvacion
154.230	7. paenitentiall psalmes
154.231	Junii Eirenicum
154.232	Junius in Epist Judae
154.233	D. Rainolds sermon
154.234	Another sermon
154.235	Beza in Seraviam
154.236	Beza de justificatione
154.237	Hermannus Renniccerus
154.238	Junius de peccato originali
154.239	Piscatoris Antidromus
154.240	Nilus de primatu Papae
154.241	Livelei annotationes quosdam prophetas
154.242	Death of Usury
154.243	Genesis Haebraice
154.244	Lauren: Valla
154.245	Jo: Cant. Archiep. perspectivae
154.246	testamentum graec 16
154.247	Bible englishe 4to

§

154.1 Eusebius fol.

Eusebius, *Pamphili, Bishop.* Probably [*Works*]. Continent: date not determined.

His major works, as distinct from the *opera*, were also published in the folio format. *Language(s)*: Latin. Appraised at 10s in 1599.

154.2 Demosthenes fol.

Demosthenes. [*Works*]. Continent: date not determined.
Language(s): Greek (probable) Latin (probable). Appraised at 16s in 1599.

154.3 T. Livius fol.

Titus Livius. [*Historiae Romanae decades*]. Continent: date not determined.

No folio editions were published in England. *Language(s)*: Latin. Appraised at 11s in 1599.

154.4 Biblia Junii fol.

The Bible. Translated and edited by Joannes Immanuel Tremellius and Franciscus Junius, *the Elder*. Britain or Continent: date not determined.

STC 2061 *et seq.* and non-STC. Earlier editions published in England were not in folio. *Language(s)*: Latin. Appraised at 10s in 1599.

154.5 Bellar. 3bus vol. fol.

Roberto Bellarmino, *Cardinal. Disputationes de controversiis christianae fidei, adversus nostri temporis haereticos.* Continent: 1586–1599.

The first volume of this work appeared in 1586 with the third appearing in 1593; individual volumes were reissued throughout the nineties. An edition of all three volumes, however, was published in 1599. The extraordinarily high valuation given to the three volumes here—exceeded only by the 38*s* valuation of the ten folio volumes of Calvin at 154.24—might suggest that this was a copy of the then new 1599 three-volume edition. Appraised at 36s in 1599. *Language(s)*: Latin.

154.6 Cemnitii Exa: fol

Martinus Chemnitius. *Examen concilii Tridentini. (Councils—Trent).* Frankfurt am Main: (different houses), date not determined.
Language(s): Latin. Appraised at 8s in 1599.

154.7 Sadielei opera fol.

Antoine La Roche de Chandieu (Antonius Sadeel). [*Works*]. Continent: date not determined.
Language(s): Latin. Appraised at 8s in 1599.

154.8 Lexicon Bas: fol.

Unidentified [*dictionary*]. Basle: (stationer unknown), date not determined.
Language(s): Latin Greek (perhaps). Appraised at 5s in 1599.

154.9 Dixtionarium Cal. fol.

Ambrogio Calepino. *Dictionarium*. Continent: date not determined.

Other vernacular languages as well, depending on the edition. *Language(s)*: Latin English (perhaps) Greek (perhaps) Hebrew (perhaps). Appraised at 4s in 1599.

154.10 Marlorat. in nov. test

Augustine Marlorat. *Novi testamenti catholica expositio ecclesiastica*. (Bible). Geneva: (different houses), 1561–1593.
Language(s): Latin. Appraised at 16s in 1599.

154.11:1 Aretius in Evan. et Acta fol.

Benedictus Aretius. [*Gospels: commentary*]. Continent: 1580–1596.
Language(s): Latin. Appraised, with one other, at 8s in 1599.

154.11:2 [See 154.11:1]

Benedictus Aretius. [*Acts: commentary*]. Continent: 1579–1596.
Language(s): Latin. Appraised, with one other, at 8s in 1599.

154.12 Aretius in Epist. fol.

Benedictus Aretius. [*Epistles and Revelation: commentary*]. Continent: 1583–1596.
Language(s): Latin. Appraised at 1s in 1599.

154.13 Aquinatis Catena fol.

Thomas Aquinas, *Saint*. [*Gospels: commentary*]. Continent: date not determined.
Language(s): Latin. Appraised at 5s in 1599.

154.14 Idem [Aquinatis] in Epistol. fol.

Thomas Aquinas, *Saint*. [*Epistles—Paul: commentary*]. Continent: date not determined.
Language(s): Latin. Appraised at 4s in 1599.

154.15 The Rhemist testa fol.

[*New Testament: text and commentary*]. (Bible). Translated by Gregory Martin, with commentary by William Fulke. London: Deputies of C. Barker, 1588.

STC 2888. The Rheims version (STC 2884) in parallel columns with the Bishops' Bible version, with confutations of the former by William Fulke; the only folio edition of the Rheims New Testament by the date of this inventory.
Language(s): English. Appraised at 8s 6d in 1599.

154.16 Lavat. in proverbia et ecclesiasten fol.

Ludwig Lavater. [*Proverbs, Ecclesiastes: commentary and text*]. (*Bible — O.T.*). Zürich: apud Christophorum Froschouerum, 1586.

Sole edition. *Language(s)*: Latin. Appraised at 3s 6d in 1599.

154.17 Mollerus in psal: fol.

Henricus Mollerus. [*Psalms: commentary*]. Geneva: apud Franciscum le Preux, 1591.

The sole folio edition by the date of this inventory. *Language(s)*: Latin. Appraised at 8s in 1599.

154.18 Pelican: in Evang et acta fol.

Conradus Pellicanus. [*Gospels, Acts: commentary*]. Zürich: Christoph Froschouer, 1537–1582.

Part of his *Commentaria Bibliorum*. *Language(s)*: Latin. Appraised at 4s 6d in 1599.

154.19 Zwinglius in Nov test. fol.

Ulrich Zwingli. [*New Testament: commentary*]. Zürich: Christoph Froschouer, 1545–1581.

The fourth volume of Zwingli's *opera*. Not on the entire New Testament. *Language(s)*: Latin. Appraised at 5s in 1599.

154.20 Whitgift and Cartw: fol.

John Whitgift, *Archbishop* and Thomas Cartwright. *The defense of the aunswere to the Admonition, against the Replie*. London: H. Binneman for H. Toye, 1574.

STC 25430 *et seq*. The book consists of large parts of Cartwright's *Replie* followed by Whitgift's refutations. See BCI, 2:799 for a series of similar manuscript entries for this work. Two editions were published in the same year. *Language(s)*: English. Appraised at 4s in 1599.

154.21 Bezae nov. testa: fol.

[*Bible — N.T.*]. Translated by Théodore de Bèze. Continent: date not determined.

Bèze's New Testament was included in a folio edition of the complete Bible (STC 2061 *et seq*.) but was not published in England separately in folio. *Language(s)*: Greek Latin. Appraised at 16s in 1599.

154.22 P. Martyr in Judic. fol

Pietro Martire Vermigli (Peter Martyr). [*Judges: commentary*]. Continent: date not determined.

Not appraised. *Language(s)*: Latin.

154.23 English bible fol.
The Bible. Britain or Continent: date not determined.
STC 2063 *et seq.* Folio editions from 1535. *Language(s)*: English. Appraised at 8s in 1599.

154.24 Calvini opera 10 vol. fol
Jean Calvin. Unidentified. Continent (probable): date not determined.
Probably not STC books. An edition of Calvin's *opera*, as such, was not published by the date of this inventory. Even if this made-up set contained all titles of Calvin published in folio in England by the date of this inventory (the *Institutes* and his sermons on Deuteronomy and on Job), the bulk of these ten volumes would had to have come from Continental printing houses, and if in Latin, all would have. *Language(s)*: Latin English (perhaps). Appraised at 38s in 1599.

154.25 Teleman Hesus: in psal fol.
Tilemannus Heshusius, *Bishop*. [*Psalms: commentary*]. Hemlstadt: excud. Jacobus Lucius, 1586–1587.
Language(s): Latin. Appraised at 6s in 1599.

154.26 Stapul: in Log: fol.
Jacobus Faber, *Stapulensis*. [*Aristotle—Selected works—Logica: commentary*]. Continent: date not determined.
Language(s): Latin. Appraised at 3s in 1599.

154.27 Idem [Stapulensis] in phys. fol.
Jacobus Faber, *Stapulensis*. [*Aristotle—Physica: commentary and paraphrase*]. Continent: date not determined.
Language(s): Latin. Appraised at 3s in 1599.

154.28 Servius in virg. folio
Publius Virgilius Maro. [*Works*]. With commentary by Servius Maurus Honoratus. Continent: date not determined.
Not appraised, with a cross in the margin, perhaps indicating that this book was not Mitchell's. *Language(s)*: Latin.

154.29 Rossinus de antiq: Rom. fol
Joannes Rosinus. *Romanarum antiquitatum corpus absolutissimum.* Continent: 1583–1585.
Language(s): Latin. Appraised at 4s in 1599.

154.30 Plutarch: Vita Engl: fol.
Plutarch. *The lives of the noble Grecians and Romanes.* Translated by Sir Thomas North. London: (different houses), 1579–1595.

STC 20065 *et seq. Language(s)*: English. Appraised at 9s in 1599.

154.31   Coperi dictionar.

Thomas Cooper, *Bishop*. *Thesaurus linguae Romanae et Britannicae*. London: (different houses), 1565–1584.

STC 5686 *et seq. Language(s)*: English. Appraised at 5s in 1599.

154.32   Zanch: de redemp:

Hieronymus Zanchius. *Tractationum theologicarum volumen*. Neustadt an der Haardt: ex officina Josuae et Wilhelmi fratrum Harnisiorum, 1597.

Though the compiler lists only Zanchius's *De redemptione* here, for several reasons the manuscript entry is taken to represent the *Tractationum theologicarum volumen*. First, *De redemptione* was published only as part of the larger work; second, the valuation would be extremely high for part of a book separated from the whole volume; and third, along with 154.34 and 154.35, Mitchell bequeathed the *Tractionum theologicarum volumen* to Queen's College, evidence that he owned the complete volume. The compiler is assumed either to have opened the volume to *De redemptione* or to have been reading from a running title. See 154.35. *Language(s)*: Latin. Appraised at 5s 6d in 1599.

154.33   Idem [Zanchius] de trib: Eloem

Hieronymus Zanchius. *De tribus Elohim*. Continent: 1572–1589.

Language(s): Latin. Appraised at 4s in 1599.

154.34   Idem [Zanchius] in Epist.

Hieronymus Zanchius. *In D. Pauli epistolam ad Ephesios, commentarius*. (*Bible—N.T*). Neustadt an der Haardt: excudebat Matthaeus Harnisius, 1594.

The manuscript entry could represent either Zanchius's commentary on Ephesians or his larger work on Philippians, Colossians, and Thessalonians; both lead with *In D. Pauli epistolam . . .*, and both were published in folio. Mitchell, however, owned Zanchius's commentary on Ephesians since he bequeathed a copy to Queen's College along with 154.32 and 154.35. *Language(s)*: Latin. Appraised at 1s in 1599.

154.35   Idem [Zanchius] de creat:

Hieronymus Zanchius. *De operibus Dei intra spacium sex dierum creatis opus*. Neustadt an der Haardt: typis Matthaei Harnisii, 1591.

Mitchell bequeathed this work to Queen's College along with 154.32 and 154.34. This edition is the only folio edition of the work published by the date of this inventory. The word "redempt" is struck through and replaced by "creat:"; see 154.32. *Language(s)*: Latin. Appraised at 4s in 1599.

154.36 Cic opera 2bus vol.
Marcus Tullius Cicero. [*Works*]. Continent: date not determined.
Though a 1585 edition of Cicero's selected works printed in England carries the title *Opera omnia*, it is not in quarto format, which the compiler assigns here along with the following thirty-six entries. *Language(s)*: Latin. Appraised at 9s 6d in 1599.

154.37 Lambin in Horat.
Quintus Horatius Flaccus. [*Works*]. Edited with a commentary by Dionysius Lambinus. Continent: date not determined.
Quarto editions range at least from 1561 to 1596. *Language(s)*: Latin. Appraised at 4s 6d in 1599.

154.38 plautus
Titus Maccius Plautus. *Comoediae*. Continent: date not determined.
At this valuation, not an individual play. *Language(s)*: Latin. Appraised at 6s in 1599.

154.39 Arist. phys. Grece
Aristotle. *Physica*. Continent: date not determined.
Language(s): Greek. Appraised at 1s in 1599.

154.40 Britannia Camdeni
William Camden. *Britannia sive florentissimorum regnorum, Angliae, Scotiae, Hiberniae chorographica descriptio*. London: [Eliot's Court Press] for G. Bishop, 1594.
STC 4506. The only quarto edition, as the book is identified by the compiler, by the date of this inventory. *Language(s)*: Latin. Appraised at 2s 8d in 1599.

154.41 Stoe his Cronicle
John Stow. [*Chronicles and annals*]. London: (different houses), 1580–1584.
STC 23333 *et seq*. Ralph Newbery was involved in printing both editions. A manuscript entry, *liber cartaceus 9 s* follows but is struck through. *Language(s)*: English. Appraised at 5s in 1599.

154.42 Guliel. parisiensis
Gulielmus, *Parisiensis, Professor*. Unidentified. Place unknown: stationer unknown, date not determined.
STC/non-STC status unknown. Less likely Gulielmus, *Arvernus, Bishop of Paris*. *Language(s)*: Latin. Appraised at 3s in 1599.

154.43 Baroes Method
Philip Barrough. *The methode of phisicke*. London: (different houses), 1590–1596.
STC 1509 *et seq*. Richard Field printed both editions, but Robert Dexter was involved with the 1596 edition. *Language(s)*: English. Appraised at 1s 8d in 1599.

154.44 antid. Wickeri
Hanss Jacob Wecker. Unidentified. Basle: (stationer unknown), date not determined.
Whether his *Antidotarium generale*, his *Antidotarium speciale*, or the composite edition of both, all issued in quarto at Basle, cannot be determined. *Language(s)*: Latin. Appraised at 2s in 1599.

154.45 Organ. pacii
Aristotle. *Organon*. With commentary by Julius Pacius. Continent: date not determined.
Language(s): Greek Latin. Appraised at 2s in 1599.

154.46 Clenard: gramm. greca.
Nicolaus Clenardus. [*Institutiones linguae graecae*]. Continent: date not determined.
No quarto edition was issued in England by the date of this inventory. *Language(s)*: Greek Latin. Appraised at 1s 8d in 1599.

154.47 Serm. disc. de tempore
Joannes Herolt (Discipulus). [*Sermones discipuli*]. Britain or Continent: date not determined.
STC 13226 and non-STC. The sole edition published in England eighty-nine years earlier is probably not likely at this valuation. *Language(s)*: Latin. Appraised at 2s in 1599.

154.48 Liber cartaceus
Unidentified. Provenance unknown: date not determined.
Manuscript. *Language(s)*: Unknown. Appraised at 1s 8d in 1599.

154.49 Udall upon the Lament.
John Udall. [*Lamentations: commentary and paraphrase*]. (*Bible—O.T.*). London: (different houses) for T. Man, 1593–1599.
STC 24494 *et seq*. *Language(s)*: English. Appraised at 2s 4d in 1599.

154.50 Dering upon Heb.
Edward Dering. [*Hebrews: commentary*]. London: (different houses), 1576–1597.
STC 6726 *et seq. Language(s)*: English. Appraised at 1s in 1599.

154.51 Beza upon can.
Théodore de Bèze. *Sermons upon the three first chapters of the Canticle of Canticles.* Translated from the French by John Harmar, *the Elder.* Oxford: J. Barnes, sould [in London by T. Cooke], 1587.
STC 2025. *Language(s)*: English. Appraised at 1s in 1599.

154.52 Wilcocks in prov.
Thomas Wilcox. *A short, yet sound commentarie; written on the Proverbes of Salomon.* London: T. Orwin for T. Man, 1589.
STC 25627. *Language(s)*: English. Appraised at 2s in 1599.

154.53 Idem [Wilcox] in psal.
Thomas Wilcox. [*Psalms: commentary*]. London: (different houses), 1586–1591.
STC 25625 *et seq.* Thomas Man was involved with both editions. *Language(s)*: English. Appraised at 2s in 1599.

154.54 Luther. in Gal. eng.
Martin Luther. [*Galatians: commentary*]. London: (different houses), 1575–1588.
STC 16965 *et seq.* Thomas Vautrollier printed all editions; the 1588 edition was in collaboration with the bookseller William Norton. *Language(s)*: English. Appraised at 1s 6d in 1599.

154.55 Cemnitii Har: 2bus vol.
Martinus Chemnitius. *Harmonia evangelica.* Edited by Polykarp Leyser. Frankfurt am Main: excudebat J. Spies, 1593.
Language(s): Latin. Appraised at 5s 6d in 1599.

154.56 Eiusdem [Chemnitii] loci communes 3bus vol.
Martinus Chemnitius. *Loci theologici.* Frankfurt am Main: excud. Johann Spies, 1591–1594.
Both editions were three-volume quartos. *Language(s)*: Latin. Appraised at 6s 8d in 1599.

154.57 Bells motives
Thomas Bell. *Thomas Bels motives: concerning romish faith.* London: J. Legate, pr. to the Univ. of Cambridge, sold in London [by Ab. Kitson], 1593.

STC 1830. *Language(s)*: English. Appraised at 2s in 1599.

154.58 Juel in Har: per Witak.

John Jewel, Bishop. *Joannis Juelli . . . adversus Thomam Hardingum, volumen*. Translated into Latin by William Whitaker. London: T. Vautrollierus, imp. T. Chardi, 1578–1588.

STC 14607.5 *et seq*. According to the STC, the 1588 edition may in fact have been printed in 1578 with the later date a misprint. Also printed on the Continent but in folio format. *Language(s)*: Latin. Appraised at 2s in 1599.

154.59 Synops: Willet

Andrew Willet. *Synopsis papismi, that is, a generall viewe of papistry*. London: (different houses), 1592–1594.

STC 25696 *et seq*. The second edition was an expanded list of Roman Catholic "errors." Thomas Man was involved as a stationer in both editions with different members of the Orwin printing family. *Language(s)*: English. Appraised at 4s 6d in 1599.

154.60 Text: Epith

Joannes Ravisius (Textor). *Epitheta*. Continent: date not determined.

Only the epitome was published in England by the date of this inventory, and that not in quarto. *Language(s)*: Latin. Appraised at 2s in 1599.

154.61 Zanch: Cate.

Hieronymus Zanchius. *De religione christiana fides*. Neustadt an der Haardt: excudebat Matthaeus Harnisch, 1585 (probable).

Not properly a catechism but rather a confession of faith divided into subjects and responses much as a catechism is. The only quarto edition by the date of this inventory; some sources give 1586 as the publication date. *Language(s)*: Latin. Appraised at 1s 6d in 1599.

154.62 Raynoldi Idol.

John Rainolds. *De romanae ecclesiae idololatria* [sic], *in cultu sanctorum, reliquiarum . . . libri duo*. Britain or Continent: 1596.

STC 20606 and non-STC. Published in Oxford and in Geneva in the same year. *Language(s)*: Latin. Appraised at 2s 4d in 1599.

154.63 Idem [Raynoldi] in Hartum

John Rainolds and John Hart, Jesuit. *The summe of the conference betwene J. Rainoldes and J. Hart*. London: (different houses), 1584–1598.

STC 20626 *et seq*. Despite the language of the manuscript entry, this necessarily is the English translation; the two Latin editions were published well after the date of this inventory, in octavo and folio. The compiler indicates quarto here.

The work is a report of a conference that the Protestant Rainolds had with Hart, an imprisoned Roman Catholic priest and Jesuit. The book was published with Hart's approval and, to that degree, Hart should be considered a collaborator. An English translation of STC 20624 (Rainolds's *Sex theses de sacra scriptura, et ecclesia*) is included. Finally, George Bishop had a stationer's role in both editions. *Language(s)*: English. Appraised at 2s 6d in 1599.

154.64   The Remonst.

A remonstrance: or plaine detection of faults in a booke, entituled, a demonstration of discipline. London: G. Bishop and R. Newberie, 1590.

STC 20881. Sometimes attributed to Matthew Sutcliffe, it was a response to STC 24499, John Udall's *Demonstration of discipline*. *Language(s)*: English. Appraised at 3s in 1599.

154.65   Bilson church gvt.

Thomas Bilson, *Bishop. The perpetual governement of Christes church.* London: Deputies of C. Barker, 1593.

STC 3065. *Language(s)*: English. Appraised at 1s 4d in 1599.

154.66   Beza et Sarav.

Hadrianus Saravia. *Defensio tractationis de diversis ministrorum evangelii gradibus, contra Responsionem T. Bezae.* London: Reg. typog. [Deputies of C. Barker and Eliot's Court Press], 1594.

STC 21748. This book includes selections from Saravia's *De diversis ministrorum evangelii gradibus* and selections from Théodore de Bèze's response to Saravia, *Ad tractationem De ministrorum evangelii gradibus* (see 154.235) as well as Saravia's rebuttal of Bèze. See the next record. *Language(s)*: Latin. Appraised at 1s 8d in 1599.

154.67   Beza de divers. grad. minist

Probably Hadrianus Saravia. *De diversis ministrorum evangelii gradibus.* London: G. Bishop and R. Newberie, 1590.

STC 21746. The manuscript entry is necessarily in error. Bèze's work (his reply to Saravia; see 154.235) was published only in octavo (this item appears in a quarto listing), and his title does not contain anything that could be represented by the word *divers*. On the other hand, Saravia's work was published in quarto (one octavo edition in Frankfurt am Main in 1593), and its title better fits what the compiler entered. The compiler, apparently aware of the exchange between Saravia and Bèze (again, see the preceding), erroneously entered the latter's name. *Language(s)*: Latin. Appraised at 2s 4d in 1599.

154.68:1 Junius in Gen: et Danielem

François Du Jon, *the Elder*. *Libri Geneseos analysis*. Heidelberg: in officina Sanctandreana, 1594.
Language(s): Latin. Appraised at 2s 8d in 1599.

154.68:2 [See 154.68:1]

François Du Jon, *the Elder*. *Expositio prophetae Danielis*. Place unknown: excudebat Gabriel Carterius, 1594.
Supplied locations include Geneva, Heidelberg, Leyden, and Lyon. *Language(s)*: Latin. Appraised at 2s 8d in 1599.

154.69 Idem [Junius] in exodum

François Du Jon, *the Elder*. *Libri II. Mosis, qui Exodus vulgo inscribitur, analytica explicatio*. Leyden: ex officina Plantiniana, apud Franciscum Raphelengium, 1597.
Language(s): Latin. Appraised at 8d in 1599.

154.70 Anlys. Typ.

Moses Pflacher. *Analysis typica omnium cum veteris tum novi Testamenti librorum historicorum*. Britain or Continent: date not determined.
STC 19826 and non-STC. A 1595 Tübingen edition is variously described as folio, quarto, and octavo by the bibliographical and library sources. The only edition uniformly identified as quarto size is the 1587 London edition. *Language(s)*: Latin. Appraised at 2s in 1599.

154.71 Offic Cic cum commentariis

Marcus Tullius Cicero. *De officiis*. Continent: date not determined.
No quarto editions were issued from English presses by the date of this inventory. *Language(s)*: Latin. Appraised at 5s in 1599.

154.72 Marlo: in Gen. 2bus vol

Augustine Marlorat. [*Genesis: commentary and text*]. (*Bible—O.T.*). Morges: (stationer not given), 1584.
This item marks the beginning of a group of books in octavo format. The other editions of the Marlorat book are in folio. *Language(s)*: Latin. Appraised at 4s in 1599.

154.73 Daneus in minor. prophet.

Lambert Daneau. *Commentariorum in Prophetas minores tomus pr.-sec.* Geneva: apud Eustathium Vignon, 1586.
Language(s): Latin. Appraised at 1s 8d in 1599.

154.74 Ecumenius in Epist.
Oecumenius, *Bishop of Tricca*. [*Epistles—Paul: commentary*]. Continent: 1547–1555.
Language(s): Latin. Appraised at 3s in 1599.

154.75 Rolochus in Epist Rom.
Robert Rollock. [*Romans: commentary*]. Britain or Continent: 1593–1596.
STC 21267 *et seq.* and non-STC. *Language(s)*: Latin. Appraised at 1s 8d in 1599.

154.76 Juel in Epist Thess.
John Jewel, *Bishop*. [*Thessalonians: commentary and text*]. (*Bible—N.T.*). London: (different houses), 1583–1594.
STC 14603 *et seq.* Despite the language of the manuscript entry, this work did not appear in Latin. Ralph Newbery was involved in all three editions represented here by the date range. *Language(s)*: English. Appraised at 1s 4d in 1599.

154.77 Beza de resur.
Théodore de Bèze. *Homiliae in historiam Domini resurrectione*. Geneva: apud Joannem Le Preux, 1593.
Gardy nos. 394–395. *Language(s)*: Latin. Appraised at 1s 6d in 1599.

154.78 Idem [Beza] de passione
Théodore de Bèze. *In historiam passionis et sepulturae Domini nostri Jesu Christi*. Geneva: excudebat Joannes Le Preux, 1592–1593.
Gardy nos. 388–389. *Language(s)*: Latin. Appraised at 1s 4d in 1599.

154.79 Zanch. de sacra scrip
Hieronymus Zanchius. *De scriptura sacra*. Continent: 1593–1598.
Two editions, one published in Heidelberg, the other in Neustadt a.d. Haardt. *Language(s)*: Latin. Appraised at 1s in 1599.

154.80 Zanch. de incarnat
Hieronymus Zanchius. *De incarnatione Filii Dei*. Neustadt an der Haardt: apud Josuam Harnisch, 1593.
Following this item is a heavily struck-through manuscript entry that appears to be *Italius Diatonus in Epist* which cannot be identified as written. *Language(s)*: Latin. Appraised at 2s in 1599.

154.81 Melanth. loci communes
Philipp Melanchthon. [*Loci communes theologici*]. Continent: date not determined.
Not appraised. *Language(s)*: Latin.

154.82 Junius de Theologica
François Du Jon, *the Elder. De theologia vera.* Leyden: ex officina Plantiniana, apud Franciscum Raphelengium, 1594.
Language(s): Latin. Appraised at 1s 4d in 1599.

154.83 Arist. Eth. greco-lat
Aristotle. *Ethica.* Continent: date not determined.
Language(s): Greek Latin. Appraised at 1s 8d in 1599.

154.84 Lawneus epitom. inst. Cal.
Jean Calvin. [*Institutio Christianae religionis—epitome*]. Abridged by Edmund Bunny, with commentary by William Lawne. London: Thomas Vautrollier, 1583–1584.
STC 4427 *et seq. Language(s)*: Latin. Appraised at 1s 2d in 1599.

154.85 Mornaeus de virit chris. releg
Philippe de Mornay. *De veritate religionis christianae liber.* Continent: 1583–1597.
Language(s): Latin. Appraised at 1s 4d in 1599.

154.86 Beza de controvers in caena domini
Théodore de Bèze. *De controversiis in coena Domini.* Geneva: apud Joannem le Preux, 1593–1594.
Gardy, nos. 397–398. Not appraised. *Language(s)*: Latin.

154.87 Aretius: examen theol.
Benedictus Aretius. *Examen theologicum.* Continent: date not determined.
Language(s): Latin. Appraised at 1s in 1599.

154.88 Zanchii loci communes
Hieronymus Zanchius. Unidentified. Continent: date not determined.
More than one of Zanchius's works contain the phrase "loci communes" in the long title, including both of the candidates for the manuscript entry at 154.34. That the compiler has struck through this entry and did not enter an appraisal may indicate that it is Zanchius's commentary on Paul's Epistles that he had already listed earlier, whichever one that may have been. *Language(s)*: Latin.

154.89:1 Spicil. [spicilegium] in prov: et eccles
Probably Georgius Remus. *Vir pius et sapiens. Hoc est, in Solomonis regis Paroimion librum, post aliorum messes spicilegium primum* [*alterum*]. Siegen: ex officina Christophori Corvini, 1596.

An unusual manuscript entry in that, if the identification is correct, the compiler has chosen to enter a minor word in the long title where one would have expected him to have selected the author's name. For this reason the identification must remain qualified, but the subjects, the dates, the sizes of the books, not to mention that the publisher apparently viewed the two works listed as companion volumes, argue that these are Remus's commentaries. Not appraised. *Language(s)*: Latin.

154.89:2 [See 154.89:1]

Probably Georgius Remus. *In Solomonis ecclesiasten, qui de vanitate rerum, et adipiscendo summo bono, spicilegium alterum*. Siegen: ex officina Christophori Corvini, 1596.

See the annotation to 154.89:1. Not appraised. *Language(s)*: Latin.

154.90   Bilson contra Alanum

Thomas Bilson, *Bishop*. *The true difference betweene christian subjection and unchristian rebellion*. London: J. Jackson and E. Bollifant, 1586.

STC 3072. A response to a work by Cardinal William Allen. An earlier edition is in quarto. *Language(s)*: English. Appraised at 2s in 1599.

154.91   Babington upon the commandments

Gervase Babington, *Bishop*. *A very fruitfull exposition of the commaundements by way of questions and answeres*. London: (different houses) for T. Charde, 1583–1590.

STC 1095 *et seq*. *Language(s)*: English. Appraised at 1s in 1599.

154.92   Idem [Babington] upon the Lo: prayer

Gervase Babington, *Bishop*. *A profitable exposition of the Lord's prayer, by way of questions and answers*. London: T. Orwin for T. Charde, 1588.

STC 1090. A second edition (1596) is in quarto. *Language(s)*: English. Appraised at 1s in 1599.

154.93   A Conferenc twixt Frailty and Faith

Gervase Babington, *Bishop*. *A briefe conference betwixt mans frailtie and faith*. London: (different houses) for T. Charde, 1583–1590.

STC 1081 *et seq*. *Language(s)*: English. Appraised at 1s in 1599.

154.94   Calvini catech

Jean Calvin. [*Catechism*]. Britain or Continent: date not determined.
STC 4375 and non-STC. *Language(s)*: Latin. Appraised at 1s 4d in 1599.

154.95 multiple   divers catechis: bound together

Unidentified [catechisms]. Places unknown: stationers unknown, date not determined.

STC/non-STC status unknown. *Language(s)*: English (probable) Latin (probable). Appraised as a group at 1s 4d in 1599.

154.96   Resolut. pars utraque

Robert Parsons. [*A book of Christian exercise*]. Britain or Continent: date not determined.

STC 19353 *et seq*. It is assumed that by *pars utraque* the compiler means both Parsons's original and Edmund Bunny's Protestant adaptation. See STC 19355 *et seq*. *Language(s)*: English. Appraised at 2s 4d in 1599.

154.97   Basting. Catechis. Engl.

Jeremias Bastingius. *A catechisme of christian religion, taught in the Low Countries, and dominions of the countie Palatine*. (*Heidelberg catechism*). Edinburgh: R. Walde-grave, 1591.

STC 1562. STC 1565–1566 also appear in octavo, but they are Bastingius's commentary without the catechism. By giving the language, the compiler distinguishes this item from the original, while also making clear in the manuscript entry the presence of the catechism itself. *Language(s)*: English. Appraised at 1s 6d in 1599.

154.98   parei Catech. 2bus vol

Zacharias Ursinus. [*Doctrinae christiana compendium*]. Edited by David Pareus. Continent: 1591–1598.

A commentary on the Heidelberg catechism, the text of which is included. The Latin edition with Pareus as editor, which the compiler identifies here, seems not to have been published in England. *Language(s)*: Latin. Appraised at 4s in 1599.

154.99   English Bible.

The Bible. Britain or Continent: date not determined.

STC 2087 *et seq*. Given the high valuation for an octavo size, perhaps a multi–volume collection or set. *Language(s)*: English. Appraised at 5s in 1599.

154.100   Hieron. biblia

The Bible. Continent: date not determined.

The only edition of the Vulgate published in England by the date of this inventory was in quarto. *Language(s)*: Latin. Appraised at 2s 6d in 1599.

154.101 Marlorati loci communes

Isaacus Feguernekinus. *Enchiridion locorum communium theologicorum*. Britain or Continent: date not determined.

STC 10747 *et seq.* and non-STC. A compilation from the *Thesaurus sacrae scripturae* by Augustine Marlorat, whose work appeared only in folio until the seventeenth century. *Language(s)*: Latin. Appraised at 1s 2d in 1599.

154.102 Danaeus in orat. dominicam

Lambert Daneau. *Orationis dominicae explicatio*. Geneva: apud Eustathium Vignon, 1582–1583.

Language(s): Latin. Appraised at 2s in 1599.

154.103 piscator in Matth.

Johann Piscator. [*Matthew: commentary and text*]. Britain or Continent: 1594–1597.

STC 19948 *et seq.* and non-STC. Refutes Cardinal Bellarmine. *Language(s)*: Latin. Appraised at 1s 10d in 1599.

154.104 piscator in reliquos evangelistas

Johann Piscator. [*Gospels—Unidentified: commentary*]. Britain or Continent: date not determined.

STC 19949 and non-STC. Whether Piscator's three remaining commentaries on the Gospels (Mark, Luke, John), or just two, and if only two, which two, cannot be determined. The different commentaries appeared in solo editions in England and on the Continent; there were no collected editions. The compiler is either grouping them together or Mitchell had them bound in one volume. The valuation, when compared to the valuation of the preceding item, does not help to identify the number of commentaries represented here. *Language(s)*: Latin. Appraised at 2s in 1599.

154.105 piscator in Epist. Rom. et Corinth.

Johann Piscator. [*Epistles—Paul: commentary*]. Britain or Continent: date not determined.

STC 19995.5 *et seq.* and non-STC. This entry is taken to be one of the several editions of Piscator's commentaries on Paul's Epistles that lead with commentaries on Romans and Corinthians, whether the smaller edition of selected commentaries or the enlarged edition of commentaries on all the Pauline Epistles. A multiple entry in which the solo editions of Piscator's commentaries on Romans and Corinthians, published on the Continent, are listed together must, however, remain a possibility, especially given that preceding this item the compiler created a multiple entry of several works. *Language(s)*: Latin. Appraised at 1s 4d in 1599.

154.106 Piscat. in reliquas Epistolas

Johann Piscator. [*Epistles: commentary*]. Britain or Continent: 1593–1598. STC 19958 *et seq.* and non-STC. This is taken to be Piscator's collection of commentaries on the non-Pauline Epistles, though it could be a collection of a variety of Piscator's individual commentaries bound or grouped together. *Language(s)*: Latin. Appraised at 2s in 1599.

154.107 Serranus in Ecclesiastem

Jean de Serres. [*Ecclesiastes: commentary and text*]. (*Bible — O.T.*). Geneva: apud Petrum Sanctandreanum, 1579–1580.
Language(s): Latin. Appraised at 1s 8d in 1599.

154.108 2ex translatio in psal.

[*Bible — O.T. — Psalms*]. Place unknown: stationer unknown, date not determined.

STC/non-STC status unknown. A frustrating manuscript entry. The only thing that can be determined is that the work listed has to do with the Psalms. Whether a commentary on the Psalms, which the phrasing suggests, cannot be determined. Indeed why the emphasis on translation by the compiler is unclear. The transcription "2ex" is itself uncertain, and what it means, if that is what the compiler wrote, is also uncertain. Conceivably it indicates that two copies (*exempla*) are listed; conceivably it is a way of suggesting a repetition of Serres as author from the preceding, which would indicate that this might be his Greek paraphrase of selections of the Psalms. See CLC B1418 and Adams B1504. *Language(s)*: Latin (probable) Greek (perhaps). Appraised at 1s 6d in 1599.

154.109 Hyperius de rat. studii theol.

Andreas Gerardus, *Hyperius. De theologo, sive De ratione studii theologici.* Continent: date not determined.
Language(s): Latin. Appraised at 1s 6d in 1599.

154.110 Zepperus

Wilhelm Zepper. Unidentified. Continent: date not determined.

His most widely published work, *De politia ecclesiastica*, was published in octavo, but other works are possible. STC 2614.5 not likely given its language, English, and its date, late 1599. *Language(s)*: Latin. Appraised at 1s 4d in 1599.

154.111 Amandus polan.

Amandus Polanus. Unidentified. Place unknown: stationer unknown, date not determined.

STC/non-STC status unknown. More likely, given the collection and the location of the item in the collection, one of his theological works. *Language(s)*: English (probable) Latin (probable). Appraised at 2s in 1599.

154.112 August. de Haeres.
Augustine, *Saint*. *De haeresibus*. Edited by Lambert Daneau. Geneva: apud Eustathium Vignon, 1576–1595.
The Vignon heirs published the 1595 edition. *Language(s)*: Latin. Appraised at 1s 4d in 1599.

154.113 fenneri loci communes
Unidentified. Continent (probable): date not determined.
STC/non-STC status unknown. The transcription is uncertain; the first word could be "feuneri," "fenueri," "ferneri," or even "fernei." But if "fenneri," perhaps a work by either Dudley Fenner or William Fenner. *Language(s)*: Latin. Appraised at 2s in 1599.

154.114 Trident. Catech.
Catechismus ex decreto Concilii Tridentini. (*Councils—Trent*). Continent: date not determined.
Language(s): Latin. Appraised at 1s 2d in 1599.

154.115 petrus Lombardus
Peter Lombard. Probably *Sententiarum libri IIII*. Continent: date not determined.
Language(s): Latin. Appraised at 1s 8d in 1599.

154.116 Melchioris Cani Loci communes
Francisco Melchor Cano, *Bishop*. *De locis theologicis*. Continent: 1564–1585.
The first edition, 1563, is variously described by sources as folio or quarto, but it is not octavo, which the compiler assigns to the item here. *Language(s)*: Latin. Appraised at 1s 2d in 1599.

154.117 Wilcocks in cantic
Thomas Wilcox. *An exposition uppon the booke of the Canticles*. London: R. Waldegrave for T. Man, 1585.
STC 25622. *Language(s)*: English. Appraised at 10d in 1599.

154.118 Hemingii catech.
Niels Hemmingsen. *Catechismi quaestiones concinnatae*. Continent: date not determined,
Language(s): Latin. Appraised at 8d in 1599.

154.119 vocabularius utriusque Juris
Vocabularius juris utriusque. Continent: date not determined.
Language(s): Latin. Appraised at 1s 4d in 1599.

154.120   Scaliger de subtil.
Julius Caesar Scaliger. *Exotericarum exercitationum liber XV.* Continent: date not determined.
A response to Girolamo Cardano's *De subtilitate rerum*, which explains the odd manuscript entry. *Language(s)*: Latin. Appraised at 2s 6d in 1599.

154.121   Fernel. 2bus vol.
Joannes Fernelius. Unidentified. Continent: date not determined.
A physician, his books were overwhelmingly on medical subjects though he did write several works on mathematics and astronomy. *Language(s)*: Latin. Appraised at 4s in 1599.

154.122   Bodini de repub.
Jean Bodin, *Bishop*. *De republica*. Continent: 1591–1594.
An earlier edition (1586) is in folio. This item is octavo according to the compiler. *Language(s)*: Latin. Appraised at 3s 6d in 1599.

154.123   Isocr: grece et Lat.
Isocrates. Probably [*Works*]. Continent: date not determined.
Language(s): Greek Latin. Appraised at 1s 8d in 1599.

154.124   Herodian gre. et Lat.
Herodian. [*Historiae*]. Continent: date not determined.
Language(s): Greek Latin. Appraised at 1s in 1599.

154.125   Suetonius
Caius Suetonius Tranquillus. *De vita Caesarum*. Britain or Continent: date not determined.
Language(s): Latin. Appraised at 10d in 1599.

154.126   pomponis Mela
Pomponius Mela. *De situ orbis*. Continent: date not determined.
The only edition published in England was in quarto and was an English translation. *Language(s)*: Latin. Appraised at 1s 3d in 1599.

154.127   Valer. Ma.
Valerius Maximus. *Facta et dicta memorabilia*. Continent: date not determined.
Language(s): Latin. Appraised at 1s 4d in 1599.

154.128   Justin. Hist.
Trogus Pompeius and Justinus, *the Historian*. [*Epitomae in Trogi Pompeii historias*]. Britain or Continent: date not determined.

STC 24287 *et seq.* and non-STC. *Language(s)*: Latin. Appraised at 1s 6d in 1599.

154.129   Sleiden. de 4or monarch.

Joannes Philippson, *Sleidanus. De quatuor summis imperiis.* Britain or Continent: date not determined.

STC 19847 and non-STC. *Language(s)*: Latin. Appraised at 2s in 1599.

154.130   Casar. Comment.

Caius Julius Caesar. *Commentarii.* Continent: date not determined.

The editions published in England were in sextodecimo, a size the compiler might have thought octavo, which format he has indicated here. Still, the item here is being treated as octavo for publication information. *Language(s)*: Latin. Appraised at 1s 8d in 1599.

154.131   Thucid.

Thucydides. *De bello peloponnesiaco.* Continent: date not determined.

Nothing of Thucydides was published in octavo in England by the date of this inventory. *Language(s)*: Latin (probable) Greek (perhaps). Appraised at 1s 6d in 1599.

154.132   Curtius

Quintus Curtius Rufus. *De rebus gestis Alexandri Magni.* Continent: date not determined.

Several English versions were published in octavo, but there is no reason to believe the item here is a translation of the Latin. *Language(s)*: Latin. Appraised at 1s 4d in 1599.

154.133   Herodotus

Herodotus. [*Historiae*]. Continent: date not determined.

No octavo edition was published in England. *Language(s)*: Latin (probable) Greek (perhaps). Appraised at 1s 6d in 1599.

154.134   pagnini thesaur.

Sanctes Pagninus. *Thesauri linguae sanctae epitome.* Continent: date not determined.

The octavo size identifies this as the epitome. *Language(s)*: Latin. Appraised at 2s in 1599.

154.135   Vigandi gramm. Heb.

Wigandus Happellius. *Linguae sanctae canones grammatici.* Basle: per Thomam Guerinum, 1561.

Language(s): Hebrew Latin. Appraised at 10d in 1599.

154.136 Udalls gramm. Heb.
Petrus Martinius. [*Mafteah leshon ha-kodesh*], *that is the key of the holy tongue*. Translated by John Udall. Leyden: F. Raphelengius, 1593.
STC 17523. The title is transliterated from the Hebrew. Essentially Martinius's grammar, Udall's work also contains a short dictionary. See also the following. *Language(s)*: English Hebrew. Appraised at 1s 6d in 1599.

154.137 Martin: Gramm Heb.
Petrus Martinius. [*Grammatica hebraica*]. Continent: 1567–1597.
This may be an edition that includes Chaldaic as well. See the preceding. *Language(s)*: Hebrew Latin. Appraised at 1s 8d in 1599.

154.138 Ceporin gramm. Grae.
Jacobus Ceporinus. *Compendium grammaticae graecae*. Britain or Continent: date not determined.
STC 4913 *et seq.* and non-STC. *Language(s)*: Greek Latin. Appraised at 1s 2d in 1599.

154.139 Rami gram. Grae.
Pierre de La Ramée. [*Grammatica*]. Continent: Andreas Wechel, 1560–1586.
The seven editions in this date range were published variously in Paris and in Frankfurt am Main. See Ong nos. 566–572. *Language(s)*: Greek Latin. Appraised at 1s in 1599.

154.140:1 Horat. bis
Quintus Horatius Flaccus. Probably [*Works*]. Britain or Continent: date not determined.
STC 13784 *et seq.* and non-STC. One of the two items indicated is likely to be the Works. Perhaps the entry represents a two-volume set, but the compiler's habit is to indicate explicitly when a single work appears in multiple volumes. *Language(s)*: Latin. Appraised with one other at 2s in 1599.

154.140:2 [See 154.140:1]
Quintus Horatius Flaccus. Perhaps [*Works*]. Britain or Continent: date not determined.
STC 13784 *et seq.* and non-STC. Perhaps a second copy of the preceding, but perhaps a copy of, say, the *Epistolae* alone. See the annotation to the preceding record. *Language(s)*: Latin. Appraised with one other at 2s in 1599.

154.141 Virgil
Publius Virgilius Maro. Probably [*Works*]. Britain or Continent: date not determined.

STC 24787 *et seq.* and non-STC. *Language(s)*: Latin. Appraised at 1s 8d in 1599.

154.142   Terentius
Publius Terentius, *Afer*. [*Works*]. Britain or Continent: date not determined.
23885.7 *et seq.* and non-STC. *Language(s)*: Latin. Appraised at 1s 6d in 1599.

154.143   Sabinus in ovid Metamorph
Publius Ovidius Naso. *Metamorphoses*. With commentary by Georgius Sabinus. Britain or Continent: date not determined.
STC 18951 and non-STC. A Cambridge edition appeared in 1584. *Language(s)*: Latin. Appraised at 2s in 1599.

154.144   Ovidii Epist
Publius Ovidius Naso. *Heroides*. Continent: date not determined.
Language(s): Latin. Appraised at 10d in 1599.

154.145   Sophocles Latin
Sophocles. [*Works*]. Continent: date not determined.
Language(s): Latin. Appraised at 1s 3d in 1599.

154.146   Homer Odyss: greco lat
Homer. *Odyssey*. Continent: date not determined.
Language(s): Greek Latin. Appraised at 2s in 1599.

154.147   Eiusdem. [Homer] Il. greco. lat
Homer. *Iliad*. Continent: date not determined.
Language(s): Greek Latin. Appraised at 2s in 1599.

154.148   Licosthenis aphth.
Conrad Lycosthenes (Conrad Wolffhart). *Apophthegmata*. Britain or Continent: date not determined.
STC 17003.3 *et seq.* and non-STC. *Language(s)*: Latin. Appraised at 1s in 1599.

154.149   A rth: ad Heren.
Marcus Tullius Cicero (spurious). *Rhetorica ad Herennium*. Britain or Continent: date not determined.
STC 5323 *et seq.* and non-STC. The first character in the manuscript entry ("A") may have been a false start. *Language(s)*: Latin. Appraised at 10d in 1599.

154.150 Quintillian

Marcus Fabius Quintilianus. Unidentified. Continent: date not determined.

The *Institutiones oratoriae* is probably more likely than the *Declamationes*, but the complete works might be intended. *Language(s)*: Latin. Appraised at 2s in 1599.

154.151 fonsecae Logica

Petrus Fonseca. *Institutionum dialecticarum libri octo*. Continent: 1564–1599.

Language(s): Latin. Appraised at 1s 8d in 1599.

154.152 Alexander ab Alexand.

Alexander ab Alexandro. *Geniales dies*. Continent: date not determined. *Language(s)*: Latin. Appraised at 1s 8d in 1599.

154.153 Latina grammatica lillii

William Lily. *Institutio compendiaria totius grammaticae*. Britain or Continent: 1544–1599.

STC 15610.8 *et seq*. Several editions listed in the STC were published on the Continent. *Language(s)*: Latin. Appraised at 8d in 1599.

154.154 Danaeus in Bell 2bus vol.

Lambert Daneau. *Ad R. Bellarmini disputationes theologicas responsio*. Geneva: apud Joannem Le Preux, 1596–1598 (single edition).

Published in two volumes; again the compiler is strikingly accurate in detail. *Language(s)*: Latin. Appraised at 3s in 1599.

154.155 Spangenbergius in Epist

Johann Spangenberg. [*Epistles (liturgical): commentary and text*]. Continent: date not determined.

Whether this is an edition of his commentary on the liturgical Epistles alone, such as that published in 1548 (see Adams S1539), or a volume separated from one of his multi-volume editions of the liturgical Gospels and Epistles cannot be determined. *Language(s)*: Latin. Appraised at 10d in 1599.

154.156 Eobani Hessi psalterium

[*Bible — O.T. — Psalms*]. Translated by Helius Eobanus, *Hessus*. Continent (probable): date not determined.

Probably not an STC book. STC 2356 and 2361 are sextodecimo editions but could have been mistaken for octavo by the compiler. *Language(s)*: Latin. Appraised at 10d in 1599.

154.157 ferus in exodum et
Joannes Ferus (Johann Wild, *Prediger zu Mainz*). [*Exodus, Numbers, Deuteronomy, Joshua, Judges: commentary*]. Cologne: (different houses), 1571–1574.
Language(s): Latin. Appraised at 1s 2d in 1599.

154.158 Machiovel princeps
Niccolò Macchiavelli. *De principe*. Translated by Sylvester Telius. Continent: date not determined.
Language(s): Latin. Appraised at 1s 3d in 1599.

154.159 Eiusdem [Macchiavelli] discursus.
Niccolò Macchiavelli. *Disputationum de republica libri iii*. Translated by Johann Niklaus Stupanus. Montbeliard: per Jacobum Foilletum, 1588–1599.
The Latin translation of the *Discorsi*. *Language(s)*: Latin. Appraised at 1s 3d in 1599.

154.160 frigii logica et
Joannes Thomas Freigius. Unidentified. Continent: date not determined,
De logica jureconsultorum and *Logica, ad vsum rudiorum in epitomen redacta* are the likeliest possibilities. Other of his works include *logica* in the long titles, some with "&" or "et" following, as in "logicae et ethicae." The manuscript entry here, however, could represent one of the first mentioned titles with another book (*et*) entirely but bound or simply grouped with it, its title accidentally omitted. *Language(s)*: Latin. Appraised at 1s 2d in 1599.

154.161 Goclenius in Eth
Rudolphus Goclenius, *the Elder. Exercitationes ethicae*. Marburg: typis Pauli Egelnolphi typographi academici, 1592–1596.
Several academic theses on Aristotle's *Ethica* were published in the 1590s that included Goclenius's contribution, all in quarto, not the size given by the compiler here. *Language(s)*: Latin. Appraised at 1s in 1599.

154.162 Idem [Goclenius] in phys.
Rudolphus Goclenius, *the Elder. Scholae, seu Disputationes physicae*. Continent: 1591–1598.
Language(s): Latin. Appraised at 10d in 1599.

154.163 Mantuanus.
Baptista Spagnuoli (Mantuanus). Unidentified. Place unknown: stationer unknown, date not determined.
STC/non-STC status unknown. There is no reason to expect an English edition of Mantuan here. *Language(s)*: Latin. Appraised at 4d in 1599.

154.164 Manutii Epist.
Paolo Manuzio (Paolo Manutius). [*Epistolae*]. Britain or Continent: date not determined.
STC 17286 *et seq.* and non-STC. The only octavo edition published in England was issued in 1573. His *Epistolae clarorum virorum selectae* is less likely, his commentary on Cicero's epistles even less so. *Language(s)*: Latin. Appraised at 8d in 1599.

154.165 Arist. Rhetorica
Aristotle. *Rhetorica*. Continent: date not determined.
Language(s): Latin (probable) Greek (perhaps). Appraised at 1s in 1599.

154.166 Arist. phys
Aristotle. *Physica*. Britain or Continent: date not determined.
STC 758 and non-STC. *Language(s)*: Latin (probable) Greek (perhaps). Appraised at 10d in 1599.

154.167 Rodolphi dial.
Probably Caspar Rhodolphus. [*Dialectica*]. Continent: date not determined.
Rodolphus Agricola's *De inventione dialectica* is a possibility. *Language(s)*: Latin. Appraised at 1s in 1599.

154.168 Institut. Justin.
Justinian I. *Institutiones*. (*Corpus juris civilis*). Continent: date not determined.
Language(s): Latin Greek (perhaps). Appraised at 10d in 1599.

154.169 codex Juris civ
Justinian I. *Codex*. (*Corpus juris civilis*). Continent: date not determined.
Language(s): Latin Greek (perhaps). Appraised at 1s 4d in 1599.

154.170 Ascami Epist
Roger Ascham. *Familiarium epistolarum libri tres*. Edited by Edward Grant. London: (different houses) for F. Coldock, 1576–1590.
STC 826 *et seq.* The 1590 edition contains a number of letters by, among others, Joannes Sturmius to Ascham. No Continental edition appeared in octavo. *Language(s)*: Latin. Appraised at 1s 3d in 1599.

154.171 Purbachii Theor.
Georg Purbach. *Novae theoricarum planetarum*. Continent: date not determined.
Language(s): Latin. Appraised at 1s 3d in 1599.

154.172 conputus astro. Skonbordii

Bartholomaeus Schönborn. *Computus vel calendarium astronomicum.* Wittenberg: (different houses), 1567–1579.
Language(s): Latin. Appraised at 10d in 1599.

154.173 proclus de sphera

Diadochus Proclus. *Sphaera.* Britain or Continent: date not determined.
STC 20398.3 and non-STC. *Language(s)*: Latin (probable) Greek (perhaps). Appraised at 1s in 1599.

154.174 Bakers Arith.

Humphrey Baker. *The well sprynge of sciences.* London: (different houses), 1562–1598.
STC 1209.5 *et seq. Language(s)*: English. Appraised at 8d in 1599.

154.175 Erasmi Adagia

Desiderius Erasmus. *Adagia.* Continent: date not determined.

This is not assumed to be one of the English-Latin editions published in England, though one is possible. In another hand and between the manuscript entry and the valuation is entered "16to" which may or may not refer to this work, editions of which were overwhelmingly published in quarto and folio sizes with the occasional octavo and apparently one duodecimo. Whether it refers to the next item and those that follow is also unclear. Except for the one item specifically described as folio (154.179) below, the books that follow are treated as if the compiler did not physically describe them until 154.189 when he provides the group heading "vellam books" for those that follow. *Language(s)*: Latin. Appraised at 3d in 1599.

154.176 Summa conciliorum

Bartholome Carranza, *Archbishop.* [*Summa conciliorum*]. Continent: date not determined.

The size of the book listed cannot be determined; see the annotation to 154.175. *Language(s)*: Latin. Appraised at 1s 2d in 1599.

154.177 Palingenius

Marcellus Palingenius (Pietro Angelo Manzolli [Stellatus]). *Zodiacus vitae.* Britain or Continent: date not determined.
STC 19138.5 *et seq.* and non-STC. The size of the book listed cannot be determined; see the annotation to 154.175. *Language(s)*: Latin. Appraised at 6d in 1599.

154.178 Canitii Summa

Petrus Canisius, *Saint*. [*Summa doctrina Christianae*]. Continent: date not determined.

All editions published in England were in English. The *Summa juris canonica* of Henricus Canisius appears to have been published too late to be in this collection. The size of the book listed cannot be determined; see the annotation to 154.175. *Language(s)*: Latin. Appraised at 10d in 1599.

154.179 Liber cartatius follio

Unidentified. Provenance unknown: date not determined.
Manuscript. *Language(s)*: Unknown. Appraised at 3s in 1599.

154.180 Irvin, paraleisis

Unidentified. Place unknown: stationer unknown, date not determined.
STC/non-STC status unknown. *Language(s)*: Latin. Appraised at 1s 2d in 1599.

154.181 Cordius de pharmacis

Valerius Cordus. [*Dispensatorium*]. Continent: date not determined.

The size of the book listed cannot be determined; see the annotation to 154.175. *Language(s)*: Latin. Appraised at 8d in 1599.

154.182 Schola Salerni

[*Regimen sanitatis Salernitatum*]. Britain or Continent: date not determined.

STC 21596 *et seq.* and non-STC. The size of the book listed cannot be determined; see the annotation to 154.175. *Language(s)*: Latin English (perhaps). Appraised at 10d in 1599.

154.183 Lemnius

Levinus Lemnius. Unidentified. Continent: date not determined.

There is no reason to expect that this, probably one of Lemnius's medical works among other such books here, is an English translation. The size of the book listed cannot be determined; see the annotation to 154.175. *Language(s)*: Latin. Appraised at 8d in 1599.

154.184 Pindarus

Pindar. Probably [*Works*]. Continent: date not determined.

The size of the book listed cannot be determined; see the annotation to 154.175. *Language(s)*: Greek (probable) Latin (probable). Appraised at 1s in 1599.

154.185 Salust
Caius Sallustius Crispus. Unidentified. Place unknown: stationer unknown, date not determined.

STC/non-STC status unknown. The size of the book listed cannot be determined; see the annotation to 154.175. *Language(s)*: Latin. Appraised at 10d in 1599.

154.186 Elianus var. Hist
Claudius Aelianus. *Varia historia*. Continent: date not determined.

The size of the book listed cannot be determined; see the annotation to 154.175. *Language(s)*: Greek (probable) Latin (probable). Appraised at 1s 2d in 1599.

154.187 Aesopi fab. graece et lat.
Aesop. *Fabulae*. Continent: date not determined.

The size of the book listed cannot be determined; see the annotation to 154.175. *Language(s)*: Greek Latin. Appraised at 1s in 1599.

154.188 Enchirid. pro animabus regendis
Alessandro Ariosto. *Enchiridion sive interrogatorium perutile pro animabus regendis*. Continent: 1513–1520.

This book provides some evidence that the sextodecimo at 154.175 may not be intended to describe all the books that follow; the five sixteenth-century editions of this work listed in *Aureliensis* are all octavo. *Language(s)*: Latin. Appraised at 2d in 1599.

154.189 Beza upon Job.
Théodore de Bèze. [*Job: commentary and paraphrase*]. (*Bible — O.T.*). Britain or Continent: 1589–1590.

STC 2019 *et seq.* and non-STC. The manuscript entry suggests the English edition, but a Latin edition is possible. Gardy, nos. 376–378. The Latin edition printed in England contains a paraphrase and commentary on *Ecclesiastes* as well. Listed under a heading: "vellam books." *Language(s)*: English Latin (perhaps). Appraised at 1s in 1599.

154.190 Aquinas in Job:
Thomas Aquinas, *Saint*. [*Job: commentary*]. Continent: 1505–1562.

A 1474 folio edition was published, but it is not likely intended here, both because of size and age. Listed under a heading: "vellam books." *Language(s)*: Latin. Appraised at 10d in 1599.

154.191 frig questiones geom

Joannes Thomas Freigius. *Quaestiones geometricae et steriometricae*. Basle: per Sebastianum Henricpetri, 1583.

Listed under a heading: "vellam books." *Language(s)*: Latin. Appraised at 10d in 1599.

154.192 The reformed cathol

William Perkins. *A reformed catholike: or, a declaration shewing how neere we may come to the present church of Rome*. London: J. Legat, pr. to the Univ. of Camb., 1597–1598.

STC 19735.8 *et seq*. Listed under a heading: "vellam books." *Language(s)*: English. Appraised at 8d in 1599.

154.193 Muffett upon the prov

Peter Muffet. [*Proverbs: commentary and text*]. (*Bible — O.T.*). London: (different houses) for R. Dexter, 1592–1596.

STC 18245 *et seq*. Listed under a heading: "vellam books." *Language(s)*: English. Appraised at 1s in 1599.

154.194 Concil: Trident

Probably *Acta Concilii Tridentini*. (*Councils — Trent*). Continent: date not determined.

Conceivably, but less likely, the *Canones et decreta Concilii Tridentini*. Listed under a heading: "stitched bookes." *Language(s)*: Latin. Appraised at 1s in 1599.

154.195 piscator in Acta

Johann Piscator. [*Acts: commentary*]. Britain or Continent: 1597.

STC 19955 and non-STC. Two editions published in the same year, one in Siegen and one in London. Listed under a heading: "stitched bookes." *Language(s)*: Latin. Appraised at 6d in 1599.

154.196 Concilii Trident gravamina

Concilii Tridentii restitutioni opposita gravamina. (*Councils — Trent*). Translated by Laurentius Tuppius. Continent: 1565–1597.

Listed under a heading: "stitched bookes." *Language(s)*: Latin. Appraised at 1s 3d in 1599.

154.197 Sandersoni Logica

John Sanderson. *Institutionum dialecticarum libri quatuor*. Antwerp: ex officina Christopheri Plantini, 1589.

The DNB gives an Oxford 1594 edition, but it is not listed in the STC. STC 21698, published in London in 1602 is, however, described as *"editio tertia"* on the title page. Listed under a heading: "stitched bookes." *Language(s)*: Latin. Appraised at 6d in 1599.

154.198 Juris quo utimur Epitome

Julius Pacius. *Juris quo utimur epitome secundum ordinem Institutionum Imperialium digesta*. Speier: Bernardus Albinus, 1589–1594.
Listed under a heading: "stitched bookes." *Language(s)*: Latin. Appraised at 4d in 1599.

154.199 An introduction to the Script

Unidentified. Britain: date not determined.
Unidentifiable in the STC. Perhaps a running-title. Listed under a heading: "stitched bookes." *Language(s)*: English. Appraised at 3d in 1599.

154.200 Gemma fabri

William Smyth. *Gemma Fabri*. London: ex typ. F. Kingstoni, imp. J. Porteri, 1598.
STC 22882. Published anonymously. John Shepery's *Summa et synopsis Novi Testamenti* (STC 22406) is reprinted in this volume. Altogether, the work consists of a verse summary of the books of the Bible, with Smyth providing the paraphrases of the Old Testament books. Laurence Humphrey edited Shepery's work. Listed under a heading: "stitched bookes." *Language(s)*: Latin. Appraised at 8d in 1599.

154.201 Ecclesiastica disciplina

Walter Travers. *Ecclesiastica disciplina*. Heidelberg: Michael Schirat, 1574.
A false imprint reads: "Rupellae, excudebat Adamus de Monte." See Shaaber T110. Listed under a heading: "stitched bookes." *Language(s)*: Latin. Appraised at 10d in 1599.

154.202 Junii politia et

François Du Jon, *the Elder*. *De politiae Mosis observatione*. Leyden: ex officina Platiniana, apud F. Raphelengium, 1593.
Listed under a heading: "stitched bookes." *Language(s)*: Latin. Appraised at 1s in 1599.

154.203 Enchirid catecheticon

Zacharias Ursinus. *Enchiridion catecheticum*. Amberg: ex officina Michaëlis Forsteri, 1596.
Related to the Heidelberg catechism. Listed under a heading: "stitched bookes." *Language(s)*: Latin. Appraised at 6d in 1599.

154.204 first part of the key of phy
Philippus Hermanni. *The first part of the key of philosophie*. London: (different houses), 1580–1596.
STC 19181.5 *et seq.* Compiled and translated by John Hester, supposedly, but not in fact, from works by Paracelsus. Listed under Paracelsus in the STC. A good part of the book is based on the work of Philippus Hermanni. First published in 1575 under a different title; see STC 19181.3. Listed under a heading: "stitched bookes." *Language(s)*: English. Appraised at 2d in 1599.

154.205 ferus in Job.
Joannes Ferus (Johann Wild, *Prediger zu Mainz*). *Jobi historiae explicatio in CXIIII conciones distributa*. Cologne: (different houses), 1571–1574.
Preceding this item, the compiler has written "Againe 8°." Unless otherwise indicated, as with 154.207, the rest of the books are assumed to be in octavo format. *Language(s)*: Latin. Appraised at 1s 8d in 1599.

154.206 Reward of religion
Edward Topsell. *The reward of religion*. London: J. Windet, 1596–1597.
STC 24127 *et seq.* Not appraised. *Language(s)*: English.

154.207 Harmonia confessionum 4to
Harmonia Confessionum fidei orthodoxarum et reformatarum ecclesiarum. (*Reformed Churches*). Edited by Jean-François Salvart. Geneva: apud Petrum Sanctandreanum, 1581.
The 1586 English translation (STC 5155) was ordered seized. *Language(s)*: Latin. Appraised at 2s 6d in 1599.

154.208 Perkins his Creed
William Perkins. *An exposition of the symbole or creed of the apostles*. London: J. Legate, pr. to the Univ. of Camb., 1597.
STC 19705. The only octavo edition, the size indicated by the compiler. *Language(s)*: English. Appraised at 2s in 1599.

154.209 Juells Lyfe
Laurence Humphrey. *Joannis Juelli Angli, episcopi Sarisburiensis vita et mors, eiusque; verae doctrinae defensio*. London: apud J. Dayum, 1573.
STC 13963. An anomaly for this list. The compiler lists this book as octavo and enters it as if it were in English when the only edition, now extant, is in quarto and in Latin. Given the accuracy and diligence the compiler demonstrates throughout the rest of the book-list, one is tempted to believe there existed an English translation, in octavo, no longer extant. A work as important as an English biography of John Jewel, however, would not likely have gone unnoticed elsewhere. BCI (2:443) cites two listings of the Latin edition, both of

which specifically identify the format as quarto. *Language(s)*: Latin. Appraised at 3s in 1599.

154.210 liber cartaceus
Unidentified. Provenance unknown: date not determined.
Manuscript. Struck through. Not appraised. *Language(s)*: Unknown.

154.211 A table of the bible
Perhaps Heinrich Bullinger. *A briefe and compendiose table in a manner of a concordaunce of the whole Bible.* (*Biblical concordance*). Translated by Walter Lynne. London: (different houses), 1550–1563.

STC 17117 *et seq.* The book also draws on the work of Leo Juda and Konrad Pellicanus as well as Bullinger. The imprecise manuscript entry, if merely descriptive, allows for other concordances. Despite its title, this work is not a concordance of the complete Bible. Listed under Lynne in the STC. *Language(s)*: English. Appraised at 4d in 1599.

154.212 Talaeus Rhetorick
Audomarus Talaeus (Omer Talon). *Rhetorica*. Continent: date not determined.

Ramus had a major role in this work. The 1592 edition published in Cambridge was not octavo. *Language(s)*: Latin. Appraised at 3d in 1599.

154.213 Marclinus Rhet
Joannes Mercklin. *Quaestionum rhetoricarum.* Continent: 1577.

RRstc2, no. 2516; editions published the same year in Basle and Amberg. RRstc2 also lists a *Quaestiones* [sic] *rhetoricarum libri duo* (Basle, 1559) by J. M. [Master Joannes?] Merclin (no. 2517), derived from a secondary source and found nowhere else. *Language(s)*: Latin. Appraised at 3d in 1599.

154.214 Macropedius
Georgius Macropedius. Unidentified. Place unknown: stationer unknown, date not determined.

STC/non-STC status unknown. There were five octavo editions of Macropedius's *Methodus de conscribendis epistolis* published in England between 1576 and 1594, making it a reasonable possibility, but other Continental works are possible. Only because Macropedius is listed here in this highly ordered booklist might the previous manuscript entry, *Marchius Rhet*, be remotely considered a garbled attempt at a reference to his *Methodus*, a work on rhetoric. *Language(s)*: Greek (probable) Latin (probable). Appraised at 2d in 1599.

154.215 Rami Logica
Pierre de La Ramée. [*Dialectica*]. Britain or Continent: date not determined.
STC 15241.7 *et seq.* and non-STC. Ong list editions in octavo from 1543. Another copy is at 154.217. *Language(s)*: Latin. Appraised at 2d in 1599.

154.216 Scribonii Logica
Gulielmus Adolphus Scribonius. Probably *Triumphus logicae Rameae*. Britain or Continent: 1583–1588.
STC 22114 *et seq.* and non-STC. Since the item is found between two of Ramus's *Logica*, this title is more likely than other of Scribonius's works that carry various forms of "logica" in their long titles. *Language(s)*: Latin. Appraised at 2d in 1599.

154.217 Rami Logica
Pierre de La Ramée. [*Dialectica*]. Britain or Continent: date not determined.
STC 15241.7 *et seq.* and non-STC. Another copy at 154.215. *Language(s)*: Latin. Appraised at 4d in 1599.

154.218 Busbequius
Ogier Ghislain de Busbecq. Unidentified. Continent: date not determined.
The Austrian ambassador to the Ottoman Empire in the mid-sixteenth century, Busbecq's most widely published work was *Legationis turcicae epistolae quatuor* but he also wrote travel literature. The monetary symbol is omitted but pence is probably intended given the valuation of the surrounding items. *Language(s)*: Latin. Appraised at 3[d?] in 1599.

154.219 De esculentis et poculentis
Gaspar Torrella. *Pro regimine seu preservatione sanitatis. De esculentis et poculentis dialogus*. Rome: per Joannem Besicken, 1506.
As the sole edition, a very old book and perhaps not in the best of condition, which may account for the compiler listing a quarto as an octavo. *Language(s)*: Latin. Appraised at 4d in 1599.

154.220 Caninius grammar graec
Angelus Caninius. *Hellenismos*. Paris: apud Joannem Bene-natum, 1578.
The title above is transliterated from the Greek. A 1555 edition appeared in quarto; the compiler, however, indicates an octavo here. *Language(s)*: Greek Latin. Appraised at 1s 3d in 1599.

154.221 De inferno tractatus

Martin Ruland, *the Elder. De inferno, seu, Cacodaemonum, damnatorumq; domicilio: tractatus.* Continent: 1594.

Sources uniformly state: "Anonymous work sent to Ruland; attributed to Philipp Heilbronner." Adams (R901) suggests Frankfurt am Main as the printing location. Not appraised. *Language(s)*: Latin.

154.222 Antichoppinus

Jean Hotman. *Antichoppinus.* Continent: 1592–1593. *Language(s)*: Latin. Appraised at 4d in 1599.

154.223 Sebastians phy.

Sebastian Verro. *Physicorum libri x.* Britain or Continent: 1581–1590.

STC 24688 *et seq.* and non-STC. *Language(s)*: Latin. Appraised at 3d in 1599.

154.224 Perkins de praedestinatione

William Perkins. *De praedestinationis modo et ordine.* Britain or Continent: 1598–1599.

STC 19682 and non-STC. See Shaaber P126 for the 1599 edition. *Language(s)*: Latin. Appraised at 2d in 1599.

154.225 De unica ratione concionandi

William Perkins. *Prophetica, sive de sacra et unica ratione concionandi tractatus.* London: ex off. J. Legate, Acad. Cantab. typog., 1592.

STC 19735 *et seq.* Two editions in 1592. The two Continental editions were published after the date of this inventory. *Language(s)*: Latin. Appraised at 2d in 1599.

154.226 The government of the tonge

William Perkins. *A direction for the government of the tongue.* Britain: 1593.

STC 19688 *et seq.* Two editions in the same year, one from London, the other from Edinburgh. *Language(s)*: English. Appraised at 1d in 1599.

154.227 Treatise of repentance

William Perkins. *Two treatises. I. Of . . . repentance. II. Of the combat of the flesh and spirit.* London: J. Legate, pr. to the Univ. of Camb., sold by (different houses), 1593–1595.

STC 19758 *et seq. Language(s)*: English. Appraised at 2d in 1599.

154.228 Ramea rhetorica

Charles Butler. *Rameae rhetoricae libri duo.* Oxford: J. Barnesius, 1597–1598.

STC 4196.5 *et seq.* One of La Ramée's works on rhetoric must, of course, also be considered, but the manuscript entry all but duplicates the Butler work. *Language(s)*: Latin. Appraised at 2d in 1599.

154.229   Sanctuary of salvacion

Levinus Lemnius. *The sanctuarie of salvation, helmet of health, and mirrour of modestie.* Translated by Henry Kinder. London: H. Singleton, 1592. STC 15454.5. *Language(s)*: English. Appraised at 4d in 1599.

154.230   7. paenitentiall psalmes

John Fisher, *Saint and Cardinal. This treatise concernynge the fruytfull saynges of Davyd in the seven penytencyall psalmes.* London: T. Marshe, 1555.

STC 10908. Published in eight editions from 1508, all in quarto except this edition, which is in octavo, the size indicated by the compiler. *Language(s)*: English. Appraised at 8d in 1599.

154.231   Junii Eirenicum

François Du Jon, *the Elder. Eirenicum de pace ecclesiae catholicae.* Leyden: ex officina Plantiniana, apud Franciscum Raphelengium, 1593.

Language(s): Latin. Appraised at 4d in 1599.

154.232   Junius in Epist Judae

François Du Jon, *the Elder.* [*Jude: commentary*]. Continent: 1584–1598. *Language(s)*: Latin. Appraised at 4d in 1599.

154.233   D. Rainolds sermon

John Rainolds. Unidentified. Britain: 1584–1586.

Unidentifiable in the STC. Doubtless one of the four books listed as STC 20621 through STC 20623.5, but which is impossible to say. *Language(s)*: English. Appraised at 1d in 1599.

154.234   Another sermon

Unidentified [*sermon*]. Britain: date not determined.

Unidentifiable in the STC. Perhaps another of Rainolds's sermons; see the preceding record. *Language(s):* English. Appraised at 1d in 1599.

154.235   Beza in Seraviam

Théodore de Bèze. *Ad tractationem De ministrorum evangelii gradibus, ab Hadriano Saravia Bela editam.* Geneva (probable): excudebat Joannes Le Preux, 1592–1593.

See 154.66–154.67 for other works involved in this exchange. Gardy nos. 390–391. *Language(s)*: Latin. Appraised at 5d in 1599.

154.236 Beza de justificatione

Théodore de Bèze. *Apologia pro justificatione per unius Christi viva fide apprehensi justitiam gratis imputatam.* Geneva: excudebat Joannes Le Preux, 1592. Gardy no. 384. *Language(s)*: Latin. Appraised at 8d in 1599.

154.237 Hermannus Renniccerus

Herman Rennecherus. Unidentified. Continent: date not determined. *Language(s)*: Latin. Appraised at 3d in 1599.

154.238 Junius de peccato originali

Unidentified. François Du Jon, *the Elder* (*Praes.*). Leyden: (different houses), 1597–1598.

Not properly the work of Du Jon; rather one of the several academic disputations with slightly different titles on the subject of original sin that he presided over while professor of theology at the University of Leyden. *Language(s)*: Latin. Appraised at 3d in 1599.

154.239 Piscatoris Antidromus

Johann Piscator. *Antidromus ad prodromum Andreae Schaafmanni.* Siegen: ex officina Christophori Corvini, 1596.

The only solo edition (see VD16). Also published as part of *Disputatio theologica de praedestinatione* (1595–1598), from which this item may have been detached given its low valuation. *Language(s)*: Latin. Appraised at 1d in 1599.

154.240 Nilus de primatu Papae

Nilus Cabasilas, *Archbishop*. *De primatu papae Romani libri duo.* Translated by Bonaventura Vulcanius. Leyden: ex off. Plantiniana, apud Franciscum Raphelengium, 1595.

Published in 1555 as *De primatu Romani Pontificis*, often erroneously treated as a different work. The manuscript entry, however, identifies this item as the 1595 edition. *Language(s)*: Greek Latin. Appraised at 4d in 1599.

154.241 Livelei annotationes quosdam prophetas

Edward Lively. *Annotationes in quinq; priores ex minoribus prophetis.* London: G. Bishop, 1587.

STC 16608. *Language(s)*: Latin. Appraised at 6d in 1599.

154.242 Death of Usury

The death of usury, or the disgrace of usurers. London: J. Legatt, pr. to the Univ. of Cambridge, sold by (different houses), 1594.

STC 6443. Published anonymously. *Language(s)*: English. Appraised at 1d in 1599.

154.243 Genesis Haebraice
[*Bible — O.T. — Genesis*]. Continent: date not determined. *Language(s)*: Hebrew. Appraised at 6d in 1599.

154.244 Lauren: Valla
Laurentius Valla. Unidentified. Continent: date not determined.
Most likely the *Elegantiae*, but other works are possible. *Language(s)*: Latin. Appraised at 8d in 1599.

154.245 Jo: Cant. Archiep. perspectivae
John Peckham, *Archbishop of Canterbury*. *Perspectiva communis*. Continent: date not determined.
With the exception of the 1504 folio edition, the many sixteenth-century editions were all issued in quarto. Editions date from 1482. *Language(s)*: Latin. Appraised at 6d in 1599.

154.246 testamentum graec 16
[*Bible — N.T.*]. Britain or Continent: date not determined.
STC 2793 *et seq.* and non-STC. *Language(s)*: Greek. Appraised at 10d in 1599.

154.247 Bible englishe 4to
The Bible. Britain or Continent: date not determined. STC 2065 et seq. and non-STC. An initial appraisal of 6*s* has been struck through. *Language(s)*: English. Appraised at 5s in 1599.

George Barton. Scholar (B.Th):
Probate Inventory. 1602

RIVES NICHOLSON

A native of Lancashire, George Barton (Burton) was a fellow of Brasenose College, Oxford, where he received his B.A. in 1588; he proceeded M.A. four years later in 1592 and was granted a B.Th. in 1600. He died on May 11, 1602, according to the inventory of his goods, and was buried from the university parish church, St. Mary's, two days later (*Alumni Oxonienses,* 1:80; Clark [Wood] 1899, 3: 238). On May 14, an inventory of his belongings was compiled for probate; the inventory includes his library of thirteen identified books and a group of some eighty "ould bookes and pomflets" that the compiler vexingly failed to list by title. Also recorded in the inventory is a sad jumble of shabby "old" articles of clothing that betray Barton's apparently humble life.

The known portion of Barton's library is that of a student of divinity whose attraction to the more heated Protestant literature of his day was balanced by a receptiveness to the devotional writings of Catholics and an openness to unorthodox views of fraught topics such as witchcraft. *The Theatre of God's judgements*, a tract by the Puritan divine Thomas Beard, based on Jean Chassanion's *Histoires memorables des grans et merveilleux jugemens et punitions de Dieu*, portions of which he appropriated in translation and then augmented further, offers lurid contemporary examples of divine punishment of sinners and a skewed account of the death of Christopher Marlowe. The commentary on the sapiential books of the Old Testament by the German reformer Lucas Osiander, *the Elder*, perhaps shares some of its fire. The heat of these texts is, however, chilled somewhat by the company of Biblical commentaries and devotional works by Protestant reformers of a less flammable temperament, among them Théodore de Bèze's paraphrase of the Psalms and Philipp Melanchthon's *Argumentorum et objectionum de praecipuis articulis doctrinae Christianae. De contemnendis mundi vanitatibus*, a popular devotional work by the Spanish Franciscan friar Diego de Estella, introduces a current of mysticism into Barton's library. And Johann

Wier's *De praestigiis daemonum*, a prescient tract on witch-hunting that argues that the objects of such crusades are foolish, simple-minded old women rather than nefarious agents of Satan, strikes a note of rational inquiry. The library is rounded out by a Greek lexicon, an English edition of Plutarch's *Lives*, and an English Bible, standbys in private libraries of the period.

The most interesting members of Barton's library may have been found among the eighty or so books and pamphlets that the compiler for whatever reason chose not to identify.

Oxford University Archives, Bodleian Library: Hyp.B.10.

§

Clark, Andrew, ed. 1899. *"Survey of the Antiquities of the City of Oxford,"* Composed in 1661–6 by Antony Wood. Vol. 3. Oxford: Printed for the Oxford Historical Society at the Clarendon Press.

§

155.1   a bible in english in 4°
155.2   a scapula in folio
155.3   Plutarcke his lives in english
155.4   Ortelius
155.5   Osiander in libros sapientiales
155.6:1:12   two paper bookes in folio, and six in 4°
155.6:2:16   [See 155.6:1]
155.7   Wierus de prestigiis
155.8   the theatre of gods judgments
155.9   Pagnini Epitome
155.10   Pezelius de articulis fidei
155.11   Bezae paraphrasis in Psalmos
155.12   Stella de contemptu mundi
155.13   Aretii Isagoge ad lectionem epistolarum divi Pauli
155.14:1–80   foure score ould bookes and pomflets

§

155.1   a bible in english in 4°
The Bible. Britain or Continent: date not determined.
STC 2063 *et seq. Language(s)*: English. Appraised at 8s in 1602.

155.2 a scapula in folio
Joannes Scapula. *Lexicon graecolatinum novum*. Continent: date not determined.
Language(s): Greek Latin. Appraised at 10s in 1602.

155.3 Plutarcke his lives in english
Plutarch. *The lives of the noble Grecians and Romanes*. Translated by Sir Thomas North. London: (different houses), 1579–1595.
STC 20065 *et seq. Language(s)*: English. Appraised at 10s in 1602.

155.4 Ortelius
Abraham Ortelius. Probably *Theatrum orbis terrarum*. Continent: date not determined.

The *Theatrum orbis terrarum* was Ortelius's most widely published work, and at 8*s*, one of the large folio editions is likely here and not the English versions of the *Epitome* in octavo format. *Language(s)*: Latin. Appraised at 8s in 1602.

155.5 Osiander in libros sapientiales
Probably Lucas Osiander, *the Elder*. Unidentified. Continent: date not determined.

Doubtless a commentary on the sapiential books of the Old Testament, but none of the commentaries by Osiander on those books was published separately or even, it appears, in a discrete volume. The best candidate is probably Osiander's large collection of biblical commentaries (Tübingen, 1586) that carries in its title, as the second item, *Liber Sapientiae*. Then again, it might be that portion of the collection separated from the whole. *Language(s)*: Latin. Appraised at 2s in 1602.

155.6:1:1–2 two paper bookes in folio, and six in 4°
Unidentified. Provenances unknown: dates not determined.
Manuscripts. *Language(s)*: Unknown. Appraised with six others at 26s in 1602.

155.6:2:1–6 [See 155.6:1]
Unidentified. Provenances unknown: dates not determined.
Manuscripts. *Language(s)*: Unknown. Appraised with two others at 26s in 1602.

155.7 Wierus de prestigiis
Johann Wier. *De praestigiis daemonum*. Continent: 1563–1586.
Language(s): Latin. Appraised at 2s in 1602.

155.8 the theatre of gods judgments

Thomas Beard, editor and translator. *The theatre of Gods judgements*. London: A. Islip, 1597.

STC 1659. A translation and augmentation of Jean Chassanion's *Histoires memorables des grans et merveilleux jugemens et punitions de Dieu*. *Language(s)*: English. Appraised at 2s 6d in 1602.

155.9 Pagnini Epitome

Sanctes Pagninus. *Thesauri linguae sanctae epitome*. Continent: 1570–1599. *Language(s)*: Hebrew Latin. Appraised at 2s 6d in 1602.

155.10 Pezelius de articulis fidei

Philipp Melanchthon. *Argumentorum et objectionum de praecipuis articulis doctrinae Christianae*. Edited by Christoph Pezel. Continent: date not determined. *Language(s)*: Latin. Appraised at 12d in 1602.

155.11 Bezae paraphrasis in Psalmos

Théodore de Bèze. [*Psalms: paraphrase*]. (*Bible — O.T.*). Britain or Continent: date not determined.

STC 2032 *et seq.* and non-STC. *Language(s)*: Latin. Appraised at 12d in 1602.

155.12 Stella de contemptu mundi

Diego de Estella. *De contemnendis mundi vanitatibus*. Cologne: (different houses), 1585–1599.

Language(s): Latin. Appraised at 8d in 1602.

155.13 Aretii Isagoge ad lectionem epistolarum divi Pauli

Benedictus Aretius. *Isagoge ad lectionem epistolarum D. Pauli*. Continent: 1574–1584.

Language(s): Latin. Appraised at 8d in 1602.

155.14:1–80 foure score ould bookes and pomflets

Unidentified. Places unknown: stationers unknown, dates not determined.

STC/non-STC status unknown. *Language(s)*: Unknown. Appraised at 13s 4d in 1602.

PRIVATE LIBRARIES IN RENAISSANCE ENGLAND 156

Richard Fisher. Scholar (M.A.):
Probate Inventory. 1602

JOSEPH L. BLACK AND JULIETTE M. CUNICO

Richard Fisher (Fysher, Fyssher) matriculated from Merton College: his father "claimed admission for him as of Founder's kin, but this claim was disallowed, and he was expressly elected on grounds of merit" (Brodrick 1885, 272). He was elected a fellow of Merton in 1577, received his Bachelor of Arts degree in February 1579, and received his Master of Arts degree in May 1583. He was elected College Proctor in January 1593, but in October 1598 was suspended from his fellowship for insubordination; he was restored a year later, in October 1599 (Clark 2:i.246, 2:iii.79; Brodrick 1885, 272; *Alumni Oxonienses*, 1:501; *Athenae Oxonienses*, 5:257). Fisher may have had a family connection to Bedford: the following inventory was made in February 1602 because, as the inventory's heading indicates, Fisher's goods came to the "hands possession & disposition of Edmond Bloffeild [Blofield] of Flitwicke in the countie of Bedford yeoman Administrator of the same."

Fisher's collection of about one hundred books focuses on law, literature, history, rhetoric, and grammar, accompanied by an interestingly diverse scattering of works on subjects such as divination, emblems, medicine, and mathematics; he owned almost no works of theology. He possessed several works in Greek, and much of his literature and history appears in Continental vernaculars, including French but particularly Italian and, more unusually, Spanish. His works in Italian include Tasso (156.12), Boccaccio (156.31 is probably an edition in Italian of *Il Filocopo*, though it could be an English translation), Paolo Giovio (156.29), collections of dialogues (156.34) and drama (156.43), and a translation of Dionysius of Halicarnassus (156.11). In Spanish he owned a Bible (156.16), Pedro Mexia's *Historia imperial y caesarea* (156.6), and an historical romance by Ginés Perez de Hita (156.42). Some unidentified books apparently in Latin (e.g., 156.7, 156.10, 156.20) may also be in one of these other languages: this cataloguer often translates vernacular titles into Latin. Other Continental literary works not found in previous Oxford (PLRE) inventories include Pietro Angelio's *Cynegetica* (156.14) and Henri Estienne's *Schediasmatum variorum* (156.25).

The manuscript of this inventory appears to be a scribal copy of the original list made onsite. While written in a professionally clear hand, the manuscript's extra distance from the books themselves is reflected in occasional scribal errors that have posed difficulties of identification. The clearly written "Judicae," "Cynrgetica," and "Fiacovanti" were ultimately identified as Judicialum, Cynegetica, and Fioravanti; however, author names such as "Gossipe" and "Mathri" so far remain (probably garbled) mysteries. An additional complication has been mentioned already: the habitual translation of vernacular titles into Latin. Some entries may also reflect the same process in reverse (e.g., 156.3). Fisher's library is mentioned by Mark Curtis, who notes its high proportion of books in Continental vernaculars (Curtis 1959, 136n and 285n).

Oxford University Archives, Bodleian Library: Hyp.B.12.

§

Brodrick, George C. 1885. *Memorials of Merton College*. Oxford Historical Society, vol. 4. Oxford: Clarendon Press.

Curtis, Mark. 1959. *Oxford and Cambridge in Transition, 1558–1642*. Oxford: Clarendon Press.

§

156.1:1–3	3 french lawbookes in folio cum Judicae Rastall
156.1:4	[See 156.1:13]
156.2	Polydorus virgilius in folio
156.3	the Storie of Saxonie imperfect
156.4	the poore mans librarye
156.5:1–4	4 statute bookes in folio
156.6	Imperiales historiae hispanice
156.7	Historia Hispanica folio
156.8	Institutiones Civiles 16°
156.9	Institutiones Canonicae 4°
156.10	Gosippe historia gallica
156.11	Halicarnasseus de civitate Romana Itallicae
156.12	Tassus ittalice
156.13	fragmenta Ciceronis
156.14:1	Angelii Cynrgetica et gramatice vetus greece
156.14:2	[See 156.14:1]
156.15	Peucerus de devinatione
156.16	Biblia hispanica
156.17	Galen de simplicibus medicamentis

156.18	Orationes Ciceronis volumen primum
156.19	Ciceronis: epistole familiares
156.20	Mathri: historia Indica
156.21	Ciceronis philosophiae duo volumnia
156.22	methodus juris
156.23	dictionarium Italicum
156.24	Epistolae Ciceronis ad Atticum
156.25	Stephani Schediasmata
156.26	Leonardi Fiacovanti medicinales
156.27	Opuscula Levini Lemini
156.28	Texita in Ciceronem ad herennium
156.29	Regionamenta de P. Jovio
156.30	Nomenclator Junii
156.31	Boccatii Phelocopo
156.32	Appothegmata Erasmi
156.33	Speculum Marantae
156.34	Baptistae Dialogus Italice
156.35	Bezae test: grec: latinae
156.36	Justinii historia
156.37	Gemma Frisii Arithmetica
156.38	Justini historia
156.39	Homelii Cliotovie
156.40	Erasmi Copia
156.41	Linacer de Emendata structura
156.42	historia de bello Civili Granad
156.43	Comed et Traged Italice
156.44	Institutiones Justiniane
156.45	historia de regno Navarre
156.46	Boccatius 16°
156.47:1	Horatius bis
156.47:2	[See 156.47:1]
156.48	Bricott in physica
156.49:1–2	2 old Canon lawbookes
156.50	Terentius
156.51	wesenbechii paratitla
156.52	Lexcion [Lexicon] Juris Civilis et Canonici
156.53	Ausonius
156.54:1	Herodote Clio graece Theodiogii gram grece
156.54:2	[See 156.54:1]
156.55	Comentaria in parva Naralia Arlis:
156.56	Faber Stapulensis in phisica
156.57	Eustratius in Ethica
156.58	Arlis: metaphisica in 4°

156.59 Ethica in 4°
156.60 Toletus de Anima
156.61 Arlis: politica in 4°
156.62 Talei Accademia
156.63 Strabeus in partitiones Ciceronis
156.64 Frigii in Orationes Ciceronis 3ia vol
156.65 Arlis: Rhetorica
156.66 Manutii epistole
156.67 Conciliatio Arlis: et platonis
156.68:1 Omphalius cum Rami Ciceronian
156.68:2 [See 156.68:1]
156.69 Caelus 2 in partitiones Cicer:
156.70 Mathiolius in Analitice
156.71 Erythraeus de Conscribend epistolis
156.72 testament: graecae 16°
156.73 multiple   a baskett with old bookes & papers
156.74:1–14   a box with locke & little desk & 14 oldbookes in the box

§

156.1:1–3   3 french lawbookes in folio cum Judicae Rastall

Unidentified. London (probable): date not determined.

Not identifiable in the STC. Fitzherbert's folio multi-volume *Grand abridgement* is a good candidate, but there are many other possibilities. *Language(s)*: Law French. Appraised as a group with one other at 6s in 1602.

156.1:4   [See 156.1:1–3]

Registrum omnium brevium tam originalium quam judicialium. Edited by William Rastell. London: (different houses), 1531–1595.

STC 20836 *et seq*. A register of legal writs. The compiler apparently transcribed "judicialium" as "Judicae" *Language(s)*: Latin. Appraised with a group of three others at 6s in 1602.

156.2   Polydorus virgilius in folio

Polydorius Vergilius. Unidentified. Continent: date not determined.

The *Anglica historia* appeared in several folio editions, but other of his works were issued in that format as well, though none from England. *Language(s)*: Latin. Appraised at 3s in 1602.

156.3   the Storie of Saxonie imperfect

Unidentified. Place unknown: stationer unknown, date not determined.

STC/non-STC status unknown. Albert Krantz's *Saxonia* is a likely candidate; this work is mentioned in contemporary printed English sources as his "storie of Saxonie," and this inventory often records books in a language other than the one in which they were printed (though usually translating vernacular to Latin). If, however, the work was in English, as suggested by the manuscript entry, nothing on Saxony is found to be extant in English from this period. *Language(s)*: English (perhaps) Latin (perhaps). Appraised at 6d in 1602.

156.4 the poore mans librarye
William Alley, *Bishop*. *Ptochomouseion. The poore mans librarie*. London: J. Daye, 1565–1571.
STC 374 *et seq. Ptochomouseion* is in Greek characters. *Language(s)*: English. Appraised at 2s in 1602.

156.5:1–4 4 statute bookes in folio
Unidentified [*England-Statutes*]. Britain: date not determined.
STC 9264 *et seq.* Likely a tattered collection (see the valuation of the folio volumes at 156.1:1–3), but precisely which statutes cannot be determined. *Language(s)*: English (probable) Latin (probable) Law French (probable). Appraised at 16d in 1602.

156.6 Imperiales historiae hispanice
Pedro Mexia. *Historia imperial y caesarea*. Continent: date not determined.
The *hispanice* in the manuscript entry is in a different hand. *Language(s)*: Spanish. Appraised at 3s 4d in 1602.

156.7 Historia Hispanica folio
Unidentified. Continent: date not determined.
The manuscript entry suggests a Latin work, but given the preceding, Spanish is possible. *Language(s)*: Latin (probable) Spanish (perhaps). Appraised at 3s 4d in 1602.

156.8 Institutiones Civiles 16°
Justinian I. *Institutiones*. (*Corpus juris civilis*). Continent: date not determined.
Another copy at 156.44. *Language(s)*: Greek Latin. Appraised at 16d in 1602.

156.9 Institutiones Canonicae 4°
Perhaps Giovanni Paolo Lancelotto. *Institutiones juris canonici*. Continent: date not determined.
At this valuation, the entire *Corpus juris canonici*, with an erroneous "Institutiones" carried over from the preceding item, is not at all likely. An alternative

to the Lancelotto is the Marcus Antonius Cucchus, *Institutionum juris canonici libri quatuor*. Given the apparent transcription problems associated with this fair copy list, a manuscript entry that should have been "Constitutiones" rather than "Institutiones" cannot be ruled out entirely. Several other works would then be possible. *Language(s)*: Latin. Appraised at 20d in 1602.

156.10   Gosippe historia gallica

Unidentified. Continent (probable): date not determined.

Probably not an STC book. Perhaps "historia gallica" is a descriptive entry rather than an actual title. Works of Richardus Dinothus and of Paulus Aemylius have been entered in such a manner; see BCI 2:275 and 2:5. *Gosippe*, whatever is intended, does not suggest these or any other known writer of French history. Very likely yet another fair copy transcription error. *Language(s)*: Latin. Appraised at 6d in 1602.

156.11   Halicarnasseus de civitate Romana Itallicae

Dionysius, *of Halicarnassus*. *Delle cose antiche della Citta di Roma*. Translated by Francesco Venturi. Venice: per Nicolo Bascarini a instantia de Michel Tramezzino, 1545.

The sole Italian translation and edition at the date of this inventory. The manuscript entry is in a precise italic hand—unlike the rest of the list which is in the secretary hand—and perhaps inserted in the list. *Language(s)*: Italian. Appraised at 8d in 1602.

156.12   Tassus ittalice

Unidentified. Continent: date not determined.

Torquato Tasso is probably more likely than Bernardo Tasso, but the latter, as well as the less widely published Faustino Tasso, is possible; all wrote and were pubished in Italian. Inserted in a different hand. *Language(s)*: Italian. Appraised at 12d in 1602.

156.13   fragmenta Ciceronis

Marcus Tullius Cicero. [*Selections—Fragmenta*]. Continent: date not determined.

Language(s): Latin. Appraised at 6d in 1602.

156.14:1 Angelii Cynrgetica et gramatice vetus greece

Pietro Angelio. *Cynegetica*. Lyon: apud haered. Sebast. Gryphii, 1561. *Language(s)*: Latin. Appraised with one other at 6d in 1602.

156.14:2 [See 156.14:1]

Unidentified [*grammar*]. Continent (probable): date not determined.

STC/non-STC status unknown. The sole Greek grammar published in England by this date was Edward Grant's in 1575 (STC 12188) and would probably not be described as "old," but it must be considered. STC 6044a.5 was published in 1520, but in Cologne. *Language(s)*: Greek Latin. Appraised with one other at 6d in 1602.

156.15 Peucerus de devinatione

Kaspar Peucer. *Commentarius de praecipuis divinationum generibus*. Continent: 1553–1593.

Language(s): Latin. Appraised at 20d in 1602.

156.16 Biblia hispanica

The Bible. Continent: date not determined.

The Spanish New Testament in octavo (STC 2959), though printed in England in 1596, is not likely intended here given the valuation and the form of the manuscript entry. *Language(s)*: Spanish. Appraised at 3s 4d in 1602.

156.17 Galen de simplicibus medicamentis

Galen. *De simplicium medicamentorum facultatibus*. Continent: date not determined.

A volume of selected works, with this title leading, is also possible. *Language(s)*: Latin. Appraised at 3d in 1602.

156.18 Orationes Ciceronis volumen primum

Marcus Tullius Cicero. [*Selected works—Orations*]. Britain or Continent: date not determined.

STC 5308 *et seq.* and non-STC. *Language(s)*: Latin. Appraised at 4d in 1602.

156.19 Ciceronis: epistole familiares

Marcus Tullius Cicero. *Epistolae ad familiares*. Britain or Continent: date not determined.

STC 5295 *et seq.* and non-STC. *Language(s)*: Latin. Appraised at 6d in 1602.

156.20 Mathri: historia Indica

Unidentified. Place unknown: stationer unknown, date not determined.

STC/non-STC status unknown. The first problem is that the manuscript entry could just as well read "Judica" as "Indica." If the latter is correct, one is tempted to read the "Mathri:" as a garbled "Martyr" for Peter Martyr (Anglerius). But the colon attached to "Mathri" suggests an abbreviation, which would not fit "Martyr." Further, Peter Martyr's *De orbe novo*, in Latin as well as English, cannot be found anywhere referred to as "Indica." If, however, the compiler intended "Judica," one is tempted to consider Pietro Martire Vermigli's commentary on Judges, but then "historia" would have no place. Once again the problem probably stems from the fair copy transcription. *Language(s)*: Latin. Appraised at 18d in 1602.

156.21   Ciceronis philosophiae duo volumnia

Marcus Tullius Cicero. [*Selected works—Philosophica*]. Continent: date not determined.

Language(s): Latin. Appraised at 16d in 1602.

156.22   methodus juris

Unidentified. Continent (probable): date not determined.

Probably not an STC book. Something by Nicolaus Vigelius is probably the best guess; several of his works (e.g., *Methodus juris feudalis*, *Methodus juris controversi*, *Methodus universi juris civilis*) might have been entered in this manner. *Language(s)*: Latin. Appraised at 10d in 1602.

156.23   dictionarium Italicum

Unidentified [*dictionary*]. Continent: date not determined.

If an Italian-English dictionary, entered for some reason by the compiler in Latin, then Florio's dictionary would be a possibility. *Language(s)*: Italian Latin. Appraised at 10d in 1602.

156.24   Epistolae Ciceronis ad Atticum

Marcus Tullius Cicero. *Epistolae ad Atticum*. Continent: date not determined.

Language(s): Latin. Appraised at 6d in 1602.

156.25   Stephani Schediasmata

Henri Estienne. *Schediasmatum variorum*. Continent: excudebat Henricus Stephanus, 1578–1589.

The place of publication is not given, but most sources supply Geneva, some Paris. *Language(s)*: Latin. Appraised at 8d in 1602.

156.26   Leonardi Fiacovanti medicinales

Leonardo Fioravanti. *Capricci medicinali*. Venice: (different houses), 1561–1595.

A 1602 edition was published in Venice, but it would hardly have been in an Oxford library inventoried in February 1602. *Language(s)*: Italian. Appraised at 6d in 1602.

156.27   Opuscula Levini Lemini

Levinus Lemnius. Unidentified. Continent: date not determined.

Nothing of Lemnius's would be described as *Opuscula* and nothing of his in Latin, the language of this item based on the manuscript entry, was published in England. Perhaps, therefore, a misreading or mishearing of his widely published *De miraculis occultis naturae libri IIII*. *Language(s)*: Latin. Appraised at 4d in 1602.

156.28   Texita in Ciceronem ad herennium

Michael Toxites. [*Cicero (spurious)—Rhetorica ad Herennium: commentary and text*]. Basle: Joannes Oporinus with (different houses), 1556–1568. *Language(s)*: Latin. Appraised at 4d in 1602.

156.29   Regionamenta de P. Jovio

Paolo Giovio, *Bishop*. *Ragionamento sopra i motti e disegni d'arme e d'amore*. Venice: appresso Giordano Ziletti, 1556–1560.

The title of the *editio princeps* (1555) is *Dialogo dell'imprese militari et amorose*. *Language(s)*: Italian. Appraised at 4d in 1602.

156.30   Nomenclator Junii

Adrian Junius. *Nomenclator*. Continent: date not determined.

Editions included various vernacular languages as well. The manuscript entry does not, however, suggest the one edition translated into English (STC 14680). *Language(s)*: German Greek Latin. Appraised at 8d in 1602.

156.31   Boccatii Phelocopo

Giovanni Boccaccio. *Il Filocopo*. Britain or Continent: date not determined.

This book need not be in Italian even though Fisher read Italian. The English version (STC 3180) included the word *Philocopo*, though it was placed well into the title. *Language(s)*: Italian (probable) English (perhaps). Appraised at 10d in 1602.

156.32   Appothegmata Erasmi

Desiderius Erasmus. *Apophthegmata*. Continent: date not determined. *Language(s)*: Latin. Appraised at 4d in 1602.

156.33   Speculum Marantae

Robertus Maranta. *Speculum aureum, et lumen advocatorum*. Continent: date not determined.

Language(s): Latin. Appraised at 16d in 1602.

156.34   Baptistae Dialogus Italice

Unidentified. Continent (probable): date not determined.

Probably not an STC book. Baptista Spagnuoli (Mantuanus) wrote *De vita beata dialogus* and *Ad Ptolemeum Gonza. contra detractores dialogus* that might be represented here, but others who wrote dialogues in Italian might be referred to in this manner, including Leon Battista Alberti, Battista Possevino, and Battista Gelli, to name but three. *Language(s)*: Italian. Appraised at 4d in 1602.

156.35   Bezae test: grec: latinae

[*Bible—N.T.*]. Edited and translated by Théodore de Bèze. Continent: date not determined.

Another Greek New Testament at 156.72. *Language(s)*: Greek Latin. Appraised at 2s in 1602.

156.36   Justinii historia

Trogus Pompeius and Justinus, *the Historian*. [*Epitomae in Trogi Pompeii historias*]. Britain or Continent: date not determined.

STC 24287 *et seq*. and non-STC. Another copy at 156.38. *Language(s)*: Latin. Appraised at 12d in 1602.

156.37   Gemma Frisii Arithmetica

Reiner Gemma, *Frisius. Arithmetica practicae methodus facilis*. Continent: date not determined.

Numerous editions from 1540. *Language(s)*: Latin. Appraised at 3d in 1602.

156.38   Justini historia

Trogus Pompeius and Justinus, *the Historian*. [*Epitomae in Trogi Pompeii historias*]. Britain or Continent: date not determined.

STC 24287 *et seq*. and non-STC. Another copy at 156.36. *Language(s)*: Latin. Appraised at 6d in 1602.

156.39   Homelii Cliotovie

Jodocus Clichtoveus. [*Homiliae*]. Continent: date not determined.
Language(s): Latin. Appraised at 3d in 1602.

156.40   Erasmi Copia

Desiderius Erasmus. *De duplici copia verborum ac rerum*. Britain or Continent: date not determined.

STC 10471.4 *et seq*. and non-STC. *Language(s)*: Latin. Appraised at 2d in 1602.

156.41   Linacer de Emendata structura

Thomas Linacre. *De emendata structura Latini sermonis libri sex*. Britain or Continent: 1524–1591.

STC 15634 and non-STC. Of the many editions, all but the first were published on the Continent. *Language(s)*: Latin. Appraised at 3d in 1602.

156.42 historia de bello Civili Granad

Ginés Perez de Hita. *Historia de los vandos de los Zegries y Abencerrajes cavalleros moros de Granada, de las civiles guerras.* Continent: 1595–1598.

This historical romance was customarily referred to as *Guerras civiles de Granada* though that actual title does not appear until the 1606 edition. As with other vernacular titles in this list, the compiler enters the information in Latin. *Language(s)*: Spanish. Appraised at 4d in 1602.

156.43 Comed et Traged Italice

Unidentified. Continent: date not determined.
Language(s): Italian. Appraised at 4d in 1602.

156.44 Institutiones Justiniane

Justinian I. *Institutiones.* (*Corpus juris civilis*). Continent: date not determined.

Another copy at 156.8. *Language(s)*: Greek Latin. Appraised at 10d in 1602.

156.45 historia de regno Navarre

Gabriel Chappuys. *L'Histoire du royaume de Navarre.* Paris: chez Nicolas Gilles, 1596.

Despite the language of the manuscript entry, no Latin translation appears to have existed at the time of this inventory. The compiler habitually enters vernacular titles in Latin. *Language(s)*: French. Appraised at 6d in 1602.

156.46 Boccatius 16°

Giovanni Boccaccio. Unidentified. Continent: date not determined.

The STC does not list any sextodecimo edition of Boccaccio though the compiler could have been in error regarding the volume's size. With Fisher, despite the Latin form of the manuscript entry, the book could have been in Italian, or even English. *Language(s)*: Unknown. Appraised at 2d in 1602.

156.47:1 Horatius bis

Quintus Horatius Flaccus. Probably [*Works*]. Britain or Continent: date not determined.

STC 13784 *et seq.* and non-STC. *Language(s)*: Latin. Appraised with one other at 4d in 1602.

156.47:2 [See 156.47:1]

Quintus Horatius Flaccus. Probably [*Works*]. Britain or Continent: date not determined.

STC 13784 *et seq.* and non-STC. *Language(s)*: Latin. Appraised with one other at 4d in 1602.

156.48 Bricott in physica

Thomas Bricot. [*Aristotle—Physica: commentary*]. Continent: date not determined.
Language(s): Latin. Appraised at 10d in 1602.

156.49:1–2 2 old Canon lawbookes

Unidentified. Continent (probable): date not determined.

Probably not STC books. Volumes so readily identifiable as books on canon law are not likely to have been published in England, though conceivably one of these might have been the widely used *Constitutiones provinciales* of Bishop William Lyndewode. *Language(s)*: Latin (probable). Appraised at 6d in 1602.

156.50 Terentius

Publius Terentius, *Afer*. [*Works*]. Britain or Continent: date not determined.
STC 23885 *et seq.* and non-STC. *Language(s)*: Latin. Appraised at 6d in 1602.

156.51 wesenbechii paratitla

Matthaeus Wesenbecius. [*Digesta: commentary*]. Continent: date not determined.
Language(s): Latin. Appraised at 12d in 1602.

156.52 Lexcion [Lexicon] Juris Civilis et Canonici

Pardoux Duprat. *Lexicon juris civilis et canonici*. Continent: date not determined.
Language(s): Latin. Appraised at 16d in 1602.

156.53 Ausonius

Decimus Magnus Ausonius. [*Works*]. Continent: date not determined.
Language(s): Latin. Appraised at 4d in 1602.

156.54:1 Herodote Clio graece Theodiogii gram grece

Herodotus. *Historiarum liber primus, Clio*. Britain or Continent: date not determined.
STC 13225 and non-STC. The sole edition printed in England appeared in 1591. *Language(s)*: Greek. Appraised with one other at 2d in 1602.

156.54:2 [See 156.54:1]

Theodorus, *Gaza*. [*Institutiones grammaticae*]. Continent: date not determined.
Language(s): Greek. Appraised with one other at 2d in 1602.

156.55   Comentaria in parva Naralia Arlis:
Unidentified. [*Aristotle—Parva naturalia: commentary*]. Continent: date not determined.
Language(s): Latin. Appraised at 12d in 1602.

156.56   Faber Stapulensis in phisica
Jacobus Faber, *Stapulensis*. [*Aristotle—Physica: commentary and paraphrase*]. Continent: date not determined.
Language(s): Latin. Appraised at 12d in 1602.

156.57   Eustratius in Ethica
Eustratius, *Archbishop of Nicaea*. [*Aristotle—Ethica: commentary and text*]. Continent: 1536–1589.
Language(s): Greek (probable) Latin (probable). Appraised at 12d in 1602.

156.58   Arlis: metaphisica in 4°
Aristotle. *Metaphysica*. Continent: date not determined.
Language(s): Latin (probable) Greek (perhaps). Appraised at 12d in 1602.

156.59   Ethica in 4°
Aristotle. *Ethica*. Continent: date not determined.
The only quarto edition of the *Ethica* published in England appeared in 1479 (STC 752) and is probably not represented here in a 1602 inventory. *Language(s)*: Latin (probable) Greek (perhaps). Appraised at 8d in 1602.

156.60   Toletus de Anima
Franciscus Toletus, *Cardinal*. [*Aristotle—De anima: commentary*]. Continent: 1574–1600.
The date range is from Lohr II. A Lyon 1602 edition would surely not be in Fisher's library, the inventory of which was taken in February 1602. *Language(s)*: Latin. Appraised at 12d in 1602.

156.61   Arlis: politica in 4°
Aristotle. *Politica*. Continent: date not determined.
The only edition published in England by the date of this inventory (STC 760) is in English and is in folio. *Language(s)*: Latin. Appraised at 12d in 1602.

156.62   Talei Accademia
Audomarus Talaeus (Omer Talon). *Academia*. Paris: (different houses), 1547–1550.
Two editions in 1550. Each edition contains one or more additional works. *Language(s)*: Latin. Appraised at 4d in 1602.

156.63 Strabeus in partitiones Ciceronis

Jacobus Lodovicus Strebaeus. [*Cicero—De partitione oratoria: commentary and text*]. Continent: date not determined.

Inserted in a different hand. *Language(s)*: Latin. Appraised at 4d in 1602.

156.64 Frigii in Orationes Ciceronis 3ia vol

Marcus Tullius Cicero. [*Selected works—Orationes*]. Edited by Joannes Thomas Freigius. Continent: 1583–1592.

These two editions, the first printed in Basle, the second in Frankfurt am Main, were both issued in three volumes. A 1602 edition published in Hanover would not have been in this collection, which was inventoried in February 1602. *Language(s)*: Latin. Appraised at 4s 6d in 1602.

156.65 Arlis: Rhetorica

Aristotle. *Rhetorica*. Continent: date not determined. *Language(s)*: Latin. Appraised at 3d in 1602.

156.66 Manutii epistole

Paolo Manuzio. *Epistolae*. Britain or Continent: date not determined.

STC 17286 *et seq.* and non-STC. The collection of classical writers, *Epistolae clarorum virorum selectae*, which Manuzio edited, is a less likely possibility. *Language(s)*: Latin. Appraised at 3d in 1602.

156.67 Conciliatio Arlis: et platonis

Gabriele Buratelli. *Praecipuarum controversiarum Arist. et Platonis conciliatio*. Venice: apud Franciscum, Gasparem Bindonum et fratres, 1573.

Language(s): Latin. Appraised at 4d in 1602.

156.68:1 Omphalius cum Rami Ciceronian

Jacobus Omphalius. Unidentified. Continent: date not determined.

Given the grouping with the Ramus, probably one of Omphalius's commentaries on Cicero's orations or his major work on rhetoric, *De elocutionis imitatione ac apparatu*, but he published various works on other subjects. *Language(s)*: Latin. Appraised with one other at 6d in 1602.

156.68:2 [See 156.68:1]

Pierre de la Ramée. *Ciceronianus*. Continent: 1557–1580.

Ong, nos. 487–491. *Language(s)*: Latin. Appraised with one other at 6d in 1602.

156.69 Caelus 2 in partitiones Cicer:
Caelius Secundus Curio. [*Cicero—De partitione oratoria: commentary* (and other works)]. Continent: date not determined.
Language(s): Latin. Appraised at 4d in 1602.

156.70 Mathiolius in Analitice
Perhaps Pietro Andrea Mattioli. Unidentified. Continent: date not determined.

Pietro Mattioli published extensively on medical subjects, areas which seem to have interested Fisher, but no commentary by him on Aristotle's *Analytics* has been found. Perhaps this manuscript entry is a garbled "Anazarbei" improperly transcribed in this fair copy. Mattioli's commentary on *Dioscorides* would then be a possibility. *Language(s)*: Latin (probable) Italian (perhaps). Appraised at 2d in 1602.

156.71 Erythraeus de Conscribend epistolis
Valentinus Erythraeus. *De ratione legendi, explicandi et scribendi epistolas libri tres.* Strassburg: (different houses), 1573–1576.

The stationer Bernhard Jobin was involved with both editions. *Language(s)*: Latin. Appraised at 4d in 1602.

156.72 testament: graecae 16°
[*Bible—N.T.*]. Britain or Continent: date not determined.

STC 2793 *et seq.* and non-STC. The sole Greek New Testament published in England at the time of this inventory was, like this item, in sextodecimo (in two editions) and edited by Bèze, whose Greek and Latin edition of the same appears elsewhere in this collection; another Greek New Testament at 156.35. *Language(s)*: Greek. Appraised at 6d in 1602.

156.73 multiple a baskett with old bookes & papers
Unidentified. Places unknown: stationers unknown, dates not determined.

STC/non-STC status unknown. *Language(s)*: Unknown. Appraised as a group, with other items, at 2s in 1602.

156.74:1–14 a box with locke & little desk & 14 oldbookes in the box
Unidentified. Places unknown: stationers unknown, dates not determined.

STC/non-STC status unknown. *Language(s)*: Unknown. Appraised as a group, with other items, at 5s in 1602.

*William Gearing. Cleric (chaplain), Scholar (M.A.):
Probate Inventory. 1607*

R. J. FEHRENBACH

A Gloucestershire native, William Gearing (Geering, Gering) matriculated from St. John's College on 10 October 1594, aged 17. Admitted B.A. on 1 February 1600 and incepted M.A. on 12 May 1603, he became chaplain at The Queen's College (*Alumni Oxonienses*, 2:556) where he died in early 1607. He was buried from the Church at St. Peter's-in-the-East, Oxford, on 4 February 1607 (Clark [Wood] 1899, 3:255), and a little over two months later, on 11 April 1607, officials compiled an inventory of his goods that included the books listed below.

Not surprisingly for a chaplain, Gearing's library of at least sixty volumes consists overwhelmingly of theological works, with more than two-thirds of the titles on that subject. Most of these works are either exegetical or polemical, the latter distinctly reformist and generally Calvinist. In addition, Gearing's library contains various classical authors, all appropriate to one a few years from his M.A. and B.A. studies, including Aristotle, Cicero, Plautus, and Quintilian along with Plutarch. Hebrew and Greek were among Gearing's languages based on the appearance of several lexicons, grammars, and a Hebrew Bible.

The compilers of the inventory recorded Gearing's books by size, doubtless following the owner's arrangement; in so doing they have provided information that helps to identify particular editions of several works, as does the description of four items as "old," a repeated notation at 157.20–157.22:2, likely made by Lancelot Waistell, a stationer who participated in the inventory. These "old" books are four of Calvin's works printed over forty years earlier by the Genevan stationer Thomas Courteau, and probably purchased by Gearing as a set. Approximately half of Gearing's books were published in England, unusual for an Oxford scholar but not perhaps for a practicing cleric in the early seventeenth century.

On the basis of the inventory, Gearing was hardly a man of means; the valuation of a trunk and all his apparel barely exceeded the value assigned his books, with only a desk and "linning and bedding" completing the description of all the "goods and chattell" of this university cleric, deceased in his thirtieth year.

Oxford University Archives, Bodleian Library: Hyp.B.13.

§

Clark, Andrew, ed. 1899. *"Survey of the Antiquities of the City of Oxford," Composed in 1661–6 by Anthony Wood.* Vol. 3. Oxford: Printed for the Oxford Historical Society at the Clarendon Press.

§

157.1	Fulke on the Rhemish Testament
157.2	Zwinglius in Evangelia et epistolas Pauli
157.3	Eusebii Historia Ecclesiastica
157.4	Scapulae Lexicon graecum
157.5	Avenarii Lexicon Hebraicum
157.6	Aristot. opera duob. vol. lat.
157.7	Perkins workes
157.8	B. Bilson of the difference betweene christian subjection and unchristian rebellion.
157.9	Morellii comment. verborum latinorum
157.10	Ursini Catechism engl.
157.11	Morney of the Church eng:
157.12	Dod on the Commandments
157.13	Dod on the 10 and 9. chapt. of the proverbs
157.14	Canons of the Church of England
157.15	Perkinsi problemata.
157.16	Gyffard on the Revelation
157.17	D. Pye de divortiis Judaeorum
157.18	Whitakeri prelectiones
157.19	Udall on Jeremie
157.20	Calvin institutiones lat. old
157.21	Idem in psalmos old
157.22	Idem in Epistolas Pauli old
157.23:1	Idem in Evang. et Acta Apostolorum old
157.23:2	[See 157.23:1]
157.24	A bible engl
157.25	Bullingeri decades
157.26	Chemnitii examen duob. vol.
157.27	Musculi loci communes
157.28	Lubbertus de papa Romano.
157.29	Melanthonis loci communes

157.30   Bezae confessio lat.
157.31   Hyperius de ratione studii Theolog.
157.32   Bonaventura de Politia Judaica
157.33   Reward of Religion
157.34   Vorstii Enchiridion
157.35   Trelcatius
157.36   Piscator in novum testam:
157.37   Sanderi demonstrao
157.38   Danei Elenchus haereticorum
157.39   Polani partitiones
157.40   Biblia Hebraica 2bus vol.
157.41   Blebelii Grammat. Hebraica
157.42   Quinitilianus
157.43   Clenardi grammat. graec.
157.44   Cic. de philosophia volum. duo.
157.45:1 Eiusdem epist. ad Atticum et fam.
157.45:2 [See 157.45:1]
157.46   Tullius de oratore
157.47   Plautus
157.48   Plutarchi vitae 3bus vol.
157.49   Eiusdem moral. vol. tantum duo
157.50   Willet on Jude
157.51   Gyffard on the Canticles
157.52   Rainoldi Theses

§

157.1   Fulke on the Rhemish Testament

The text of the New Testament translated by the papists. (*Bible*). London: (different houses), 1589–1601.

STC 2888 *et seq*. Rheims and The Bishops' Bible versions in parallel columns, with commentary by William Fulke, refuting the Roman glosses, which are also included. *Language(s)*: English. Appraised at 8s in 1607.

157.2   Zwinglius in Evangelia et epistolas Pauli

Ulrich Zwingli. *In evangelicam historiam de Jesu Christo annotationes.* Edited by Leo Juda. Zürich: excud. Christophorus Froschouerus, 1539.

The collected commentaries of Zwingli on the New Testament, with additions by Caspar Megander. Adams Z236. *Language(s)*: Latin. Appraised at 18d in 1607.

157.3 Eusebii Historia Ecclesiastica

Eusebius, *Pamphili, Bishop. Historia ecclesiastica.* Continent: date not determined.
Language(s): Latin. Appraised at 5s in 1607.

157.4 Scapulae Lexicon graecum

Joannes Scapula. *Lexicon graecolatinum novum.* Continent: date not determined.
Language(s): Greek Latin. Appraised at 8s in 1607.

157.5 Avenarii Lexicon Hebraicum

Johann Habermann (Joannes Avenarius). *Liber radicum seu lexicon ebraicum.* Wittenberg: (different houses), 1568–1589.

The printers were Johann Crato for the 1568 edition and his heirs for the 1589 edition. *Language(s)*: Hebrew Latin. Appraised at 3s in 1607.

157.6 Aristot. opera duob. vol. lat.

Aristotle. [*Works*]. Continent: date not determined.
Language(s): Latin. Appraised at 3s in 1607.

157.7 Perkins workes

William Perkins. *The works of that famous and worthie minister of Christ, in the universitie of Cambridge, M. W. Perkins: gathered into one volume, and newly corrected according to his owne copies.* Cambridge: J. Legat, pr. to the Univ. of Camb., 1603 (1602) 1605.

STC 19647 *et seq.* Other publishers of the 1603 edition mentioned are J. Porter and R. Jackson, who died in 1601; Simon Waterson of London is identified as bookseller on the 1605 title page. STC 19646 (1600) is in quarto; the compiler describes this item as folio. *Language(s)*: English. Appraised at 5s in 1607.

157.8 B. Bilson of the difference betweene christian subjection and unchristian rebellion.

Thomas Bilson, *Bishop. The true difference betweene christian subjection and unchristian rebellion.* Oxford: J. Barnes, 1585.

STC 3071. A London 1586 edition was in octavo, not quarto as the compiler assigns here. *Language(s)*: English. Appraised at 2s 6d in 1607.

157.9 Morellii comment. verborum latinorum

Gulielmus Morelius. *Verborum latinorum cum graecis gallicisque conjunctorum, commentarii.* Continent: 1558–1578.

This is not the 1583 London edition (STC 18101), which replaced French with English, since that edition was issued in folio, and this item is identified as a quarto. The valuation is not out of line with other quarto books in this section of Gearing's collection; see the preceding item, definitely a quarto and valued at 2s 6d, as well as the next. See also considerably higher valuations (8s to 11s 6d) of the folio editions of this work cited in booklists in BCI 2:555. *Language(s)*: French Greek Latin. Appraised at 2s 8d in 1607.

157.10   Ursini Catechism engl.

Zacharias Ursinus. *The summe of christian religion*. Edited by Richard Crosse. English translation by Henry Parry, *Bishop*. Oxford and London: J. Barnes, sold [by J. Broome, London], 1601.

STC 24536. Originally in German, the Latin translation by David Pareus is included in this sole quarto edition published before the date of this inventory. The long title of this edition continues: "delivered by Zacharias Ursinus, in his Lectures upon the Catechisme." Ursinus's name does not feature in any of the English translations of the Heidelberg catechism (STC 13028 *et seq.*) despite his role in the creation of the original. *Language(s)*: English Latin. Appraised at 2s in 1607.

157.11   Morney of the Church eng:

Philippe de Mornay. *A treatise of the church*. Translated by J. Molle. London: L. S[nowden] for G. Potter, 1606.

STC 18162. A different translation was published several times between 1579 and 1581 but not in quarto, which the compiler assigns here. *Language(s)*: English. Appraised at 18d in 1607.

157.12   Dod on the Commandments

John Dod and Robert Cleaver. *A plaine and familiar exposition of the Ten commandements, with a methodicall short catechisme*. London: (different houses) for T. Man, 1604–1607.

STC 6968 *et seq.* The 1603 edition (with a second issue) was published anonymously, and therefore, the compiler, unless he was unusually well acquainted with the literature, would not have entered the item with Dod's name. The 1603 quarto remains, however, a possibility. *Language(s)*: English. Appraised at 10d in 1607.

157.13   Dod on the 10 and 9. chapt. of the proverbs

John Dod and Robert Cleaver. *A plaine and familiar exposition of the ninth and tenth chapters of the Proverbs of Salomon*. (*Bible — O.T.*). London: (different houses) for T. Man, 1606.

STC 6954 *et seq.* Two editions in 1606. *Language(s)*: English. Appraised at 3d in 1607.

157.14 Canons of the Church of England
[*Church of England—Constitutions and Canons*]. London: (different houses), 1571–1604.

STC 10062.5 *et seq.* The canons of 1603 (STC 10068 *et seq.*) are more likely than the sixteenth-century issues. *Language(s)*: English (probable) Latin (perhaps). Appraised at 3d in 1607.

157.15 Perkinsi problemata.
William Perkins. *Problema de Romanae fidei ementito catholicismo*. Edited by Samuel Ward, *of Cambridge*. Cambridge and London: ex officina J. Legat, extant Londini ap. S. Waterson, 1604.

STC 19734. The 1604 edition published in Hanau was in octavo (Shaaber P139), not quarto as indicated by the compiler here. *Language(s)*: Latin. Appraised at 6d in 1607.

157.16 Gyffard on the Revelation
George Gifford. *Sermons upon the whole booke of the Revelation*. London: (different houses), 1596–1599.

STC 11866 *et seq. Language(s)*: English. Appraised at 20d in 1607.

157.17 D. Pye de divortiis Judaeorum
Thomas Pie. *Epistola ad ornatissimum virum D. Johannem Housonum qua dogma eius novum et admirabile de Judaeorum divortiis refutatur*. London: excudebat Arn. Hatfieldus, 1603.

STC 19899. The running title reads: "De Divortiis Judaeorum." Written in response to STC 13886 (John Howson, *Bishop*). *Language(s)*: Latin. Appraised at 2d in 1607.

157.18 Whitakeri prelectiones
William Whitaker. *Praelectiones . . . in quibus tractatur controversia de ecclesia*. Edited by John Allenson. Cambridge: ex off. J. Legat, acad. Cantab. typog., 1599.

STC 25368. Includes a work of Abdias Ashton. Other editions of this work and other titles with "Praelectiones" leading were all published in octavo, not quarto as the compiler indicates here. *Language(s)*: Latin. Appraised at 16d in 1607.

157.19 Udall on Jeremie
John Udall. *A commentarie upon the Lamentations of Jeremy*. (*Bible—O.T.*). London: (different houses) for T. Man, 1593–1599.

STC 24494 *et seq*. With selections of the text. *Language(s)*: English. Appraised at 4d in 1607.

157.20   Calvin institutiones lat. old

Jean Calvin. *Institutio Christianae religionis*. Britain or Continent: date not determined.

STC 4414 and non–STC. *Language(s)*: Latin. Appraised at 14d in 1607.

157.21   Idem in psalmos old

Jean Calvin. *In librum Psalmorum commentarius*. Geneva: excudebant Nicolaus Barbirius et Thomas Courteau, 1564.

The only octavo edition. *Language(s)*: Latin. Appraised at 16d in 1607.

157.22   Idem in Epistolas Pauli old

Jean Calvin. *Commentarii in epistolas Pauli atque in ep. ad Hebraeos et omnes epistolas canonicas*. Geneva: excudebat Thomas Curteus, 1565.

The only octavo edition among six editions before the date of this inventory; the 1565 date would qualify as "old." *Language(s)*: Latin. Appraised at 18d in 1607.

157.23:1   Idem in Evang. et Acta Apostolorum old

Jean Calvin. *Harmonia ex tribus evangelistis, adjuncto Joanne*. Geneva: excudebant Nicolaus Barbirius et Thomas Courteau, 1563–1564 (single edition).

The only octavo edition among six published before the date of this inventory, probably bound with the following. *Language(s)*: Latin. Appraised with one other at 18d in 1607.

157.23:2   [See 157.23:1]

Jean Calvin. *Commentarii in Acta Apostolorum*. Geneva: excudebant Nicolaus Barbarius et Thomas Courteau, 1564.

The only octavo edition among seven editions printed before the date of this inventory. Probably bound with the preceding. *Language(s)*: Latin. Appraised with one other at 18d in 1607.

157.24   A bible engl

The Bible. Britain or Continent: 1566–c.1607.

STC 2098.5 *et seq*. All of the English Bibles published in the octavo format during the date range were the Geneva version with the exception of the c.1566 edition, a Great Bible version. The valuation is unusually high for a book in octavo. *Language(s)*: English. Appraised at 2s 6d in 1607.

157.25   Bullingeri decades

Heinrich Bullinger. *Sermonum decades*. London: excudebat Henricus Midletonus, impensis Radulphi Newberii et Hugonis Jaksoni, 1587.

STC 4076. Staedtke no. 189. According to Staedtke's census, the sole octavo edition of this title. *Language(s)*: Latin. Appraised at 20d in 1607.

157.26 Chemnitii examen duob. vol.
Martinus Chemnitius. *Examen concilii Tridentini*. (*Councils — Trent*). Continent: date not determined.
The Frankfurt am Main 1566 octavo edition of two volumes (Adams C1436 and C1437) is a good possibility. *Language(s)*: Latin. Appraised at 4s in 1607.

157.27 Musculi loci communes
Wolfgang Musculus. *Loci communes*. Continent: date not determined.
Loci communes sacri by Andreas Musculus, less widely published and with all editions apparently in folio size, is not likely since the compiler lists this item among octavo volumes. *Language(s)*: Latin. Appraised at 22d in 1607.

157.28 Lubbertus de papa Romano.
Sibrandus Lubbertus. *De Papa Romano libri decem*. Franeker: apud Aegidium Radaeum, 1594–1595.
Language(s): Latin. Appraised at 18d in 1607.

157.29 Melanthonis loci communes
Philipp Melanchthon. [*Loci communes theologici*]. Continent: date not determined.
Language(s): Latin. Appraised at 6d in 1607.

157.30 Bezae confessio lat.
Théodore de Bèze. *Confessio christianae fidei*. Britain or Continent: 1560–1595.
STC 2006 *et seq.* and non–STC. Gardy nos. 114–122. *Language(s)*: Latin. Appraised at 4d in 1607.

157.31 Hyperius de ratione studii Theolog.
Andreas Gerardus, *Hyperius*. *De theologo, sive De ratione studii theologici*. Britain or Continent: date not determined.
Language(s): Latin. Appraised at 6d in 1607.

157.32 Bonaventura de Politia Judaica
Bonaventure Corneille Bertram. *De politia judaica*. Geneva: apud Eustathium Vignon, 1574–1580.
Language(s): Latin. Appraised at 2d in 1607.

157.33 Reward of Religion
Edward Topsell. *The reward of religion*. London: J. Windet, 1596–1601.
STC 24127 *et seq. Language(s)*: English. Appraised at 4d in 1607.

157.34 Vorstii Enchiridion

Conrad Vorstius. *Enchiridion controversium: seu index errorum ecclesiae Romanae, una cum antidoto.* Oxford: J. Barnesius, 1606.

STC 24881. Issued with the next (Trelcatius) by Barnes; it is assumed to have been separated as the two are listed and valued separately. The 1604 Steinfurt edition must remain a possibility, but the presence of the Trelcatius strongly argues for the Oxford edition. *Language(s)*: Latin. Appraised at 2d in 1607.

157.35 Trelcatius

Lucas Trelcatius, *the Younger. Scholastica et methodica locorum communium s. theologiae institutio, didactice et elenctice in epitome explicata.* Oxford: J. Barnesius, 1606.

STC 24263. The manuscript entry could represent STC 24262, published in 1604 by J. Bill, but since this title was issued with the preceding by Barnes, it is assumed to be part of the composite 1606 edition and was separated as the two are listed and valued separately. A 1604 Leyden edition was in quarto, not octavo as indicated here; BN lists an octavo edition published in Saumur in 1607, which must be considered a remote possibility. *Language(s)*: Latin. Appraised at 3d in 1607.

157.36 Piscator in novum testam:

Johann Piscator. Unidentified. Place unknown: stationer unknown, date not determined.

STC/non–STC status unknown. The first collected edition of Piscator's commentaries on the New Testament appeared in 1613. This item, therefore, probably represents several of the many octavo volumes of Piscator's individual commentaries on the Gospels and the Epistles issued both from the Continent and in England during the 1590s and the early 1600s. The valuation would be unusually high for a single octavo volume. Which volumes the compiler lumped together (or Gearing had bound together) as "in novum testam:" cannot be determined. By way of comparison, see BCI's citation of an unidentified collection "Piscator 5 vol:" in a 1614 inventory valued at 8*s* (BCI, 2:621). *Language(s)*: Latin. Appraised at 4s in 1607.

157.37 Sanderi demonstrao

William Whitaker. *Ad Nicolai Sanderi demonstrationes quadraginta, in octavo visibilis Monarchiae positas, responsio.* London: T. Vautrollerius, imp. T. Chardi, 1583.

STC 25357. A response to the last part of Nicholas Sanders's *De visibili monarchia Ecclesiae, libri octo*, which is included. For Sanders's work, see Shaaber S2124. *Language(s)*: Latin. Appraised at 6d in 1607.

157.38 Danei Elenchus haereticorum

Lambert Daneau. *Elenchi haereticorum*. Geneva: Eustathius Vignon, 1573–1592.

The 1592 edition was published by Vignon's heirs. *Language(s)*: Latin. Appraised at 3d in 1607.

157.39 Polani partitiones

Amandus Polanus. *Partitiones theologicae juxta naturalis methodi leges conformatae duobus libris*. Britain or Continent: 1590–1607.

STC 20083.5 and non–STC. *Language(s)*: Latin. Appraised at 6d in 1607.

157.40 Biblia Hebraica 2bus vol.

[*Bible—O.T.*]. Continent: date not determined.
Language(s): Hebrew. Appraised at 3s in 1607.

157.41 Blebelii Grammat. Hebraica

Thomas Blebelius. *Grammaticae hebraeae sanctae linguae institutiones*. Wittenberg: apud haered. Johannis Cratonis, 1587.

Language(s): Hebrew Latin. Appraised at 4d in 1607.

157.42 Quinitilianus

Marcus Fabius Quintilianus. Unidentified. Continent: date not determined.

The *Institutiones oratoriae* is more likely than the *Declamationes*, but the complete works might be intended. *Language(s)*: Latin. Appraised at 12d in 1607.

157.43 Clenardi grammat. graec.

Nicolaus Clenardus. [*Institutiones linguae graecae*]. Britain or Continent: date not determined.

STC 5400.5 *et seq*. and non–STC. *Language(s)*: Greek. Appraised at 3d in 1607.

157.44 Cic. de philosophia volum. duo.

Marcus Tullius Cicero. [*Selected works—Philosophica*]. Continent: date not determined.

Language(s): Latin. Appraised at 14d in 1607.

157.45:1 Eiusdem epist. ad Atticum et fam.

Marcus Tullius Cicero. *Epistolae ad Atticum*. Continent: date not determined.

Language(s): Latin. Appraised with one other at 8d in 1607.

157.45:2 [See 157.45:1]
Marcus Tullius Cicero. *Epistolae ad familiares*. Britain or Continent: date not determined.
STC 5295 *et seq.* and non–STC. *Language(s)*: Latin. Appraised with one other at 8d in 1607.

157.46   Tullius de oratore
Marcus Tullius Cicero. *De oratore*. Britain or Continent: date not determined.
STC 5290 and non–STC. *Language(s)*: Latin. Appraised at 6d in 1607.

157.47   Plautus
Titus Maccius Plautus. *Comoediae*. Continent: date not determined.
Necessarily from the Continent since the only Plautus published in England by this date, the *Menaechmi*, was in quarto. *Language(s)*: Latin. Appraised at 8d in 1607.

157.48   Plutarchi vitae 3bus vol.
Plutarch. *Vitae parallelae*. Continent: date not determined.
Language(s): Latin (probable) Greek (perhaps). Appraised at 2s in 1607.

157.49   Eiusdem moral. vol. tantum duo
Plutarch. *Moralia*. Continent: date not determined.
Apparently a broken set: two volumes only (*vol. tantum duo*). *Language(s)*: Latin. Appraised at 14d in 1607.

157.50   Willet on Jude
Andrew Willet. *A catholicon, that is, a generall preservative or remedie against the pseudocatholike religion, gathered out of the epistle of S. Jude*. Cambridge and London: J. Legat, pr. to the Univer. of Camb., sold by S. Waterson, 1602.
STC 25673. Waterson's shop was in London. *Language(s)*: English. Appraised at 4d in 1607.

157.51   Gyffard on the Canticles
George Gifford. *Fifteene sermons, upon the Song of Salomon*. London: (different houses) for T. Man, 1598–1600.
STC 11854 *et seq. Language(s)*: English. Appraised at 4d in 1607.

157.52   Rainoldi Theses
John Rainolds. *Sex theses de sacra scriptura, et ecclesia*. Britain or Continent: 1580–1603.
STC 20624 *et seq.* and non–STC. See Shaaber R4. *Language(s)*: Latin. Appraised at 8d in 1607.

Abel Trefry. Scholar (M.A.): Probate Inventory. 1610

JOSEPH L. BLACK AND JULIETTE M. CUNICO

Abel Trefry (Treffry, Trefrie) came to Oxford from Trefry, Cornwall, where he was born in 1577. He received a Bachelor of Arts degree from St. Alban's Hall on 30 October 1598 and a Master of Arts degree on 1 July 1601; he was a fellow of All Souls' College (*Alumni Oxonienses* 4:1405). The following inventory and appraisal were made on 10 December 1610.

The strengths of Trefry's collection of a handful more than forty books are Reformed theology (including Calvin, Zacharias Ursinus, Hieronymus Zanchius, and Amandus Polanus) and classics (mainly classical history with some philosophy and rhetoric, but including the plays of Terence and the first copy of Petronius to appear in the PLRE Oxford inventories). Some common works of rhetoric, medicine, and law round out Trefry's expected quota of the more standard texts. But the scarce Petronius is not the only one of Trefry's books to display a more individual taste: a surprising number of books in this rather small library make few or no appearances elsewhere in the Oxford (PLRE) and Cambridge (BCI) inventories. Trefry owned a copy of Ben Jonson's *Sejanus*, perhaps for the interest of its imaginative treatment of Roman history; he also owned Fulvio Orsini's imagination-spurring collection of images of famous Greeks and Romans. The appeal of Richard Carew's *Survey of Cornwall* likely lay in its more personal connections. Ramón Lull's *Ars magna* (or its abridgement), a significant work on logic and mathematics, makes a rare appearance here, as does John Florio's Italian dictionary, the neo-Latin orations of the Jesuit Franciscus Bencius, Henry Garnet's *Treatise of Renunciation* (printed on a secret recusant press in London), the versified version of the Bible by the eccentric (and sometime Separatist) Henoch Clapham, and Peter Bales's introduction to shorthand, the *Arte of Brachygraphie*. The variety of books present here but not commonly found in earlier academic inventories is a suggestive reminder of the ongoing expansion of private libraries in range as well as size as they begin to reflect developments in the book trade and in collecting practices in the early seventeenth century. Almost one quarter of Trefry's books (at least) are in English, for example, a percentage that would have been quite unusual in an academic collection a decade or so earlier.

Trefry's collection is mentioned as "a small arts and theology library" by Mark Curtis (1959, 136n, 253 and 285n) and for his ownership of Tacitus by Mordechai Feingold (1997, 356).

Oxford University Archives, Bodleian Library: Hyp.B.19.

§

Curtis, Mark H. 1959. *Oxford and Cambridge in Transition, 1558–1642*. Oxford: Clarendon Press.
Feingold, Mordechai. 1997. "Oriental Studies." *Seventeenth–Century Oxford*, ed. Nicholas Tyacke. Volume 4 of *The History of the University of Oxford*, gen. ed. T.H.Aston. Oxford: Oxford University Press, pp. 449–503.

§

158.1	Tremeli bib follio latt
158.2	bible englishe
158.3	calvins Institution foll
158.4	ursinus englishe
158.5	Thomas. thomasi
158.6	Polanus de verbo dei
158.7	zanchi de nature dei
158.8	[zanchi] de religione
158.9	[zanchi] compendium
158.10	Tullii opera 2 voll
158.11	Plutarchi moraliae
158.12	[Plutarchi] vitae
158.13	Aristo: metaphis
158.14	[Aristo:] phisi
158.15	[Aristo:] retoricke
158.16	regius with aristo pollitickes
158.17	Tacitus with lipsius
158.18	valerius perterculis
158.19	florius frutes
158.20	Justinus historic
158.21	Campianis reasons et whittac
158.22	bentii oratio.
158.23	Pantalion.
158.24	clarke de aulico
158.25	rami gramatica.

158.26	Illustrimon imag
158.27	terrentius
158.28	Albertus de secretis
158.29	Lulli Ars
158.30	Petronis arbiter.
158.31	herodianus
158.32	tulli de oratore
158.33	fenestella de magistr
158.34	Camdenus brittania
158.35	Talei retorica.
158.36	L. foris
158.37	Bocace
158.38	sorvay cor walle
158.39	A treatise of renuntiation
158.40	A brife of the bible
158.41	bales brage
158.42:1–2	2 paper bookes foll
158.43	1 paper booke
158.44	littleton frenche
158.45	Sejanus

§

158.1　Tremeli bib follio latt

The Bible. Translated and edited by Joannes Immanuel Tremellius and François Du Jon, *the Elder*. Britain or Continent: date not determined.

STC 2061 *et seq.* and non–STC. *Language(s)*: Latin. Appraised at 12s in 1610.

158.2　bible englishe

The Bible. Britain or Continent: 1535–1610.

STC 2063 *et seq.* and non–STC. *Language(s)*: English. Appraised at 4s in 1610.

158.3　calvins Institution foll

Jean Calvin. *Institutio Christianae religionis*. Continent (probable): date not determined.

Probably not an STC book, but see STC 4415 *et seq.* The compiler appears to identify items as English if the expectation is otherwise; see the items preceding and following this work (158.2 and 158.4). But the English translation must remain a possibility. *Language(s)*: Latin English (perhaps). Appraised at 6s in 1610.

158.4 ursinus englishe

Zacharias Ursinus. Probably *The summe of christian religion*. Britain: 1587–1601.

STC 24532 *et seq*. This standard text, repeatedly published prior to the date of this inventory (five editions from 1587 to 1601), is considerably more likely than the two other available works by Ursinus translated into English. Those two (STC 24527 and STC 24528) are both smaller by far, making them much less likely to be valued at 5*s* 6*d* as this item is. Even less likely is the pseudonymous Joachim Ursinus, *The Romane conclave* (STC 24526). *Language(s)*: English. Appraised at 5s 6d in 1610.

158.5 Thomas. thomasi

Thomas Thomas. *Dictionarium linguae Latinae et Anglicanae*. Britain: 1587–1610.

STC 24008 *et seq*. After 1596, some editions carried a Greek supplement. *Language(s)*: English Latin Greek (perhaps). Appraised at 3s 4d in 1610.

158.6 Polanus de verbo dei

Amandus Polanus. *De verbo Dei didascalia in sex disputationes tributa*. Basle: per Conrad Waldkirch, 1593.

Language(s): Latin. Appraised at 2d in 1610.

158.7 zanchi de nature dei

Hieronymus Zanchius. *De natura Dei, seu de divinis attributis, libri V*. Continent: 1577–1598.

Language(s): Latin. Appraised at 5s in 1610.

158.8 [zanchi] de religione

Hieronymus Zanchius. *De religione christiana fides*. Britain or Continent: 1586 (probable)–1605.

STC 26121 and non–STC. Some sources supply 1585 for the *editio princeps*. *Language(s)*: Latin. Appraised at 1s 2d in 1610.

158.9 [zanchi] compendium

Hieronymus Zanchius. *Compendium praecipuorum capitum doctrinae Christianae*. Neustadt an der Haardt: apud viduam Wilhelmi Harnisii, 1598.

A synopsis of Calvin's *Institutes*. *Language(s)*: Latin. Appraised at 1s 4d in 1610.

158.10 Tullii opera 2 voll

Marcus Tullius Cicero. [*Works*]. Continent: date not determined.

The STC titles listed under [*Works*] (STC 5265.7 *et seq*.) are not the entire *opera* but rather selected works. *Language(s)*: Latin. Appraised at 10s in 1610.

158.11 Plutarchi moraliae
Plutarch. *Moralia*. Continent: date not determined. *Language(s)*: Latin. Appraised at 5s 6d in 1610.

158.12 [Plutarchi] vitae
Plutarch. *Vitae parallelae*. Continent: date not determined. *Language(s)*: Latin. Appraised at 5s in 1610.

158.13 Aristo: metaphis
Aristotle. *Metaphysica*. Continent: date not determined. *Language(s)*: Latin. Appraised at 8d in 1610.

158.14 [Aristo:] phisi
Aristotle. *Physica*. Continent: date not determined.
The several titles listed under [*Physica*] in the STC are either commentaries with text or a paraphrase. *Language(s)*: Latin. Appraised at 1s 2d in 1610.

158.15 [Aristo:] retoricke
Aristotle. *Rhetorica*. Continent: date not determined. *Language(s)*: Latin. Appraised at 3d in 1610.

158.16 regius with aristo pollitickes
Aristotles politiques, or discourses of government. Translated by I.D. London: A. Islip, 1598.
STC 760. From a French version by Louis Le Roy of Aristotle's *Politica*. Le Roy, identified as "Regius," on the title page, included material from other writers, among them Plato. The English translation is generally attributed to John Dee. *Language(s)*: English. Appraised at 2s 6d in 1610.

158.17 Tacitus with lipsius
Publius Cornelius Tacitus. [*Works*]. Edited and with commentary by Justus Lipsius. Continent: 1574–1608.
See CTC 6:100–102 for a bibliography (by Robert W. Ulery, Jr.) of Tacitus's *Works* with Lipsius's commentary. *Language(s)*: Latin. Appraised at 5s in 1610.

158.18 valerius perterculis
Caius Velleius Paterculus. *Historiae Romanae duo volumina*. Continent: date not determined.
Language(s): Latin. Appraised at 8d in 1610.

158.19 florius frutes
John Florio. Probably *Florios second frutes, . . . to which is annexed his Gardine of recreation*. London: [T. Orwin] for T. Woodcock, 1591.

STC 11097. Given this compiler's carelessness and often illegible hand, it is risky to identify this item as STC 11097 when it could be *Florio his first fruites* (STC 11096), a different work. The spelling of "frutes" suggests STC 11097, but Elizabethan spelling, even in diligent practice, was irregular. The compiler's spelling of Florio's name as "Florius," however, is a different matter. Florio's name is not even unconventionally latinized, and, therefore, "Florius" is taken to be an error for "Florios," the first word in the title of STC 11097. *Language(s)*: English Italian. Appraised at 6d in 1610.

158.20   Justinus historic

Trogus Pompeius and Justinus, *the Historian*. [*Epitomae in Trogi Pompeii historias*]. Britain or Continent: date not determined.

STC 24287 *et seq.* and non–STC. *Language(s)*: Latin. Appraised at 2s in 1610.

158.21   Campianis reasons et whittac

Edmund Campion. *Rationes decem*. Continent: date not determined.

The Campion–Whitaker exchange has a complicated printing history. In 1581, Campion's work was published alone, and then later with William Whitaker's response which had also been published solo in 1581 as *Ad rationes decem Edmundi Campiani jesuitae, responsio* (STC 25358). Further exchanges followed. The two original works appeared as well in collections by others (see ARCR 1: pp. 24–26). What is represented here is taken to be one of the editions that contains Campion's *Rationes decem* with Whitaker's response, first published together in 1582. This could also be a double entry of a solo edition of Campion and one of the solo editions of Whitaker (STC 25358–59) or even Whitaker's response (STC 25362) to Campion's reply. What is clear is that both arguments—the Roman Catholic and the Protestant—were, in some form, in Trefry's collection. *Language(s)*: Latin. Appraised at 1s in 1610.

158.22   bentii oratio.

Franciscus Bencius. Unidentified. Continent: date not determined.

Several of Bencius's works might be abbreviated in such a manner. *Language(s)*: Latin. Appraised at 1s 4d in 1610.

158.23   Pantalion.

Unidentified. Continent: date not determined.

The prolific Heinrich Pantaleon is most likely, but Pantaleon Barteleone Raverinus, and Panthaleon, *de Confluentis*, both of whom have been cited in booklists as "Pantaleon" (see BCI 2:595 and 2:657) are necessarily possibilities. *Language(s)*: Latin. Appraised at 6d in 1610.

158.24 clarke de aulico

Baldassare Castiglione, *Count*. *De curiali sive aulico libri quatuor ex Italico sermone in Latinum conversi*. Translated by Bartholomew Clerke. Britain or Continent: 1571–1606.

STC 4782 *et seq.* and non–STC. *Language(s)*: Latin. Appraised at 1s 2d in 1610.

158.25 rami gramatica.

Pierre de La Ramée. [*Grammatica*]. Britain or Continent: date not determined.

STC 15251.3 *et seq.* and non–STC. Trefry could have owned either the Latin or the English translation. It is also possible that what is represented here is either the *Grammatica graeca, quatenus a Latina differt*, or the *Rudimenta graeca*; however, Trefry's library shows no evidence of any other works in Greek. *Language(s)*: Latin English (perhaps). Appraised at 3d in 1610.

158.26 Illustrimon imag

Fulvio Orsini. [*Illustrium imagines*]. Continent: 1570–1606.

This book of engravings of classical figures appeared with text by Orsini first in 1570 and then again in 1602 in folio editions. Quarto editions were issued with added material by Theodore Galle and by Joannes Fabri, *Bishop of Vienna* in 1598 and in 1606. Given the location of the book in the collection and its valuation, one of the quarto editions is more likely, particularly since the titles of those editions are closer to the manuscript entry however nearly illegible it is. *Language(s)*: Latin. Appraised at 3d in 1610.

158.27 terrentius

Publius Terentius, *Afer*. [*Works*]. Britain or Continent: date not determined.

STC 23885 *et seq.* and non–STC. *Language(s)*: Latin (probable). Appraised at 10d in 1610.

158.28 Albertus de secretis

Albertus Magnus. *De secretis mulierum et virorum*. Britain or Continent: date not determined.

STC 258 *et seq.* and non–STC. Various editions, STC 258 among them, include *De virtutibus herbarum*. *Language(s)*: Latin. Appraised at 8d in 1610.

158.29 Lulli Ars

Ramón Lull. Unidentified. Continent: date not determined.

Either the *Ars Magna* or its abridgement, the *Ars brevis*, the latter perhaps more likely given the valuation, but this could be a tattered copy of the larger work. *Language(s)*: Latin. Appraised at 4d in 1610.

158.30   Petronis arbiter.
Petronius Arbiter. [*Satyricon*]. Continent: date not determined.
Language(s): Latin. Appraised at 1s in 1610.

158.31   herodianus
Herodian. [*Historiae*]. Continent: date not determined.
Language(s): Latin. Appraised at 6d in 1610.

158.32   tulli de oratore
Marcus Tullius Cicero. *De oratore*. Britain or Continent: date not determined.
STC 5290 *et seq.* and non–STC. *Language(s)*: Latin. Appraised at 4d in 1610.

158.33   fenestella de magistr
Andreas Dominicus Floccus (Lucius Fenestella). *De magistratibus sacerdotiisque Romanorum*. Continent: date not determined.
Language(s): Latin. Appraised at 3d in 1610.

158.34   Camdenus brittania
William Camden. *Britannia sive florentissimorum regnorum, Angliae, Scotiae, Hiberniae chorographica descriptio*. Britain or Continent: 1586–1607.
STC 4503 *et seq.* and non–STC. *Language(s)*: Latin. Appraised at 3s 4d in 1610.

158.35   Talei retorica.
Audomarus Talaeus (Omer Talon). *Rhetorica*. Britain or Continent: date not determined.
STC 23659.3 *et seq.* and non–STC. *Language(s)*: Latin. Appraised at 2d in 1610.

158.36   L. foris
Lucius Annaeus Florus. [*Epitomae de Tito Livio bellorum omnium annorum*]. Continent: date not determined.
The *Epitomae* was a standard text in scholars's libraries, and that in combination with the compiler's habitual scribal carelessness making "foris" a likely attempt at Florus, urges this identification. *Language(s)*: Latin. Appraised at 1s 2d in 1610.

158.37   Bocace
Giovanni Boccaccio. Unidentified. Britain or Continent: date not determined.

STC/non–STC status unknown. Only because of the presence of the Florio work in Trefry's collection (158.19) is Italian a possibility. *Language(s)*: English (probable) Italian (perhaps) Latin (perhaps). Appraised at 1s 3d in 1610.

158.38   sorvay cor walle

Richard Carew. *The survey of Cornwall*. London: S. S[tafford] for J. Jaggard, 1602.

STC 4615. *Language(s)*: English. Appraised at 6d in 1610.

158.39   A treatise of renuntiation

Henry Garnet. *A treatise of christian renunciation*. London: [Fr. Garnet's first press], 1593.

STC 11617.8. Anonymously and secretly published. ARCR 2: no. 322. *Language(s)*: English Latin. Appraised at 4d in 1610.

158.40   A brife of the bible

Henoch Clapham. *A briefe of the Bible, drawne first into English poësy, and then illustrated by apte annotations*. Britain: 1596–1608.

STC 5332 *et seq*. *A bryefe summe of the whole Byble* (STC 3017) cannot be entirely dismissed. *Language(s)*: English. Appraised at 4d in 1610.

158.41   bales brage

Peter Bales. *The arte of brachygraphie*. London: G. Shawe and R. Blower for T. Charde, 1597.

A scribal flourish is at the end of the manuscript entry and is likely a mark of abbreviation in an attempt to represent "brachygraphie," a word the compiler understandably may not have been keen to write out. An earlier edition is titled *The writing schoolemaster* (STC 1312) with *The arte of brachygraphie* buried deep in its long title unlike the 1597 edition here, whose title page leads with and displays prominently what the compiler must have been reading. *Language(s)*: English. Appraised at 3d in 1610.

158.42:1–2   2 paper bookes foll

Unidentified. Provenances unknown: dates not determined.
Manuscripts. *Language(s)*: Unknown. Appraised at 4s in 1610.

158.43   1 paper booke

Unidentified. Provenance unknown: date not determined.
Manuscript. *Language(s)*: Unknown. Appraised at 6d in 1610.

158.44   littleton frenche

Sir Thomas Littleton. [*Tenures*]. Britain or Continent: date not determined.
STC 15719 *et seq*. *Language(s)*: Law French. Appraised at 4d in 1610.

158.45   Sejanus
Benjamin Jonson. *Sejanus his fall*. London: G. Elld for T. Thorpe, 1605. STC 14782. *Language(s)*: English. Appraised at 4d in 1610.

Walter Brown. Cleric, Scholar (B.Th.): Probate Inventory. 1613

JOSEPH L. BLACK

Walter Brown (Browne), of Eastwick Park, Great Bookham, Surrey, was born in either 1575 or 1576 and matriculated in 1590 at the age of 14 from Corpus Christi College. He graduated B.A. in 1595, was elected Fellow of Corpus Christi, supplicated M.A. in 1598, was admitted B.Th. and given his license to preach in 1606, and named rector of Kiddington (Cuddington), Oxford, in 1611. After his death Brown was commemorated with a "little white stone" in the outer chapel at Corpus Christi; this memorial, along with others, was subsequently removed into the Cloisters (*Alumni Oxonienses*, 1:198; Clark, 2:ii.178, 2:iii.187; *Athenae Oxonienses* 5:i.317; Wood 1786, 1:279, 408; Warton 1783, 11; Brayley 1850, 4.470; Fowler 1893, 392). The following inventory and appraisal were made by University stationer Dionise Edwards and yeoman beadle Richard Reed on 27 April 1613.

Brown's was an unusually substantial private library: numbering almost 600 books, his is among the largest collections listed in either the Oxford (PLRE) or Cambridge (BCI) inventories. It contains what one would expect of a library this size put together by a bookish scholar/cleric: a solid collection of the standard classical and patristic texts; a great deal of history, theology, and theological controversy; and a working selection of books in fields such as medicine, law, astronomy, geography, mathematics, and linguistics. This last category is particularly strong: in addition to many works in French, Italian, and Spanish, Brown owned more than a dozen Hebrew grammars as well as introductions to Arabic and Syriac.

But Brown's library is also unusual in several respects. To begin with, it includes more literature, vernacular as well as classical, than is commonly found in these inventories: more than ten percent of the entire collection is literary. In addition to a good selection of Greek drama and Latin poetry, Brown owned works in English by Chaucer (159.57), Ben Jonson (159.171), Thomas Middleton

(159.173), Thomas Heywood (159.206), Samuel Daniel (159.177 and probably 159.313), Michael Drayton (159.55), George Gascoigne (159.127, 159.133), and possibly Shakespeare (159.200) and Spenser (159.207); he owned Tottell's *Miscellany* (159.274), Bacon's *Essays* (159.381, 159.502), the *Mirror for Magistrates* (159.122), the neo-Latin verse of John Owen (159.524), John Grange's *Golden Aphroditis* (159.148), and such anthologies as William Painter's *Palace of Pleasure* (159.121) and the *Forrest of Fancy* (159.163). He also owned, sometimes in English translation, a number of literary works by Continental writers, including Petrarch (159.44), Boccaccio (159.47, 159.492), Montaigne (159.250), Tasso (159.532), Castiglione (159.304), Marot (159.444), and the *Amadis de Gaule* (159.46).

Much, though not all, of this vernacular literature was published in the 1570s, which may suggest that Brown inherited a collection to which he added. But it is also possible that he simply liked older books, since another unusual aspect of this library is that Brown appears to have been something of a collector. Many books in this library date from the mid-sixteenth century or earlier, including several printed before 1525 (e.g., 159.30, 159.31, 159.34, 159.37, 159.123) and at least two incunables (159.115, 159.167). Two books, by Sir Richard Morison and Constantinus Felicius (159.107, 159.125), appear only once before in the Oxford PLRE inventories, in the library of William Brown (d. 1558), a Fellow of Merton College. There is no evidence of family relation between the two men: the older Brown came to Oxford from the West Country. But it is possible that some of the older Brown's books had lingered in the book trade in Oxford and were bought by the younger Brown, a scholar with antiquarian interests. Other authors represented in both libraries (e.g., Johann von Tritheim and Jacobus Omphalius, as well as some of the more standard classical authors) may also reflect overlap between the two collections. Brown's bibliographical interests are also suggested by his copy of the printed catalogue of Thomas Bodley's library (159.89): his is the only copy listed among the Oxford inventories, and the only other owner listed so far in PLRE is Sir Edward Dering (PLRE 4.570).

Finally, Brown owned a great number of books by Roman Catholic theologians and controversialists. Their presence in his collection may be explained by his professional responsibilities in a period during which the Church of England continued to fight to define itself doctrinally. But the scores of Catholic works here, including devotional texts and Jesuit commentaries, could raise suspicions about the direction of Brown's sympathies. Some members of Brown's college in fact accused him with being Catholic in depositions made in about 1603 during an investigation of the actions of another College Fellow, Ralph Barlow (British Library MS Add. 28, 571, fols. 181–186; cited in Tyacke 1986, 65–66). Most likely, these charges arose out of disputes over doctrinal shifts within the English church that had begun to gather steam in early seventeenth-century Oxford. Brown appears to have been a member of the incipiently anti-Calvinist or "Arminian" circle associated with John Howson and William Laud (Tyacke 1997,

574); four works by Jacobus Arminius appear in the library (159.321, 159.323, 159.325, 129.401). Nonetheless, this belief within the Oxford community that Brown had been a closet Catholic would later give him and his library a role in one of the major political events of the British civil wars, the 1644 trial and execution of (by then) Archbishop William Laud.

The first charge laid against Laud was that he was "generally reputed" to be Catholic and had sought to reconcile the English Church with Rome. Among the evidences produced to support the charge was Laud's friendship with Walter Brown. According to Laud's account of the trial, Sir Nathaniel Brent, who was Proctor of Oxford when Brown received his license to preach, testified that Laud "was acquainted with one Mr. Brown, Fellow of Corpus Christi College in Oxford, who was suspected to be a Papist, and after his Death proved to be one by a Book that was found in his Study, proving that a Man might be a Roman-Catholick, and yet go to Church and Conform in England." Laud defended both his friendship with Brown and Brown's ownership of the book in question:

> I was acquainted with this Man; he was a very good Scholar and an Honest man, and a good Protestant, for ought I know. For the Tract found after his Death among his Papers, that's no Proof: For Scholars get all the Papers they can, especially such as belong to their own Profession. And the more strange the Opinions are, the more do they labour to get them. Nor is it any Proof that the Tract was of his making, because written in his own Hand, as 'tis urged. For the arguments being so foul and dangerous, it could not be safe for him, nor any way fit, to commit it to any other to write for him. Nor is there any Proof that I knew he had such a tract by him; neither indeed did I. The Opinion is very base and unworthy, and was first broached by the Jesuit Azorius, and it seems some of his Fellows had inlarged him, and made this Tract out of his Principles (Laud 1695, 380–81).

The book is 159.79, a manuscript, apparently in Brown's hand (according to the account offered in Laud's trial), of the opinions of the Jesuit Juan Azor. Laud is to some extent persuasive with his argument that owning such a work was no proof of confessional sympathy because scholars like to get their hands on "all the papers they can," the more strange the opinions they contain the better. But Brent's testimony reflects the opinion of some of Brown's contemporaries at Oxford, and reminds us that they too sought to read the implications of book ownership. To them, the discovery of this manuscript during the inventory "proved" their suspicions that Brown had been a Catholic. Brown may even have taken some measures to thwart hostile curiosity about his books: among his possessions was "a locke & key for his study dore" valued at five shillings, a somewhat unusual presence in these university inventories.

Brown's library is mentioned (under the spelling "Browne") in articles by Mordechai Feingold and Nicholas Tyacke in the *History of the University of*

Oxford, who cite the collection as evidence of his skills in languages and interest in history (Feingold 1997, 275, 344–345; Tyacke 1997, 578). It is also listed in Jayne, though incorrectly under the name "William" Browne.

Oxford University Archives, Bodleian Library: Hyp.B.20.

§

Brayley, Edward Wedlake. 1850. *A Topographical History of Surrey*. 5 vols. London: G. Willis.
Feingold, Mordechai. 1997. "Oriental Studies." *Seventeenth–Century Oxford*, ed. Nicholas Tyacke. Volume 4 of *The History of the University of Oxford*, gen. ed. T.H. Aston. Oxford: Oxford University Press, pp. 449–503.
Fowler, Thomas. 1893. *The History of Corpus Christi College*. Oxford: The Oxford Historical Society.
Laud, William. 1695. *The History of the Troubles and Tryal*. London.
Tyacke, Nicholas. 1986. *The Anti-Calvinists: The Rise of English Arminianism*. Oxford: Oxford University Press.
Tyacke, Nicholas. 1997. "Religious Controversy." *Seventeenth-Century Oxford*, ed. Nicholas Tyacke. Volume 4 of *The History of the University of Oxford*, gen. ed. T.H. Aston. Oxford: Oxford University Press, pp. 569–619.
Warton, Thomas. 1783. *Specimen of a History of Oxfordshire*. 2nd ed., corrected and enlarged. London.
Wood, Anthony à. 1786. *The History and Antiquities of the Colleges and Halls in the University of Oxford*. Continued by John Gutch. Oxford: Clarendon Press.

§

159.1	St Augustines workes in five volumes fol
159.2	Cardinall Baronius his workes in vi vol: fol
159.3	all Bellarmines workes iii volumes fol
159.4	Suares metaphi foll
159.5	Arias Montanus his interliniari bible fo
159.6	Gregorius de valentia iiii vol fo
159.7	Aristotels workes fo: i vol
159.8	Pererius upon Genni
159.9	Maldonat upon the foure Evangelistes fo
159.10	Baradius in ii tomes
159.11	Demostines workes in gree and lat: fol
159.12	Pagnines hebrue lex fol
159.13	Dionisius Halacarn: gree et lat fo
159.14	Luchetus fo
159.15	Basill in Gree fo

159.16	Tho: Aqinnus Summes fo
159.17	Bibliotheca sextisenen fo
159.18	Tullie his workes ii vol fol:
159.19	Junius & Tremelius bible fo
159.20	Sigonius fo
159.21	a Frenche bible
159.22	Heroditus in gree and latine with certaine other workes fo
159.23	Origen fo: sum parte
159.24	Zerbis anotomia fo
159.25	Polidor virgill fo
159.26	Walsinghams historie
159.27	Zenophon gree et latine
159.28	Agrippa de oculta philosophia fo
159.29	Sextus Impericus fo
159.30	Rainerii de Pisis fo
159.31	Ante Lutherus fo
159.32	Jeroms bible fo
159.33	St Barnards workes fo
159.34	Dionisius Cistertiencis fo:
159.35	the fourthe tome of Jeroms workes fo
159.36	Molina fo
159.37	Scotus metaphi: fo
159.38	Baronii tomus decem fo
159.39	Coquei Examen fo
159.40	the workes of Sr Tho: more fo
159.41:1–4	iiii paper bookes fo
159.42	Epephanius lat fo: unbound
159.43	a Dictionari in frenche et latine fo
159.44	Petrarckes workes fo
159.45	ii tomes of Bellarmine fo
159.46	Som parte of Amidis de Gaule fo
159.47	Bockcas his workes fo
159.48	Comines in frenche fo
159.49	Fabritius fo
159.50	the diall of Princes fo
159.51	Licostines de prodigiis
159.52	legend sanctorum fo
159.53	Hookers Eclesiasticall polit
159.54	Guicciardines History in English
159.55	draitons polyolbion
159.56	part of Cornelius Tacitus
159.57	Chauchers workes
159.58	damasceni opuscula

159.59	Scapulus lexicon
159.60	a discription of Italie in Italian
159.61	Concordantia bib:
159.62	Parreus upon Gen
159.63	Herodian gree et latin
159.64	Collet de anima
159.65	suarez opuscula
159.66	Corpus Juris civilis
159.67	Connimbricensis Phys:
159.68	Molina de libero arbitrio
159.69	Junctini Tabulae Astronomi
159.70	Bucaei opera 2 vol
159.71	Catalogus Tritemii Eccles script.
159.72	Connimbric Log.
159.73	Collection of Statutes
159.74	Lipsius saturnal.
159.75	Maginus Geogr:
159.76	Latimers sermons
159.77	Huttons reasons for refusal of subscrip.
159.78	Bilsons Apology
159.79	Arocius his notes of Phys M.S.
159.80	Mercers haeb grammer
159.81	Copi Dialogi
159.82	Elias Levita his Hebr. Gramm.
159.83	Tollets log:
159.84	Scoti quaest. in Metaph.
159.85	Stapletons Controv. in Whitaker
159.86	Osiander Eccles. Hist. in 5 vol:
159.87	Medulla Patrum pars 1a
159.88	Baptist. Porta de furt. lit. notis
159.89	Catalog libr. Bibl. Oxon.
159.90	Feild of the Church
159.91	Torturi Torti
159.92	Lissius de Gratia
159.93	Mortons Apolog.
159.94	Macchiavels art of warr
159.95	Th. James of the Corrup. of the Fathers
159.96	Dr Howson in Pius
159.97	Physick against Fortune
159.98	Dr Coosins answer to the abstract
159.99	Mr Twines antiquity
159.100	Mr Jacksons Eternall truth
159.101	Colloquium Ratisbonense

159.102	The French Academy
159.103	Poultons abstract
159.104	Boterus in italian
159.105	Lipsius Electa
159.106	Elienses contra Bellarm
159.107	Cochlaei Apomaxis
159.108	Eliots French grammer
159.109	Precepta Juris Civilis
159.110	Broughtons concent of scripture
159.111	Dr Benfeild lectures
159.112:1	Justa Oxoniensis et Cant
159.112:2	[See 159.112:1]
159.113	Boteri Amphitreatrid
159.114	Ariae Mont. Jud. Antiq.
159.115	Francisci de platea
159.116:1	Cantuariens perspect with Arith Salign
159.116:2	[See 159.116:1]
159.117	Benius de libero arbitrio
159.118	A Sasfron Bible
159.119	Appian in English
159.120	Edens decads
159.121	The 2 Tom. of the Palace of Pleasure
159.122	the mirrour of Magistrates
159.123	A booke of Battels of Pavy
159.124	Ferrarius Commonwealth
159.125	Catlines Conspiracyes In English
159.126	Monardus
159.127	Gascoines workes
159.128	Osorius Nobility Engl.
159.129	Tho: diction graecolat.
159.130	The Picture of a Papist
159.131	Dr Allens treasons
159.132	Politicke Discourses
159.133	The steele glasse
159.134	Civil wars in Flanders
159.135	Alablaster on the Revelation
159.136	Sanderi responsio
159.137	Bishops Blossoms
159.138	Dr Cosins apol. engl
159.139	Fentons Treatise of usury
159.140	Tragicall Discourses
159.141	Haddons Orations & Poems
159.142	Fornerius selections

159.143	Mortons Satisfaction
159.144	Wasseri Institut. ling. Syrae
159.145	Flacius logicus
159.146	Calvins Institut
159.147	A Paper booke
159.148	The golden Aphroditis
159.149	Campi* Conference
159.150	The Apology of the Prince of Orenge
159.151	The acknowledge of wars
159.152	4 Sermons at Hampt. Court
159.153	Alphabet Arab
159.154	Trial of wits
159.155	Concio Lat. Episc. eliens.
159.156	Caussaub. Resp.
159.157	Brought. Respons
159.158	Brusi comment
159.159	Neroes Trag.
159.160	Lex levita
159.161	Becani disput
159.162	Meschlini examen
159.163	The forrest of fancy
159.164	wegelini disput
159.165	Nordens spec. brit.
159.166	quaesti Jurid. per cook
159.167	Politiani Nutricia
159.168	the Queens Injunctions
159.169	Polonica electio
159.170	Catalog Marts
159.171	Sejanus
159.172	Cardans comfort
159.173	A tricks to catch the old one
159.174	Smiths Common wealth
159.175	Bilsons church governm
159.176	Bulckleies Apolog with others
159.177	Daniels Histor. of Engl
159.178	Catalog. of Bishops
159.179	A Survey of pretended discipline
159.180	Anticotton
159.181	Answer to Downams sermon
159.182	Bancrofts sermon
159.183	Benfeilds sermon
159.184	booke of Canons
159.185	Sr Edwins Sands Relation

159.186	Oxfords answer to the ministers Petition
159.187	Christ descension into hell
159.188	B Elies Serm
159.189	Apology for the oth of Allegiance
159.190	B Elies Serm 2
159.191	Downfal of Popery
159.192	Wilkes eccles union
159.193:1	Dr Howsons 2 sermons
159.193:2	[See 159.193:1]
159.194	Service in the low countries
159.195	Passions of the mind
159.196	Duello
159.197	Meredith Serm.
159.198	Romish Judas
159.199	A copy of a letter
159.200	The History of Henr. 4
159.201	Sardus de nummis
159.202	Gentilis de potestate regis
159.203	Art of navigation
159.204	Discovery of Guiana
159.205	Franci Insignium
159.206	Edward the fourth
159.207	Shepheards Kalendar
159.208	Art of dialling
159.209	Navigators supply
159.210	Lixivium
159.211	Parraeis conciones
159.212	Leede sabbato
159.213	spanish grammer
159.214	Picture of puritan
159.215	Lubbertus de fide
159.216	Bilson de gubernationes ecclesiae
159.217	Bellarmini Gram: Heb:
159.218:A	Histor. Orient: Eccles: Gal.
159.218:B	[See 159.218:A]
159.219	Cicer: Epist:
159.220	Diction: Concionatoris
159.221	Tho: Diction:
159.222	Lucii Flores
159.223	Becani Enchiridion
159.224	Nubigensis hist:
159.225	Sarisburiens: Policraticus
159.226	Machav: de Rep:

159.227	Fulke against martin
159.228	Costeri Enchiridion
159.229	Ferus in genes:
159.230	Terentius Varro
159.231	Ameyen in Virgil
159.232	Clen: gram
159.233	Hom: odiss: grae. lat.
159.234	Lucan: Bersman:
159.235	Magir Ethic:
159.236	Cajeton in parab:
159.237	Bez: Testament: grae lat:
159.238	Euseb: Dialog:
159.239	Sleid: Comment:
159.240	Sum: virtut: et vitior:
159.241	Sanchez concion:
159.242	Bencius orationes
159.243	Pagnini Epitome
159.244	Artopius Psalteri Heb: lat: grae
159.245	Peraldi Homiliae
159.246	Hieron: Bibl: lat
159.247	Phrases Lin: lat:
159.248	Bib: french
159.249	Paraphras Riccob: in Rhetori Arist.
159.250	Mount: essais in french
159.251	Blebelius heb: gram:
159.252	Lodovicios vivis
159.253	stories of the fathers
159.254	Canini de locis scriptu:
159.255	Fuccius Instituti
159.256	Bucanon Hist: Scotland
159.257	Cannonis gram:
159.258	Junius Ecclesiast:
159.259	Marloret: Enchirid:
159.260	August: Enchirid:
159.261	de tripl: coena disput:
159.262	delrio disquisitions mag.
159.263	Elenchus haeret
159.264	Chrisologus
159.265	Macha: discourses
159.266	Sleid: de 4 imper
159.267	Lucia: dialogi
159.268	Chitraeus de affecti: moven:
159.269	Praeteol: narra: consil

159.270	Gemmes: de reg: juris
159.271	Althameri concilat: scrip:
159.272	corpus leg:
159.273	Reg: france lib: duo
159.274	Earle of Surreis sonnets
159.275	Osorius contra Had
159.276	Chittraeus de Stud: theol
159.277	Acta Apostol:
159.278	Omphalius
159.279	Stephani Prodopeia
159.280	Becani disputat:
159.281	plutar: de ira
159.282	Eliots governour
159.283	French schoolemaister
159.284	vindiciae cont tiran:
159.285	discipl: eccle: anglic:
159.286	Manutius de legib
159.287	Epictet
159.288	Acan: partiti
159.289	Serar: de Herod
159.290	Osiand: cont: Calvinist:
159.291	Machievil: prin:
159.292	Schind: Heb. gram
159.293	Campens: gram: heb:
159.294	Buteo de quadrat: circul:
159.295	Epistolae claror: vir:
159.296	Circes eng.
159.297	Fuccius in Hipp: Aphorismi:
159.298	Scultet Ethic:
159.299	Junius in Corinth:
159.300	Brant titul: Juris
159.301	Brutus fulmen
159.302	Ascams scholemaister
159.303	Ital: diction
159.304	the courtier in Span:
159.305	Tenterbelly
159.306	Lucian: dial:
159.307	Cajet: in epist:
159.308	Jun: Heb: gram
159.309	Scaliger de subtili
159.310	Plaut: Paraei
159.311	Ausonius
159.312	Lullii opera

159.313	Philotas
159.314	Eedes sermons
159.315	Mans: in eng.
159.316	Trelcat
159.317	Mascharenas de gratia
159.318	Antimariana gal:
159.319	the mir: france gal
159.320	Index expurgat
159.321	Armin: theses
159.322	Ferus in math:
159.323	Armin: in cap 7 ea [epistolae] Rom
159.324	Barcleius de potestat: papae
159.325	Armin: examen
159.326	Widrington Apolog:
159.327	Stapleton: promptuar: morale vol. 2
159.328	Lawes of Eng:
159.329	Fulleri miscelanea
159.330	Stapleton promptuar Cathol
159.331	Reibadeneira princepis christian
159.332	Justus Baron: adversus Heret:
159.333	Termes of the law
159.334	Kecker: Rhetor:
159.335	Scala coeli
159.336	Bucanani Poemata
159.337	Becani opuscula vol. 2
159.338	Ovid: metamor: Bersman
159.339	Macha: homil: graec: lat
159.340	Becanus de deo
159.341	Matthaeus de Rispolis
159.342	Ferus in exod:
159.343	Respons: adversus Anticoton
159.344	Concilium tridentinus
159.345	Fabul: Joan: papae
159.346	Kecker: theolog
159.347	Morton de notis eccles:
159.348	Marquarles
159.349	Enchiridion Remed
159.350	Barth: amabilia
159.351	Burhilli con: Becanus
159.352	Cudseni de caus: Calvi:
159.353	delrio Vindicid
159.354	Calsand: consultat:
159.355	Ciprian tom: 2us

159.356	Epitome Variani
159.357	Sphinx philosophica
159.358	Aristotle: Rhetori:
159.359	Thesaurus poemat
159.360	Baronius de monar: Ciciliae
159.361	Baldwini Conciones
159.362	Piloti gram. gal
159.363	Contarenus de rep: Venet
159.364	Vasseii Anotomeia
159.365	Joannes de Indag:
159.366	Danaei Isagoges
159.367	Scalig: de causis ling: lat:
159.368	Ferroneus de reb: gall:
159.369	Coment: rer: gallici
159.370	Tittleman: phisic:
159.371	Cornel: tacit
159.372	Sigon: de rep: hebr:
159.373	Lessii consulti
159.374	Trugilli conciones
159.375	Plutar: mor: 3 vol
159.376	Lipsius epist:
159.377	Pet: Lumbard
159.378	Keckerman: logic
159.379	August. de heresib
159.380	Decius londinus
159.381	Bacons essais
159.382	Ferus in Johannes
159.383	Granatens. de ratio: concion:
159.384	Doctor et student
159.385	Cani loci commu:
159.386	Fulgentius
159.387	Thesauri: Polit:
159.388	Lipsius polit
159.389	description of the low countries
159.390	Testament graec
159.391	Euclid element
159.392	Chitraei chronicon
159.393	A recusantes satisfaction
159.394	Practica linfranci
159.395	Recogni libr: Bellarm:
159.396	Blackwels examination
159.397	Wickliff against friers
159.398	Verronis Phisica

159.399	Portae mag: natural
159.400	Deming: de grati:
159.401	Arminii orationes
159.402	Aristopha: grae lat:
159.403	Aristot polit:
159.404	Velleius Paterculus
159.405	Pacii organon
159.406	Thucid: lat
159.407:A	Juven et Pers:
159.407:B	[See 159.407:A]
159.408	Textor: officin:
159.409	Thernellii opera
159.410	Sallust
159.411	Livius opera
159.412	Plutar: vit:
159.413	Traged sen:
159.414	Ital: testament
159.415	Gentilis de legat
159.416	Homer: Iliad
159.417	Pindarus grae: lat
159.418	Euripid. grae: lat
159.419	Drusii observationes
159.420	Catul: tibul:
159.421	Reusneri Simbol
159.422	In plaut: annotaton
159.423	Euripides 2 vol
159.424	Heliadorus
159.425	The breviat of britaine
159.426	bonds horac
159.427	Stepani appologia
159.428	Parraselsus 1 tom
159.429	Acosta conciones
159.430	didacus de lavega 5 voll
159.431	Bosquier 6 voll
159.432	Horrac
159.433	Mortons appollogi
159.434	Mallius malliff
159.435	Textors Epist:
159.436	Polibbius
159.437	Terrence
159.438	Pollider Virgill
159.439:1	ii greecke testam
159.439:2	[See 159.439:1]

159.440	Jeuels Appollog
159.441	Jani Anglorum
159.442	Suetonius
159.443	Epitomi Radicum Hebraic
159.444	Clement Marot
159.445	Quintus Curt
159.446	Histor: Brit:
159.447	Beda Hist Eccle:
159.448	Specculum politicum
159.449	Frischlini facetiae
159.450	Voelli generali officium
159.451	Henricus octavus contra Luther
159.452	Ars Chimica
159.453	Valerius Maximus
159.454	Ante Machevell
159.455	Bodines method
159.456	an ould test: Eng
159.457	Canisie summa
159.458	Petter marter prayers frenche
159.459	Theater of the world in frenche
159.460	Fenistella
159.461	Agripp de vanit scienticar
159.462	Aulus gelius
159.463	Ransovius de conservand valitudine
159.464	Molanus de fide hereticorum
159.465	Epistol: Plin:
159.466	Summa consiliorum
159.467	Pascasius
159.468	Dr Gwinns oration
159.469	The Imag of government
159.470	meditationes Bruni 4 voll
159.471	Psalmes in Italian
159.472	figurae bib:
159.473	Josephus ii vol
159.474	Testament in frenche
159.475	the minor poets
159.476	Gildas
159.477	Lucian the second tome
159.478	Alberti compendium theolog
159.479	Coelum philos
159.480	Epigram Marcial
159.481	Haebru Psalter
159.482	Daneus Apharism

159.483	Hues de Globis
159.484	Piscators aforis
159.485	Widenburgia philosophia
159.486	Columb: anotomia
159.487	Symbolatria
159.488	Breviarum
159.489	Rudiment: fid
159.490	Carions Croni:
159.491	Problem Arist
159.492	Boccas
159.493	Jani Anglo
159.494	Calvinus Judaizance
159.495	Fulcke againste Bristowe
159.496	Aronis purgat
159.497	Sacrabos
159.498	Dorhoff apodix
159.499:A	Juvinall et Perscius
159.499:B	[See 159.499:A]
159.500	Boys on the Leturg:
159.501	Parradines Emblemes french
159.502	Bacons Essayes
159.503	Argenterius de urinis
159.504	Piscator de predestinat
159.505	Concordia Anglicana
159.506	Sandersons log:
159.507	Erasm: Coll
159.508	An answere to a Jesuited gent
159.509	Antidoton
159.510	Lentulus Gram Italian
159.511	Nullus et nemo
159.512	Parreus de Jure Regum
159.513	Limbo mastix
159.514	Martinius Gram Heb:
159.515	a discoveri of Jesuits
159.516	Pratum Lacus
159.517	varietractatus
159.518	Seranus de fide
159.519	Commineus frenche
159.520	Arist: prob: Eng
159.521	Aron purgatus
159.522	the discoveri of a gulphe
159.523	Chrisostums Homilyes
159.524	Epigram Owen

159.525   Hypomnesis polit
159.526   Vincentius
159.527   Carolus de lorma
159.528   Erasm: similes
159.529   Papa non papa
159.530   Miracula chimica
159.531   Becanus de sacraficia
159.532   Godfre of Bullame
159.533:1–24   Ould Pamflets xxiiii tyed up altogeather
159.534   the Imag of government
159.535   Magna carta
159.536   tremelius psalter
159.537   Mirror of the world french
159.538   littletons teniors
159.539:1–18   xviii smale bookes tyed togeather
159.540 multiple   other smale bookes afterward found
159.541 multiple   certaine bookes in Mr Vicechancelors custody

§

159.1   St Augustines workes in five volumes fol

Augustine, *Saint*. [*Works*]. Continent: date not determined.

Editions of Augustine were issued and bound in varying numbers of volumes; this copy was not necessarily complete. *Language(s)*: Latin. Appraised at £4 in 1613.

159.2   Cardinall Baronius his workes in vi vol: fol

Cesare Baronius, *Cardinal*. *Annales ecclesiastici*. Continent: date not determined.

Originally issued in twelve volumes. A stray *"tomus decem"* of this work is listed at 159.38. *Language(s)*: Latin. Appraised at £5 in 1613.

159.3   all Bellarmines workes iii volumes fol

Roberto Bellarmino, *Cardinal. Disputationes de controversiis christianae fidei, adversus nostri temporis haereticos*. Continent: date not determined.

Issued in varying numbers of parts, and his only work issued in folio. The word *all* in the manuscript entry cannot, therefore, refer to Bellarmine's entire corpus. See also 159.45. *Language(s)*: Latin. Appraised at 30s in 1613.

159.4   Suares metaphi foll

Francisco Suarez. [*Aristotle—Metaphysica: commentary*]. Continent: 1597–1610.

Language(s): Latin. Appraised at 12s in 1613.

159.5 Arias Montanus his interliniari bible fo
The Bible. Continent: date not determined.

Probably an edition of *Biblia hebraica*, first published 1584 (the Old Testament translated by Sanctes Pagninus, the New Testament translated and the whole edited by Benito Arias Montano); possibly a copy of a single volume from the Antwerp polyglot Bible (1569); possibly a copy of Arias Montano's interlinear Greek-Latin New Testament, often issued separately. *Language(s)*: Greek Latin Hebrew (probable). Appraised at 20s in 1613.

159.6 Gregorius de valentia iiii vol fo
Gregorius de Valentia. [*Aquinas—Summa theologica: commentary*]. Continent: 15911612.
Language(s): Latin. Appraised at 40s in 1613.

159.7 Aristotels workes fo: i vol
Aristotle. [*Works*]. Continent: date not determined.
Possibly one (or the first) volume of a set. *Language(s)*: Latin (probable) Greek (perhaps). Appraised at 18s in 1613.

159.8 Pererius upon Genni
Benedictus Pererius. [*Genesis: commentary*]. Continent: 1590–1612.
At this valuation and given its location in the list, probably a folio, issued only in the seventeenth century. *Language(s)*: Latin. Appraised at 16s in 1613.

159.9 Maldonat upon the foure Evangelistes fo
Joannes Maldonatus. [*Gospels: commentary and text*]. Continent: 1596–1611.
Struck through and not appraised. *Language(s)*: Latin.

159.10 Baradius in ii tomes
Sebastianus Barradas. *Commentariorum in concordiam et historiam evangelicam.* Continent: 1591–1613.
Issued in four parts. *Language(s)*: Latin. Appraised at 20s in 1613.

159.11 Demostines workes in gree and lat: fol
Demosthenes. [*Works*]. Continent: date not determined.
Language(s): Greek Latin. Appraised at 13s 4d in 1613.

159.12 Pagnines hebrue lex fol
Sanctes Pagninus. *Thesaurus linguae sanctae.* Continent: date not determined.

The size and valuation identify this as the unabridged *Lexicon hebraicum*. See also 159.80. *Language(s)*: Hebrew Latin. Appraised at 32s 8d in 1613.

159.13 Dionisius Halacarn: gree et lat fo
Dionysius, *of Halicarnassus. Antiquitates sive origines Romanae*. Continent: date not determined.

Possibly the Greek and Latin edition edited by Fridericus Sylburgius (Frankfurt, 1546), but possibly also an edition with Latin introduction and Greek text. *Language(s)*: Greek Latin. Appraised at 10s in 1613.

159.14 Luchetus fo
Franciscus Lychetus. Probably [John Duns, *Scotus — Sentences: commentary*]. Continent: date not determined.

Lychetus's commentaries on Duns, *Scotus* appear to have been his only works published in folio, and there were several folio editions of his commentaries on the commentaries by Duns on Lombard. Both Lombard and Duns are represented elsewhere in Brown's collection. *Language(s)*: Latin. Appraised at 2s 6d in 1613.

159.15 Basill in Gree fo
Basil, *Saint, the Great*. Probably [*Works*]. Continent: date not determined.

Conceivably a smaller collection; see, for example, Adams B344 ff. *Language(s)*: Greek. Appraised at 8s in 1613.

159.16 Tho: Aqinnus Summes fo
Thomas Aquinas, *Saint. Summa theologica*. Continent: date not determined. *Language(s)*: Latin. Appraised at 20s in 1613.

159.17 Bibliotheca sextisenen fo
Sisto, *da Siena. Bibliotheca sancta*. Continent: 1566–1610. *Language(s)*: Latin. Appraised at 8s in 1613.

159.18 Tullie his workes ii vol fol:
Marcus Tullius Cicero. [*Works*]. Continent: date not determined. *Language(s)*: Latin. Appraised at 13s 4d in 1613.

159.19 Junius & Tremelius bible fo
The Bible. Translated by François Du Jon, *the Elder* and Joannes Immanuel Tremellius. Britain or Continent: 1575–1607.

STC 2061 *et seq*. and non–STC. Their Latin translation of the Old Testament and Apocrypha was first published in five parts (1575–1579); later editions were accompanied by the translation of the Syriac New Testament by Tremellius, or the Latin version of the Greek New Testament by Beza, or both. *Language(s)*: Latin Syriac (perhaps). Appraised at 13s 4d in 1613.

159.20   Sigonius fo
Carlo Sigonio. Unidentified. Continent: date not determined. *Language(s)*: Latin. Appraised at 6s in 1613.

159.21   a Frenche bible
The Bible. Continent: date not determined. *Language(s)*: French. Appraised at 10s in 1613.

159.22   Heroditus in gree and latine with certaine other workes fo
Herodotus. [*Historiae*]. Continent: date not determined.

Perhaps the edition of Herodotus, first published in 1592, containing excerpts from Xenophon, Plutarch, and others. The compiler could, however, have grouped together entirely different books with the Herodotus volume here cited. *Language(s)*: Greek Latin. Appraised at 6s in 1613.

159.23   Origen fo: sum parte
Origen. [*Works* (part)]. Continent: date not determined. *Language(s)*: Latin. Appraised at 4s in 1613.

159.24   Zerbis anotomia fo
Gabriel Zerbus. *Liber anathomie corporis humani*. Venice: (different houses), 1502–1533.

Sources differ on the publishing information, but Bonetus Locatellus and the heirs of Octavianus Scotus were responsible for the 1502 and certainly Locatellus for the 1533 edition. *Language(s)*: Latin. Appraised at 2s in 1613.

159.25   Polidor virgill fo
Polydorus Vergilius. Probably *Anglica historia*. Continent: 1534–1570.

Anglica historia appeared in several folio editions; his *Proverbiorum* (1500) and *Adagiorum liber* (1521) were each published once in folio. *Language(s)*: Latin. Appraised at 2s 5d in 1613.

159.26   Walsinghams historie
Thomas Walsingham. *Historia brevis Thomae Walsingham, ab Edwardo primo, ad Henricum quintum*. Edited by Matthew Parker, *Archbishop*. London: apud H. Binneman, 1574.

STC 25004. *Language(s)*: Latin. Appraised at 3s in 1613.

159.27   Zenophon gree et latine
Xenophon. [*Works*]. Continent: date not determined.

Language(s): Greek Latin. Appraised at 5s in 1613.

159.28   Agrippa de oculta philosophia fo
Henricus Cornelius Agrippa. *De occulta philosophia*. Place not given: stationer unknown, 1533.
Adams supplies Basle; others supply Cologne. *Language(s)*: Latin. Appraised at 18d in 1613.

159.29   Sextus Impericus fo
Sextus, *Empiricus*. [*Works*]. Translated by Gentian Hervet and Henri Estienne, *the Younger*. Paris: apud Martinum Juvenem, 1569.
This item, the only volume of Sextus issued in folio, was not published as his *Opera*, but it contains the only extant works of Sextus: *Adversus mathematicos* (the leading title and by which this volume is frequently cited) and *Pyrrhoniarum hypotyposeon libri tres*, the first translated by Hervet, the second by Estienne. Erasmus's translation of *Galeni contra academicos* is also included. Two variant issues carry the Plantin imprint (Antwerp), but they were likewise actually printed by Juvenis. *Language(s)*: Latin. Appraised at 2s 4d in 1613.

159.30   Rainerii de Pisis fo
Rainerius, *de Pisis*. *Pantheologia, sive Summa universae theologiae*. Continent: 1473–1519.
Language(s): Latin. Appraised at 2s in 1613.

159.31   Ante Lutherus fo
Jodocus Clichtoveus. *Antilutherus*. Paris: ex officina Simon Colinaei, 1524.
Sole folio edition. See VHc. *Language(s)*: Latin. Appraised at 12d in 1613.

159.32   Jeroms bible fo
The Bible. Continent: date not determined.
St. Jerome's Vulgate. Another copy is listed at 159.246. *Language(s)*: Latin. Appraised at 2s 6d in 1613.

159.33   St Barnards workes fo
Bernard, *Saint*. [*Works*]. Continent: date not determined.
Language(s): Latin. Appraised at 8s in 1613.

159.34   Dionisius Cistertiencis fo:
Dionysius, *Cisterciensis*. *Liber in quatuor sententiarum*. Edited by Joannes Maceriensis. Paris: venund. a P. le Preux, c.1505.
Sole work of this author. Undated, and sources supply a variety of dates from 1505 to 1520. *Language(s)*: Latin. Appraised at 12d in 1613.

159.35 the fourthe tome of Jeroms workes fo

Jerome, *Saint*. [*Works* (part)]. Continent: date not determined. *Language(s)*: Latin. Appraised at 5s in 1613.

159.36 Molina fo

Unidentified. Continent: date not determined.

Potentially by any number of authors named Molina, Molino, Molanus, or Du Moulin, though see 159.68 for a work by Ludovico Molina, *Jurist*. *Language(s)*: Unknown. Appraised at 8s in 1613.

159.37 Scotus metaphi: fo

John Duns, *Scotus*. [*Aristotle—Metaphysica: commentary*]. Continent: 1497–1520.

Another copy is listed at 159.84. *Language(s)*: Latin. Appraised at 2s in 1613.

159.38 Baronii tomus decem fo

Cesare Baronius, *Cardinal*. *Annales ecclesiastici* (part). Continent: date not determined.

Apparently a stray volume of the set listed at 159.2. Language(s): Latin. Appraised at 10s in 1613.

159.39 Coquei Examen fo

Léonard Coqueau. *Examen praefationis monitoriae Jacobi I praemissae apologiae suae pro juramento fidelitatis*. Freiburg: apud Joannem Strasserum, 1610–1611. *Language(s)*: Latin. Appraised at 3s in 1613.

159.40 the workes of Sr Tho: more fo

Sir Thomas More. *The workes of Sir T. More . . . wrytten by him in the Englysh tongue*. Edited by William Rastall. London: at the costes of J. Cawood, J. Waly, and R. Tottell, 1557.

STC 18076. Possibly one of the Latin *Opera* (Louvain, 1565–1566), though the form of the title points strongly to the English edition. *Language(s)*: English. Appraised at 10s in 1613.

159.41:1–4 iiii paper bookes fo

Unidentified. Provenances unknown: dates not determined.

Manuscripts. *Language(s)*: Unknown. Appraised as a group at 6s in 1613.

159.42 Epephanius lat fo: unbound

Epiphanius, *Bishop of Constantia*. Probably *Contra octoginta haereses*. Continent: date not determined.

Size and Latin as sole language strongly suggest this identification. *Language(s)*: Latin. Appraised at 3s in 1613.

159.43   a Dictionari in frenche et latine fo
Unidentified [dictionary]. Continent: date not determined. *Language(s)*: French Latin. Appraised at 2s in 1613.

159.44   Petrarckes workes fo
Francesco Petrarca. [*Works*]. Continent: date not determined. *Language(s)*: Latin (probable) Italian (perhaps). Appraised at 10s in 1613.

159.45   ii tomes of Bellarmine fo
Roberto Bellarmino, *Cardinal*. Unidentified. Continent: date not determined.
Bellarmine wrote the preface to the Clementine Bible, first published in two folio volumes in 1592. Otherwise, his only folio publication was the *Disputationes* (see 159.3). *Language(s)*: Latin. Appraised at 18s in 1613.

159.46   Som parte of Amidis de Gaule fo
Amadis, *de Gaule*. Probably *Le tresor des livres* (part). Continent: date not determined.
No folio English editions (STC 541 *et seq.*) were issued by the date of this inventory. Many more folio editions, the format indicated here by the compiler, were published in French than in other vernacular languages. Language(s): French (probable). Appraised at 2s in 1613.

159.47   Bockcas his workes fo
Giovanni Boccaccio. Unidentified. Britain (perhaps): date not determined.
Unidentifiable in the STC. If an English volume, "workes" in the manuscript entry must be a general rather than a precise term. Possibly one of the folio editions of *De casibus* (STC 3175 *et seq.*). *Language(s)*: English (probable) Italian (probable). Appraised at 2s in 1613.

159.48   Comines in frenche fo
Philippe de Comines. Probably [*Memoires*]. Continent: date not determined.
Another copy is listed at 159.519. *Language(s)*: French. Appraised at 2s in 1613.

159.49   Fabritius fo
Unidentified. Continent (probable): date not determined.
Probably not an STC book. Since "Fabritius" and "Fabricius" were often interchangeable, many authors are possible, including also variations on Fabrizzi,

Le Fèvre, Fabri, and Faber. *Language(s)*: Latin (probable). Appraised at 2s in 1613.

159.50 the diall of Princes fo

Antonio de Guevara, *Bishop*. *The diall of princes*. Translated by Sir Thomas North. London: (different houses), 1557–1568.

STC 12427 *et seq*. The stationer Thomas Marsh was involved in printing both folio editions. *Language(s)*: English. Appraised at 2s 6d in 1613.

159.51 Licostines de prodigiis

Conrad Lycosthenes (Conrad Wolfhart). *Prodigiorum ac ostentorum chronicon*. Basle: per H. Petri, 1557.

Published only in folio, this title is not identified as a folio volume by the compiler; it is, however, between two books that are, as are all the volumes that precede this item in the list. *Language(s)*: Latin. Appraised at 3s in 1613.

159.52 legend sanctorum fo

Jacobus de Voragine. *Legenda aurea sanctorum*. Continent (probable): date not determined.

Probably not an STC book, but see STC 24873 *et seq*. The English version would probably not be entered in this manner. *Language(s)*: Latin. Appraised at 2s 6d in 1613.

159.53 Hookers Eclesiasticall polit

Richard Hooker. *Of the lawes of ecclesiasticall politie*. London: (different houses), 1593–1611.

STC 13712 *et seq*. *Language(s)*: English. Appraised at 5s in 1613.

159.54 Guicciardines History in English

Francesco Guicciardini. *The historie of Guicciardin, conteining the warres of Italie*. Translated by Sir Geoffrey Fenton. London: (different houses), 1579–1599.

STC 12458 *et seq*. *Language(s)*: English. Appraised at 8s in 1613.

159.55 draitons polyolbion

Michael Drayton. *Poly-Olbion*. London: [H. Lownes] for M. Lownes, J. Browne, J. Helme, J. Busbie, 1612 (probable)–1613.

STC 7226 *et seq*. Struck through, including the appraisal. *Language(s)*: English.

159.56 part of Cornelius Tacitus

Publius Cornelius Tacitus. Unidentified. Place unknown: stationer unknown, date not determined.

STC/non–STC status unknown. *Language(s)*: Latin (probable) English (perhaps). Appraised at 2s in 1613.

159.57   Chauchers workes

Geoffrey Chaucer. *The workes.* London: (different houses), 1532–1602.

STC 05068 *et seq.* Possibly one of the incunable editions of *The Canterbury Tales* (STC 5082 *et seq.*). But more likely an edition with *Works* in the title. *Language(s)*: English. Appraised at 2s 6d in 1613.

159.58   damasceni opuscula

Probably John, *of Damascus, Saint.* Unidentified. Continent: date not determined.

Several *Opera* and collections of works were published by Saint John *of Damascus*, but no edition found with "Opuscula" in the title. Other authors published under variations of the name Damasceni. *Language(s)*: Latin (probable) Greek (perhaps). Appraised at 12d in 1613.

159.59   Scapulus lexicon

Joannes Scapula. *Lexicon graecolatinum novum.* Continent: date not determined.

The entries for the previous five items have been squeezed into a blank space the compiler had left before adding the centered heading "in 4°." Presumably, the compiler considered books before this entry to be folios (and labeled most of them as such), and books from this entry forward to be quartos (though without indicating so individually). The five previous items appear to have turned up later in the cataloguing process and were added to the folio section. The section listing octavos begins with 159.217. The appearance of any given book within a given section is no guarantee of its actual format. *Language(s)*: Greek Latin. Appraised at 6s in 1613.

159.60   a discription of Italie in Italian

Probably Leandro Alberti. *Descrittione di tutta Italia.* Continent: 1550–1596.

Language(s): Italian. Appraised at 5s in 1613.

159.61   Concordantia bib:

Unidentified [Biblical concordance]. Continent: date not determined. *Language(s)*: Latin. Appraised at 8s in 1613.

159.62   Parreus upon Gen

David Pareus. Probably *In genesin Mosis commentarius.* Frankfurt am Main: impensis J. Rhodii, typis Joannis Lancelloti, 1609.

Positiones theologicae miscellaneae ex secundo capite Geneseos (Heidelberg, 1602) is a remote possibility. Lancellotus, who printed the Pareus book, worked in Heidelberg. *Language(s)*: Latin. Appraised at 10s in 1613.

159.63 Herodian gree et latin

Herodian. [*Historiae*]. Continent: date not determined. *Language(s)*: Greek Latin. Appraised at 2s in 1613.

159.64 Collet de anima

Probably Jacobus Colerus. *De animarum immortalitate.* Wittenberg: typis Clementis Schleich, 1587.

The manuscript entry clearly reads *Collet*, necessitating a small degree of doubt about the Colerus identification. *Language(s)*: Greek Latin. Appraised at 18d in 1613.

159.65 suarez opuscula

Francisco Suarez. *Varia opuscula theologica.* Continent: 1599–1612. *Language(s)*: Latin. Appraised at 4s in 1613.

159.66 Corpus Juris civilis

Justinian I. *Corpus juris civilis.* Continent: date not determined. *Language(s)*: Latin Greek (perhaps). Appraised at 10s in 1613.

159.67 Connimbricensis Phys:

[*Aristotle — Physica: commentary*]. (*Coimbra. Collegium Societatis Jesu*). Continent: 1592–1610.

Date range from Lohr II. See 159.72. *Language(s)*: Latin. Appraised at 3s in 1613.

159.68 Molina de libero arbitrio

Ludovicus Molina, *Jesuit. Concordia liberi arbitrii cum gratia donis* …. Continent: 1588–1609.

Some editions are titled "Liberi arbitrii." 159.36 is an undentified title by "Molina," possibly another work by this author. *Language(s)*: Latin. Appraised at 2s 6d in 1613.

159.69 Junctini Tabulae Astronomi

Franciscus Junctinus. *Tabulae resolutae astronomicae.* Lyon: (different houses), 1573–1583.

Appended to Junctinus's *Speculum astrologiae,* but since the tables appear in several repositories alone (see, e.g., Adams J437), they may have been issued solo. Alternatively, this section may have become separated from *Speculum astrologiae,* or the compiler was reading from the caption title and the larger work was in Brown's collection. *Language(s)*: Latin. Appraised at 2s in 1613.

159.70   Bucaei opera 2 vol
Unidentified. Continent (probable): date not determined
Probably not an STC book. *Language(s)*: Latin. Appraised at 6s 8d in 1613.

159.71   Catalogus Tritemii Eccles script.
Johann von Tritheim. *Catalogus scriptorum ecclesiasticorum*. Cologne: per me Petrum Quentell, 1531.
The only edition that includes the word "Catalogus" in the title. *Language(s)*: Latin. Appraised at 12d in 1613.

159.72   Connimbric Log.
[*Aristotle—Logica: commentary*]. (*Coimbra. Collegium Societatis Jesu*). Continent: 1604–1607.
See 159.67. *Language(s)*: Latin. Appraised at 4s in 1613.

159.73   Collection of Statutes
Unidentified. [*England—Statutes*]. Britain: date not determined.
STC 9264 *et seq. Language(s)*: English (probable) Latin (probable) Law French (probable). Appraised at 4s in 1613.

159.74   Lipsius saturnal.
Justus Lipsius. *Saturnalium sermonum libri duo*. Continent: 1582–1607. *Language(s)*: Latin. Appraised at 2s in 1613.

159.75   Maginus Geogr:
Claudius Ptolemy. *Geographia*. Edited by Giovanni Antonio Magini. Continent: 1596–1608.
Language(s): Latin. Appraised at 8s in 1613.

159.76   Latimers sermons
Hugh Latimer. [*Sermons*]. London: (different houses), 1549–1607.
STC 15274 *et seq*. According to the note to STC 15724, early editions of individual sermons were usually bound with collections of other sermons, but STC 15724 is the first to print multiple sermons. *Language(s)*: English. Appraised at 2s in 1613.

159.77   Huttons reasons for refusal of subscrip.
Thomas Hutton. *Reasons for refusal of subscription to the booke of common praier, under the hands of certaine ministers of Devon, and Cornwall*. Oxford: J. Barnes, sold by S. Waterson, 1605.

STC 14035. Less likely but possible: STC 14036. *Language(s)*: English. Appraised at 2s in 1613.

159.78   Bilsons Apology

Thomas Bilson, *Bishop. The true difference betweene christian subjection and unchristian rebellion.* Britain: 1585–1586.

STC 3071 *et seq.* The phrase "against the popish Apology for English Catholics" appears in the long title. See also BCI 2:129. *Language(s)*: English. Appraised at 3s 6d in 1613.

159.79   Arocius his notes of Phys M.S.

Juan Azor. *Institutiones morales* (part). Provenance unknown: date not determined.

Manuscript. See introduction. Sir Nathaniel Brent, the proctor of Oxford, testified at the trial of William Laud that a manuscript in Brown's hand of the opinions of "the Jesuit Azorius" was found in Brown's study after his death. For some contemporaries, the discovery confirmed their suspicions that Brown harbored Catholic sympathies. Laud denied that conclusion, but was familiar with the manuscript in question and described it as a collection of "Principles" extracted from Azor's *Institutiones morales*, the most "foul and dangerous" of which was the argument "that a Man might be a *Roman-Catholick*, and yet go to Church and Conform in England" (Laud 1695, 380–81). The title recorded by the compiler, "notes of Phys," might reflect an effort by Brown to disguise the manuscript's contents. *Language(s)*: Latin (probable). Appraised at 18d in 1613.

159.80   Mercers haeb grammer

Joannes Mercerus, *Professor of Hebrew. Tabulae in Chaldaeam grammaticen.* Continent: 1550–1602.

Sanctes Pagninus's *Thesaurus linguae sanctae: sive lexicon Hebraicum* (see 159.12) lists Mercerus on the title page, but Pagninus's work is not likely intended here. *Language(s)*: Aramaic Hebrew Latin Syriac. Appraised at 2s in 1613.

159.81   Copi Dialogi

Nicholas Harpsfield. *Dialogi sex contra summi pontificatus, monasticae vitae, sanctorum, sacrarum imaginum oppugnatores, et pseudomartyres.* Edited by Alan Cope. Antwerp: ex officina C. Plantini, 1566–1573.

Shaaber H93–H94. *Language(s)*: Latin. Appraised at 2s in 1613.

159.82   Elias Levita his Hebr. Gramm.

Elias, *Levita. Grammatica hebraica.* Continent: date not determined. *Language(s)*: Hebrew Latin. Appraised at 6d in 1613.

159.83   Tollets log:
Franciscus Toletus, *Cardinal*. [*Aristotle — Selected works — Logic: commentary*]. Continent: date not determined.
Language(s): Latin. Appraised at 2s in 1613.

159.84   Scoti quaest. in Metaph.
John Duns, *Scotus*. [*Aristotle — Metaphysica: commentary*]. Continent: 1497–1520.
Some commentaries on Aristotle's *Metaphysica* attributed to Duns are probably by other writers (see Harris, 1722). Another copy is listed at 159.37. *Language(s)*: Latin. Appraised at 18d in 1613.

159.85   Stapletons Controv. in Whitaker
William Whitaker and Thomas Stapleton. Unidentified. Britain or Continent: date not determined.
Stapleton, professor at Douai and Louvain, and Whitaker, Regius Professor of Divinity at Cambridge, exchanged five works of controversy between 1588 and 1600. This manuscript entry could refer to any one or to more than one, perhaps bound together. See STC 25366, 25363, 25370; Shaaber S306, S316 [ARCR 1: nos. 1142, 1154]. *Language(s)*: Latin. Appraised at 6s in 1613.

159.86   Osiander Eccles. Hist. in 5 vol:
Lucas Osiander, *the Elder*. *Epitomes historiae ecclesiasticae*. Continent: 1592–1613.
Language(s): Latin. Appraised at 20s in 1613.

159.87   Medulla Patrum pars 1a
Abraham Scultetus. *Medulla theologiae patrum* (part 1). Amberg: ex typo. Forsteriano, 1598.
Subsequent parts published in different cities through to 1613. Language(s): Latin. Appraised at 3s 4d in 1613.

159.88   Baptist. Porta de furt. lit. notis
Giovanni Battista della Porta. *De furtivis literarum notis*. Britain or Continent: 1563–1602.
STC 20118 *et seq.* and non-STC. Editions after 1602 carried a title with *De occultis* leading rather than *De furtivis*. *Language(s)*: Latin. Appraised at 12d in 1613.

159.89   Catalog libr. Bibl. Oxon.
Thomas James, *D.D. Catalogus librorum bibliothecae publicae quam Thomas Bodleius in academia Oxoniensi nuper instituit*. Oxford: apud J. Barnesium, 1605.

STC 14449. STC 14449.5 is another issue, reimposed in broadsheet form, nine pages per sheet, for posting on the ends of shelves in the Bodleian. *Language(s)*: Latin. Appraised at 2s in 1613.

159.90   Feild of the Church

Richard Field. *Of the church, five bookes*. London: (different houses) for S. Waterson, 1606.

STC 10857 *et seq*. Actually only four books. Two editions bear a 1606 imprint, but STC 10857.5 may have been published in 1614 according to the STC, too late for this book-list. *Language(s)*: English. Appraised at 2s 4d in 1613.

159.91   Torturi Torti

Lancelot Andrewes, *Bishop*. *Tortura Torti: sive, ad Matthaei Torti librum responsio*. Britain or Continent: 1609–1610.

STC 626 *et seq*. and non–STC. *Language(s)*: Latin. Appraised at 2s in 1613.

159.92   Lissius de Gratia

Leonardus Lessius. *De gratia efficaci decretis divinis libertate arbitrii et praescientia Dei conditionata*. Continent: 1610.

Editions from Antwerp and Barcelona in the same year. *Language(s)*: Latin. Appraised at 2s 6d in 1613.

159.93   Mortons Apolog.

Thomas Morton, *Bishop*. *Apologiae catholicae, in qua paradoxa, haereses, blasphemiae, scelera, quae Jesuitae impingunt, diluuntur*. London: (different houses), 1605–1606.

STC 18173.5 *et seq*. One of the 1606 editions was printed abroad for a London stationer. Not appraised. See 159.433 for another copy; 159.347 is another work by Morton issued with his *Apologiae*. *Language(s)*: Latin.

159.94   Macchiavels art of warr

Niccolò Machiavelli. *The arte of warre*. Translated by Peter Whitehorne. London: (different houses), 1560–1588.

STC 17164 *et seq*. *Language(s)*: English. Appraised at 16d in 1613.

159.95   Th. James of the Corrup. of the Fathers

Thomas James, D.D. *A treatise of the corruption of scripture, councels, and fathers, by the prelats, of the Church of Rome*. London: H. L[ownes] for M. Lownes, 1611–1612.

STC 14462 *et seq*. *Language(s)*: English. Appraised at 18d in 1613.

159.96   Dr Howson in Pius

John Howson, *Bishop*. *Uxore dimissa propter fornicationem aliam non licet superinducere . . . Accessit eiusdem theseos defensio contra reprehensiones T. Pyi.* Oxford: excudebat J. Barnesius, et veneunt Londini apud S. Watersonum, 1606.

STC 13887. The reply to Thomas Pie is by Robert Burhill. See the STC for other matter included in this augmented edition. *Language(s)*: Latin. Appraised at 12d in 1613.

159.97   Physick against Fortune

Francesco Petrarca. *Phisicke against fortune, as well prosperous, as adverse.* Translated by Thomas Twyne. London: [T. Dawson for] R. Watkyns, 1579.

STC 19809. *Language(s)*: English. Appraised at 2s in 1613.

159.98   Dr Coosins answer to the abstract

Richard Cosin. *An answer to the two first and principall treatises of a certeine factious libell, An abstract of certeine acts of Parlement.* London: H. Denham for T. Chard, 1584.

STC 5819.5 *et seq.* Also issued with the imprint: for T. Chard. *Language(s)*: English. Appraised at 16d in 1613.

159.99   Mr Twines antiquity

Brian Twyne. *Antiquitatis academiae Oxoniensis apologia.* Oxford: J. Barnesius, 1608.

STC 24405. *Language(s)*: Latin. Appraised at 18d in 1613.

159.100   Mr Jacksons Eternall truth

Thomas Jackson, *Dean of Peterborough*. *The eternall truth of scriptures.* London: W. Stansby and (different houses), 1613.

STC 14308 *et seq.* Issued with two imprints: W. Stansby, sold by J. Budge; W. Stansby, for E. Crossley. *Language(s)*: English. Appraised at 2s 6d in 1613.

159.101   Colloquium Ratisbonense

Unidentified. Continent: date not determined.

Colloquies were held in Ratisbon in 1541 and 1601. This entry could refer to the published *Acta* of either, or to any of the various works published after each Colloquy with these words in the title. *Language(s)*: Latin. Appraised at 12d in 1613.

159.102   The French Academy

Pierre de La Primaudaye. *The French academie.* Translated by Thomas Bowes. London: (different houses), 1586–1602.

STC 15233 *et seq.* A "second part" was published in 1594 (STC 15238 *et seq.*) and a third volume in 1601 (STC 15240). *Language(s)*: English. Appraised at 4s in 1613.

159.103   Poultons abstract

An abstract of all the penall statutes. (*England—Statutes—Abridgements and Extracts*). Compiled by Ferdinand Pulton. London: (different houses), 1577–1600.

STC 9526.7 *et seq. Language(s)*: English. Appraised at 2s in 1613.

159.104   Boterus in italian

Giovanni Botero. Unidentified. Continent: date not determined.

His most widely published work was *Relationi universali*. *Language(s)*: Italian. Appraised at 3s 6d in 1613.

159.105   Lipsius Electa

Justus Lipsius. *Electa*. Antwerp: Christopher Plantin, 1580–1585. *Language(s)*: Greek Latin. Appraised at 5d in 1613.

159.106   Elienses contra Bellarm

Lancelot Andrewes, *Bishop*. *Responsio ad Apologiam cardinalis Bellarmini, contra praefationem monitoriam Jacobi regis*. London: R. Barkerus, 1610.

STC 604. Dedication signed "L. Eliensis" (Andrewes was at the time Bishop of Ely). *Language(s)*: Latin. Appraised at 18d in 1613.

159.107   Cochlaei Apomaxis

Sir Richard Morison. *Apomaxis calumniarum, convitiorumque, quibus Joannes Cocleus, . . . Henrici octavi, famam impetere, . . . studuit*. London: in aedibus T. Bertheleti, 1537.

STC 18109. *Language(s)*: Latin. Appraised at 5d in 1613.

159.108   Eliots French grammer

John Eliot. *Ortho-epia Gallica. Eliots fruits for the French: which teacheth to speake the French-tongue*. London: [R. Field for] J. Wolfe, 1593.

STC 7574. *Language(s)*: English French. Appraised at 5d in 1613.

159.109   Precepta Juris Civilis

Unidentified. Continent: date not determined.

Perhaps Garcia Fortunius, *Tractatus de ultimo fine juris civilis et canonici: de principio et subsequentibus praeceptibus, de derivatione, et differentiis juris*, published in several editions. But the words "juris civilis" appear in a multitude of titles, and "precepta" may be descriptive. *Language(s)*: Latin. Appraised at 5d in 1613.

159.110 Broughtons concent of scripture

Hugh Broughton. *A concent of scripture*. London: (different houses), 1588–c.1612.

STC 3850 *et seq.* The manuscript entry indicates an English language edition. The 1602 Latin edition published in Hanau with a similar title, *Concentus SS. Scripturae* (Shaaber B682), should, however, be mentioned as a possibility. The stationer William White possibly had a hand in all English editions. *Language(s)*: English. Appraised at 12d in 1613.

159.111 Dr Benfeild lectures

Sebastian Benefield. *Doctrinae christianae sex capita, totidem praelectionibus in Schola Theologica Oxoniae*. Oxford: J. Barnesius, 1610.

STC 1867. *Language(s)*: Latin. Appraised at 12d in 1613.

159.112:1 Justa Oxoniensis et Cant

Justa Oxoniensium. (Lachrymae Oxoniensis stillantes in tumulum principis Henrici). (Oxford University—Verses, Addresses). [Edited by Samuel Fell?]. Oxford: [E. Griffin?] impensis J. Bill, 1612.

STC 19021 *et seq.* The collection published by Oxford to commemorate the death of Prince Henry, apparently either bound or listed together with the similar work published by Cambridge (see next entry). *Language(s)*: Latin English. Appraised with one other at 16d in 1613.

159.112:2 [See 159.112:1]

Epicedium Cantabrigiense, in obitum ... Henrici, principis Walliae. (Cambridge University). Cambridge: ex officina C. Legge, 1612.

STC 4481 *et seq.* The collection of verse published by Cambridge to commemorate the death of Prince Henry, apparently either bound or listed with the similar work published by Oxford (see previous entry). There were two issues in 1612, one of which contains Latin and French verses, another offering Latin and English. *Language(s)*: Latin English (perhaps) French (perhaps). Appraised with one other at 16d in 1613.

159.113 Boteri Amphitreatrid

Giovanni Botero. *Amphitheatridion*. Continent: 1597–1600.

The second part of Botero's *Relationi universali*, first published in Latin as *Mundus imperiorum* in 1596. *Language(s)*: Latin. Appraised at 8d in 1613.

159.114 Ariae Mont. Jud. Antiq.

Benito Arias Montano. *Antiquitatum Judaicarum libri IX*. Leyden: ex officina Plantiniana, apud Franciscum Raphelengium, 1593.

Language(s): Latin. Appraised at 2s 6d in 1613.

159.115 Francisci de platea

Franciscus de Platea. *Opus restitutionum, usurarum, et excommunicationum.* Continent: 1472–1489.
Language(s): Latin. Appraised at 6d in 1613.

159.116:1 Cantuariens perspect with Arith Salign

John Peckham, *Archbishop of Canterbury. Perspectiva communis.* Continent: date not determined.
Shaaber P78–P90. *Language(s)*: Latin. Appraised with one other at 10d in 1613.

159.116:2 [See 159.116:1]

Bernardus Salignacus. Unidentified. Continent: date not determined.
Either his *Tractatus arithmetici partium et alligationis* or his *Arithmeticae libri II.* *Language(s)*: Latin. Appraised with one other at 10d in 1613.

159.117 Benius de libero arbitrio

Paolo Beni. *Qua tandem ratione dirimi possit controversia quae inpraesens de efficaci Dei auxilio et libero arbitrio inter nonnullos catholicos agitatur.* Padua: in officina L. Pasquati, 1603.
Language(s): Latin. Appraised at 12d in 1613.

159.118 A Sasfron Bible

The Bible. Place unknown: stationer unknown, date not determined.
STC/non–STC status unknown. The only certainty is that the item listed is a Bible. The compiler may have intended to write "Saffron" instead of *Sasfron*, describing thereby the color of the binding as some form of yellow. Less likely, he intended to write "A Saxon Bible," but no Bible in Anglo-Saxon had appeared by the date of this inventory. An Anglo-Saxon and English translation of the Gospels had (STC 2961), but that would not have been identified as a Bible. *Language(s)*: Unknown. Appraised at 12d in 1613.

159.119 Appian in English

Appian, *of Alexandria. An auncient historie and exquisite chronicle of the Romanes warres.* Translated by W.B[arker?]. London: 1578.
STC 712.5 *et seq.* Henry Bynneman was the printer; he shares the imprint in two issues with Ralph Newbery. *Language(s)*: English. Appraised at 2s in 1613.

159.120 Edens decads

Petrus Martyr Anglerius (Peter Martyr). *The decades of the newe worlde or west India.* Translated by Richard Eden. London: (different houses), 1555–1612.
STC 645 *et seq.* The 1612 edition includes five additional decades translated by Michael Lok. *Language(s)*: English. Appraised at 2s 6d in 1613.

159.121 The 2 Tom. of the Palace of Pleasure

William Painter. *The second tome of the palace of pleasure*. London: (different houses), 1567–1580?

STC 19124 *et seq*. At the valuation of 18*d* almost certainly not two volumes. Further, compilers, including this one, do not customarily use the phrase "two tomes" to identify two books, but rather "two volumes." *Language(s)*: English. Appraised at 18d in 1613.

159.122 the mirrour of Magistrates

William Baldwin, John Higgins, Thomas Blenerhasset [and others]. *A myrroure for magistrates*. London: (different houses), 1559 (probable)–1610.

STC 1247 *et seq*. *Language(s)*: English. Appraised at 12d in 1613.

159.123 A booke of Battels of Pavy

Franciscus Taegius. *Le siege de Pavie ensemble les assaulx: sailliez: Escarmouchex et battailes*. Place unknown: stationer unknown, 1525.

Language(s): French. Appraised at 12d in 1613.

159.124 Ferrarius Commonwealth

Joannes Ferrarius. *A woorke of Joannes Ferrarius Montanus, touchynge the good orderynge of a common weale*. Translated by William Bavande. London: J. Kingston for J. Wight, 1559.

STC 10831. *Language(s)*: English. Appraised at 12d in 1613.

159.125 Catlines Conspiracyes In English

Constantius Felicius. *The conspiracie of Lucius Catiline*. Translated by Thomas Paynell. London: (different houses), 1541–1557.

STC 10751 *et seq*. Ben Jonson's *Catiline his conspiracy* (1611; STC 14759) is tempting; Brown did own of a copy of Jonson's *Sejanus his fall* (159.171). The phrasing of the manuscript entry ("In English") does, however, indicate that the original is in a language other than English. *Language(s)*: English. Appraised at 6d in 1613.

159.126 Monardus

Nicolas Monardes. Unidentified. Place unknown: stationer unknown, date not determined.

STC/non-STC status unknown. One of the several English editions of Monardes's work on medicinal plants between 1577 and 1596 is likely, but the manuscript entry is too imprecise to be certain, and it does suggest a Latin text. *Language(s)*: English (probable) Latin (probable). Appraised at 10d in 1613.

159.127 Gascoines workes

George Gascoigne. [*Works*]. London: (different houses), 1573 (probable)–1587.

STC 11635 *et seq*. First published as *A hundreth sundrie flowres bounde up in one small poesie* (1573), revised and augmented as *The posies of George Gascoigne esquire* (1575), and eventually published, with additions, under the titles *The whole woorkes* and *The pleasauntest workes* (both 1587). Language(s): English. Appraised at 18d in 1613.

159.128 Osorius Nobility Engl.

Jeronimo Osorio da Fonseca, *Bishop*. *The five bookes . . . contayninge a discourse of civill, and christian nobilitie*. Translated by William Blandy. London: T. Marsh, 1576.

STC 18886. Language(s): English. Appraised at 6d in 1613.

159.129 Tho: diction graecolat.

Thomas Thomas. *Dictionarium linguae Latinae et Anglicanae . . . cum Graecarum dictionum adjectione auctior*. Britain: 1596–1606.

STC 24011 *et seq*. First published in 1587 (STC 24008); the fifth (1596; STC 24011) and seventh (1606; STC 24013) editions appear to be the only ones by the date of this inventory to contain the Greek supplement. Another copy (perhaps without the Greek supplement) is listed at 159.221. Language(s): English Greek Latin. Appraised at 6s in 1613.

159.130 The Picture of a Papist

Oliver Ormerod. *The picture of a papist: or, a relation of the damnable heresies*. London: [R. Bradock] for N. Fosbrooke, 1606.

STC 18850. Language(s): English. Appraised at 6d in 1613.

159.131 Dr Allens treasons

Probably G.D. *A briefe discoverie of doctor Allens seditious drifts, contrived in a pamphlet*. London: J. W[olfe] for F. Coldock, 1588.

STC 6166. Language(s): English. Appraised at 4d in 1613.

159.132 Politicke Discourses

Perhaps Pierre de la Place. *Politique discourses, treating of the differences and inequalities of vocations*. Translated by Aegremont Ratcliffe. London: [T. Dawson?] for E. Aggas, 1578.

STC 15230.5. Published anonymously, which would explain the absence of an author's name. In addition, "Politique discourses" is displayed prominently at the top of the title page, whereas a less likely possibility, Matthieu Coignet, *Politique discourses upon trueth and lying* (1586; STC 5486), carries the name of the author and features the titular phrase less prominently. *Language(s)*: English. Appraised at 6d in 1613.

159.133 The steele glasse

George Gascoigne. *The steele glas. A satyre*. London: (H. Binneman) for R. Smith, 1576.

STC 11645. *Language(s)*: English. Appraised at 4d in 1613.

159.134 Civil wars in Flanders

A tragicall historie of the troubles and civile warres of the lowe countries, otherwise called Flanders. Translated by T. S(tocker). London: J. Kyngston [and T. Dawson] for T. Smith, 1583 (probable).

STC 17450.3. Listed in the STC under Philips van Marnix van Sant Aldegonde, but with the note that the attribution is "doubtful." Sometimes attributed to Carolus Rijckewaert (called Theophilius). The French edition (of an originally Dutch work), on which the English translation is based, is sometimes attributed to Jean François Le Petit. All versions partly based on a work by Adam Henricpetri. *Language(s)*: English. Appraised at 12d in 1613.

159.135 Alablaster on the Revelation

William Alabaster. *Apparatus in revelationem Jesu Christi*. Antwerp: ex officina Arnoldi Conincx, 1607.

Shaaber A78. *Language(s)*: Latin. Appraised at 2s in 1613.

159.136 Sanderi responsio

William Whitaker. *Ad Nicolai Sanderi demonstrationes quadraginta, in octavo visibilis Monarchiae positas, responsio*. London: T. Vautrollerius impensis T. Chardi, 1583.

STC 25357. Includes and answers Nicholas Sanders's *De visibili monarchia ecclesiae*. *Language(s)*: Latin. Appraised at 3d in 1613.

159.137 Bishops Blossoms

John Bishop. *Beautifull blossomes, gathered... from the best trees of all kyndes, divine, philosophicall, astronomicall*. London: [H. Middleton] for H. Cockyn, 1577.

STC 3091. Running-title reads "Byshops blossoms." *Language(s)*: English. Appraised at 10d in 1613.

159.138 Dr Cosins apol. engl

Richard Cosin. *An apologie: of, and for sundrie proceedings by jurisdiction ecclesiasticall*. London: Deputies of C. Barker, 1591–1593.

STC 5820 *et seq*. Published anonymously. The manuscript entry originally read "Bishop of Elies apol. engl." suggesting that the compiler apparently thought the work an English version of the Latin text by Lancelot Andrewes mentioned in the work's full title (see the STC note to 5821). Andrewes was Bishop of Ely when this inventory was made. The compiler then corrected the entry to "Dr. Cosins," but left the now unnecessary "engl." Only about forty copies were printed of the 1591 edition. *Language(s)*: English. Appraised at 18d in 1613.

159.139   Fentons Treatise of usury

Roger Fenton. *A treatise of usury, divided into three bookes*. London: F. Kyngston for W. Aspley, 1611–1612.

STC 10806 *et seq. Language(s)*: English. Appraised at 6d in 1613.

159.140   Tragicall Discourses

Probably Matteo Bandello. *Certaine tragicall discourses*. Translated by Sir Geoffrey Fenton. London: T. Marshe, 1567–1579.

STC 1356.1 *et seq*. Running-title reads: "Tragicall discourses." *Language(s)*: English. Appraised at 12d in 1613.

159.141   Haddons Orations & Poems

Walter Haddon. *Lucubrationes passim collectae, et editae*. Edited by Thomas Hatcher. London: (different houses), 1567–1592.

STC 12596 *et seq*. Issued in two parts. Part one contains orations and epistles; part two contains the poems. The rearranged and enlarged editions from 1576 forward are titled *Poematum*. Possibly bound-together copies of STC 12596.3 and 12596.7, the separately published *Oratio* (1555) and *Poëmata* (1567). *Language(s)*: Latin. Appraised at 12d in 1613.

159.142   Fornerius selections

Gulielmus Fornerius. [*Selectiones*]. Continent: 1565–1611.

Language(s): Latin. Appraised at 6d in 1613.

159.143   Mortons Satisfaction

Thomas Morton, *Bishop*. *A full satisfaction concerning a double Romish iniquitie; hainous rebellion, and more then heathenish aequivocation*. London: R. Field for E. Weaver, 1606.

STC 18185. *Language(s)*: English. Appraised at 8d in 1613.

159.144   Wasseri Institut. ling. Syrae

Caspar Waser and Andreas Masius. *Institutio linguae Syrae*. Leyden: ex officina Plantiniana, apud Franciscum Raphelengium, 1593–1594.

Language(s): Aramaic Latin Syriac. Appraised at 3d in 1613.

159.145   Flacius logicus

Matthias Flacius, *Illyricus*. Unidentified. Continent: date not determined.

Either *Opus logicum in organon Aristotelis stagiritae* or *Compendium logicae*. *Language(s)*: Latin. Appraised at 2s in 1613.

159.146 Calvins Institut

Jean Calvin. *Institutio Christianae religionis*. Britain or Continent: date not determined.

STC 4414 *et seq.* and non-STC. *Language(s)*: Latin (probable) English (perhaps). Appraised at 4s in 1613.

159.147 A Paper booke

Unidentified. Provenance unknown: date not determined.

Manuscript. Perhaps a notebook. *Language(s)*: Unknown. Appraised at 12d in 1613.

159.148 The golden Aphroditis

John Grange, *Student in the Common Law*. *The golden Aphroditis: a pleasant discourse*. London: (H. Bynneman), 1577.

STC 12174. Includes *Granges Garden*, in verse. *Language(s)*: English. Appraised at 3d in 1613.

159.149 Campi* Conference

Alexander Nowell, William Day, *Bishop*, and Edmund Campian. *A true report of the disputation or rather private conference had in the Tower of London, with E. Campion, Jesuite*. London: C. Barker, 1583.

STC 18744 *et seq*. "Campion" in book's title; "Campian" as name in STC. *Language(s)*: English. Appraised at 4d in 1613.

159.150 The Apology of the Prince of Orenge

Attributed to Pierre Loyseleur, revised by Hubert Languet. *The apologie or defence, of the most noble prince William*. Anonymously translated. Britain or Continent: 1581–1584 (probable).

STC 15207.5 *et seq*. The imprints of all three editions claim Delft as place of printing, though at least one was actually printed in London. Listed under Languet in the STC. *Language(s)*: English. Appraised at 2d in 1613.

159.151 The acknowledge of wars

Probably T.P. *Of the knowledge and conducte of warrres, two bookes*. London: in aedibus Richardi Tottelli, 1578.

STC 20403. Listed by the STC under Thomas Proctor, *Poet* with a note that it is "probably by a different Procter." *Language(s)*: English. Appraised at 2d in 1613.

159.152   4 Sermons at Hampt. Court

William Barlow, *Bishop of Rochester and Lincoln. One of the foure sermons preached before the kings majestie, at Hampton Court.* London: imprinted by J.W[indet] for Matthew Law, 1606–1607.

STC 1451 *et seq.* The two 1607 editions are titled *The first of the foure sermons preached before the kings majestie, at Hampton Court.* This was the only one of Barlow's four Hampton Court sermons to be published. *Language(s)*: English. Appraised at 8d in 1613.

159.153   Alphabet Arab

Unidentified. Continent: date not determined.

Either Jakob Christmann, *Alphabetum Arabicum: cum Isagoge scribendi legendique arabice* (Naples, 1582) or the anonymous *Alphabetum Arabicum* (Rome, 1592). *Language(s)*: Arabic Latin (probable). Appraised at 2d in 1613.

159.154   Trial of wits

Juan Huarte. *Examen de ingenios. The examination of mens wits.* London: (different houses), 1592?–1604.

STC 13889.5 *et seq.* Two different translations: unattributed in the 1592? edition, and the work of Richard Carew in editions from 1594 forward. Running-title reads "Trial of Wits" in all editions. *Language(s)*: English. Appraised at 12d in 1613.

159.155   Concio Lat. Episc. eliens.

Lancelot Andrewes, *Bishop. Concio Latinè habita coram regia majestate.* London: R. Barkerus, 1610.

STC 596. The title "Bishop of Ely" does not appear in the book, but Andrewes held that position at the time this inventory was made. *Language(s)*: Latin. Appraised at 2d in 1613.

159.156   Caussaub. Resp.

Isaac Casaubon. *Isaaci Casauboni ad epistolam illustr. cardinalis Perronii responsio.* Britain or Continent: 1612.

STC 4740 *et seq.* In all three editions published in 1612, the imprint reads "Londini: J. Norton." But while John Norton did publish at least one edition, probably in collaboration with Eliot's Court Press, the STC speculates that the two others were actually printed in Paris. *Language(s)*: Latin. Appraised at 4d in 1613.

159.157   Brought. Respons

Hugh Broughton. *Responsum ad epistolam Judaei sitienter expetentis cognitionem fidei christianorum.* Amsterdam: (stationer unknown), 1606.

Shaaber B689. *Language(s)*: Hebrew Latin. Appraised at 2d in 1613.

159.158   Brusi comment

Probably Antonio Brucioli. *A commentary upon the canticle of canticles*. London: R. F[ield] for T. Man, 1598.

STC 3928. If Brucioli, this single octavo volume is in accord with the valuation, unlike any one of the seven folio volumes published on the Continent in Italian. See CLC B2471. *Language(s)*: English. Appraised at 2d in 1613.

159.159   Neroes Trag.

Probably Matthew Gwinne. *Nero tragaedia nova*. London: [R. Read,] imp. E. Blounte, 1603.

STC 12551. Possibly STC 2406363a, *The tragedie of Claudius Tiberius Nero, Romes greatest tyrant* (1607). *Language(s)*: Latin. Appraised at 6d in 1613.

159.160   Lex levita

Elias, *Levita*. Unidentified. Continent: date not determined.

Either his *Lexicon Hebraicum* or *Lexicon Chaldaicum*. *Language(s)*: Latin Chaldaic (perhaps) Hebrew (perhaps). Appraised at 2d in 1613.

159.161   Becani disput

Martinus Becanus. Unidentified. Continent: date not determined.

Beginning in the late 1590s, Becanus published several works of theological controversy that contain some variation of "disputatio" in their titles. 159.280 lists either a different book with the same short title or another copy. *Language(s)*: Latin. Appraised at 4d in 1613.

159.162   Meschlini examen

Unidentified. Continent (probable): date not determined.

Probably not an STC book. Perhaps a garbled attempt at Philipp Melanchthon, *Examen eorum qui audiuntur ante ritum publicae ordinationis*. *Language(s)*: Latin. Appraised at 3d in 1613.

159.163   The forrest of fancy

H.C. *The forrest of fancy. Wherein is conteined very prety apothegmes, and pleasaunt histories, both in meeter and prose*. London: T. Purfoote, 1579.

STC 4271. Sometimes attributed to Henry Constable. *Language(s)*: English. Appraised at 4d in 1613.

159.164   wegelini disput

Unidentified. Continent: date not determined.

Balthasar Wegelin, Thomas Wegelin, and Joannes Wegelin all contributed to academic disputations published in German university cities between 1593 and 1607. *Language(s)*: Latin. Appraised at 4d in 1613.

159.165   Nordens spec. brit.

John Norden. Unidentified. London: (different houses), 1593–1598.

Unidentifiable in the STC. STC 18635, STC 18637, and STC 18638 are equal possibilities. Each was printed by a different London stationer. *Language(s)*: English. Appraised at 3d in 1613.

159.166   quaesti Jurid. per cook

James Cooke. *Juridica trium quaestionum ad majestatem pertinentium determinatio; opposita praecipue epistolae cuidam dedicatoriae.* Oxford: J. Barnesius, 1608.

STC 5671. *Language(s)*: Latin. Appraised at 2d in 1613.

159.167   Politiani Nutricia

Angelus Politianus (Angelo Ambrogini). *Silva cui titulus Nutricia. Silvae.* Continent: 1491.

Two editions printed in the same year, one in Bologna, the other in Florence. *Language(s)*: Latin. Appraised at 2d in 1613.

159.168   the Queens Injunctions

Injunctions geven by the quenes majestie. (England, Church of—*Injunctions, General, 1559*). London: (different houses), 1559 (probable)–1600 (probable).

STC 10099.5 *et seq. Language(s)*: English. Appraised at 2d in 1613.

159.169   Polonica electio

De polonica electione, in comitiis Warsauiensibus, anni 1587 acta: et quae secuta sunt, usque ad coronationem Sigismundi III et captum Maximilianum. Place not given: stationer unknown, 1588.

Language(s): Latin. Appraised at 1d in 1613.

159.170   Catalog Marts

Probably Thomas Worthington. Unidentified. Continent (probable): date not determined.

STC/non-STC status unknown. Two works associated with Worthington are the best candidates. *A catalogue of martyrs in England* (STC 26000.8) is said to have been a collection edited by Worthington though published anonymously (ARCR 2: no. 846). A Latin work first published in 1610 and also attributed to Worthington, *Catalogus martyrum pro religione Catolica in Anglia* (ARCR 1: no. 1416), is equally possible. Neither apparently was published in England. It is not clear if the Latin work is a translation of the earlier collection. For another though less likely possibility, see STC 25771. *Language(s)*: English (probable) Latin (probable). Appraised at 2d in 1613.

159.171   Sejanus

Benjamin Jonson. *Sejanus his fall.* London: G. Elld for T. Thorp, 1605.

STC 14782. *Language(s)*: English. Appraised at 6d in 1613.

159.172 Cardans comfort

Girolamo Cardano. *Cardanus comforte translated into Englishe*. Translated by Thomas Bedingfield. London: T. Marshe, 1573–1576.

STC 4607 *et seq. Language(s)*: English. Appraised at 4d in 1613.

159.173 A tricks to catch the old one

Thomas Middleton. *A trick to catch the old-one*. London: (different houses), 1608.

STC 17896 *et seq.* George Eld printed both issues; Henry Rocket's name appears on the second as bookseller. *Language(s)*: English. Appraised at 2d in 1613.

159.174 Smiths Common wealth

Sir Thomas Smith, *Doctor of Civil Laws. The common-welth of England, and maner of government thereof.* London: (different houses), 1589–1612.

STC 22859 *et seq. Language(s)*: English. Appraised at 3d in 1613.

159.175 Bilsons church governm

Thomas Bilson, *Bishop. The perpetual governement of Christes church.* London: (different houses), 1593–1610.

STC 3065 *et seq. Language(s)*: English. Appraised at 12d in 1613.

159.176 Bulckleies Apolog with others

Edward Bulkeley. *An apologie for religion, or an answere to an unlearned pamphlet intituled: Certain articles, or forcible reasons.* London: (different houses) for A. Johnson, 1602–1608.

STC 4025 *et seq.* The title of the enlarged 1608 edition is changed to *An apologie for the religion established in the church of England* and includes substantial additions mentioned on the title page which may explain the "with others" in the manuscript entry. Alternatively, the phrase may refer to Thomas Wright's *Certain articles* (1600), reprinted in Bulkeley's work, or to other, unnamed texts bound with this volume or simply included in a group valuation. Whatever the compiler intended by the phrase, his citation to Bulkeley's polemic is clear. *Language(s)*: English. Appraised at 16d in 1613.

159.177 Daniels Histor. of Engl

Samuel Daniel. *The first part of the historie of England.* London: (different houses), 1612–1613.

STC 6246 *et seq. Language(s)*: English. Appraised at 12d in 1613.

159.178 Catalog. of Bishops

Francis Godwin, *Bishop. A catalogue of the bishops of England, with a briefe history of their lives and actions.* London: [Eliot's Court Press,] imp. G. Bishop, 1601.

STC 11937. *Language(s)*: English. Appraised at 2s in 1613.

159.179   A Survey of pretended discipline
Richard Bancroft, *Archbishop*. *A survay of the pretended holy discipline*. London: J. Wolfe, 1593.
STC 1352. Published anonymously. *Language(s)*: English. Appraised at 18d in 1613.

159.180   Anticotton
Anti-Coton, or a refutation of Cottons Letter declaratorie: touching the killing of kings. Translated by G.H. [George Hakewill?]. London: T. S[nodham] for R. Boyle, 1611.
STC 5861 *et seq*. "Usually attributed to C. de Plaix; sometimes also to J. Du Bois, P. du Coignet, and P. du Moulin" (STC). Two editions in 1611. *Language(s)*: English. Appraised at 2d in 1613.

159.181   Answer to Downams sermon
An answere to a sermon preached the 17 of April 1608, by G. Downame, . . . intituled, A sermon defendinge the honorable function of bishops. Amsterdam: J. Hondius [part 1], G. Thorp [part 2], 1609.
STC 20605. Listed in the STC under John Rainolds, but with a note that the book is not by him. *Language(s)*: English. Appraised at 6d in 1613.

159.182   Bancrofts sermon
Richard Bancroft, *Archbishop*. *A sermon preached at Paules Crosse the 9. of Februarie, 1588*. London: (different houses) for G. Seton, 1588.
STC 1346 *et seq*. Two editions in 1588 (old style). *Language(s)*: English. Appraised at 2d in 1613.

159.183   Benfeilds sermon
Sebastian Benefield. *A sermon preached in St Maries Oxford, March xxiv. MDCX. at the inauguration of king James*. Oxford: (different houses), 1611–1613.
STC 1870 *et seq*. Both editions printed by Joseph Barnes, the second with the imprint "sold by John Barnes," Joseph's son. *Language(s)*: English. Appraised at 2d in 1613.

159.184   booke of Canons
Probably *A booke of certaine canons, concernyng some parte of the discipline of the churche of England*. London: J. Daye, 1571 (probable).
STC 10062.5 *et seq*. *Language(s)*: English. Appraised at 6d in 1613.

159.185   Sr Edwins Sands Relation
Sir Edwin Sandys. *A relation of the state of religion: and with what hopes and pollicies it hath beene framed, and is maintained in the severall states of these westerne parts of the world*. London: (different houses) for S. Waterson, 1605.

STC 21716 *et seq.* Three editions in 1605, published anonymously. *Language(s)*: English. Appraised at 16d in 1613.

159.186   Oxfords answer to the ministers Petition

The answere of the vicechancelour, the doctors, both the proctors, and other the heads of houses in the universitie of Oxford. To the humble petition of the ministers of the Church of England, desiring reformation of certaine ceremonies and abuses. (*Oxford University — Official Documents*). Oxford: (different houses), 1603–1604.

STC 19010 *et seq.* All five editions printed by Joseph Barnes; some imprints note "sold by" Simon Waterson, in London. *Language(s)*: English. Appraised at 1d in 1613.

159.187   Christ descension into hell

Unidentified. Britain (probable): date not determined.

Unidentifiable in the STC. Possibilities include works by Thomas Bilson, Hugh Broughton, Christopher Carlile, John Higgins, Adam Hill, Alexander Hume, Thomas Morton, and Richard Parkes. *Language(s)*: English. Appraised at 2d in 1613.

159.188   B Elies Serm

Lancelot Andrewes, *Bishop*. Unidentified. London: date not determined.

Unidentifiable in the STC. All of Andrewes's numerous sermons published singly, or in pairs, by the date of this inventory were published by Robert Barker. The valuation seems too low to refer to a sermon collection, though Andrewes had published some by this date. See also 159.190. *Language(s)*: English. Appraised at 3d in 1613.

159.189   Apology for the oth of Allegiance

James I, *King of England. An apologie for the oath of allegiance: first set forth without a name, now acknowledged by James, King.* London: R. Barker, 1609.

STC 14401 *et seq.* Perhaps STC 14400, the first edition, published anonymously with the lead title *Triplici nodo, triplex cuneus. Or an apologie for the oath of allegiance* (1607). *Language(s)*: English. Appraised at 4d in 1613.

159.190   B Elies Serm 2

Lancelot Andrewes, *Bishop*. Unidentified. London: date not determined.

Unidentifiable in the STC. See also 159.188, particularly the annotation. *Language(s)*: English. Appraised at 4d in 1613.

159.191   Downfal of Popery

Thomas Bell. *The downefall of poperie: proposed by way of a new challenge to English jesuits.* London: (different houses), 1604–1608.

STC 1818 *et seq. Language(s)*: English. Appraised at 4d in 1613.

159.192 Wilkes eccles union

William Wilkes. *Obedience or ecclesiasticall union*. London: G. Elde for Roger Jackson, 1605.

STC 25633. Subsequent issues (1608, 1609) were published under the title *A second memento for magistrates*, but with the running-title "Obedience or ecclesiastical union" appearing in both, one of them just possibly might be intended here. *Language(s)*: English. Appraised at 3d in 1613.

159.193:1 Dr Howsons 2 sermons

John Howson, *Bishop*. *A sermon preached at Paules Crosse the 4. of December. 1597. [Showing] that all buying and selling of spirituall promotion is unlawfull*. Oxford: (different houses) for T. Adams, 1597.

STC 13881 *et seq*. See also 159.193:2. In addition to these two sermons, delivered and marketed as a pair, Howson published only one other sermon. *Language(s)*: English. Appraised with one other at 4d in 1613.

159.193:2 [See 159.193:1]

John Howson, *Bishop*. *A second sermon, preached at Paules Crosse, the 21. of May, 1598. Concluding a former sermon*. London: A. Hatfield for T. Adams, 1598.

STC 13883. See the annotation to the preceding entry. *Language(s)*: English. Appraised with one other at 4d in 1613.

159.194 Service in the low countries

Thomas Digges. *A briefe report of the militarie services done in the Low Countries, by the erle of Leicester: written by one that served in good place there*. London: A. Hatfield for G. Seton, 1587.

STC 7285 *et seq*. Listed in the STC under Robert Dudley, *Earl of Leicester*, though with a note that the text was written by Digges. Two editions in 1587. *Language(s)*: English. Appraised at 1d in 1613.

159.195 Passions of the mind

Thomas Wright, *Priest*. *The passions of the minde*. London: (different houses), 1601–1604.

STC 26039 *et seq*. Stationers Valentine Simmes and Walter Burre had a hand in both possible editions. *Language(s)*: English. Appraised at 16d in 1613.

159.196 Duello

John Selden. *The duello or single combat*. London: G. E[ld] for J. Helme, 1610.

STC 22171. *Language(s)*: English. Appraised at 2d in 1613.

159.197 Meredith Serm.
Richard Meredeth. *Two sermons preached before his majestie*. London: G. Eld for S. Waterson, 1606.
STC 17832. Meredeth's only publication. *Language(s)*: English. Appraised at 2d in 1613.

159.198 Romish Judas
John Rawlinson. *The Romish Judas. A sermon*. London: W. Hall for J. Hodgets, 1611.
STC 20775. *Language(s)*: English. Appraised at 2d in 1613.

159.199 A copy of a letter
Unidentified. Britain (probable): date not determined.
Unidentifiable in the STC. Numerous possibilities. *Language(s)*: English. Appraised at 1d in 1613.

159.200 The History of Henr. 4
Probably William Shakespeare. *The Hystorie, of Henrie the fourth*. London: (different houses), 1598 (probable)–1613.
STC 22279a *et seq*. Possibly Sir John Hayward, *The first part of the life and raigne of king Henrie the IIII* (editions 1599 to c.1610), though the title of Shakespeare's play offers a closer match for the entry. A less likely possiblity is Edmond Skory, *An extract out of the historie of the last French king Henry the fourth* (1610). *Language(s)*: English. Appraised at 6d in 1613.

159.201 Sardus de nummis
Alessandro Sardi. *Liber de nummis: in quo antiqua pecunia romana et graeca metitur precio eius, quae nunc est in usu*. Mainz: per Casparum Behem, 1579.
Sometimes mistakenly attributed to John Selden because of late seventeenth-century re-issues published under his name. *Language(s)*: Latin. Appraised at 1d in 1613.

159.202 Gentilis de potestate regis
Albericus Gentilis. *Regales disputationes tres: id est, De potestate regis absoluta, De unione regnorum Britanniae, De vi civium in regem semper injusta*. Britain or Continent: [W. Antonius, sold], ap. T. Vautrollerium, 1605.
STC 11741. Printed in Hanau, sold in London. *Language(s)*: Latin. Appraised at 4d in 1613.

159.203 Art of navigation
Unidentified. London (probable): date not determined.
Unidentifiable in the STC. Probably either Pedro de Medina, *The arte of navigation* (editions in 1581 and 1595) or Martin Cortes, *The arte of navigation,*

conteynyng a compendious description of the sphere (editions from 1561 to 1609). Possibly one of Antonio de Guevara, *A booke of the invention of the art of navigation* (1578); John Dee, *General and rare memorials perteyning to the perfect arte of navigation* (1577); or Anthony Linton, *Newes of the complement of the art of navigation* (1609). *Language(s)*: English. Appraised at 6d in 1613.

159.204 Discovery of Guiana

Sir Walter Raleigh. *The discoverie of the large, rich, and bewtiful empire of Guiana*. London: R. Robinson, 1596.

STC 20634 *et seq.* Three editions in 1596. *Language(s)*: English. Appraised at 4d in 1613.

159.205 Franci Insignium

Abraham Fraunce. *Abrahami Fransi insignium, armorum, emblematum, hieroglyphicorum, et symbolorum, explicatio*. London: T. Orwinus, imp. T. Gubbin et T. Newman, 1588.

STC 11342. *Language(s)*: Latin. Appraised at 4d in 1613.

159.206 Edward the fourth

Thomas Heywood. *The first and second partes of king Edward the fourth*. London: 1599–1613.

STC 13341 *et seq.* Published anonymously. The ballad *A merrie and delectable historie, betweene king Edward the fourth, and a tanner of Tamworth* (STC 7503 *et seq.*) is an unlikely possibility. Struck through, with an "X" in the margin, and not appraised. *Language(s)*: English.

159.207 Shepheards Kalendar

Perhaps Edmund Spenser. *The shepheardes calendar conteyning twelve aeglogues proportionable to the twelve monethes*. London: (different houses), 1579–1611.

STC 23089 *et seq.* Possibly the [*Shepherds' Kalendar*] (STC 22407 *et seq.*), a popular almanac. But editions of the almanac with this form of the title, published from c.1570 to 1611, were all published in folio, and the books in this section of the catalogue (beginning at 159.59) appear to be quartos. Also, valued at 4*d*, this item is not likely to be a folio book. Some early sixteenth-century editions of the almanac were published in quarto, but only under variations of the title *The kalender of shepeherdes*. The five editions of Spenser's work to 1597 were published in quarto. *Language(s)*: English. Appraised at 4d in 1613.

159.208 Art of dialling

Probably John Blagrave. *The art of dyalling in two parts*. London: N. O[kes] for S. Waterson, 1609.

STC 3116. Perhaps Thomas Fale, *Horologiographia. The art of dialling: teaching an easie and perfect way to make dials* (1593). Edward Wright's *The arte of dialing* (1614) was entered after Brown's death. *Language(s)*: English. Appraised at 12d in 1613.

159.209   Navigators supply
William Barlow, *Archdeacon of Salisbury*. *The navigators supply. Conteining many things belonging to navigation*. London: G. Bishop, R. Newbery and R. Barker, 1597.
STC 1445. *Language(s)*: English. Appraised at 4d in 1613.

159.210   Lixivium
Jacob Gretser. *Lixivium pro abluendo male sano capite anonymi cuiusdam fabulatoris, et, ut vocant novellantis, qui caedem christianissimi Galliae et Navarrae Regis Henrici IV. in Jesuitas, partim aperte partem tacite confert*. Ingolstadt: ex typographeo Adami Sartorii, 1610.
Includes a work by Henry IV, in German, in defense of the Jesuits. *Language(s)*: German Latin. Appraised at 2d in 1613.

159.211   Parraeis conciones
Henry Parry, *Bishop*. *De regno Dei, et victoria christiana, conciones duae*. London: ex typog. Kyngstoniano, imp. C. Burbaei et E. Weaver, 1606.
STC 19335. According to the STC, some copies read "Felix Kyngstoniano" in the imprint. *Language(s)*: Latin. Appraised at 2d in 1613.

159.212   Leede sabbato
Unidentified. Place unknown: stationer unknown, date not determined.
STC/non-STC status unknown. *Language(s)*: Latin (probable). Appraised at 8d in 1613.

159.213   spanish grammer
Unidentified. Place unknown: stationer unknown, date not determined.
STC/non-STC status unknown. Perhaps Richard Percyvall, *A spanish grammar* (1599); other STC possibilities include grammars by Antonio del Corro and Lewis Owen. The entry could also describe any number of Continental texts. *Language(s)*: Spanish. Appraised at 4d in 1613.

159.214   Picture of puritan
Oliver Ormerod. *The picture of a puritane: or, a relation of the opinions, and practises of the Anabaptists in Germanie, and of the puritanes in England*. London: E. A[llde] for N. Fosbroke, 1605.
STC 18851 *et seq*. Two editions in 1605. *Language(s)*: English. Appraised at 3d in 1613.

159.215 Lubbertus de fide
Sibrandus Lubbertus and Pierre Bertius. *Epistolica disceptatio de fide justificante*. Delft: apud Joannem Andreae, 1612.
Language(s): Latin. Appraised at 8d in 1613.

159.216 Bilson de gubernationes ecclesiae
Thomas Bilson, *Bishop*. *De perpetua ecclesiae christi gubernatione*. London: [R. Field,] impensis J. Billii, 1611.
STC 3067. A translation of STC 3065. A manuscript entry that follows this item is heavily crossed out; a gap in the list then follows before continuing with the next item. *Language(s)*: Latin. Appraised at 2s in 1613.

159.217 Bellarmini Gram: Heb:
Roberto Bellarmino, *Cardinal*. *Institutiones linguae hebraicae*. Continent: 1578–1609.
A gap precedes this entry in the manuscript, marking the conclusion of the quarto listings that began at 159.59 and the start of a section listing octavos. The appearance of any given book within a given section is not, however, a guarantee of actual format. *Language(s)*: Hebrew Latin. Appraised at 12d in 1613.

159.218:A Histor. Orient: Eccles: Gal.
Antonius de Gouveaus. *Histoire orientale des grans progres de l'eglise Cathol. apost. et Rom.* Continent: 1609 (composite publication).
Published in Antwerp and Brussels. As elsewhere in this inventory, "gal" indicates that a work is in French. *Language(s)*: French. Appraised [a composite volume] at 2s 6d in 1613.

159.218:B [See 159.218:A]
Aleixo de Menezes. *Le messe des anciens chrestiens dicts de S. Thomas, en l'Evesche d'Angamal, es Indes Orientales*. [Composite publication].
This work seems always to have been published with Gouveaus's work; see the annotation to 159.218:A. *Language(s)*: French. Appraised [a composite volume] at 2s 6d in 1613.

159.219 Cicer: Epist:
Marcus Tullius Cicero. [*Selected works—Epistolae*]. Continent: date not determined.
The *Epistolae ad familiares*, printed in England as well as on the Continent, is also a possibility. *Language(s)*: Latin. Appraised at 8d in 1613.

159.220 Diction: Concionatoris
Pietro Ridolfi. [*Dictionarium concionatorum pauperum*]. Continent: 1580–1610.

Title varies; earlier editions begin *Dictionarium pauperum*, but the titles of all editions somewhere contain "concionatorum" or "concionatoribus." *Language(s)*: Latin. Appraised at 2s 6d in 1613.

159.221   Tho: Diction:
Thomas Thomas. *Dictionarium linguae Latinae et Anglicanae*. Britain: 1587 (probable)–1610.

STC 24008 *et seq.* Some editions contain a Greek supplement; a copy of one of these editions is listed at 159.129. *Language(s)*: English Latin Greek (perhaps). Appraised at 2s in 1613.

159.222   Lucii Flores
Lucius Annaeus Florus. [*Epitomae de Tito Livio bellorum omnium annorum*]. Continent: date not determined.

Language(s): Latin. Appraised at 8d in 1613.

159.223   Becani Enchiridion
Martinus Becanus. *Enchiridion variarum disputationum*. Mainz: ex officina Joannis Albini, 1606.

Language(s): Latin. Appraised at 18d in 1613.

159.224   Nubigensis hist:
William, *of Newburgh*. *Rerum anglicarum libri quinque*. Continent: 1567–1610.

Language(s): Latin. Appraised at 8d in 1613.

159.225   Sarisburiens: Policraticus
John, *of Salisbury, Bishop of Chartres*. *Policraticus de nugis curialium*. Continent: 1481–1595.

Language(s): Latin. Appraised at 18d in 1613.

159.226   Machav: de Rep:
Niccolò Machiavelli. *Disputationum de republica libri III*. Translated by Johann Niklaus Stupanus. Continent: 1588–1608.

The Latin translation of the *Discorsi*. *Language(s)*: Latin. Appraised at 12d in 1613.

159.227   Fulke against martin
William Fulke. *A defense of the sincere and true translations of the holie scriptures into the English tong, against G. Martin*. London: H. Bynneman for G. Bishop, 1583.

STC 11430 *et seq.* A variant title page omits Bishop's name, which appears in the colophon. *Language(s)*: English. Appraised at 18d in 1613.

159.228 Costeri Enchiridion

Franciscus Costerus. *Enchiridion controversiarum de religione.* Continent: 1585–1612.
Language(s): Latin. Appraised at 2s in 1613.

159.229 Ferus in genes:

Joannes Ferus (Johann Wild, *Prediger zu Mainz*). *In totam Genesim enarrationes.* (*Bible — O.T.*). Continent: 1564–1573.
Language(s): Latin. Appraised at 2s in 1613.

159.230 Terentius Varro

Marcus Terentius Varro. *De re rustica.* Continent: date not determined.
Language(s): Latin. Appraised at 18d in 1613.

159.231 Ameyen in Virgil

Publius Virgilius Maro. [*Works*]. Edited by Joannes a Meyen. Continent: 1576–1608.

With this entry, the hand in the manuscript changes: the two compilers switched roles. They reverse duties again at 159.423. *Language(s)*: Latin. Appraised at 2s in 1613.

159.232 Clen: gram

Nicolaus Clenardus. Unidentified. Continent: date not determined.

Either *Institutiones linguae graecae* or *Tabula in grammaticen hebraeam*, both widely published. Brown's library contains an unusual amount of Hebrew, making Clenard's Hebrew grammar as likely as his Greek. *Language(s)*: Latin Greek (perhaps) Hebrew (perhaps). Appraised at 10d in 1613.

159.233 Hom: odiss: grae. lat.

Homer. *Odyssey.* Continent: date not determined.
Language(s): Greek Latin. Appraised at 18d in 1613.

159.234 Lucan: Bersman:

Marcus Annaeus Lucanus. *Pharsalia.* Edited by Gregorius Bersmanus. Leipzig: imprim. haered. Joannis Steinmanni, impens. Henningi Grosii, 1589.
Language(s): Latin. Appraised at 12d in 1613.

159.235 Magir Ethic:

John Magirus. [*Aristotle — Ethica: commentary*]. Frankfurt am Main: proponitum in Collegio Musarum Paltheniano, 1601–1608.

Includes the text, in Greek and Latin. *Language(s)*: Greek Latin. Appraised at 3s in 1613.

159.236   Cajeton in parab:
Thomas de Vio Cajetanus, *Cardinal*. [*Proverbs, Ecclesiastes, Isaiah: commentary*]. Continent: 1542–1545.
Language(s): Latin. Appraised at 12d in 1613.

159.237   Bez: Testament: grae lat:
[*Bible—N.T.*]. Translated and edited by Théodore de Bèze. Continent: date not determined.
Language(s): Greek Latin. Appraised at 2s 6d in 1613.

159.238   Euseb: Dialog:
Nicolaus Barnaud (Eusebius, *Philadelphus*, pseudonym). *Dialogi ab Eusebio Philadelpho cosmopolita in Gallorum et caeterarum nationum gratiam compositi*. Edinburgh: ex typ. J. Jamaei, 1574.
STC 1463. The imprint is false; the book was printed abroad. The printer name is a pseudonym for Bernhard Jobin of Strassburg and other unidentified Continental printers. *Language(s)*: Latin. Appraised at 6d in 1613.

159.239   Sleid: Comment:
Joannes Philippson, *Sleidanus*. *De statu religionis et reipublicae, Carolo Quinto, Caesare, commentarii*. Britain or Continent: 1555–1612.
STC 19848 *et seq.* and non-STC. Both editions of the English translation were published in folio, making these a less likely match than one of the Continental editions: all the books for some distance on either side of this entry seem likely to have been octavo editions. *Language(s)*: Latin (probable) English (perhaps). Appraised at 3s 6d in 1613.

159.240   Sum: virtut: et vitior:
Probably Gulielmus Peraldus. *Summa virtutum ac vitiorum*. Continent: date not determined.
Other books bear similar, but not identical, titles, for example the anonymous *Summarium summae virtutum et vitiorum*, or Dionysius, *Carthusianus*, *Summa vitiorum et virtutum*. Another of Peraldus's works is in Brown's collection; see 159.245. *Language(s)*: Latin. Appraised at 12d in 1613.

159.241   Sanchez concion:
Gaspar Sanchez, *de Granada*. *Conciones in Dominicis, et feriis quadragesimae*. Continent: 1597–1609.
Language(s): Latin. Appraised at 2s in 1613.

159.242   Bencius orationes
Franciscus Bencius. Unidentified. Continent: date not determined.

His most frequently published work was *Orationes et carmina*, but this could also be his *Orationes duae et elegiae totidem in obitum Alexandri Farnesii*, or *Orationes XXII . . . De stylo et scriptione disputatio*. *Language(s)*: Latin. Appraised at 12d in 1613.

159.243   Pagnini Epitome
Sanctes Pagninus. *Thesauri linguae sanctae epitome*. Continent: 1570–1609. *Language(s)*: Hebrew Latin. Appraised at 2s in 1613.

159.244   Artopius Psalteri Heb: lat: grae
[*Bible — O.T. — Psalms*]. Edited with commentary by Petrus Artopoeus (Peter Becker). Basle: (different houses), 1545–1569.
Language(s): Greek Hebrew Latin. Appraised at 2s 4d in 1613.

159.245   Peraldi Homiliae
Gulielmus Peraldus. *Homeliae sive sermones eximii, praestantesque super Evangelia Dominicalia totius anni*. Lyon: apud Carolum Pesnot, 1576.

The only collection of his sermons with "Homiliae" in the title. See also 159.240. *Language(s)*: Latin. Appraised at 18d in 1613.

159.246   Hieron: Bibl: lat
The Bible. Continent: date not determined.
St. Jerome's Vulgate. Another copy is listed at 159.32. *Language(s)*: Latin. Appraised at 2s 6d in 1613.

159.247   Phrases Lin: lat:
Unidentified. Place unknown: stationer unknown, date not determined.
STC/non-STC status unknown. Works by Aldo Manuzio, *the Elder*, by Antonius Schorus, and by Estienne Dolet are among books with titles that a compiler might enter in this manner. Manuzio's *Phrases linguae latinae*, with an English translation of the Latin phrases, was repeatedly printed in England and, therefore, may be marginally more likely here. *Language(s)*: Latin. Appraised at 8d in 1613.

159.248   Bib: french
The Bible. Continent: date not determined.
Language(s): French. Appraised at 2s 6d in 1613.

159.249   Paraphras Riccob: in Rhetori Arist.
Antonio Riccoboni. [*Aristotle — Rhetorica: commentary and paraphrase*]. Continent: 1588–1606.
Language(s): Latin. Appraised at 6d in 1613.

159.250   Mount: essais in french
Michel de Montaigne. *Les essais*. Continent: 1580–1611.
Language(s): French. Appraised at 2s in 1613.

159.251   Blebelius heb: gram:
Thomas Blebelius. *Grammatices hebraeae sanctae linguae institutiones*. Wittenberg: apud haered. Joannis Cratonis, 1587.
Language(s): Hebrew Latin. Appraised at 12d in 1613.

159.252   Lodovicios vivis
Joannes Ludovicus Vives. Unidentified. Place unknown: stationer unknown, date not determined.
STC/non-STC status unknown. *Language(s)*: Latin (probable) English (perhaps). Appraised at 16d in 1613.

159.253   stories of the fathers
Thomas Hayne (attributed). Probably *A briefe discourse of the scriptures: declaring the severall stories, lives, and deaths of the fathers, from Adam, unto Joseph*. London: W. White, 1614.
STC 12975. Running-title reads "Stories of the fathers, from Adam to Joseph." While the imprint is 1614, this book was entered in the Stationers' Register in May 1613. The text, with some alterations, follows part of STC 12981, Thomas Hayne, *The times, places, and persons of the holie scripture* (1607), but neither the title nor running-title of this book matches this entry. Listed in the STC under Hayne, but with a note that it is not by him, and that it is possibly by somebody connected with Hugh Broughton. *Language(s)*: English. Appraised at 1s in 1613.

159.254   Canini de locis scriptu:
Angelus Caninius. *De locis s. scripturae hebraicis*. Edited by Gaspar Bellerus. Continent: 1600.
A composite volume containing *Loci aliquot Novi Testamenti cum Hebraeorum originibus* by Caninius (Angelo Canini), *Quinquagena* by Aelius Antonius Nebrissensis (Antonio de Nebrija), and *De Orphira regione in sacris litteris disputatio* by Gaspar Barreiros (Caspar Varrerius), as well as some shorter documents. Published simultaneously in Antwerp and Louvain. *Language(s)*: Latin. Appraised at 8d in 1613.

159.255   Fuccius Instituti
Leonard Fuchs. *Institutionum medicinae*. Continent: 1555–1605.
A revision of his *Methodus seu ratio compendiara cognoscendi veram solidamque medicinam*. *Language(s)*: Latin. Appraised at 16d in 1613.

159.256   Bucanon Hist: Scotland
George Buchanan. *Rerum Scoticarum historia*. Britain or Continent: 1582–1594.
STC 3991 *et seq.* and non-STC. More likely one of the octavo editions published in Frankfurt, rather than one of the folio editions published in Edinburgh and Antwerp: this section of the inventory lists books in octavo and elsewhere tends to indicate in the entry if a book is a folio. *Language(s)*: Latin. Appraised at 20d in 1613.

159.257   Cannonis gram:
Perhaps Angleus Caninius. *Hellenismos*. Britain or Continent: 1555–1613.
STC 4566 and non-STC. A Greek grammar. The title is transliterated from Greek characters. But the entry perhaps refers to Giovanni Battista Cantalicio's frequently published (under varying titles) *Canones grammatices*. *Language(s)*: Greek Latin. Appraised at 10d in 1613.

159.258   Junius Ecclesiast:
François Du Jon, *the Elder*. *Ecclesiastici sive de natura et administrationibus ecclesiae Dei*. Frankfurt am Main: apud Andream Wechelum, 1581.
Language(s): Latin. Appraised at 18d in 1613.

159.259   Marloret: Enchirid:
Isaacus Feguernekinus. *Enchiridion locorum communium theologicorum*. Britain or Continent: 1586–c.1604.
STC 10747 *et seq.* and non-STC. The title page lists Marlorat's name first, noting that Feguernekinus based this work on Marlorat's *Thesaurus sacrae sripturae* (as well as on work by Christoph Obenheim). The 1604 date is supplied; a few sources give 1610. *Language(s)*: Latin. Appraised at 18d in 1613.

159.260   August: Enchirid:
Augustine, *Saint*. *Enchiridion*. Britain or Continent: date not determined.
STC 921.5 and non-STC. The sole English edition is a remote possibility in this library, but it must be considered. *Language(s)*: Latin (probable) English (perhaps). Appraised at 2s in 1613.

159.261   de tripl: coena disput:
Martinus Becanus. *Disputatio theologica de triplici coena: Calvinistica, Lutherana, Catholica*. Mainz: ex officina Joannis Albini, 1608.
Language(s): Latin. Appraised at 12d in 1613.

159.262   delrio disquisitions mag.
Martin Antonio Delrio. *Disquisitionum magicarum libri sex*. Continent: 1599–1612.

Language(s): Latin. Appraised at 4s in 1613.

159.263   Elenchus haeret

Gabriel Du Preau (Prateolus). *Elenchus haereticorum omnium*. Cologne: apud Arnoldum Quentelium, 1605.

Earlier editions (from 1569) have a different title: *De vitis, sectis, et dogmatibus omnium haereticorum*. *Language(s)*: Latin. Appraised at 4d in 1613.

159.264   Chrisologus

Peter Chrysologus. [*Sermones*]. Continent: date not determined. *Language(s)*: Latin. Appraised at 17d in 1613.

159.265   Macha: discourses

Niccolò Macchiavelli. [*Discorsi*]. Britain or Continent: date not determined.

STC 17159 *et seq.* and non-STC. Despite "discourses" of the entry, the first English translation was not published until 1636. Probably one of the French editions published under the title *Les discours*, but the manuscript entry could be a general descriptive phrase in English, which would allow for the Italian or Latin versions as well. *Language(s)*: French (probable) Italian (perhaps) Latin (perhaps). Appraised at 6d in 1613.

159.266   Sleid: de 4 imper

Joannes Philippson, *Sleidanus*. *De quatuor summis imperiis*. Britain or Continent: 1556–1613.

STC 19847 and non-STC. Printed in London in 1584. *Language(s)*: Latin. Appraised at 8d in 1613.

159.267   Lucia: dialogi

Lucian, *of Samosata*. Probably [*Dialogues — Selected*]. Britain or Continent: date not determined.

STC 16891 *et seq.* and non-STC. A low appraisal for the collected works. See 159.306 and 159.477 for other copies. *Language(s)*: Latin (probable) Greek (perhaps). Appraised at 4d in 1613.

159.268   Chitraeus de affecti: moven:

Nathan Chytraeus. *Ethe kai pathe, seu de affectibus movendis, Aristotelis ex II. rhetoricorum doctrina explicat*. Herborn: excud. Christophorus Corvinus, 1586.

The first part of the title is transliterated from Greek characters. *Language(s)*: Latin. Appraised at 4d in 1613.

159.269   Praeteol: narra: consil

Gabriel Du Preau (Prateolus). *Narratio historica conciliorum omnium ecclesiae christianae*. Leyden: ex typ. Henrici ab Haestens, 1610.

Language(s): Latin. Appraised at 6d in 1613.

159.270   Gemmes: de reg: juris
Unidentified. Continent (probable): date not determined.

Probably not an STC book. No authors of books bearing the key titular phrase "De regulis juris," among whom the most widely published were Dinus, *Mugello* and Felippo Decio, can be identified with "Gemmes." *Language(s)*: Latin. Appraised at 2d in 1613.

159.271   Althameri concilat: scrip:
Andreas Althamer. *Conciliatio locorum scripturae*. Continent: date not determined.

Language(s): Latin. Appraised at 12d in 1613.

159.272   corpus leg:
[*Brachylogus juris civilis, sive Corpus legum*]. Continent: date not determined. *Language(s)*: Latin. Appraised at 2d in 1613.

159.273   Reg: france lib: duo
Charles de Grassaille. *Regalium Franciae libri duo*. Continent: 1538–1545. *Language(s)*: Latin. Appraised at 4d in 1613.

159.274   Earle of Surreis sonnets
Henry Howard, *Earl of Surrey. Songes and sonettes, written by Henry Haward late earle of Surrey, and other.* London: (different houses), 1557–1587.

STC 13860 *et seq*. Usually known as "Tottell's Miscellany," from Richard Tottell, the publisher of editions up to 1574. Contains poems by Surrey, as well as by Sir Thomas Wyatt and Nicholas Grimald, along with selections from various others. *Language(s)*: English. Appraised at 4d in 1613.

159.275   Osorius contra Had
Jeronimo Osorio da Fonseca, *Bishop. In Gualterum Haddonum magistrum libellorum supplicum libri tres*. Britain or Continent: 1567–1589.

STC 18889 and non-STC. *Language(s)*: Latin. Appraised at 6d in 1613.

159.276   Chittraeus de Stud: theol
David Chytraeus. *De studio theologiae recte inchoando*. Continent: 1560–1580.

Chytraeus's *Oratio, De studio theologiae, exercitiis verae pietatis et virtutis* (1582), given its limited printing and comparative minor status, is but a slim possibility. *Language(s)*: Latin. Appraised at 3d in 1613.

159.277   Acta Apostol:

Unidentified. Probably [*Acts: commentary*]. Continent (probable): date not determined.

Probably not an STC book. More likely a commentary than a solo edition of Acts; the possibilities with or without text are numerous. *Language(s)*: Latin. Appraised at 3d in 1613.

159.278   Omphalius

Jacobus Omphalius. Unidentified. Continent: date not determined.

De elocutionis imitatione ac apparatu was Omphalius's most frequently published work. *Language(s)*: Latin. Appraised at 4d in 1613.

159.279   Stephani Prodopeia

Henri Estienne. *Ad Senecae lectionem proodopoeia*. Geneva (probable): H. Stephanus, 1586.

Geneva is supplied by most sources; some give Paris. *Language(s)*: Latin. Appraised at 8d in 1613.

159.280   Becani disputat:

Martinus Becanus. Unidentified. Continent: date not determined.

Beginning in the late 1590s, Becanus published several works of theological controversy that contain some variation of "disputatio" in their titles. See 159.161 for either another copy or a different book with the same short title. *Language(s)*: Latin. Appraised at 8d in 1613.

159.281   plutar: de ira

Plutarch. *De non irascendo*. Continent: date not determined.

Probably one of the editions by Desiderius Erasmus (published 1520 and 1525) or Willibald Pirckheimer (published 1523). Perhaps one of the many collections of selected *Moralia*. *Language(s)*: Latin (probable) Greek (perhaps). Appraised at 3d in 1613.

159.282   Eliots governour

Sir Thomas Elyot. *The boke named the governour*. London: (different houses), 1531–1580.

STC 7635 *et seq*. *Language(s)*: English. Appraised at 8d in 1613.

159.283   French schoolemaister

Claude Desainliens (Claude Holyband). *Frenche schoolemaister, wherin is shewed, the pronouncing of the Frenche tongue*. London: (different houses), 1573–1612.

STC 6748 *et seq*. *Language(s)*: English French. Appraised at 6d in 1613.

159.284 vindiciae cont tiran:
Hubert Languet (Stephanus Junius Brutus, *pseudonym*). *Vindiciae contra tyrannos*. Continent: 1579–1608.
STC 15211 *et seq.* and non-STC. This work has also been attributed to Philippe de Mornay and to Théodore de Bèze. The "Edimburgi" imprint in STC 15211 is false; the STC supplies Basle as the place of printing. *Language(s)*: Latin. Appraised at 4d in 1613.

159.285 discipl: eccle: anglic:
Liber quorundam canonum disciplinae ecclesiae Anglicanae. (*Church of England—Articles*). London: [J. Day], 1571–c.1576.
STC 10037.5 *et seq*. A separately published second part of the Church of England's 39 Articles of 1562. *Language(s)*: Latin. Appraised at 4d in 1613.

159.286 Manutius de legib
Paolo Manuzio. *Antiquitatum Romanarum liber de legibus*. Continent: date not determined.
Language(s): Latin. Appraised at 8d in 1613.

159.287 Epictet
Epictetus. [*Enchiridion*]. Continent: date not determined.
Probably not an STC book, but see STC 10423. In this library, an English translation is unlikely but it must be considered. *Language(s)*: Latin (probable) English (perhaps) Greek (perhaps). Appraised at 2d in 1613.

159.288 Acan: partiti
Georgius Acanthius. [*Cicero (spurious)—Rhetorica ad Herennium: commentary*]. Continent: 1549–1554.
Language(s): Latin. Appraised at 2d in 1613.

159.289 Serar: de Herod
Nicolaus Serarius. *Rabbini et Herodes, seu De tota rabbinorum gente*. Mainz: e typographeo Balthasaris Lippii, 1607.
Language(s): Latin. Appraised at 8d in 1613.

159.290 Osiand: cont: Calvinist:
Lucas Osiander, *the Younger*. *Enchiridion controversiarum, quas Augustanae confessionis theologi habent cum Calvinianis*. Continent: 1603–1609.
Language(s): Latin. Appraised at 6d in 1613.

159.291 Machievil: prin:
Niccolò Macchiavelli. *De principe*. Continent (probable): date not determined.

STC 17167 and non-STC. One Italian edition was published in London, under a false imprint (STC 17167), with a title that reads *Il prencipe . . .*, as did many Continental Italian editions. The manuscript entry spelling favors either a Latin version (translation by Telius), as given here, or a Continental Italian version with the title spelled *Il principe*. *Language(s)*: Latin (probable) Italian (perhaps). Appraised at 6d in 1613.

159.292   Schind: Heb. gram

Valentin Schindler. [*Institutiones hebraicae*]. Wittenberg: (different houses), 1575–1612.

Whether the earlier version, *Libri V* (to 1596), or the later, *Libri VI* (1603 and 1612), cannot be determined. The less widely published abridgement, *Compendium grammatices Hebraeae* (1603 and 1613), is not as likely but remains a possibility given the "*gram*" in the manuscript entry, which, for purposes of identification, is taken to be descriptive. See BCI 2:692 for a 1589 abbreviated citation of the *Institutionum hebraicarum libri V* entered almost exactly as it is here. *Language(s)*: Hebrew Latin. Appraised at 8d in 1613.

159.293   Campens: gram: heb:

Joannes Campensis. [*Grammatica hebraica*]. Continent: date not determined.

Based on the Hebrew grammar of Elias, *Levita*. *Language(s)*: Hebrew Latin. Appraised at 4d in 1613.

159.294   Buteo de quadrat: circul:

Joannes Buteo, *pseudonym* (Jean Borrel). *De quadratura circuli libri duo*. Lyon: apud Gulielmum Rouillium, 1559.

Language(s): Latin. Appraised at 10d in 1613.

159.295   Epistolae claror: vir:

Probably [*Clarorum virorum epistolae*]. Edited by Johann Reuchlin. Continent: date not determined.

Other less widely published works with similar titles may be intended; these include a collection edited by Joannes Michael Brutus (Adams E277) and an Aldine collection of classical writers (Adams E256, E278–79). *Language(s)*: Greek Hebrew Latin. Appraised at 6d in 1613.

159.296   Circes eng.

Giovanni Battista Gelli. *Circes of John Baptista Gello, Florentyne*. Translated by Henry Iden. London: J. Cawoode, 1557–c.1558.

STC 11708 *et seq*. *Language(s)*: English. Appraised at 4d in 1613.

159.297 Fuccius in Hipp: Aphorismi:

Leonard Fuchs. [*Hippocrates—Aphorismi: commentary and text*]. Translated by Leonard Fuchs, with his explanations of Galen's commentary on the text. Continent: 1558–1559.

Earlier editions (1544–1549) seem not to have included the commentary. *Language(s)*: Greek Latin. Appraised at 12d in 1613.

159.298 Scultet Ethic:

Abraham Scultetus. *Ethicorum libri duo*. Continent: 1593–1603.
Language(s): Latin. Appraised at 8d in 1613.

159.299 Junius in Corinth:

S. Pauli Apostoli ad Corinthios Epistolae duae. (*Epistles—Corinthians*). Translated and edited by François Du Jon, *the Elder*. Place not given: apud Joannem Mareschallum, 1578.

Place of publication variously supplied as Heidelberg, Lyon, and Paris. *Language(s)*: Latin. Appraised at 4d in 1613.

159.300 Brant titul: Juris

Sebastian Brant. [*Expositiones omnium titulorum juris tam civilis quam canonici*]. Continent: date not determined.
Language(s): Latin. Appraised at 6d in 1613.

159.301 Brutus fulmen

François Hotman. *P. Sixti fulmen brutum in Henricum sereniss. Regem Navarrae et illustrissimum Henricum Borbonium, Principem Condaeum*. Continent: 1585–1604.
Language(s): Latin. Appraised at 4d in 1613.

159.302 Ascams scholemaister

Roger Ascham. *The scholemaster or plaine and perfite way of teachyng children, the Latin tong*. Edited by Margaret Ascham. London: (different houses), 1570–1589.

STC 832 *et seq. Language(s)*: English Latin. Appraised at 6d in 1613.

159.303 Ital: diction

Unidentified [dictionary]. Continent: date not determined.
Language(s): Italian. Appraised at 8d in 1613.

159.304 the courtier in Span:

Baldassare Castiglione, *Count*. [*El cortesano*]. Translated by Juan Boscán. Continent: 1534–1581.

Language(s): Spanish. Appraised at 8d in 1613.

159.305 Tenterbelly

Joseph Hall, *Bishop*. *The discovery of a new world, or a description of the South Indies, by an English Mercury*. Translated by John Healey. London: [G. Eld] for E. Blount and W. Barret, 1609?

STC 12686. The caption title of the first book reads "The discovery of the land of Tenter-belly. . ." and the running-title reads "The description of Tenter-belly." The [1613–14] issue (STC 12686.3) almost certainly did not appear in time to be inventoried here. Published anonymously. *Language(s)*: English. Appraised at 8d in 1613.

159.306 Lucian: dial:

Lucian, *of Samosata*. Probably [*Dialogues — Selected*]. Britain or Continent: date not determined.

STC 16891 *et seq.* and non-STC. A low appraisal for the collected works. See 159.267 and 159.477 for other copies. *Language(s)*: Latin (probable) Greek (perhaps). Appraised at 4d in 1613.

159.307 Cajet: in epist:

Thomas de Vio Cajetan, *Cardinal*. [*Epistles — Paul: commentary and text*]. (*Bible — N.T.*). Continent: 1531–1588.

Language(s): Latin. Appraised at 18d in 1613.

159.308 Jun: Heb: gram

François Du Jon, *the Elder*. *Grammatica hebraeae linguae*. Continent: 1580–1596.

Language(s): Hebrew Latin. Appraised at 8d in 1613.

159.309 Scaliger de subtili

Julius Caesar Scaliger. *Exotericarum exercitationum liber XV*. Continent: 1557–1612.

"De subtilitate" is in the work's long title; it is the title of the work by Girolamo Cardano that Scaliger is countering. *Language(s)*: Latin. Appraised at 2s 6d in 1613.

159.310 Plaut: Paraei

Titus Maccius Plautus. *Comoediae*. Edited by Johann Philipp Pareus. Frankfurt am Main: impensis Jonae Rhodii, 1610.

In several sources a 1523 edition appears, a misprint for an edition published in 1623. *Language(s)*: Latin. Appraised at 3s 6d in 1613.

159.311 Ausonius

Decimus Magnus Ausonius. [*Works*]. Continent: date not determined. *Language(s)*: Latin. Appraised at 8d in 1613.

159.312 Lullii opera
Ramón Lull. [*Works*]. Strassburg: sumptibus L. Zetzneri, 1598?–1609.
Perhaps one of several other collections of Lull's selected works, though none of them has "opera" in the title. *Language(s)*: Latin. Appraised at 3s 6d in 1613.

159.313 Philotas
Probably Samuel Daniel. *The tragedie of Philotas*. London: M. Bradwood for E. Blount, 1607.
STC 6263. Daniel's *A defence of ryme* is appended. *Philotas* first appeared in several collections of Daniel's works: see STC 6239, 6240, 6242, and 6243. Much less likely Felix Fidler, *Philotas ecloga* (Augsburg? 1550) and the anonymous *Philotus* (1603), STC 19888, which is in Scots. *Language(s)*: English. Appraised at 10d in 1613.

159.314 Eedes sermons
Richard Eedes. *Six learned and godly sermons*. London: A. Islip for E. Bishop, 1604.
STC 7526. *Language(s)*: English. Appraised at 6d in 1613.

159.315 Mans: in eng.
Probably Dominicus Mancinus. [*De quatuor virtutibus*]. London: (different houses), 1520?–1568.
STC 17241 *et seq*. Of the four editions and three translations available — with different English titles — STC 17421, in quarto, and STC 17244, in octavo, are more likely than the intervening folio editions at the valuation given here. STC 17244, Turberville's translation, is in verse. See a manuscript entry in BCI 2:520 for Mancinus spelled Man*s*inus. *Language(s)*: English. Appraised at 4d in 1613.

159.316 Trelcat
Unidentified. Place unknown: stationer unknown, date not determined.
STC/non-STC status unknown. Either Lucas Trelcatius, *the Younger* or Lucas Trelcatius, *the Elder*, both of whose works were overwhelmingly on theological subjects. The son's work was, however, published in England in the original Latin as well as in an English translation (STC 24261 *et seq*.). *Language(s)*: English (probable) Latin (probable). Appraised at 6d in 1613.

159.317 Mascharenas de gratia
Fernando Martins Mascarenhas. *Tractatus de auxiliis divinae gratiae ad actus supernaturales*. Lyon: H. Cardon, 1605.
A folio edition was published in Lisbon in 1604. But the cataloguers usually note if a book is a folio, and the books for some distance on either side of this entry appear generally to be in octavo. *Language(s)*: Latin. Appraised at 10d in 1613.

159.318   Antimariana gal:
Michel Roussel. *L'Antimariana, ou réfutation des propositions de Mariana.* Continent: 1610.

Two editions in the same year; published in Paris and Rouen. The "gal" in the manuscript entry indicates French. *Language(s)*: French. Appraised at 12d in 1613.

159.319   the mir: france gal
Unidentified. Continent: date not determined.

Probably either *Le miroir Francois, representant la face de ce siècle corrumpu* (1598), or Nicolas Barnaud, *Le miroir des Francois, compris en trois livres* (1581 and 1582). *Language(s)*: French. Appraised at 10d in 1613.

159.320   Index expurgat
[*Index librorum prohibitorum*]. Continent: date not determined. *Language(s)*: Latin. Appraised at 12d in 1613.

159.321   Armin: theses
Jacobus Arminius. Unidentified. Continent: date not determined.

Probably either *Theses theologicae de natura dei* (Leyden, 1603) or *Theses theologicae de primo primi hominis peccato* (Leyden, 1604). Both were published by Jan Jacobszoon Paets. *Language(s)*: Latin. Appraised at 16d in 1613.

159.322   Ferus in math:
Joannes Ferus (Johann Wild, *Prediger zu Mainz*). [*Matthew: commentary*]. Continent: date not determined.

Language(s): Latin. Appraised at 2s 4d in 1613.

159.323   Armin: in cap 7 ea [epistolae] Rom
Jacobus Arminius. *De vero et genuino sensu cap. VII Epistolae ad Romanos dissertatio.* Leyden: ex officina Godefridi Basson, 1612.

Language(s): Latin. Appraised at 8d in 1613.

159.324   Barcleius de potestat: papae
William Barclay, *Professor of Civil Law. De potestate papae.* Probably edited by John Barclay. Britain or Continent: 1609–1612.

STC 1408 *et seq.* and non-STC. *Language(s)*: Latin. Appraised at 10d in 1613.

159.325   Armin: examen
Jacobus Arminius. *Examen modestum libelli.* Leyden: ex officina Godefridi Basson, 1612.

An attack on a work by William Perkins on predestination. *Language(s)*: Latin. Appraised at 12d in 1613.

159.326 Widrington Apolog:

Roger Widdrington, *pseudonym* (Thomas Preston). Probably *Apologia cardinalis Bellarmini pro jure principum*. Britain or Continent: 1611.

STC 25596 *et seq*. Two editions in the same year (London: Richard Field and Paris: Denis Binet?), though both editions bear the same fictitious imprint (Cosmopoli: apud Theophilum Pratum). Possibly STC 25997, *Rogeri Widdringtoni catholici Angli responsio apologetica ad libellum* (London, 1612; Paris, 1613). *Language(s)*: Latin. Appraised at 12d in 1613.

159.327 Stapleton: promptuar: morale vol. 2

Thomas Stapleton. [*Gospels (liturgical): commentary*]. Continent: 1591–1613.

Often published as a two-volume set; the manuscript entry might mean that Brown owned only the second volume. Shaaber S336–S348. *Language(s)*: Latin. Appraised at 4s in 1613.

159.328 Lawes of Eng:

Probably [*Institutions*]. (*England—Statutes—General Collections*). Britain: (different houses), 1538?–1611.

STC 9290 *et seq*. The only general collection of statutes to include "laws" prominently in the title. Title varies; sample titles include *Institutions in the lawes of England*, *The principal lawes and statutes of England*, *Institutions, or principall lawes and statutes of Englande*. Of the nearly two dozen editions published during the date range, all but one were printed in London. See 159.530 for the other major general collection of statutes, *Magna Carta cum statutis*. *Language(s)*: English. Appraised at 6d in 1613.

159.329 Fulleri miscelanea

Nicholas Fuller, *Prebendary*. *Miscellaneorum theologicorum libri III*. Heidelberg: sumptibus Lazari Zetzneri, 1612.

Published eventually in Oxford (STC 11461), but three years after Brown's death. Fuller's *Miscellaneorum sacrorum* . . . was not published until 1622. *Language(s)*: Latin. Appraised at 10d in 1613.

159.330 Stapleton promptuar Cathol

Thomas Stapleton. [*Promptuarium catholicum*]. Continent: 1589–1613.

Commentary on the liturgical gospels for preaching. Shaaber S317–S334. *Language(s)*: Latin. Appraised at 2s in 1613.

159.331 Reibadeneira princepis christian

Pedro de Ribadeneira. *Princeps christianus adversus Nicolaum Machiavellum.* Translated by Joannes Oranus. Continent: 1603–1604. *Language(s)*: Latin. Appraised at 18d in 1613.

159.332 Justus Baron: adversus Heret:

Justus Baronius. *Praescriptionum adversus haereticos perpetuarum ex SS. Orthodoxis potissimum patribus tractatus VI.* Mainz: Joannes Albinus, 1602–1605. *Language(s)*: Latin. Appraised at 18d in 1613.

159.333 Termes of the law

John Rastell, *Barrister and Printer. The exposicions of the termes of the lawes of England, with divers rules.* London: (different houses), 1563–1609.

STC 20703.5 *et seq.* The title changes in 1579 to *An exposition of certaine difficult and obscure words, and termes of the lawes of this realme. Language(s)*: English. Appraised at 10d in 1613.

159.334 Kecker: Rhetor:

Bartholomaeus Keckermann. Unidentified. Continent: date not determined.

Either his *Rhetoricae ecclesiasticae, sive artis formandi et habendi conciones sacras libri duo* or his *Systema rhetoricae*, both published in several editions prior to the date of this inventory. *Language(s)*: Latin. Appraised at 6d in 1613.

159.335 Scala coeli

Unidentified. Place unknown: stationer unknown, date not determined.

STC/non-STC status unknown. Possibilities include: Lancelot Andrewes, *Scala coeli. Nineteene sermons concerning prayer* (editions 1611–1612), Gabriele Inchino, *Scala coeli: seu concionis* (1609), and Joannes Gobius, *Scala Coeli* (editions 1476 to 1485). *Language(s)*: English (probable) Latin (probable). Appraised at 12d in 1613.

159.336 Bucanani Poemata

George Buchanan. [*Selected works*]. Continent: date not determined.

The word "poemata" appears deep in the long titles of Buchanan's early collections that lead with the title *Franciscanus et fratres*. Since, however, the word does not appear prominently on the title pages, and since the compiler could have entered "poemata" descriptively, it is difficult to determine which edition of his verse is intended here, including subsequent editions that do not carry "poemata" on the title pages. Collections published in England and Scotland prominently titled *Poemata* did not appear until after the date of this inventory. See Shaaber B697 *et seq. Language(s)*: Latin Greek (perhaps). Appraised at 12d in 1613.

159.337 Becani opuscula vol. 2
Martinus Becanus. *Opuscula theologica* (part). Mainz: ex officina Joannis Albini, 1610.

This is assumed to be the second volume, not two volumes. Three parts, in various arrangements, had been published by the date of this inventory. *Language(s)*: Latin. Appraised at 4s in 1613.

159.338 Ovid: metamor: Bersman
Publius Ovidius Naso. *Metamorphoses*. Edited by Gregorius Bersmanus. Continent: date not determined.

Bersmanus's first edition appeared in 1582. *Language(s)*: Latin. Appraised at 3s in 1613.

159.339 Macha: homil: graec: lat
Macarius, *Aegyptius. Homiliae spirituales quinquaginta*. Frankfurt am Main: apud Joan. Wecheli viduam, impensis Nicolai Bassaei, 1594.

The earlier editions, from 1559, are either in Greek or in Latin alone; the 1594 edition prints parallel columns of Greek and Latin. *Language(s)*: Greek Latin. Appraised at 12d in 1613.

159.340 Becanus de deo
Martinus Becanus. Perhaps *Tractatus de Deo et attributis divinis*. Mainz: ex officina Joannis Albini, 1611.

Either the above, or his *De fide deo servanda* (Mainz, 1611), published in octavo by the same printer. *Language(s)*: Latin. Appraised at 12d in 1613.

159.341 Matthaeus de Rispolis
Joannes Matthaeus de Rispolis. *Status controversiae praedefinitionum et praedeterminationum cum libero arbitrio*. Paris: apud Reginaldum Chaudiere, 1609.

Language(s): Latin. Appraised at 8d in 1613.

159.342 Ferus in exod:
Joannes Ferus (Johann Wild, *Prediger zu Mainz*). [*Exodus, Numbers, Deuteronomy, Joshua, Judges: commentary*]. Cologne: apud haeredes Arnoldi Birckmanni, 1571–1574.

The 1571 edition was printed by the heirs of Arnold Birckman in collaboration with Franciscus Behem; the 1574 by Birckman alone. *Language(s)*: Latin. Appraised at 2s in 1613.

159.343 Respons: adversus Anticoton
Responsio apologetica adversus Anticotini, et sociorum criminationes. Translated by Joannes Perpezatius. Lyon: sumptibus Horatii Cardon, 1611.

A translation of *Response apologetique a l'Anticoton* (editions 1610 and 1611), attributed to François Bonald or Pierre Cotton (sometimes Coton). *Language(s)*: Latin. Appraised at 16d in 1613.

159.344 Concilium tridentinus

Probably *Acta Concilii Tridentini*. (*Councils — Trent*). Continent: date not determined.

First published in 1546. Perhaps the *Canones et decreta Concilii Tridentini*; see Adams C2783–89. *Language(s)*: Latin. Appraised at 12d in 1613.

159.345 Fabul: Joan: papae

Florimond de Raemond. *Fabula Joannae quae pontificis Romani sedem occupasse falso credita est*. Translated by Jean-Charles de Raemond. Bordeaux: apud Simonem Millangium, 1601–1605.

Language(s): Latin. Appraised at 8d in 1613.

159.346 Kecker: theolog

Bartholomaeus Keckermann. *Systema S.S. theologiae, tribus libris adornatum*. Continent: 1602–1611.

Language(s): Latin. Appraised at 12d in 1613.

159.347 Morton de notis eccles:

Thomas Morton, *Bishop*. *De notis ecclesiae*. Britain or Continent: 1605–1606.

STC 18173.5 *et seq*. Not published separately; issued with the (varyingly titled) editions of his *Apologiae catholicae* (see 159.93 and 159.433). The stationer John Norton was involved with all editions, one of which was printed abroad for him. *Language(s)*: Latin. Appraised at 16d in 1613.

159.348 Marquarles

Unidentified. Continent (probable): date not determined.

Almost certainly not an STC book. No author's name matches the manuscript entry exactly, but possibilities include Joannes Marquardus, Marquardus de Susanis, Marquardus Freherus, Giovanni Marquale, and Jaime de Marquilles, none of which was published in England by the date of this inventory. *Language(s)*: Unknown. Appraised at 8d in 1613.

159.349 Enchiridion Remed

Walther Hermann Ryff. *Enchiridion remediorum*. Frankfurt am Main: excudebat Joannes Wolffius, impensis Gulielmi Hoffmani, 1610.

Language(s): Latin. Appraised at 6d in 1613.

159.350 Barth: amabilia

Caspar von Barth. *Amabilium libri IV.* Hanau: typis Willerianis, 1612. *Language(s)*: Latin. Appraised at 3d in 1613.

159.351 Burhilli con: Becanus

Robert Burhill. Probably *Contra Martini Becani, jesuitae Moguntini, Controversiam Anglicanam.* London: Edwardus Griffin, impensis Nathanielis Butter, 1613.

STC 4116. Possibly his *Pro Tortura Torti, contra Martinum Becanum jesuitam, responsio* (1611). *Language(s)*: Latin. Appraised at 10d in 1613.

159.352 Cudseni de caus: Calvi:

Petrus Cudsemius. [*De desperata Calvini causa tractatus brevis*]. Continent: 1609–1613.

Language(s): Latin. Appraised at 12d in 1613.

159.353 delrio Vindicid

Martin Antonio Delrio. *Vindiciae areopagiticae contra Josephum Scaligerum.* Antwerp: ex officina Plantiniana, apud Joannem Moretum, 1607.

Language(s): Latin. Appraised at 12d in 1613.

159.354 Calsand: consultat:

Georgius Cassander. *Consultatio de articulis religionis inter catholicos et protestantes controversis.* Continent: 1577–1612.

The 1612 edition also includes Cassander's *De officio pii ac publicae tranquillitatis vere amantis viri. Language(s)*: Latin. Appraised at 12d in 1613.

159.355 Ciprian tom: 2us

Cyprian, *Saint.* [*Works*]. Continent: date not determined.

Probably the second volume only of a set. *Language(s)*: Latin. Appraised at 18d in 1613.

159.356 Epitome Variani

Perhaps Joachim Vadianus. [*Epitome trium terrae partium*]. Continent: 1533–1569.

Some later editions were published as *Epitome topographica totius orbis. Language(s)*: Latin. Appraised at 8d in 1613.

159.357 Sphinx philosophica

Johann Heidfeld. [*Sphinx philosophica*]. Herborn: (different houses), 1600–1612.

Language(s): Latin. Appraised at 18d in 1613.

159.358 Aristotle: Rhetori:

Aristotle. *Rhetorica*. Continent: date not determined.
Language(s): Latin (probable) Greek (perhaps). Appraised at 10d in 1613.

159.359 Thesaurus poemat

Joannes Buchler. [*Thesaurus poeticus*]. Continent: date not determined.
Widely printed, often with Jacob Pontanus's *Institutio poetica*. *Language(s)*: Latin. Appraised at 6d in 1613.

159.360 Baronius de monar: Ciciliae

Cesare Baronius, *Cardinal*. *Tractatus de monarchia Siciliae*. Paris: apud Hadrianum Beys, 1609.
Published originally in folio as part of *Annales ecclesiastici* (see 159.2 and 159.38). *Language(s)*: Latin. Appraised at 8d in 1613.

159.361 Balduini Conciones

Balduinus Junius. [*Conciones super evangelia*]. Antwerp: (different houses), 1610–1613.
The heirs of Martin Nutius were involved in the printing of all editions. *Language(s)*: Latin. Appraised at 8d in 1613.

159.362 Piloti gram. gal

Joannes Pilotus. *Gallicae linguae institutio*. Continent: 1550–1581.
Language(s): French Latin. Appraised at 3d in 1613.

159.363 Contarenus de rep: Venet

Gasparo Contarini, *Cardinal*. *De magistratibus et republica Venetorum*. Continent: 1543–1599.
Language(s): Latin. Appraised at 6d in 1613.

159.364 Vasseii Anotomeia

Ludoicus Vassaeus. *In anatomen corporis humani tabulae quatuor*. Continent: date not determined.
Language(s): Latin. Appraised at 2d in 1613.

159.365 Joannes de Indag:

Joannes ab Indagine. [*Chiromantia*]. Continent (probable): date not determined.
Probably not an STC book, but see STC 14705 *et seq*. Dutch, French, and German are all possibilities, but not likely. Nor are the English editions, which the compiler is in the habit of identifying. *Language(s)*: Latin (probable). Appraised at 3d in 1613.

159.366   Danaei Isagoges
Lambert Daneau. [*Christianae isagoges*]. Geneva: (different houses), 1583–1591.
All editions were printed by Eustathius Vignon save for the last, which his heirs produced. *Language(s)*: Latin. Appraised at 4s in 1613.

159.367   Scalig: de causis ling: lat:
Julius Caesar Scaliger. *De causis linguae latinae libri tredecim*. Continent: 1540–1609.
Language(s): Latin. Appraised at 16d in 1613.

159.368   Ferroneus de reb: gall:
Arnoldus Ferronus. *De rebus gestis Gallorum*. Paris: (different houses), 1549–1555.
Seems always to have been published with Paulus Aemilius's *De rebus gestis Francorum*, but this may have separated, or it may be a solo edition. *Language(s)*: Latin. Appraised at 12d in 1613.

159.369   Coment: rer: gallici
Unidentified. Place unknown: stationer unknown, date not determined.
STC/non-STC status unknown. The manuscript entry's "gallici" is taken to indicate that the subject concerns France, not that the item is in French. Caesar's *Commentarii* should be given thought as a possibility. If, however, that work is intended here, the manuscript entry represents an extremely unusual form, particularly since among the nearly one hundred citations of the work in BCI (2:167–168) and PLRE, not one contains any form of the word "rerum." *Language(s)*: Latin. Appraised at 6d in 1613.

159.370   Tittleman: phisic:
Franz Titlemann. [*Aristotle—Selected works—Philosophia naturalis: commentary*]. Continent: date not determined.
Language(s): Latin Greek (perhaps). Appraised at 6d in 1613.

159.371   Cornel: tacit
Publius Cornelius Tacitus. Unidentified. Continent: date not determined.
If not the *opera*, probably the *Annales* or the *Historiae*, both of which are substantial, which the valuation suggests this item is. *Language(s)*: Latin. Appraised at 2s 6d in 1613.

159.372   Sigon: de rep: hebr:
Carlo Sigonio. *De republica Hebraeorum libri VII*. Continent: 1582–1608.
Language(s): Latin. Appraised at 10d in 1613.

159.373 Lessii consulti

Leonardus Lessius. *Quae fides et religio sit capessenda, consultatio.* Continent: 1609–1612.
Language(s): Latin. Appraised at 8d in 1613.

159.374 Trugilli conciones

Thomas de Truxillo. [*Sermones*]. Continent: date not determined.
One of his many volumes of sermons, and perhaps, at the valuation of 5s, a collection of several volumes. Also, conceivably, though less likely, a copy of his *Thesauri concionatorum*. *Language(s)*: Latin. Appraised at 5s in 1613.

159.375 Plutar: mor: 3 vol

Plutarch. [*Moralia*]. Continent: date not determined.
Thomas Blundville's English translation (though an English version is not indicated here) was published in three parts, as were some Continental editions. *Language(s)*: Latin Greek (perhaps). Appraised at 5s in 1613.

159.376 Lipsius epist:

Justus Lipsius. Unidentified. Continent (probable): date not determined.
Probably not an STC book, but see STC 15697 *et seq*. More than one of Lipsius's letter collections could be so entered, even the English editions, though they are not likely here. *Language(s)*: Latin. Appraised at 2s 6d in 1613.

159.377 Pet: Lumbard

Peter Lombard. *Sententiarum libri IIII.* Continent: date not determined.
Language(s): Latin. Appraised at 2s 6d in 1613.

159.378 Keckerman: logic

Bartholomaeus Keckermann. Unidentified. Place unknown: stationer unknown, date not determined.
STC/non-STC status unknown. Several possibilities, including *Gymnasium logicum* (published in London and on the Continent), *Resolutio systematis logici*, *Praecognita logica*, and *Systema logicae*. *Language(s)*: Latin. Appraised at 2s in 1613.

159.379 August. de heresib

Augustine, *Saint. De haeresibus.* Edited with commentary by Lambert Daneau. Geneva: (different houses), 1576–1595.
All three editions were published by Eustathius Vignon or his heirs. *Language(s)*: Latin. Appraised at 12d in 1613.

159.380 Decius londinus

Unidentified. Place unknown: stationer unknown, date not determined.

STC/non-STC status unknown. Perhaps an erroneously entered Judocus Ludovicus Decius. The word *londinus* allows an English publication to be a possibility, however remote. *Language(s)*: Latin (probable). Appraised at 12d in 1613.

159.381 Bacons essais

Francis Bacon, *Viscount St. Albans. Essayes*. London: (different houses), 1597–1613.

STC 1137 *et seq*. Another copy is listed at 159.502. *Language(s)*: English Latin (perhaps). Appraised at 8d in 1613.

159.382 Ferus in Johannes

Joannes Ferus (Johann Wild, *Prediger zu Mainz*). [*John: commentary*]. Continent: 1545–1577.

Language(s): Latin. Appraised at 18d in 1613.

159.383 Granatens. de ratio: concion:

Luis, *de Granada. Ecclesiasticae rhetoricae, sive de ratione concionandi libri VI.* Continent: 1576–1611.

Sometimes printed with other works as leading title. *Language(s)*: Latin. Appraised at 16d in 1613.

159.384 Doctor et student

Christopher Saint German. [*Doctor and student*]. Britain: (different houses), 1530?–1613.

STC 21561 *et seq*. *Language(s)*: English. Appraised at 6d in 1613.

159.385 Cani loci commu:

Francisco Melchor Cano, *Bishop. De locis theologicis*. Continent: 1563–1603.

The 1603 edition includes *De locis theologicis praelectiones* by Seraphino Razzi (Seraphinus Ractius). *Language(s)*: Latin. Appraised at 2s 6d in 1613.

159.386 Fulgentius

Probably Fulgentius, *Bishop of Ruspa*. [*Works*]. Continent: date not determined.

Perhaps one of the several works by the often published mythographer Fabius Planciades Fulgentius, though given the theological cast of Brown's collection, the saint seems more likely. *Language(s)*: Latin. Appraised at 2s in 1613.

159.387 Thesauri: Polit:

Probably Ventura Comino. *Thesaurus politicus*. Translated by Gaspar Ens. Cologne: G. Grevenbruch, 1609–1613.

Language(s): Latin. Appraised at 2s in 1613.

159.388 Lipsius polit

Justus Lipsius. *Politicorum sive civilis doctrinae libri sex*. Britain or Continent: date not determined.

STC 15700.7 *et seq.* and non-STC. The manuscript entry would permit this to be the English translation, *Sixe bookes of politickes or civil doctrine*, but the compiler's habit has been to note if a work is in a vernacular. Lipsius's *Monita et exempla politica* is also a remote possibility. *Language(s)*: Latin (probable) English (perhaps). Appraised at 10d in 1613.

159.389 description of the low countries

Ludovico Guicciardini. *The description of the Low countreys gathered into an epitome*. Translated and edited by Thomas Danett. London: P. Short for T. Chard, 1593.

STC 12463. *Language(s)*: English. Appraised at 6d in 1613.

159.390 Testament graec

[*Bible — N.T.*]. Britain or Continent: date not determined.

STC 2793 *et seq.* and non-STC. *Language(s)*: Greek. Appraised at 8d in 1613.

159.391 Euclid element

Euclid. *Elementa*. Continent: date not determined.

Language(s): Latin (probable) Greek (perhaps). Appraised at 8d in 1613.

159.392 Chitraei chronicon

David Chytraeus. [*Chronicon Saxoniae*]. Continent: 1588–1611. *Language(s)*: Latin. Appraised at 6d in 1613.

159.393 A recusantes satisfaction

Francis Savage. *A conference betwixt a mother a devout recusant, and her sonne a zealous protestant, seeking by humble and dutifull satisfaction to winne her unto the trueth*. Cambridge: J. Legat, pr. to the Univ. of Camb., 1600.

STC 21781. With the running-title "A satisfaction for a devout recusant." *Language(s)*: English. Appraised at 4d in 1613.

159.394 Practica linfranci

Lanfrancus de Oriano. [*Practica Lanfranci*]. Continent: date not determined.

Sometimes attributed to Lanfranc, *Archbishop of Canterbury*. *Language(s)*: Latin. Appraised at 6d in 1613.

159.395 Recogni libr: Bellarm:
Roberto Bellarmino, *Cardinal. Recognitio librorum omnium*. Ingolstadt: ex typographeo Adami Sartorii, 1608.
Language(s): Latin. Appraised at 6d in 1613.

159.396 Blackwels examination
George Blackwell. Probably *A large examination taken at Lambeth, of M. G. Blakwell*. London: R. Barker, 1607.

STC 3104. STC 3105, *Mr George Blackwel . . . his answeres upon sundry his examinations* (1607), also printed by Robert Barker, is a less likely possibility. The Latin translation of these two works, STC 3103, is even less likely. *Language(s)*: English. Appraised at 6d in 1613.

159.397 Wickliff against friers
John Wiclif. *Two short treatises, against the orders of the begging friars*. Edited by Thomas James. Oxford: J. Barnes, 1608.

STC 25589. According to the STC, issued with STC 14445, Thomas James, D.D., *An apologie for John Wickliffe*. But apparently not as a composite volume: extant copies often do not contain both, though the two are bound together in some collections. *Language(s)*: English. Appraised at 6d in 1613.

159.398 Verronis Phisica
Sebastian Verro. *Physicorum libri X*. Britain or Continent: 1581–1590.

STC 24688 *et seq.* and non-STC. The one edition published outside Britain is Basle, 1581. *Language(s)*: Latin. Appraised at 4d in 1613.

159.399 Portae mag: natural
Giovanni Battista della Porta. *Magiae naturalis*. Continent: date not determined.

Language(s): Latin. Appraised at 18d in 1613.

159.400 Deming: de grati:
Unidentified. Continent (probable): date not determined.

Probably not an STC book. Possibly a mishearing or miswriting of Nicolaus Hemmingius, *Tractatus de gratia universalis*. See BCI (2:415) for a similarly abbreviated manuscript entry of that title, but here the compiler has clearly written "Deming." Domingo de Soto is not referred to by his given name (see BCI, 2:712–713), but his *De natura et gratia* should at least be considered. *Language(s)*: Latin. Appraised at 4d in 1613.

159.401 Arminii orationes
Jacobus Arminius. *Orationes, itemque tractatus insigniores aliquot*. Leyden: (different houses), 1611–1613.

Members of the Dutch Basson printing family were involved in the two editions. *Language(s)*: Latin. Appraised at 10d in 1613.

159.402   Aristopha: grae lat:
Aristophanes. Probably [*Works*]. Continent: date not determined. *Language(s)*: Greek Latin. Appraised at 18d in 1613.

159.403   Aristot polit:
Aristotle. *Politica*. Continent: date not determined. *Language(s)*: Latin. Appraised at 18d in 1613.

159.404   Velleius Paterculus
Caius Velleius Paterculus. *Historia Romana duo volumina*. Continent: date not determined.
Language(s): Latin. Appraised at 12d in 1613.

159.405   Pacii organon
Aristotle. *Organon*. Edited by Julius Pacius. Continent: date not determined.
Whether an edition with or without commentary, or whether his commentary alone, cannot be determined. *Language(s)*: Greek Latin. Appraised at 20d in 1613.

159.406   Thucid: lat
Thucydides. *De bello peloponnesiaco*. Continent: date not determined. *Language(s)*: Latin. Appraised at 16d in 1613.

159.407:A   Juven et Pers:
Decimus Junius Juvenalis. [*Works*]. Britain or Continent: date not determined (composite publication).
STC 14889 and non-STC. Another copy is found at 159.499. *Language(s)*: Latin. Appraised [a composite volume] at 8d in 1613.

159.407:B   [See 159.407:A]
Aulus Persius Flaccus. [*Works*]. [Composite publication].
STC 14889 and non-STC. Another copy is found at 159.499. *Language(s)*: Latin. Appraised [a composite volume] at 8d in 1613.

159.408   Textor: officin:
Joannes Ravisius (Textor). [*Officina*]. Continent: date not determined. *Language(s)*: Latin. Appraised at 2s 4d in 1613.

159.409 Thernellii opera

Unidentified. Place unknown: stationer unknown, date not determined.

STC/non-STC status unknown. Perhaps a garbled Tremellius, but nothing of his would be described as "opera." Given that this is a section of standard classical works, perhaps "Therentii" for Terentius was intended. *Language(s)*: Latin. Appraised at 2s 6d in 1613.

159.410 Sallust

Caius Sallustius Crispus. Probably [*Works*]. Britain or Continent: date not determined.

STC 21622.8 and non-STC. *De bello Jugurthino* and *De conjuratione Catilinae* are possible as well. *Language(s)*: Latin. Appraised at 8d in 1613.

159.411 Livius opera

Titus Livius. [*Historiae Romanae decades*]. Britain or Continent: date not determined.

STC 16611.5 *et seq.* and non–STC. *Language(s)*: Latin. Appraised at 4s 6d in 1613.

159.412 Plutar: vit:

Plutarch. [*Vitae parallelae*]. Continent: date not determined.
Language(s): Latin Greek (perhaps). Appraised at 5s in 1613.

159.413 Traged sen:

Lucius Annaeus Seneca. *Tragoediae*. Britain or Continent: date not determined.

STC 22217 *et seq.* and non-STC. Struck through. *Language(s)*: Latin. Appraised at 12d in 1613.

159.414 Ital: testament

[*Bible—N.T.*]. Continent: date not determined.
Language(s): Italian. Appraised at 10d in 1613.

159.415 Gentilis de legat

Albericus Gentilis. *De legationibus, libri tres*. Britain or Continent: 1585–1607.

STC 11737 and non-STC. See Shaaber G174–175. *Language(s)*: Latin. Appraised at 12d in 1613.

159.416 Homer: Iliad

Homer. *Iliad*. Britain or Continent: date not determined.

STC 13629 and non-STC. An English edition is a possibility but, without an indication by the compiler, unlikely. *Language(s)*: Latin (probable) Greek (perhaps). Appraised at 16d in 1613.

159.417   Pindarus grae: lat
Pindar. [*Works*]. Continent: date not determined.
Language(s): Greek Latin. Appraised at 12d in 1613.

159.418   Euripid. grae: lat
Euripides. Probably [*Works*]. Continent: date not determined.
No appraisal amount recorded. *Language(s)*: Greek Latin.

159.419   Drusii observationes
Joannes Drusius. [*Observationes*]. Continent: 1584–1594.
The 1594 edition is expanded from twelve to sixteen books. *Language(s)*: Latin. Appraised at 12d in 1613.

159.420   Catul: tibul:
Caius Valerius Catullus, Albius Tibullus, and Sextus Propertius. [*Works*]. Continent: date not determined.
Language(s): Latin. Appraised at 8d in 1613.

159.421   Reusneri Simbol
Nicolaus Reusner. [*Symboli imperatorii*]. Continent: 1588–1607.
Perhaps his far less often published *Symbolorum heroicorum liber singularis*, which treats the iconography of the Holy Roman Emperors; the title above treats the Roman Emperors. *Language(s)*: Latin. Appraised at 2s in 1613.

159.422   In plaut: annotaton
Unidentified. [*Comoediae: commentary*]. Continent (probable): date not determined.
Almost certainly not an STC book. An unidentified commentary on Plautus. *Language(s)*: Latin. Appraised at 4d in 1613.

159.423   Euripides 2 vol
Euripides. [*Works*]. Continent: date not determined.
With this entry, the compilers switch duties again; the previous change of scribal hands was at 159.231. *Language(s)*: Latin (probable) Greek (perhaps). Appraised at 3s 6d in 1613.

159.424   Heliadorus
Heliodorus. *Historia Aethiopica*. Continent (probable): date not determined.

Probably not an STC book, but see STC 13041 *et seq. Language(s)*: Latin (probable) Greek (perhaps). Appraised at 10d in 1613.

159.425   The breviat of britaine

A breviat cronicle contaynynge all the kinges from brute to this daye. Britain: (different houses), 1552 (probable)–1561 (probable).

STC 9968 *et seq.* The [1561] edition does not contain the word "breviat" in the title and, therefore, is less likely to have been intended here. *Language(s)*: English. Appraised at 4d in 1613.

159.426   bonds horac

Quintus Horatius Flaccus. [*Works*]. Edited by John Bond. London: (different houses), 1606–1611.

STC 13790a *et seq. Language(s)*: Latin. Appraised at 8d in 1613.

159.427   Stepani appologia

Henri Estienne. *L'introduction au traité de la conformité des merveilles anciennes avec les modernes: ou, traité préparatif à l'apologie pour Hérodote*. Continent (probable): 1566–1607.

Almost certainly not an STC book, but see STC 10553 *et seq.* Given the low valuation and the location of the book in the collection, an octavo edition published only in French seems more likely than the two Latin editions in folio (1566, 1594) and the English editions (1607, 1608) also published in folio. Further, the Latin version was not issued separately but appeared only in editions of Herodotus, *Historiae libri IX*. Though the manuscript entry may indicate the Latin version, citations in English books of the period suggest that contemporaries used the Latin title even when citing the "gallic" edition. Estienne's *Apologeticum pro veteri ac germana linguae graecae pronuntiatione* (1579) was published without Estienne's name and, in any case, would probably not be listed as "appologia." *Language(s)*: French (probable) Latin (perhaps). Appraised at 4d in 1613.

159.428   Parraselsus 1 tom

Paracelsus. Unidentified. Continent (probable): date not determined.

Probably not an STC book, but see STC 19179.5 *et seq.* In the absence of a title identification, an English translation is possible but not likely, especially given the hint of a Latin work with "*1 tom.*" *Language(s)*: Latin (probable) English (perhaps). Appraised at 8d in 1613.

159.429   Acosta conciones

Joseph de Acosta. Unidentified. Continent: date not determined.

Acosta published three collections of sermons with "conciones" in the title, beginning in 1596. *Language(s)*: Latin. Appraised at 3s in 1613.

159.430   didacus de lavega 5 voll
Diego Covarruvias a Leyva, *Bishop of Segovia*. Unidentified. Continent: date not determined.

No potentially five-volume work found, though several editions were published of a two-volume *Opera omnia*. Perhaps a collection of some of the author's other works either bound together or catalogued as a set. *Language(s)*: Latin. Appraised at 8s in 1613.

159.431   Bosquier 6 voll
Philippe Bosquier. Unidentified. Continent: date not determined.

Bosquier did not publish any work in six volumes. The entry likely refers to a collection of separately published works either bound together or catalogued as a set. *Language(s)*: French (probable) Latin (probable). Appraised at 7s in 1613.

159.432   Horrac
Quintus Horatius Flaccus. Probably [*Works*]. Britain or Continent: date not determined.

STC 13874 *et seq.* and non-STC. *Language(s)*: Latin. Appraised at 4d in 1613.

159.433   Mortons appollogi
Thomas Morton, *Bishop*. *Apologiae catholicae, in qua paradoxa, haereses, blasphemiae, scelera, quae Jesuitae impingunt diluuntur*. London: (different houses), 1605–1606.

STC 18173.5 *et seq.* One edition was printed on the Continent for John Norton. Another copy is found at 159.93; 159.347 lists a title by Morton issued with the *Apologiae*. *Language(s)*: Latin. Appraised at 18d in 1613.

159.434   Mallius malliff
Jacob Sprenger and Heinrich Kraemer. *Malleus maleficarum*. Continent: date not determined.

Language(s): Latin. Appraised at 4d in 1613.

159.435   Textors Epist:
Joannes Ravisius (Textor). *Epistolae*. Britain or Continent: date not determined.

STC 20761.2 and non-STC. *Language(s)*: Latin. Appraised at 6d in 1613.

159.436   Polibbius
Polybius. *Historiae*. Continent: date not determined.

Language(s): Latin (probable) Greek (perhaps). Appraised at 12d in 1613.

159.437 Terrence
Publius Terentius, *Afer*. Probably [*Works*]. Britain or Continent: date not determined.

STC 23885 *et seq.* and non-STC. Likely English only if one of the diglot editions published in England. Possibly selected works only. *Language(s)*: Latin English (perhaps). Appraised at 6d in 1613.

159.438 Pollider Virgill
Polydorus Vergilius. Unidentified. Place unknown: stationer unknown, date not determined.

STC/non-STC status unknown. *Language(s)*: Latin (probable) English (perhaps). Appraised at 8d in 1613.

159.439:1   ii greecke testam
[*Bible—N.T.*]. Britain or Continent: date not determined.

STC 2793 *et seq.* and non–STC. *Language(s)*: Greek. Appraised with one other at 18d in 1613.

159.439:2 [See 159.439:1]
[*Bible—N.T.*]. Britain or Continent: date not determined.

STC 2793 *et seq.* and non-STC. *Language(s)*: Greek. Appraised with one other at 18d in 1613.

159.440 Jeuels Appollog
John Jewel, *Bishop*. *Apologia ecclesiae anglicanae*. Britain or Continent: 1562–1606.

STC 14581 *et seq.* and non-STC. *Language(s)*: English (probable) Latin (probable). Appraised at 4d in 1613.

159.441 Jani Anglorum
John Selden. *Jani Anglorum facies altera*. London: typis T. S[nodham] procur. J. Helme, imp. auctor, 1610.

STC 22174. Another copy is listed at 159.493. *Language(s)*: Latin. Appraised at 4d in 1613.

159.442 Suetonius
Caius Suetonius Tranquillus. *De vita Caesarum*. Continent: date not determined.

Absent a compiler's note, almost certainly not an English translation, first published in 1606. *Language(s)*: Latin. Appraised at 12d in 1613.

159.443 Epitomi Radicum Hebraic

Johann Buxtorf, *the Elder. Epitome radicum hebraicarum.* Basle: per Conradum Waldkirch, 1600.

Expanded in 1607 to include Chaldaic but with an expanded title, not likely here unless the compiler truncated the manuscript entry. Variously described by sources as octavo and duodecimo. *Language(s)*: Hebrew Latin. Appraised at 12d in 1613.

159.444 Clement Marot

Clément Marot. [*Works*]. Continent: date not determined.

Earlier editions were published under the title *L'Adolescence clémentine*. *Language(s)*: French. Appraised at 6d in 1613.

159.445 Quintus Curt

Quintus Curtius Rufus. *De rebus gestis Alexandri Magni.* Continent (probable): date not determined.

Probably not an STC book, but see STC 6145.5 *et seq.* An English translation would probably be identified in some manner by the compiler. *Language(s)*: Latin. Appraised at 6d in 1613.

159.446 Histor: Brit:

Unidentified. Place unknown: stationer unknown, date not determined.

Several possibilities, primarily Johann Theodor Clain, *Historia Britannica*, also attributed to John Clapham. Perhaps Ludovicus Virunius Ponticus, *Britannicae historiae libri sex* (STC 20109 and non-STC), an abridgement of Geoffrey, *of Monmouth*. John Clapham, *The historie of Great Britannie* (STC 5348) and John Speed, *The history of Great Britaine* (STC 23045), a large folio atlas, seem less likely possibilities. *Language(s)*: Latin (probable). Appraised at 4d in 1613.

159.447 Beda Hist Eccle:

Beda, *the Venerable. Historia ecclesiastica gentis anglorum.* Continent: date not determined.

Probably one of the duodecimo editions (1566–1601) rather than one of the earlier folios. *Language(s)*: Latin. Appraised at 8d in 1613.

159.448 Specculum politicum

Unidentified. Continent (probable): date not determined.

Probably not an STC book. Possibilities include the anonymous *Speculi aulicarum atque politicarum observationum libelli*, Nicolaus Selneccer, *Speculum conjugale et politicum*, and Piero Calefati, *Speculum verae politicae nobilitatis*. *Language(s)*: Latin. Appraised at 10d in 1613.

159.449 Frischlini facetiae

Nicodemus Frischlin. *Facetiae selectiores*. Continent: 1600–1609. *Language(s)*: Latin. Appraised at 4d in 1613.

159.450 Voelli generali officium

Joannes Voellus. [*Generale artificium orationis cuiuscunque componendae*]. Continent: 1588–1613.

Many editions include the work *De ratione conscribendi epistolas*, given by some sources to Voellus and by others to Justus Lipsius. *Language(s)*: Latin. Appraised at 4d in 1613.

159.451 Henricus octavus contra Luther

Henry VIII, *King of England. Assertio septem sacramentorum adversus M. Lutherum*. Britain or Continent: 1521–1562.

STC 13078 *et seq*. *Language(s)*: Latin. Appraised at 6d in 1613.

159.452 Ars Chimica

Hermes, *Trismegistus. Ars chemica, quod sit licita recte exercentibus*. Commentary by Joannes Garlandius (Hortulanus). Strassburg: excudebat Samuel Emmel, 1566.

Language(s): Latin. Appraised at 4d in 1613.

159.453 Valerius Maximus

Valerius Maximus. *Facta et dicta memorabilia*. Continent: date not determined.

Language(s): Latin. Appraised at 6d in 1613.

159.454 Ante Machevell

Probably Innocent Gentillet. *Commentariorum de regno aut quovis principatu recte administrando libri tres. Adversus N. Machiavellum*. Continent: date not determined.

Probably not an STC book, but see STC 11743 *et seq*. The English translation by Simon Patrick was published in folio, not likely at 12d and in this section of the collection. Without a language identification, the Latin version is assumed most likely. *Language(s)*: Latin (probable) French (perhaps). Appraised at 12d in 1613.

159.455 Bodines method

Jean Bodin, *Bishop. Methodus ad facilem historiarum cognitionem*. Continent: 1566–1610.

Language(s): Latin. Appraised at 6d in 1613.

159.456 an ould test: Eng

[*Bible—O.T.*]. Place unknown: stationer unknown, date not determined.

Unidentifiable in the STC. If a separately published Old Testament in English, then the Douai translation (1609) is the only possibility (STC 2207). This item, however, could be the Old Testament separated from any number of complete English Bibles, perhaps from an edition bound in two volumes. Finally, as phrased, the manuscript entry could even be describing an "old" New Testament. *Language(s)*: English. Appraised at 6d in 1613.

159.457 Canisie summa

Unidentified. Continent (probable): date not determined,

Almost certainly not an STC book. Either Petrus Canisius, *Summa doctrinae christianae*, also published in English as *A summe of christian doctrine* (STC 4571.5 *et seq.*); or Henricus Canisius, *Summa juris canonici*. *Language(s)*: Latin (probable). Appraised at 6d in 1613.

159.458 Petter marter prayers frenche

Pietro Martire Vermigli (Peter Martyr). *Sainctes prieres recueillies des pseaumes de David*. Continent: 1577–1581.

Some sources give a 1575 edition, but it has been shown to be an error for the 1577 *editio princeps*. *Language(s)*: French. Appraised at 4d in 1613.

159.459 Theater of the world in frenche

Pierre Boaistuau. *Le theatre du monde*. Britain or Continent: 1558–1609.

STC 3166 *et seq.* and non-STC. *Language(s)*: French. Appraised at 3d in 1613.

159.460 Fenistella

Andreas Dominicus Floccus (Lucius Fenestella). *De magistratibus sacerdotiisque Romanorum*. Continent: date not determined.

Language(s): Latin. Appraised at 3d in 1613.

159.461 Agripp de vanit scienticar

Henricus Cornelius Agrippa. *De incertitudine et vanitate scientiarum*. Continent: date not determined.

Language(s): Latin. Appraised at 4d in 1613.

159.462 Aulus gelius

Aulus Gellius. *Noctes Atticae*. Continent: date not determined.

Language(s): Latin. Appraised at 12d in 1613.

159.463 Ransovius de conservand valitudine

Henricus Ransovius (Heinrich Rantzau). *De conservanda valetudine liber.* Edited by Dethlerus Sylvius. Continent: 1576–1604.
Language(s): Latin. Appraised at 4d in 1613.

159.464 Molanus de fide hereticorum

Joannes Molanus. *Pontificii et regii librorum censoris, libri quinque.* Cologne: apud Godefridium Kempensem, 1584.

Editio princeps, with "De fine haereticis servanda, tres" leading and prominent on the title page; this text does not feature on the title pages of subsequent editions. *Language(s)*: Latin. Appraised at 4d in 1613.

159.465 Epistol: Plin:

Pliny, *the Younger. Epistolae.* Continent: date not determined.
Language(s): Latin. Appraised at 12d in 1613.

159.466 Summa consiliorum

Bartolome Carranza, *Archbishop.* [*Summa conciliorum*]. Continent: 1546–1601.
Language(s): Latin. Appraised at 16d in 1613.

159.467 Pascasius

Unidentified. Continent (probable): date not determined.

Probably not an STC book. Possibly any number of authors, such as Justus Pascasius, Radbertus Paschasius, Etienne Pasquier (Stephanus Paschasius), and Caspar Schoppe (Grosippus Pascasius). Pasquier is the only author to have been published in England by the date of this inventory, and then in English, not likely here. *Language(s)*: Latin (probable). Appraised at 3d in 1613.

159.468 Dr Gwinns oration

Matthew Gwinne. *Orationes duae Londini habitae in aedibus Greshamiis, 1598.* London: R. Field, 1605.

STC 12554. Gwinne's inaugural lectures at Gresham College (ODNB). *Language(s)*: Latin. Appraised at 2d in 1613.

159.469 The Imag of government

Sir Thomas Elyot. *The image of governance compiled of the actes of Alexander Severus.* London: (different houses), 1541–1556.

STC 7664 *et seq.* Based on and translated freely by Elyot from Aelius Lampridius, *Historiae Augustae scriptores.* Another copy is found at 159.534. *Language(s)*: English. Appraised at 6d in 1613.

159.470 meditationes Bruni 4 voll

Vincenzo Bruno. Unidentified. Continent (probable): date not determined.

Probably not an STC book, but see STC 3941.1 *et seq*. It is impossible to identify which of his books with titles leading with "Meditationes" (some on the Virgin Mary, some on Christ) these four volumes represent. The English translation by Richard Gibbons of the *Meditationes de praecipuis mysteriis vitae et passionis domini nostri Jesu Christi*, published c.1599 in four parts on Fr. Henry Garnet's secret recusant press in London, is not likely since the manuscript entry suggests one of the Continental Latin or Italian editions. *Language(s)*: Latin (probable) Italian (perhaps). Appraised at 3s in 1613.

159.471 Psalmes in Italian

[*Bible—O.T.—Psalms*]. Continent: date not determined.
Language(s): Italian. Appraised at 4d in 1613.

159.472 figurae bib:

Antonius de Rampegollis. *Figurae Bibliae*. Continent: date not determined.
Language(s): Latin. Appraised at 6d in 1613.

159.473 Josephus ii vol

Flavius Josephus. Probably [*Works*]. Continent (probable): date not determined.

Probably not an STC book, but see STC 14809 *et seq*. *Language(s)*: Latin (probable). Appraised at 2s in 1613.

159.474 Testament in frenche

[*Bible—N.T.*]. Britain or Continent: date not determined.
STC 2957.6 *et seq*. and non-STC. *Language(s)*: French. Appraised at 10d in 1613.

159.475 the minor poets

Unidentified. Place unknown: stationer unknown, date not determined.

STC/non-STC status unknown. The manuscript entry suggests an English title, but no work of this title can be found. If, however, the compiler was simply being descriptive, the item could be one of any number of books, including, for example, one of the many anthologies of the classical poets known as the "poetae minores." See Adams P1688 *et seq*. *Language(s)*: Unknown. Appraised at 12d in 1613.

159.476 Gildas

Gildas. *Liber querulus de excidio Britanniae*. Britain or Continent: c.1525–1568.

STC 11892 *et seq.* The c.1525 edition was probably printed in Antwerp; it is listed as STC 11892, but the STC notes that it is "not an STC book." The two subsequent editions that appeared by the date of this inventory were both printed by John Day. *Language(s)*: Latin. Appraised at 4d in 1613.

159.477 Lucian the second tome

Lucianus, *of Samosata*. Perhaps *Works*. Continent: date not determined.

Probably a volume from one of the many multi-volume *Works*. No English edition of Lucian was published in more than one volume by the time of this inventory. See 159.267 and 159.306 for other copies. Struck through. *Language(s)*: Greek (probable) Latin (probable). Appraised at 10d in 1613.

159.478 Alberti compendium theolog

Albertus Magnus. *Compendium theologicae veritatis*. Continent: date not determined.

Also attributed to Hugo, *Argentinensis*. Almost certainly not one of the many folio incunables. *Language(s)*: Latin. Appraised at 6d in 1613.

159.479 Coelum philos

Philippus Ulstadius. *Coelum philosophorum*. Continent: 1526–1572. *Language(s)*: Latin. Appraised at 6d in 1613.

159.480 Epigram Marcial

Marcus Valerius Martialis. *Epigrammata*. Continent: date not determined. *Language(s)*: Latin. Appraised at 6d in 1613.

159.481 Haebru Psalter

[*Bible—O.T.—Psalms*]. Continent: date not determined. *Language(s)*: Hebrew. Appraised at 4d in 1613.

159.482 Daneus Apharism

Lambert Daneau. *Politicorum aphorismorum silva*. Continent: 1583–1612. *Language(s)*: Latin. Appraised at 3d in 1613.

159.483 Hues de Globis

Robert Hues. *Tractatus de globis et eorum usu*. Britain or Continent: 1594–1613?

STC 13906 *et seq*. *Language(s)*: Latin. Appraised at 6d in 1613.

159.484 Piscators aforis

Jean Calvin. *Aphorismi doctrinae christianae*. Edited by Johann Piscator. Britain or Continent: date not determined.

STC 4372.5 and non-STC. An abridgement by Johann Piscator of Calvin's *Institutio*, published in Latin in Britain and the Continent, and in an English translation by Henry Holland (STC 4374), not likely here. *Language(s)*: Latin. Appraised at 3d in 1613.

159.485 Widenburgia philosophia

Hieronymus Wildenbergius (Hieronymus Gürtler). Probably *Totius philosophiae humanae digestio*. Continent: date not determined.

Probably not a copy of his *Totius naturalis philosophiae in physicam Aristotelis epitome*: if so, the cataloguer would likely have mentioned Aristotle. *Language(s)*: Latin. Appraised at 4d in 1613.

159.486 Columb: anotomia

Realdus Columbus. *De re anatomica*. Continent: 1559–1593. *Language(s)*: Latin. Appraised at 8d in 1613.

159.487 Symbolatria

Unidentified. Place unknown: stationer unknown, date not determined.

STC/non-STC status unknown. Perhaps STC 25267 *et seq.*, William West's often printed *Symbolaeographia* (also published as *Symboleography*) with the compiler mishearing the title. There are, however, numerous texts with such titles as *Symbolarum*, *Symbolae*, and *Symbolum*, one of which might be intended here. *Language(s)*: Unknown. Appraised at 3d in 1613.

159.488 Breviarum

[*Liturgies—Latin Rite—Breviaries*]. Britain or Continent: date not determined.

STC 15794 *et seq.* and non-STC. Possibly use of Salisbury (Sarum), but just as likely a more contemporary Continental edition. *Language(s)*: Latin. Appraised at 6d in 1613.

159.489 Rudiment: fid

Jean Calvin. [*Catechism*]. Britain or Continent: date not determined.

STC 4375 *et seq.* and non-STC. The London editions were published under the title *Catechismus ecclesiae Genevensis*; one of the Continental editions, published under the title *Rudimenta fidei christianae, sive catechismus*, seems more likely. *Language(s)*: Latin. Appraised at 4d in 1613.

159.490 Carions Croni:

Johann Carion. [*Chronica*]. Continent (probable): date not determined.

Probably not an STC book, but see STC 4626. *The three bokes of cronicles*, the English translation by Walter Lynne, was published in 1550, but the compiler would have probably identified an English edition. *Language(s)*: Latin. Appraised at 3d in 1613.

159.491 Problem Arist

Aristotle (spurious). *Problemata*. Britain or Continent: date not determined. STC 761 and non-STC. *Language(s)*: Latin. Appraised at 4d in 1613.

159.492 Boccas

Giovanni Boccaccio. *Unidentified*. Continent (probable): date not determined.

Probably not an STC book, but see STC 3172 *et seq*. An English edition would probably have been so identified. *Language(s)*: Latin (probable). Appraised at 12d in 1613.

159.493 Jani Anglo

John Selden. *Jani Anglorum facies altera*. London: typis T. S[nodham] procur. J. Helme, imp. auctor, 1610.

STC 22174. Another copy is listed at 159.441. *Language(s)*: Latin. Appraised at 3d in 1613.

159.494 Calvinus Judaizance

Aegidius Hunnius. *Calvinus Judaizans*. Wittenberg: (different houses), 1593–1604.

Language(s): Latin. Appraised at 4d in 1613.

159.495 Fulcke againste Bristowe

William Fulke. Probably *A retentive, to stay good christians, against the motives of R. Bristow*. London: T. Vautrollier for G. Bishop, 1580.

STC 11449. If the compiler's entry is purely descriptive, then STC 11448, Fulke's *A rejoynder to Bristows Replie* (1581), is possible. The word "againste" in the manuscript entry, however, makes STC 11449 likely. *Language(s)*: English. Appraised at 6d in 1613.

159.496 Aronis purgat

Franciscus Moncaeus. *Aaron purgatus sive de vitulo aureo libri duo*. Arras: Gulielmus Riverius, 1605–1606.

Another copy is listed at 159.521. *Language(s)*: Latin. Appraised at 12d in 1613.

159.497 Sacrabos

Unidentified. Continent: date not determined,

A work by either the astronomer Joannes Sacrobosco (John Holywood) or the theologian Christophorus Sacrobosco (Christopher Holywood); in this inventory, either is plausible, but the Jesuit controversialist, particularly in this section of Brown's collection, seems more likely. *Language(s)*: Latin (probable). Appraised at 3d in 1613.

159.498 Dorhoff apodix

Hermann Bosendorf (Bernard Doerhoff, *pseudonym*). *Apodixes, sive demonstrationes tres horrendarum blasphemiarum ecclesiae a Calvino reformatae.* Münster: excudebat Lambertus Rassfeldt, 1608.
Language(s): Latin. Appraised at 8d in 1613.

159.499:A Juvinall et Perscius

Decimus Junius Juvenalis. [*Works*]. Britain or Continent: date not determined (composite publication).
STC 14889 and non-STC. Another copy is listed at 159.407. *Language(s)*: Latin. Appraised [a composite volume] at 6d in 1613.

159.499:B [See 159.499:A]

Aulus Persius Flaccus. [*Works*]. [Composite publication].
STC 14889 and non-STC. Another copy is listed at 159.407. *Language(s)*: Latin. Appraised [a composite volume] at 6d in 1613.

159.500 Boys on the Leturg:

John Boys. Probably *An exposition of al the principall scriptures used in our English liturgie*. London: F. Kingston, sold by W. Aspley, 1609–1610.
STC 3455 *et seq*. The first of the four single editions was printed by Kingston for Martin Clarke. Perhaps, but less likely, one of STC 3458 *et seq.*, *An exposition of the dominical epistles and gospels used in our English liturgie*, published in three separate parts. *Language(s)*: English. Appraised at 6d in 1613.

159.501 Parradines Emblemes french

Claude Paradin. [*Devises heroiques*]. Continent: date not determined.
Language(s): French. Appraised at 4d in 1613.

159.502 Bacons Essayes

Francis Bacon, *Viscount St. Albans*. *Essayes*. London: (different houses), 1597–1613.
STC 1137 *et seq*. Another copy is listed at 159.381. *Language(s)*: English Latin (perhaps). Appraised at 2d in 1613.

159.503 Argenterius de urinis

Joannes Argenterius. *De urinis liber.* Heidelberg: ex off. Sanctandreana, 1591.
Language(s): Latin. Appraised at 1d in 1613.

159.504   Piscator de predestinat

Probably Johann Piscator. *Disputatio theologica de praedestinatione.* Herborn: typis C. Corvini, 1595–1598.

Possibly one of the disputations on this subject over which Piscator presided, and possibly, but less likely, Peter Piscator, *Disputatio de aeterna praedestinatione salvandorum*, considerably less widely published. *Language(s)*: Latin. Appraised at 2d in 1613.

159.505   Concordia Anglicana

Richard Harris. *Concordia Anglicana de primatu ecclesiae regio; adversus Becanum De dissidio Anglicano.* London: G. Hall, imp. R. Redmer, 1612.

STC 12814. *Language(s)*: Latin. Appraised at 2d in 1613.

159.506   Sandersons log:

John Sanderson. *Institutionum dialecticarum libri quatuor.* Britain or Continent: 1589–1609.

STC 21698 *et seq.* and non-STC. See Shaaber S30 for the 1589 edition. The earliest extant, and apparently first, edition of Robert Sanderson's *Logicae artis compendium* (Oxford, 1615) appeared two years after this inventory was compiled. *Language(s)*: Latin. Appraised at 3d in 1613.

159.507   Erasm: Coll

Desiderius Erasmus. *Colloquia.* Britain or Continent: date not determined.

STC 10450.6 *et seq.* and non-STC. *Language(s)*: Latin. Appraised at 4d in 1613.

159.508   An answere to a Jesuited gent

Anthony Copley. *An answere to a letter of a jesuited gentleman.* London: [F. Kingston], 1601.

STC 5735. Published under the initials "A.C." and sometimes attributed to Anthony Champny. *Language(s)*: English. Appraised at 3d in 1613.

159.509   Antidoton

Henoch Clapham. *Antidoton: or a soveraigne remedie against schisme and heresie: from that parable of tares.* London: [F. Kingston for] J. Wolfe, 1600.

STC 5330. *Language(s)*: English. Appraised at 1d in 1613.

159.510   Lentulus Gram Italian

Scipio Lentulo. [*Italicae grammatices*]. Britain or Continent: date not determined.

STC 15469 *et seq.* and non-STC. The English version (editions 1575–1587) is by Henry Grantham. *Language(s)*: Italian English (probable) Latin (perhaps). Appraised at 2d in 1613.

159.511 Nullus et nemo
Andreas Jurgiewicius. *Quinti evangelii professores antiquissimi et celeberrimi Nullus et Nemo.* Continent: 1599–1611.
Language(s): Latin. Appraised at 3d in 1613.

159.512 Parreus de Jure Regum
David Pareus. *Quaestiones controversae theologicae, de jure regum et principum contra papam romanum.* Amberg: ex officina typographica Schönfeldiana, 1612.
Language(s): Latin. Appraised at 3d in 1613.

159.513 Limbo mastix
Andrew Willet. *Limbo-mastix: that is, a canvise of Limbus patrum, shewing that Christ descended not in soule to hell.* London: [F. Kingston] for T. Man, 1604.
STC 25692. *Language(s)*: English. Appraised at 2d in 1613.

159.514 Martinius Gram Heb:
Petrus Martinius. [*Grammatica hebraica*]. Continent: 1567–1612.
STC 17523 and non-STC. If a post-1590 edition, it includes his Chaldaic grammar. STC 17523, the expanded English version by John Udall, is not likely to have been entered in this manner. *Language(s)*: Hebrew Latin Chaldaic (perhaps). Appraised at 3d in 1613.

159.515 a discoveri of Jesuits
Probably *A discoverie of the most secret and subtile practises of the Jesuits.* London: [G. Eld] for R. Boulton, 1610.
STC 14528. An anonymous translation from the French; original author unknown. Perhaps STC 25126, William Watson, *A sparing discoverie of our English jesuits, and of F. Parsons* (1601). *Language(s)*: English. Appraised at 2d in 1613.

159.516 Pratum Lacus
Charles Estienne. *Pratum, lacus, arundinetum.* Paris: apud Simonem Colinaeum, et Franciscum Stephanum, 1543.
Issued as a children's book. *Language(s)*: Latin. Appraised at 4d in 1613.

159.517 varietractatus
Unidentified. Place unknown: stationer unknown, date not determined.
STC/non-STC status unknown. The single-word manuscript entry is assumed to have been intended as two words. Possibly multiple books, but at the valuation probably a single item. See PLRE 2.102, PLRE 2.145, PLRE 11.7, and PLRE Ad1.57 for single works with such a title. *Language(s)*: Unknown. Appraised at 6d in 1613.

159.518 Seranus de fide
Jean de Serres. *De fide catholica*. Paris: (different houses), 1597–1607.
Given the valuation, the 1607 octavo edition is more likely than the 1597 folio. *Language(s)*: Latin. Appraised at 4d in 1613.

159.519 Commineus frenche
Philippe de Comines. Probably [*Memoires*]. Continent: date not determined.
Another copy listed at 159.48. *Language(s)*: French. Appraised at 6d in 1613.

159.520 Arist: prob: Eng
Aristotle (spurious). *The problemes of Aristotle, with other philosophers and phisitions*. Britain: 1595–1607.
STC 762 *et seq*. *Language(s)*: English. Appraised at 6d in 1613.

159.521 Aron purgatus
Franciscus Moncaeus. *Aaron purgatus sive de vitulo aureo libri duo*. Arras: Gulielmus Riverius, 1605–1606.
Another copy is listed at 159.496. *Language(s)*: Latin. Appraised at 12d in 1613.

159.522 the discoveri of a gulphe
John Stubbs. *The discoverie of a gaping gulf whereinto England is like to be swallowed by an other French mariage*. London: [H. Singleton for W. Page], 1579.
STC 23400. Published anonymously and suppressed. *Language(s)*: English. Appraised at 2d in 1613.

159.523 Chrisostums Homilyes
John, *Chrysostom, Saint*. [*Homiliae*]. Britain or Continent: date not determined.
STC 14634 *et seq*. and non-STC. *Language(s)*: Latin (probable) Greek (perhaps). Appraised at 3d in 1613.

159.524 Epigram Owen
John Owen. *Epigrammatum libri tres*. Britain or Continent: 1606–1613.
STC 18984.5 *et seq*. and non-STC. See also Shaaber O82–O85. *Language(s)*: Latin. Appraised at 3d in 1613.

159.525 Hypomnesis polit
Francesco Guicciardini. *Hypomneses politicae*. Continent: 1595–1598.
Language(s): Latin. Appraised at 2d in 1613.

159.526 Vincentius
Unidentified. Place unknown: stationer unknown, date not determined.
STC/non-STC status unknown. Many possible authors. *Language(s)*: Unknown. Appraised at 3d in 1613.

159.527 Carolus de lorma
Charles de Lorme. *Pteleinodaphneiai. Hoc est, laureae apollinares a prima ad supremam, sive enneas quaestionum medicinum.* Paris: apud Adrianum Beys, 1608. *Language(s)*: Latin. Appraised at 3d in 1613.

159.528 Erasm: similes
Desiderius Erasmus. *Parabolae sive similia.* Britain or Continent: date not determined.
STC 10502.5 and non-STC. *Language(s)*: Latin. Appraised at 3d in 1613.

159.529 Papa non papa
Andreas Osiander, *the Younger. Papa non papa.* Continent: 1599–1610. *Language(s)*: Latin. Appraised at 4d in 1613.

159.530 Miracula chimica
Philipp Müller. *Miracula chymica et misteria medica.* Continent: 1610–1611. *Language(s)*: Latin. Appraised at 3d in 1613.

159.531 Becanus de sacraficia
Martinus Becanus. *De triplici sacrificio, naturae, legis, gratiae.* Mainz: ex officina Joannis Albini, 1610.
Language(s): Latin. Appraised at 6d in 1613.

159.532 Godfre of Bullame
Torquato Tasso. *Godfrey of Bulloigne, or the recoverie of Hierusalem.* Translated by Richard Carew. London: J. Windet for (different houses), 1594.
STC 23697 *et seq.* The translation by Edward Fairfax that appeared in 1600 without the Italian text was published in folio; neither the valuation nor the location of this item in Brown's collection would suggest a book in that large format. *Language(s)*: English Italian. Appraised at 6d in 1613.

159.533:1–24 Ould Pamflets xxiiii tyed up altogeather
Unidentified. Places unknown: stationers unknown, dates not determined.
STC/non-STC status unknown. *Language(s)*: Unknown. Appraised as a group at 2s 6d in 1613.

159.534   the Imag of government

Sir Thomas Elyot. *The image of governance compiled of the actes of Alexander Severus*. London: (different houses), 1541–1556.

STC 7664 *et seq*. Based on and translated freely by Elyot from Aelius Lampridius, *Historiae Augustae scriptores*. Another copy is listed at 159.469. *Language(s)*: English. Appraised at 6d in 1613.

159.535   Magna carta

[*Magna Carta cum statutis*]. (*England—Statutes—I. General Collections*). London: (different houses), 1508–c.1608.

STC 9266 *et seq*. *Language(s)*: English (probable) Latin (probable) Law French (probable). Appraised at 4d in 1613.

159.536   tremelius psalter

Psalmi Davidis ex Hebraeo in Latinum conversi. (*Bible—O.T.*). Translated by Joannes Immanuel Tremellius and François Du Jon, *the Elder*. London: (different houses), 1580.

STC 2359 *et seq*. *Language(s)*: Latin. Appraised at 3d in 1613.

159.537   Mirror of the world french

Peeter Heyns. *Le miroir du monde*. Continent: 1579–1598.

A "pocket edition" of Abraham Ortelius's *Theatrum orbis terrarum*. The word "french" has been added to the manuscript entry. *Language(s)*: French. Appraised at 18d in 1613.

159.538   littletons teniors

Sir Thomas Littleton. [*Tenures*]. Britain or Continent: date not determined.

STC 15719 *et seq*. One early edition was published in Rouen; the rest were printed in London. *Language(s)*: English (probable) Law French (probable). Appraised at 6d in 1613.

159.539:1–18   xviii smale bookes tyed togeather

Unidentified. Places unknown: stationers unknown, dates not determined.

STC/non-STC status unknown. *Language(s)*: Unknown. Appraised as a group at 2s 6d in 1613.

159.540 multiple   other smale bookes afterward found

Unidentified. Places unknown: stationers unknown, dates not determined.

STC/non-STC status unknown. *Language(s)*: Unknown. Appraised as a group at 2s in 1613.

159.541 multiple   certaine bookes in Mr Vicechancelors custody

Unidentified. Places unknown: stationers unknown, dates not determined.

STC/non-STC status unknown. The Vice-Chancellor of Oxford from 1611 to 1614 was Thomas Singleton, *D.D.*, Principal of Brasenose College. Not appraised. *Language(s)*: Unknown.

PRIVATE LIBRARIES IN RENAISSANCE ENGLAND 160

Edward Homer. Scholar (M.A.):
Probate Inventory. 1614

STUART GILLESPIE

Edward Homer (Holdmore, Holmer), a Worcestershire native, matriculated from St. John's College on 16 February 1598–9 at the age of eighteen, pointing to a date of birth in 1581. Admitted B.A. at New College on 14 June 1602 and licensed M.A. from St. John's on 31 May 1606 (*Alumni Oxonienses* 2:739), he died in 1614. His will was proved on 2 November 1614 (*Alumni Oxonienses* 2:739), and his goods, including the books listed below, were inventoried for probate earlier that same year on 20 July.

His collection of more than sixty books is about two-thirds theological: there are the expected Bibles (including a Greek testament) and psalters; liturgies, homilies, and sermons; the occasional contemporary work of controversy; a modest range of biblical and other commentary. A relatively high proportion of this material is in English. Some of it can be dated to the years immediately preceding Homer's death. Beyond this, a handful of standard texts and textbooks, perhaps in his possession from the not very distant time of Homer's own training, cover Greek grammar, rhetoric, and metaphysics. The literary material which makes up a half-dozen further entries is mainly classical, and mainstream. There are, however, one or two hints of an interest in the contemporary literary world on Homer's part. A volume of Oxford elegies (in Latin) in memory of Elizabeth I was published in 1603, while 'Neroes Tragedie' is most likely the tragic drama *Nero tragaedia nova*, published in the same year by the St. John's figure Matthew Gwinne. Both, then, may belong to Homer's salad days. Gwinne's play was never performed, but as a member of the college Homer would have encountered the strong traditions of academic drama at St. John's at this time.

Oxford University Archives, Bodleian Library: Hyp.B.14.

§

160.1	Ferus Coment upon Mathew
160.2	Cases phi
160.3	An Englishe bible
160.4	Comistoris historia
160.5	Theophilact uppon the 4 Evang
160.6	St Peters prophesie
160.7	Pezelius upon part of Melanc
160.8	Chaney metaphi
160.9	The Doctrine of the Sabboth
160.10	A greeke Testament
160.11	Doctor Pryces foure Sermons in one
160.12:A	Trelcasius et Vastius
160.12:B	[See 160.12:A]
160.13	Aristotles Metaphi
160.14	St Augustin de consensu Evang
160.15	A piece of Boys on the Litturgie
160.16	Oxonien funebre Officium
160.17	Keckirmans divinitie
160.18	Roiardi homilie
160.19	The second parte of Tull: philo:
160.20	Homers Illi
160.21	Camdens grammer
160.22	Vivoldus de veritate Contritionis
160.23	Campions x reasons
160.24	Stella de Contemptu mundi
160.25	Yates upon Seneca
160.26	Luther on the Galath
160.27	Tractatus de Salomonis nuptiis
160.28:1–12	xii stitcht bookes
160.29	Neroes Tragedie
160.30	Hull his third worcke of Mercye
160.31	Dr Boys on the Epistle and Gospell
160.32:1	Psalter and psalmes
160.32:2	[See 160.32:1]
160.33	Tullyes Rhetorick
160.34	Cattullus Tibullus
160.35	Haymons homil
160.36	Bucha: psalter
160.37	Augustin de fide
160.38	Tullies Epistles
160.39	Virgill
160.40	A service book
160.41	Mar Maurulus

160.42:1–3   Granatensis 2. 3. 4. tomi
160.43   Testamentum latinum
160.44   Clitovii logic
160.45   Seneca his Tragedie
160.46   Virgill
160.47   Granatensis de doctrina spirituali
160.48:1–5 Fyve bookes

§

160.1   Ferus Coment upon Mathew

Joannes Ferus (Johann Wild, *Prediger zu Mainz*). [*Matthew: commentary*]. Continent: 1559–1609.
Language(s): Latin. Appraised at 12d in 1614.

160.2   Cases phi

John Case. [*Aristotle—Physica: commentary*]. Britain or Continent: 1599–1612.
STC 4754 *et seq.* and non-STC. Either his *Lapis philosophicus seu commentarius in 8° lib: phys: Aristot: in quo arcana physiologiae examinantur* (STC 4756) or the epitome *Ancilla philosophiae, seu epitome in octo libros physicorum Aristotelis*. At the valuation, the former, a much larger work, is more likely. The two were published together in at least one edition (Shaaber C141). *Language(s)*: Latin. Appraised at 2s in 1614.

160.3   An Englishe bible

The Bible. Britain or Continent: date not determined.
STC 2063 *et seq. Language(s)*: English. Appraised at 6s in 1614.

160.4   Comistoris historia

Petrus, *Comestor. Historia scholastica*. Continent: date not determined.
Language(s): Latin. Appraised at 12d in 1614.

160.5   Theophilact uppon the 4 Evang

Theophylact, *Archbishop of Achrida*. [*Gospels: commentary and text*]. (*Bible—N.T.*). Continent: date not determined.
Language(s): Latin. Appraised at 10d in 1614.

160.6   St Peters prophesie

John Hull. *Saint Peters prophesie of these last dayes*. London: [W. Stansby] for Nathaniel Fosbrooke, 1610–1611.
STC 13933 *et seq. Language(s)*: English. Appraised at 18d in 1614.

160.7 Pezelius upon part of Melanc

Philipp Melanchthon and Christoph Pezel. *Examen theologicum*. Neustadt an der Haardt: (different houses), 1587–1597.

A school edition with notes by Pezel. *Language(s)*: Latin. Appraised at 12d in 1614.

160.8 Chaney metaphi

James Cheyne, *Canon of Tournai*. [*Aristotle—Metaphysica: commentary*]. Continent: 1577–1607.

Language(s): Latin. Appraised at 6d in 1614.

160.9 The Doctrine of the Sabboth

George Widley. *The doctrine of the sabbath, handled in foure treatises*. London: F. Kyngston for T. Man, 1604.

STC 25610. *Language(s)*: English. Appraised at 6d in 1614.

160.10 A greeke Testament

[*Bible—N.T.*]. Britain or Continent: date not determined.

STC 2793 *et seq.* and non-STC. *Language(s)*: Greek. Appraised at 8d in 1614.

160.11 Doctor Pryces foure Sermons in one

Daniel Price. Probably *Spirituall odours to the memory of prince Henry, in foure of the last sermons*. Oxford: Jos. Barnes, sold by John Barnes, 1613.

STC 20304 *et seq.* Two editions in one year. Joseph Barnes of Oxford is cited as printer for both editions, though the STC indicates that the second edition was really printed by G. Eld in London; both editions were sold by John Barnes, London. This manuscript entry may represent four miscellaneous sermons bound together rather than this collection, but the four sermons on the death of Henry, just published, are more likely. *Language(s)*: English. Appraised at 4d in 1614.

160.12:A Trelcasius et Vastius

Lucas Trelcatius, *the Younger*. *Scholastica et methodica locorum communium s. theologiae institutio, didactice et elenctice in epitome explicata*. Britain or Continent: 1604–1611 (composite publication).

STC 24263 *et seq.* and non-STC. Issued with the next. *Language(s)*: Latin. Appraised with one other at 6d in 1614.

160.12:B [See 160.12:A]

Conrad Vorstius. *Enchiridion controversiarum: seu index errorum ecclesiae Romanae, una cum antidoto*. [Composite publication].

STC 24263 *et seq.* and non-STC. Issued with the preceding. *Language(s)*: Latin. Appraised with one other at 6d in 1614.

160.13 Aristotles Metaphi

Aristotle. *Metaphysica*. Continent: date not determined.
Language(s): Latin (probable) Greek (perhaps). Appraised at 8d in 1614.

160.14 St Augustin de consensu Evang

Augustine, Saint. *De consensu evangelistarum*. Continent: date not determined.
Language(s): Latin. Appraised at 4d in 1614.

160.15 A piece of Boys on the Litturgie

John Boys. *An exposition of al the principall scriptures used in our English liturgie*. London: Felix Kingston for William Aspley, 1609–1613.
STC 3455 *et seq*. Martin Clarke was an assigned bookseller of the first edition along with Aspley. See 160.31. *Language(s)*: English. Appraised at 6d in 1614.

160.16 Oxonien funebre Officium

Oxoniensis Academiae funebre officium in memoriam Elisabethae reginae. (Oxford University—Verses, Addresses) Oxford: J. Barnesius, 1603.
STC 19018. *Language(s)*: French Greek Hebrew Latin. Appraised at 4d in 1614.

160.17 Keckirmans divinitie

Bartholomaeus Keckermann. *Systema S.S. theologiae, tribus libris adornatum*. Continent: 1602–1611.
The only work of Keckermann's that would be so described. *Language(s)*: Latin. Appraised at 8d in 1614.

160.18 Roiardi homilie

Joannes Royardus. [*Homiliae*]. Continent: date not determined.
Some editions include the texts of the liturgical epistles. *Language(s)*: Latin. Appraised at 6d in 1614.

160.19 The second parte of Tull: philo:

Marcus Tullius Cicero. [*Selected works—Philosophica* (part)]. Continent: date not determined.
Language(s): Latin. Appraised at 4d in 1614.

160.20 Homers Illi

Homer. *Iliad*. Britain or Continent: date not determined.
STC 13629 *et seq*. and non-STC. *Language(s)*: English (probable) Greek (probable) Latin (probable). Appraised at 12d in 1614.

160.21 Camdens grammer

William Camden. *Institutio Graecae grammatices compendiaria, in usum regiae scholae Westmonasteriensis.* London: (different houses), 1595–1613.
STC 4511 *et seq. Language(s)*: Greek Latin. Appraised at 3d in 1614.

160.22 Vivoldus de veritate Contritionis

Joannes Lodovicus Vivaldus. *Aureum opus de veritate contritionis.* Continent: date not determined.
Language(s): Latin. Appraised at 4d in 1614.

160.23 Campions x reasons

Edmund Campian. *Rationes decem.* Britain or Continent: 1581–1607.
STC 4536.5 and non-STC. ARCR 1: nos. 135.1–161. *Language(s)*: Latin. Appraised at 2d in 1614.

160.24 Stella de Contemptu mundi

Diego de Estella. *De contemnendis mundi vanitatibus.* Cologne: (different houses), 1585–1611.
Language(s): Latin. Appraised at 4d in 1614.

160.25 Yates upon Seneca

Unidentified. [*Seneca—Unidentified: commentary*]. Place unknown: stationer unknown, date not determined.

STC/non-STC status unknown. If the author is truly an unidentified "Yates," then the work was almost certainly published in England and may have been in English. But no commentator on Seneca with the name of "Yates" can be found during this period, and therefore, despite the legibility of the manuscript entry, unless the work is no longer extant, the author's name may very well have been quite different from what the compiler wrote. *Language(s)*: Unknown. Appraised at 10d in 1614.

160.26 Luther on the Galath

Martin Luther. [*Galatians: commentary*]. Britain or Continent: date not determined.

STC 16965 *et seq.* and non-STC. The compiler sometimes enters a Latin edition in English. *Language(s)*: English (probable) Latin (probable). Appraised at 12d in 1614.

160.27 Tractatus de Salomonis nuptiis

Andrew Willet. *Tractatus de Salomonis nuptiis.* Britain or Continent: 1612–1613.
STC 25707 and non-STC. Shaaber W95. *Language(s)*: Latin. Appraised at 2d in 1614.

160.28:1–12   xii stitcht bookes

Unidentified. Places unknown: stationers unknown, dates not determined. STC/non-STC status unknown. Probably meant to indicate unbound books. *Language(s)*: Unknown. Appraised as a group at 2s in 1614.

160.29   Neroes Tragedie

Unidentified. London: date not determined.

Unidentifiable in the STC. Either *Nero tragaedia nova*, by Matthew Gwinne, printed [by Richard Read] for Edward Blount, London, 1603 (STC 12551), or *The tragedie of Claudius Tiberius Nero, Romes greatest tyrant*, Anonymous, printed [by Edward Allde] for Francis Burton, London, 1607 (STC 24063). *Language(s)*: Unknown. Appraised at 4d in 1614.

160.30   Hull his third worcke of Mercye

William Hull. [*The third worke of mercy*]. London: Printed N. O[kes] for S. Rand, 1612–1614.

STC 13938 *et seq.* Probably the 1612 edition, since in 1614 the title in the manuscript entry becomes a subtitle. *Language(s)*: English. Appraised at 3d in 1614.

160.31   Dr Boys on the Epistle and Gospell

John Boys. Probably *An exposition of the dominical epistles and gospels used in our English liturgie*. London: (different houses) for William Aspley, 1610–1613.

STC 3458 *et seq.* Boys's exposition on the Festival Epistles and Gospels (STC 3462) appeared in only one edition (1613) before the date of this inventory, whereas his exposition on the Dominical Epistles and Gospels saw a number of editions between 1610 and 1613, which makes this identification marginally more probable than the other. See 160.15. *Language(s)*: English. Appraised at 8d in 1614.

160.32:1   Psalter and psalmes

[*Liturgies—Latin Rite—Psalters*]. Britain or Continent: date not determined.

STC 16253 *et seq.* and non-STC. An unusual manuscript entry. Were the second item not listed, one would be tempted to identify this as a collection of the Psalms, but the compiler's entry clearly distinguishes one from the other, identifying the second as the Old Testament book. *Language(s)*: Latin. Appraised at 6d in 1614.

160.32:2   [See 160.32:1]

[*Bible—O.T.—Psalms*]. Britain or Continent: date not determined.

STC 2351.7 *et seq.* and non-STC. *Language(s)*: English (probable) Latin (probable). Appraised with one other at 6d in 1614.

160.33 Tullyes Rhetorick
Marcus Tullius Cicero. Probably [*Selected works — Rhetorica*]. Continent: date not determined.

Conceivably the spurious *Rhetorica ad Herennium*. *Language(s)*: Latin. Appraised at 6d in 1614.

160.34 Cattullus Tibullus
Caius Valerius Catullus, Albius Tibullus, Sextus Propertius. [*Works*]. Continent: date not determined.

Language(s): Latin. Appraised at 3d in 1614.

160.35 Haymons homil
Haymo, *Bishop of Halberstadt*. [*Homiliae*]. Continent: date not determined. *Language(s)*: Latin. Appraised at 6d in 1614.

160.36 Bucha: psalter
George Buchanan. [*Psalms: paraphrase*.] (*Bible — O.T.*). Britain or Continent: 1565–1611.

STC 3983 *et seq.* and non-STC. Some editions include Buchanan's tragedies. *Language(s)*: Latin. Appraised at 2d in 1614.

160.37 Augustin de fide
Augustine, *Saint*. *De fide et operibus*. Continent: date not determined. *Language(s)*: Latin. Appraised at 3d in 1614.

160.38 Tullies Epistles
Marcus Tullius Cicero. [*Selected works — Epistolae*]. Continent: date not determined.

STC 5295 *et seq.* and non-STC. *Language(s)*: Latin. Appraised at 4d in 1614.

160.39 Virgill
Publius Virgilius Maro. Probably [*Works*]. Britain or Continent: date not determined.

STC 24787 *et seq.* and non-STC. Another copy at 160.46. *Language(s)*: Latin (probable) English (perhaps). Appraised at 2d in 1614.

160.40 A service book
Unidentified [liturgy]. Place unknown: stationer unknown, date not determined.

STC/non-STC status unknown. *Language(s)*: Unknown. Appraised at 6d in 1614.

160.41 Mar Maurulus
Marko Marulic. Unidentified. Continent: date not determined. *Language(s)*: Latin. Appraised at 4d in 1614.

160.42:1–3 Granatensis 2. 3. 4. tomi
Luis, *de Granada*. Unidentified. Continent: date not determined.
Several of this author's works were divided into four or more volumes. Many of his works were translated into English and printed in England, but the form of the manuscript entry suggests a Latin edition. See 160.47 for what may be a separated part of the collection here. *Language(s)*: Latin. Appraised at 3s in 1614.

160.43 Testamentum latinum
[*Bible—N.T.*]. Britain or Continent: date not determined.
STC 2799 *et seq.* and non-STC. *Language(s)*: Latin. Appraised at 6d in 1614.

160.44 Clitovii logic
Jodocus Clichtoveus. *Fundamentum logicae*. Continent: date not determined.
An introduction to Aristotle's *Logica*. *Language(s)*: Latin. Appraised at 2d in 1614.

160.45 Seneca his Tragedie
Lucius Annaeus Seneca. Unidentified. Britain or Continent: date not determined.
STC 22221 *et seq.* and non-STC. Either one or all of the *Tragoediae*; appraised price probably suggests one only, as do other probabilities. There seem to be no plays or other works *called* "Seneca" by this date. Languages are based on form of manuscript entry and the multiple possibilities of English versions (all ten plays translated) by this date. *Language(s)*: English (probable) Latin (perhaps). Appraised at 1d in 1614.

160.46 Virgill
Publius Virgilius Maro. Probably [*Works*]. Britain or Continent: date not determined.
STC 24787 *et seq.* and non-STC. Another copy at at 160.39. *Language(s)*: Latin (probable) English (perhaps). Appraised at 2d in 1614.

160.47 Granatensis de doctrina spirituali
Luis, *de Granada*. *De doctrina sive disciplina vitae spiritualis libellus*. Translated from the Spanish by Antonius Dulcken. Cologne: apud Joannem Crithium, 1607.

Perhaps separated from the several volumes at 160.42. *Language(s)*: Latin. Appraised at 4d in 1614.

160.48:1–5   Fyve bookes

Unidentified. Places unknown: stationers unknown, dates not determined.

STC/non-STC status unknown. *Language(s)*: Unknown. Appraised at 6d in 1614.

Thomas Hudson. Scholar (B.A.): Probate Inventory. 1618

RIVES NICHOLSON

Like many of his colleagues at Oxford, Thomas Hudson, a native of Cumberland, is a dim, obscure figure, his academic attainments shaded by poverty, his potential achievements blotted out by illness and early death. He matriculated from Queen's College, Oxford, on 17 January 1612, "aged 18" (*Alumni Oxonienses*, 2:279). Elected "pauper puer," a title that denotes lowly status as a servitor, on 2 July 1615, Hudson received his B.A. later that year on 7 November (Magrath 1921, 1:227n). Two years afterwards he surfaces in a note in the Queen's College records indicating that "50s is allowed to domino Hudson aegrotanti" (Magrath 1921, 1:227), a suggestion of the illness to which he evidently succumbed a short time later. In an inventory of "such goods as we can find of Thomas Hudsons," he is described as "late of queenes college"; the administration of these effects, including the books listed below, was granted on 2 October 1618 (Magrath 1921, 1:227n).

Hudson's small collection of twelve books comprises standard commentaries on Aristotle's *Physica*, *Logica*, and *Physiologiae* by Franciscus Toletus, John Case, and John Magirus respectively and a Greek grammar by Nicolaus Clenardus, as well as a Latin version of Thomas More's *Utopia* and pietistic and controversial works that add a certain tang to the library's generally muted academic flavor. Hudson owned a speech by Sir Edward Coke denouncing official corruption, a work suppressed the day after publication and quickly repudiated by Coke, and the astringent *A counter-snarle for Ishmael Rabshacheh*, a defense of the Puritan divine William Crashaw by Sir Edward Hoby, the soldier, diplomat, and scholar who became a favorite of James VI of Scotland after his mission to that country in 1584. But other religious works in the library by Hieronymus Zanchius (*De operibus Dei intra spacium sex dierum creatis opus*) and Johann Schroeder (*Opusculum theologicum*) are less pungently adversarial, and suggest that Hudson's religious character was likely that of a scholar with contemplative leanings, not that of a firebrand hothead. It is tempting, but probably imprudent, to speculate that the Hoby work, along with *Tractatus de justificatione hominis coram Deo* by Joannes Scharpius, the Presbyterian minister banished by James VI in 1606 for taking part in the general assembly at Aberdeen in 1605, suggests an interest in Scottish political and religious affairs, of which Hudson may have been aware due to his home county's proximity to Scotland.

Oxford University Archives, Bodleian Library: Hyp.B.20.

§

Magrath, John Richard. 1921. *The Queen's College*. 2 vols. Oxford: Clarendon Press.

§

161.1	i English Bible
161.2	Zancheus de operibus dei
161.3	Tollettes Phissiks
161.4	Magerus Physsiks
161.5	Democritus Christianus
161.6	Scroderi opuscula
161.7	Sharpius de justificatione
161.8	Clenards grammar
161.9	Utopiae Tho: mori
161.10:1	the L: Cookes spech a contersnarle for Rabshe
161.10:2	[See 161.10:1]
161.11	And old case logick

§

161.1   i English Bible

The Bible. Britain or Continent: date not determined.

STC 2063 *et seq*. At the valuation, almost certainly a folio edition. *Language(s)*: English. Appraised at 10s in 1618.

161.2   Zancheus de operibus dei

Hieronymus Zanchius. *De operibus Dei intra spacium sex dierum creatis opus*. Continent: 1591–1602.

At the valuation, likely one of the two folio editions from Neustadt an der Haardt printed there in different printing houses. *Language(s)*: Latin. Appraised at 6s in 1618.

161.3 Tollettes Phissiks

Franciscus Toletus, *Cardinal*. [*Aristotle—Physica: commentary*]. Continent: date not determined.
Language(s): Latin. Appraised at 2s 6d in 1618.

161.4 Magerus Physsiks

John Magirus. *Physiologiae peripateticae libri sex*. Continent: 1597–1618.
Language(s): Latin. Appraised at 22d in 1618.

161.5 Democritus Christianus

Pierre de Besse. *Democritus christianus, id est, Contemptus vanitatum mundi*. Translated from the French by Matthias Martinez van Waucquier. Cologne: apud Joannem Kinckium, 1616–1618.
Language(s): Latin. Appraised at 4d in 1618.

161.6 Scroderi opuscula

Johann Schroeder. *Opusculum theologicum*. Schweinfurt: imprimebat Casparus Kemlinus, 1605.
Language(s): Latin. Appraised at 8d in 1618.

161.7 Sharpius de justificatione

Joannes Scharpius. *Tractatus de justificatione hominis coram Deo*. Geneva: (different houses), 1609–1618.
See Shaaber S209–211. *Language(s)*: Latin. Appraised at 4d in 1618.

161.8 Clenards grammar

Nicolaus Clenardus. [*Institutiones linguae graecae*]. Britain or Continent: date not determined.
STC 5400.5 *et seq*. and non-STC. A false start of "Sharpius" is struck out. *Language(s)*: Greek Latin. Appraised at 4d in 1618.

161.9 Utopiae Tho: mori

Sir Thomas More. *Utopia*. Continent: date not determined.
The manuscript entry indicates the Latin original. *Language(s)*: Latin. Appraised at 4d in 1618.

161.10:1 the L: Cookes spech a contersnarle for Rabshe

Sir Edward Coke. *The lord Coke his speech and charge (at the assises of Norwich). With a discoverie and the abuses and corruption of officers*. Edited by Robert Pricket. London: [R. Raworth and N. Okes] for (different houses), 1607.
STC 05491 *et seq*. Actually written by Pricket who supposedly reconstructed it from his memory of Coke's speech. The work was suppressed the day after

publication, and shortly afterwards, Coke repudiated it. Two editions in 1607. *Language(s)*: English. Appraised with one other at 4d in 1618.

161.10:2 [See 161.10:1]

Sir Edward Hoby. *A counter-snarle for Ishmael Rabshacheh*. London: [G. Eld and T. Snodham] for N. Butter, by the authoritie of superiors, 1613.

STC 13539 *et seq*. *Language(s)*: English. Appraised with one other at 4d in 1618.

161.11   And old case logick

John Case. *Summa veterum interpretum in universam dialecticam Aristotelis*. Britain or Continent: 1584–1606.

STC 4762 *et seq*. and non-STC. *Language(s)*: Latin. Appraised at 3d in 1618.

PRIVATE LIBRARIES IN RENAISSANCE ENGLAND 162

Richard Kilby. Scholar (D.Th.):
Inventory (Bequest). 1620

JOSEPH L. BLACK AND R. J. FEHRENBACH

Born in Redcliffe in Leicestershire, Kilby (Kilbye, Kilbie) matriculated from Lincoln College on 20 December 1577 at the age of sixteen and was elected a fellow of the college in January the following year. He received his Bachelor of Arts on 9 December 1578 and his Master of Arts on 2 July 1582. In December 1590 he was appointed rector of Lincoln College. He received the degrees of Bachelor and Doctor of Theology on 7 July 1596, and on 28 September 1601 was installed as prebendary of Lincoln Cathedral. From 1610 until his death a decade later he held Oxford's regius professorship of Hebrew. Kilby was buried in the chancel of All Saints' Church, Oxford, on 7 November 1620 (*ODNB*, *DNB*, *Athenae Oxonienses*, 2:287, *Alumni Oxonienses*, 1:849).

Arguably "the most learned Hebrew scholar Oxford had produced to that date," Kilby was widely respected by contemporaries for his learning. Isaac Casaubon, one of the most learned men of his age, described his acquaintance Kilby approvingly as "a man of some reading beyond the common" (Tyacke 1997, 455). Kilby was best known however not for his own publications, which consist of just one funeral sermon (STC 14957), but for his membership on the team of translators who produced the "Authorized Version" of the Bible commissioned by King James in 1604: he was on the Oxford committee responsible for the text of the Old Testament from Isaiah through to the end of the prophetic books. Izaak Walton tells a story about a sermon Kilby once heard in a parish church in Derbyshire while visiting a friend with his pupil Robert Sanderson (later bishop of Lincoln). The hapless young preacher spent much of his allotted hour taking exceptions against "the late Translation of several words (not expecting such a hearer as Dr. *Kilbie*) and shew'd three Reasons why a particular word should have been otherwise translated." The unsuspecting minister subsequently found himself dining with Kilby that evening, where he was told that he "might have preach'd more useful Doctrine, and not fill'd his Auditors ears with needless Exceptions against the late Translation; and for that word, for which he offered to that poor Congregation three Reasons, why it ought to have been translated, as he said; he and others had considered all them, and found thirteen more considerable Reasons, why it was translated as now printed" (Walton 1678, sig. A7r–v).

Kilby did have plans for other projects: he prepared but never published a continuation of Jean Mercier's commentary on Genesis (*Athenae Oxonienses*, 2:287), and at his death he left a manuscript commentary on Exodus, now in Lincoln College Library, that employed "almost 100 Hebrew sources, many of them rare" (*ODNB*). Some of these sources likely appear in the following booklist, which is not a probate inventory but an inventory made by Kilby himself of a bequest to Lincoln College. Kilby did not give the College his entire library, which would have been larger and more varied than this collection of a little more than forty books. Following the entry for the works of John Chrysostom, Kilby notes that if this book were already in the library, then they did not need his copy (see 162.39). He appears therefore to have selected books he was fairly sure Lincoln did not already have. Many are valuable: Kilby judged his copy of the eight-volume Antwerp Polyglot Bible as worth twenty pounds, and assigned values of eight and five pounds to other multi-volume folio works. (He made only a few valuations of his own: there were no formal appraisals because the books were not being inventoried for probate.) Many, particularly the works in Hebrew, would indeed be rare sources for English scholars, and do not appear elsewhere in the Oxford (PLRE) and Cambridge (BCI) inventories.

The collection consists mainly of editions, commentaries, and reference books, with an emphasis on collected works: a selection of authoritative texts from a serious scholar's working library that he thought would prove useful in an institutional setting. Almost half the books listed here either are in Hebrew or contain some Hebrew: in addition to the Polyglot Bible, Kilby left Lincoln his four-volume *Biblia Rabbinica*, the two-volume Bible annotated by Franciscus Vatablus, the *Midrash Rabbah*, works by Maimonides (probably his *Mishneh Torah* in four volumes), the *Seder 'Olam* edited by Gilbertus Genebrardus, Pietro Galatino's study of the cabbala, commentaries by Levi ben Gershon, Moses Nachmanides, Abraham ben Jacob Saba, and Samuel Jaffe (the *Yepheh mareh*), and Hebrew dictionaries and lexicons by David Kimchi, Nathan ben Jehiel, and others. The other half comprise collected editions, often multi-volume, of works by patristic writers (Chrysostom, Tertullian, Origen, Cyril of Alexandria, Theodoret, Athanasius, Gregory I) and later philosophers and theologians (Gulielmus Parisiensis, Alexander de Ales, Hugo de Sancto Victore, Hugo de Sancto Caro, Stanislaus Hozyusz, Alfonsus Salmeron, Juan Azor, Martin Luther), along with such works as a collection of documents connected with Church Councils and Matthias Flacius's edition of the *Magdeburg Centuries* in eight volumes. The remaining books include an Arabic dictionary and other standard works, usually of reference, by writers such as Paolo Giovio, Domingo de Soto, Matthias Flacius, and Raphael Maffeius. Again, Kilby's complete library would have contained a much wider variety of books: this collection is overwhelmingly theological and contains no works in English (including no English Bibles) or any other vernacular, no dictionaries other than Hebrew and Arabic, almost no controversy or history, no literature, and no classical texts in any field; furthermore, every book was printed abroad.

This inventory poses several difficulties of identification. Kilby's hand is somewhat shaky and he makes extensive use of abbreviations: the manuscript can be difficult to decipher in places. More troublesome is Kilby's habit of using descriptive Latin titles for Hebrew books and his own transliterations of Hebrew names in forms often distant from those used in modern catalogues. In a few cases, identification has been helped by the discovery that some titles in this list are present in Lincoln College Library. The identifications are not definite: the copies of these books in Lincoln appear not to contain any markings that would link them conclusively with Kilby. But the scarcity of these titles, the matched numbers of volumes in some sets, and in two cases the presence of the same separately published works bound together all make it probable that 162.6, 162.7:1–2, 162.10:1, 162.11:1–2, 162.17, and possibly 162.19 are the same books as those currently at Lincoln. None of these books is catalogued electronically, and we would like to thank the Librarian, Fiona Piddock, for her help with these identifications. Other books in Kilby's list seem definitely not to be in the current library: the Library's donors register was unfortunately lost some time ago, so it is not possible to tell how many of these books actually went to Lincoln at his death.

Kilby's library is mentioned in volume 3 of the *History of University of Oxford* (Greenslade 1986, 316–17), and discussed more fully by Mordechai Feingold in volume 4 (1997, 454–55).

Oxford University Archives, Bodleian Library: Hyp.B.20.

§

Feingold, Mordechai. 1997. "Oriental Studies," in *Seventeenth–Century Oxford*, ed. Nicholas Tyacke. Volume 4 of *The History of the University of Oxford*, gen. ed. T.H. Aston. Oxford: Oxford University Press, pp. 449–503.
Greenslade, S.L . 1986. "The Faculty of Theology," in *The Collegiate University*, ed. James McConica. Volume 3 of *The History of the University of Oxford*, gen. ed. T.H. Aston. Oxford: Oxford University Press, pp. 295–334.

§

162.1	Biblia philippi regis hebra: chal: Grec: Lat: in 8. Vol:
162.2	Biblia Venetiana cum Rabbins 4. Vol:
162.3	Moses Maimon 4. Vol:
162.4	dictionarium R. [Rabbi] Nathanis hebraicum 2. Vol

162.5	dictionarium Talmudicum 2. Vol
162.6	Levi ben Gersom in pentateucham 2. Vol.
162.7:1	Explicatio legis quam midrash: Rabba vocant postea ei annectitur in eodem volumine insignis commentator in pentateucham scil: [scilicet] Moses Gerund**
162.7:2	[See 162.7:1]
162.8	R: [Rabbi] Jepha Marrha. diversos tractatus ipsius Talmud explicans.
162.9	liber precum et dimissionum Judaicarum in folio
162.10:1	R: [Rabbi] Seba in pentateucham et ei annectitur R: [Rabbi] Bohoi optimi legis interpres. liber questionum et responsionum legalium Judaicarum in 2: Vol:
162.10:2	[See 162.10:1]
162.11:1	d: Chimghi in psalmos, et eius lib: radicum simul
162.11:2	[See 162.11:1]
162.12	dictionarium hebraicum magnum. 2.
162.13	Opera Lutheri in 8 Vol:
162.14	Centuriatores in 8 Vol:
162.15	Hugo Card: [Cardinalis] in vetus et novum testamentum in 5. vol:
162.16	Azorius in 2. Vol:
162.17	Salmeron in 8 Vol:
162.18	Antoninus in 5. Vol:
162.19	Paulus Jovius in 2. Vol:
162.20	Genebrardi cronal: in uno magno Volumine
162.21	Catalogus testium in uno mag: Vol:
162.22	Omnia Concil in 5. Vol.
162.23	Origines in 2. Vol:
162.24	Cirillius in 2. Vol.
162.25	H: de Sancto Vict: in 3 Vol:
162.26	Opera Stanislaii hosii in uno Vol:
162.27	Biblia Vatabli in 2. Vol:
162.28	Opera Tertulliani in 1. Vol.
162.29	opera Theodoreti in 2. Vol.
162.30	Opera Athanasii 2. Vol.
162.31	dictionarium Arabicum
162.32	Gulielmus parisiensis.
162.33	Alexander de Ales in 4. Vol
162.34	Gregor: magnus
162.35	Volaterranus.
162.36	dominicus Soto de jure et Fide
162.37	Galatinnus de secretis Judeorum
162.38	Index Talmudicus
162.39	Opera cresostosmi in 5. Volm.

§

162.1 Biblia philippi regis hebra: chal: Grec: Lat: in 8. Vol:

Biblia Sacra Hebraice, Chaldaice, Graece, et Latine, Philippi II Reg. (*The Bible*). Edited by Benito Arias Montano. Antwerp: excud. Christoph. Plantin, 1569–1572 (single edition).

Now known as the Antwerp Polyglot, it was produced under the patronage of Philip II of Spain. For a detailed description of this historically notable edition, including notes on the number of copies printed and their selling price, see DM no. 1422. *Language(s)*: Chaldaic Greek Hebrew Latin. Valued at £20 in 1620.

162.2 Biblia Venetiana cum Rabbins 4. Vol:

[*Bible — O.T.*]. Venice: Daniel Bomberg, 1517–1548.

The *Biblia Rabbinica*, it appeared in three folio editions and three quarto editions during the date range given. See DM nos. 5083, 5095, and 5093 for the folio editions, one of which, at the value Kilby gives, is likely represented here. *Language(s)*: Hebrew. Valued at £8 in 1620.

162.3 Moses Maimon 4. Vol:

Moses *ben Maimon* (Maimonides). Probably *Mishneh Torah*. Venice: Alvise Bragadini, 1574–1575 (single edition).

No *opera* of Maimonides was published by 1620. His *Mishneh Torah* published in four volumes by Bragadini would fit the valuation given by Kilby, and that is what is almost certainly cited here. The item could, however, be a collection of Maimonides's individually published works. Adams at M169 gives the dates as 1574–1576. *Language(s)*: Hebrew. Valued at £5 in 1620.

162.4 dictionarium R. [Rabbi] Nathanis hebraicum 2. Vol

Nathan ben Jehiel. [*Lexicon Talmudico-Rabbinico*]. Continent: date not determined.

No two-volume edition has been found; the set listed here may therefore include one of the several supplements or abbreviations published by other writers. The Lincoln College library does own a copy (Basle: Konrad von Waldkirch, 1599, in folio), but there is no evidence, including the notations in Latin and Hebrew in the book, to tie that copy to Kilby. Not valued. *Language(s)*: Aramaic Hebrew.

162.5 dictionarium Talmudicum 2. Vol

Unidentified [dictionary]. Continent: date not determined.

Possibilities include Talmudic dictionaries in various languages by Sanctes Pagninus and by Elijah Levita, as well as another copy of the preceding by

Nathan ben Jehiel. Not valued. *Language(s)*: Hebrew (probable) Aramaic (perhaps) Latin (perhaps).

162.6   Levi ben Gersom in pentateucham 2. Vol.

Levi ben Gershon. *Perush 'al hat-Torah*. Venice: [Daniel Bomberg], 1547.

A Venice, 1547 edition of this commentary on the Pentateuch was published in two folio volumes; Lincoln College owns one volume of that edition, and it may be a remaining book of the set Kilby gave the college. The title transliterated from the Hebrew and the publication information provided come from that edition. Not valued. *Language(s)*: Hebrew. *Current location*: Lincoln College, Oxford (probable).

162.7:1   Explicatio legis quam midrash: Rabba vocant postea ei annectitur in eodem volumine insignis commentator in pentateucham scil: [scilicet] Moses Gerund**

Midrash Rabbah. Continent: date not determined.

"The Great Midrash," or a collection of a number of commentaries on books of the Old Testament. This and the following are bound together in the Lincoln College library as Kilby's copies were and may be the books that Kilby gave to the college. A third work, however, is now bound with them at Lincoln. Not valued. *Language(s)*: Hebrew Aramaic (probable). *Current location*: Lincoln College, Oxford (perhaps).

162.7:2   [See 162.7:1]

Moses Nachmanides (Moses Gerund). [*Pentateuch: commentary*]. Continent: date not determined.

Editions from as early as 1469. See Goff Heb8689. See the preceding for the possibility that this is the copy Kilby gave to Lincoln College. Not valued. *Language(s)*: Hebrew. *Current location*: Lincoln College, Oxford (perhaps).

162.8   R: [Rabbi] Jepha Marrha. diversos tractatus ipsius Talmud explicans.

Samuel Jaffe, *ben Isaac Ashkenazy. Yepheh mareh*. Continent: 1587–1590.

Aggadic portions of the Palestinian Talmud with commentary by Jaffe. Not valued. *Language(s)*: Hebrew. *Current location*: Lincoln College, Oxford (probable).

162.9   liber precum et dimissionum Judaicarum in folio

Unidentified. Continent: date not determined.

Probably either a liturgy or a prayer book, neither of which was published in England by the date of Kilby's list. Not valued. *Language(s)*: Hebrew.

162.10:1   R: [Rabbi] Seba in pentateucham et ei annectitur R: [Rabbi] Bohoi optimi legis interpres. liber questionum et responsionum legalium Judaicarum in 2: Vol:
Abraham ben Jacob Saba. [*Pentateuch: commentary*]. Continent: 1522–1595.
A 1546 Venice edition of this cabbalistic commentary is in the Lincoln library bound with a copy of Bahya ben Asher's commentary on the Pentateuch. Although a reading of the manuscript entry might allow for a work by Bahya ben Asher, the second work is not described as a commentary on the Pentateuch. There is no internal evidence to confirm that either book was Kilby's. Conceivably three works are listed, not two. Not valued. *Language(s)*: Hebrew.

162.10:2   [See 162.10:1]
Unidentified. Continent: date not determined.
See the annotation to 162.10:1, particularly the observation that three works rather than two might be represented here. Not valued. *Language(s)*: Hebrew.

162.11:1   d: Chimghi in psalmos, et eius lib: radicum simul
[*Bible — O.T. — Psalms*]. Commentary by David Kimchi. Isny: (stationer not given), 1542.
This work is in the Lincoln College library bound with the next. Though there is no evidence to connect it with Kilby, the assumption is that these works, bound in one, are the books that Kilby describes in the same manner that he gave to Lincoln. See CLC B1317 and Adams B1352–53, where the dates are given as 1541, 1542. Not valued. *Language(s)*: Hebrew. *Current location*: Lincoln College, Oxford (probable).

162.11:2   [See 162.11:1]
David Kimchi. *Sefer hash-shorashim*. Venice: Marcantonio Giustiniani, 1546.
Commonly referred to as a Hebrew "Book of Roots" or "Liber radicum." The title is transliterated from the Hebrew. See the annotation to 162.11:1. Not valued. *Language(s)*: Hebrew. *Current location*: Lincoln College, Oxford (probable).

162.12   dictionarium hebraicum magnum. 2.
Unidentified [dictionary]. Continent: date not determined.
Not valued. *Language(s)*: Hebrew Latin (probable).

162.13   Opera Lutheri in 8 Vol:
Martin Luther. [*Works*]. Continent: date not determined.
There were several editions of Luther's *opera* issued in seven volumes; if this is such a set, then another of his works is here included by Kilby. Not valued. *Language(s)*: Latin.

162.14 Centuriatores in 8 Vol:

Matthias Flacius, *Illyricus* (editor). *Ecclesiastica historia*. (*Magdeburg centuriators*). Basle: Joannes Oporinus, 1559–1574.

Johann Hervagius or his heirs played an occasional role in the publication of the many volumes. Not valued. *Language(s)*: Latin.

162.15 Hugo Card: [Cardinalis] in vetus et novum testamentum in 5. vol:

Hugo, *de Sancto Caro*. [*Postilla*]. (*The Bible*). Continent: 1504–1600.

With the text. Most likely the 1600 edition, which bore the title *Opera omnia in universum Vetus et Novum Testamentum*, published in eight volumes, but there were other editions from at least 1504 published in multi-volume sets. Not valued. *Language(s)*: Latin.

162.16 Azorius in 2. Vol:

Juan Azor. *Institutiones morales*. Continent: date not determined.

Published in several multi-volume editions from 1586. Not valued. *Language(s)*: Latin.

162.17 Salmeron in 8 Vol:

Alfonsus Salmeron. *Commentarii in Evangelicam historiam, et in Acta Apostolorum*. Cologne: apud Antonium Hierat, et Joan. Gymni[cum], 1602–1604 (single edition).

This edition, in sixteen volumes in eight, is in the Lincoln College library. According to the librarian, Fiona Piddock, on the endpaper of the first volume there are various illegible words followed by "Salmeron 8 tomis" with no other markings in the other volumes. Though this in itself is not evidence that this set is Kilby's, no other copy of Salmeron in eight volumes is in the Lincoln College library. Not valued. *Language(s)*: Latin. *Current location*: Lincoln College, Oxford (probable).

162.18 Antoninus in 5. Vol:

Unidentified. Continent: date not determined.

Several possible authors, including: Antoninus, *Archbishop of Florence*; Antoninus, *Augustus*; Antoninus, *Liberalis*; even Marcus Aurelius Antoninus, though the last would probably not be entered in this manner. Some of the works by the first named did appear in multiple volumes. Not valued. *Language(s)*: Latin.

162.19 Paulus Jovius in 2. Vol:

Paolo Giovio, *Bishop*. Unidentified. Continent: date not determined.

His widely published *Historiarum sui temporis* is a good possibility, especially since it appeared in multiple volumes, but given the large number of Giovio's works, these two volumes could easily be two different titles. In that regard, Giovio's *Elogia vivorum literis illustrium* (Basle, 1577) and his *Opera quotquot extant omnia* (Basle, 1578) are in the library of Lincoln College, but there is no evidence to connect them with Kilby, though they may be the two Giovio works Kilby bequeathed to Lincoln. Not valued. *Language(s)*: Latin.

162.20   Genebrardi cronal: in uno magno Volumine

Chronologia hebraeorum major. (Seder 'Olam). Translated by Gilbertus Genebrardus, *Archbishop*. Continent: date not determined.

Only a few editions were published in folio, the format indicated by the manuscript entry; the larger volumes were among the later issues, particularly those issued in the seventeenth century. Because the volume is described as "magno," Genebrardus's *Chronographia*, always published in folio and with the similar titular word, must be considered, but given the spelling of "cron*al*" in the manuscript entry, that work is an unlikely possibility. Not valued. *Language(s)*: Hebrew Latin.

162.21   Catalogus testium in uno mag: Vol:

Matthias Flacius, *Illyricus. Catalogus testium veritatis.* Continent: 1562–1608.

The date range includes folio editions only as indicated by "magno" in the manuscript entry. Not valued. *Language(s)*: Latin.

162.22   Omnia Concil in 5. Vol.

Concilia omnia tam generalia quam particularia. (Councils of the Church). Continent: date not determined.

See Adams C2773 (1585) for an edition published in five volumes. What is here, however, may be five volumes collected from smaller sets. Not valued. *Language(s)*: Latin.

162.23   Origines in 2. Vol:

Origen. [*Works*]. Continent: date not determined.
Not valued. *Language(s)*: Latin.

162.24   Cirillius in 2. Vol.

Cyril, *of Alexandria, Saint*. Probably [*Works*]. Continent: date not determined

Not only was Cyril, *of Alexandria* more widely published than Cyril, *of Jerusalem* but nothing of the latter's seems to have been published in two volumes. The former's commentary on the Gospel of John was published in two volumes, but his *opera*, always published in multiple volumes, and sometimes in two, would more likely be intended here. Not valued. *Language(s)*: Latin.

162.25   H: de Sancto Vict: in 3 Vol:

Hugo, *de Sancto Victore*. [*Works*]. Continent: 1526–1617.

The date range includes three-volume editions only, all in folio. Not valued. *Language(s)*: Latin.

162.26   Opera Stanislaii hosii in uno Vol:

Stanislaus Hozyusz, *Cardinal*. [*Works*]. Continent: 1562–1584. Struck through. *Language(s)*: Latin.

162.27   Biblia Vatabli in 2. Vol:

The Bible. Annotated by Franciscus Vatablus. Heidelberg: ex officina Commeliniana, 1599–1616.

A 1587 edition did not include the New Testament but there is no indication of that omission on the title page. All editions were published in two volumes. See DM no. 1424. Not valued. *Language(s)*: Greek Hebrew Latin.

162.28   Opera Tertulliani in 1. Vol.

Quintus Tertullianus. [*Works*]. Continent: date not determined. Not valued. *Language(s)*: Latin.

162.29   opera Theodoreti in 2. Vol.

Theodoret, *Bishop*. [*Works*]. Continent: 1567–1617.

All editions published in two volumes, though the 1617 edition was issued as two volumes in one. Not valued. *Language(s)*: Latin.

162.30   Opera Athanasii 2. Vol.

Athanasius, *Saint*. [*Works*]. Continent: date not determined. Not valued. *Language(s)*: Latin Greek (perhaps).

162.31   dictionarium Arabicum

Unidentified [dictionary]. Continent: date not determined. Not valued. *Language(s)*: Arabic Latin (probable).

162.32   Gulielmus parisiensis.

Gulielmus, *Parisiensis, Professor*. [*Gospels and Epistles (liturgical): commentary and text*]. Continent: date not determined.

That this would be anything other than his repeatedly published *Postilla* is extremely unlikely. Goff gives over sixty editions in the fifteenth century alone. Not valued. *Language(s)*: Latin.

162.33   Alexander de Ales in 4. Vol

Alexander, *de Ales*. *Summa universae theologiae*. Continent: 1481–1576.

Not only his major work, but also published in four-volume editions; see Shaaber A197–A200. Not valued. *Language(s)*: Latin.

162.34 Gregor: magnus

Gregory I, *Saint, Pope*. Probably [*Works*]. Continent: date not determined. Not valued. *Language(s)*: Latin.

162.35 Volaterranus.

Raphael Maffeius, *Volaterranus*. Probably *Commentariorum urbanorum octo et triginta libri*. Continent: date not determined.

A vast encyclopedia on a wide range of subjects, this is his most often published work with at least a dozen editions before the date of this inventory. His collected *Works* is possible but less likely. Not valued. *Language(s)*: Latin.

162.36 dominicus Soto de jure et Fide

Domingo de Soto. *De justitia et jure libri decem*. Continent: date not determined.

The word "fide" appears deep in the long title. Not valued. *Language(s)*: Latin.

162.37 Galatinnus de secretis Judeorum

Pietro Galatino (Petrus Columna, *Galatinus*). *Opus de arcanis catholicae veritatis*. Continent: 1518–1612.

Later editions appeared in a composite volume with Johann Reuchlin's *De arte cabalistica libri tres* whom Galatino defended in this work in dialogue form. Not valued. *Language(s)*: Hebrew Latin.

162.38 Index Talmudicus

Talmud (index). Continent: date not determined.
Not valued. *Language(s)*: Hebrew.

162.39 Opera cresostosmi in 5. Volm.

John, *Chrysostom, Saint*. [*Works*]. Continent: date not determined.

Following this manuscript entry, Kilby writes: "if opera crisostome be **** in the librarie then the[y] neide not myne." Not valued. *Language(s)*: Latin.

John Read. Manciple:
Probate Inventory. 1623

RIVES NICHOLSON

Virtually nothing can be said about John Read (Rede, Reed) except that he was manciple of Lincoln College, and that he died sometime before the end of March, 1623. Recorded on 30 March 1623 by stationer Dion Edwards and Richard Read, perhaps a relative, the inventory of Read's possessions is short on books and long on items of apparel rather more sumptuous than the clothing that a scholar at Oxford and Cambridge tended to possess.

The slim contents of his library — an English Bible, a jumble of "divers prayer bookes," and other unidentified works, probably devotional in nature — suggest that his concern with the things of the mind and the spirit was perfunctory, as perhaps befits a man charged with the prosaic business of filling scholars' stomachs rather than nourishing their intellects. Indeed, the valuation of those books at 10*s* was woefully meager when compared with the appraisal of £11 10*s* assigned to four "cloakes" and four "sutes of Apparell," just a portion of his clothing.

Oxford University Archives, Bodleian Library: Hyp.B.18.

§

163.1:1   a bible, divers prayer bookes, with other smale bookes
163.1:2 multiple   [See 163.1:1]
163.1:3 multiple   [See 163.1:1]

§

163.1:1   **a bible, divers prayer bookes, with other smale bookes**
   The Bible. Britain or Continent: date not determined.

STC 02063 *et seq*. In the third decade of the seventeenth century, a layman's Bible would have been in English, not Latin. *Language(s)*: English. Appraised with two other groups of books at 10s in 1623.

163.1:2 multiple [See 163.1:1]

Unidentified. Places unknown: stationers unknown, dates not determined.

STC/non-STC status unknown. Likely service books rather than meditations. *Language(s)*: English (probable). Appraised with one other book and one other group of books at 10s in 1623.

163.1:3 multiple [See 163.1:1]

Unidentified. Places unknown: stationers unknown, dates not determined.

STC/non-STC status unknown. *Language(s)*: English (probable). Appraised with one other book and one other group of books at 10s in 1623.

PRIVATE LIBRARIES IN RENAISSANCE ENGLAND 164

Anonymous. Scholar (Probable):
Inventory. c.1650

WILLIAM M. ABBOTT

There is little that we can conclude with certainty about this anonymous scholar. According to Simon Bailey, Archivist of Oxford University, we can assume that the inventory of the scholar's more than seventy books was made "under the authority of the Vice-Chancellor and the Chancellor's court, although not necessarily as part of probate; it may have been part of some other proceedings (e.g. debt)." The books, most of which were appraised, were treated as inventoried personal property. The inventory cannot be earlier than 1640, as Brerewood on Aristotle's *Ethica* (164.16) is the first and only edition. The form of the appraisal entries, however, together with the resemblance of the handwriting to that of two other inventories dated 1652, suggest that this inventory could be some years later than 1640, and 1650 therefore appears a reasonable approximate date for it.

Owning over thirty works by ancient Roman or Greek authors, together with more than a dozen dictionaries, grammars, or rhetorical guides, and a number of Renaissance-era commentaries on ancient authors (mostly on Aristotle), this anonymous Oxford scholar was a thoroughgoing classicist whose interests would appear to have focused primarily on Rome. Included in his list are Terence, Cicero, Cornelius Nepos, Sallust, Virgil, Horace, Ovid, Seneca, Valerius Maximus, Quintilian, Tacitus, Pliny, *the Younger,* Juvenal, Suetonius, Lucius Annaeus Florus, Herodian, and Claudianus. The list includes Aristotle's *Ethics, Organon,* and *Physics,* although most of these works, like the commentaries on Aristotle, are in Latin. To judge from the several Greek-Latin dictionaries, this scholar read Greek, but the only other Greek authors in his list besides Aristotle and Herodian are Aesop, Sophocles, and Isocrates. Other texts in this collection include Aquinas's *Summa theologica,* a Greek New Testament, Erasmus's *Adagia,* and several works on logic.

That he could live through so tumultuous an era as the 1630s and 1640s and not include in his collection even one of the many controversial tracts produced during these decades suggests an apolitical nature. Like the great majority of English people during these decades of shifting political fortunes, however, he may simply have been prudent rather than politically disengaged.

Oxford University Archives, Bodleian Library: Hyp.B.10.

§

164.1	Perotti Cornucopia
164.2	Virgilius cum Comment
164.3	Erasmi Adagia
164.4	Aquinatis Summa
164.5	Crispini Lexicon glat.
164.6	Riders Dictionary old
164.7	The Atticke Antiquit.
164.8	Hispani Logica
164.9	Terence English
164.10	Tacitus English fol.
164.11	Jullius Pollux glat.
164.12	Lubinus in Juven:
164.13	Casi Politica
164.14	Gulsoni Rhetorica glat.
164.15	Holyokes Dictionary
164.16	Brerewood Ethic:
164.17	Buridani Ethica
164.18	Conimbrisiensis imperfect
164.19	Ruvii Logica
164.20	Pacii C*ment in Arist. Organon glat. 4° 2 vol.
164.21	Dictionarium Poeticum
164.22	Jewish & Rom: Antiqu:
164.23	Herodianus glat.
164.24	Senecae Opera 8°
164.25	Natalis Comes
164.26	Piccolominei Ethica
164.27	Pacii Phisica
164.28	Scoti Gram: Graec.
164.29	Rulandi Synonima grae:
164.30:1	2 Greeke Testaments 8°
164.30:2	[See 164.30:1]
164.31	Virgilius
164.32	Horacius
164.33	Quintilianus
164.34	Clavis l. graec:

164.35	Textoris Epithet:
164.36	Juvenall
164.37	Camdeni Gram: graec:
164.38	Susenbrotus Rheth:
164.39	Manutii Epistolae
164.40	Salustius
164.41	AEsopi Fabulae
164.42	Sophoclis graec:
164.43	Scheibleri Compend:
164.44	Ovid de tristibus
164.45	Pacius in Arist: de Anima gl:
164.46	Bertii Logica
164.47	Molinaei Logica
164.48	Clavis Homerica
164.49	Silva Synonimorum
164.50	Ruseneri Symbolum
164.51	Heinsii Orationes
164.52	Terence
164.53	Ovids Epistles
164.54	Isocratis 3s [tres] orat.
164.55:1	2 Magiri Ethica glat.
164.55:2	[See 164.55:1]
164.56	2 volumes of Tulls Orat:
164.57	Casi Logica
164.58	Scaliger de caus: l. lat:
164.59	Ovidii Metaphors:
164.60	Casi Ethica
164.61	AEmilius Probus
164.62	Plinii Eplae [Epistolae]
164.63	Formulae Orator:
164.64	Tacitus
164.65	Florus
164.66	Suetonius
164.67	Tull: Sentent:
164.68	Claudianus
164.69	Val. Maximus
164.70	Luciani Dialog:
164.71	Smiths Log:
164.72	Brerew: Elementa Log:

§

164.1 Perotti Cornucopia

Nicolaus Perottus. *Cornucopia*. Continent: date not determined. *Language(s)*: Latin. Appraised at 1s in c.1650.

164.2 Virgilius cum Comment

Publius Virgilius Maro. Probably [*Works*]. Britain or Continent: date not determined.

STC 24788 *et seq.* and non-STC *Language(s)*: Latin. Appraised at 1s 6d in c.1650.

164.3 Erasmi Adagia

Desiderius Erasmus. *Adagia*. Britain or Continent: date not determined.

STC 10437 *et seq.* and non-STC. *Language(s)*: Latin. Appraised at 4s 6d in c.1650.

164.4 Aquinatis Summa

Thomas Aquinas, *Saint*. *Summa theologica*. Continent: date not determined. *Language(s)*: Latin. Appraised at 6s in c.1650.

164.5 Crispini Lexicon glat.

Jean Crespin. *Lexicon graecolatinum*. Britain or Continent: 1566–1615.

STC 6037 and non-STC. *Language(s)*: Greek Latin. Appraised at 1s in c.1650.

164.6 Riders Dictionary old

John Rider, *Bishop*. *Bibliotheca scholastica*. Britain: 1589–1649.

STC 21031.5 *et seq.* and Wing R1442 *et seq.* For the relationship of this dictionary, represented here by the title of its *editio princeps*, to the *Dictionarium etymologicum latinum*, also in this collection (164.15), see Starnes (239–71). There Starnes describes the process whereby Rider's dictionary became a Rider-Holyoke dictionary. The first edition to carry the title *Riders dictionarie* was issued in 1606; the manuscript entry, however, may be descriptive, which, additionally, renders the meaning of "old" by the compiler as uncertain. Not appraised. *Language(s)*: English Latin.

164.7 The Atticke Antiquit.

Francis Rous, *the Younger*. *Archaeologiae Atticae libri tres. Three bookes of the Attick antiquities*. Britain: 1637–1649.

STC 21350 and Wing R2032 *et seq. Language(s)*: English. Appraised at 4d in c.1650.

164.8 Hispani Logica
John XXI, *Pope* (Petrus, *Hispanus*). [*Summulae logicales*]. Continent: date not determined.
Not appraised. *Language(s)*: Latin.

164.9 Terence English
Publius Terentius, *Afer.* [*Works*]. Britain: 1598–1641.
STC 23894 *et seq.* and Wing T751. Conceivably one of the several editions of individual plays or selected works in English and Latin, but the date range represents the entire *opera*. Wing T751 (1641) carries at the top of the title page *Terence in English*, not unlike the manuscript entry. *Language(s)*: English Latin. Appraised at 10d in c.1650.

164.10 Tacitus English fol.
Publius Cornelius Tacitus. [*Works*]. Britain: 1591–1640.
STC 23642 *et seq.* The works in the several editions vary. See 164.64 for another "Tacitus," assumed to be a Latin edition since it is not identified as being in English as is this one. *Language(s)*: English. Appraised at 3s in c.1650.

164.11 Jullius Pollux glat.
Julius Pollux. *Onomasticon*. Continent: date not determined.
Language(s): Greek Latin. Appraised at 2s 6d in c.1650.

164.12 Lubinus in Juven:
Eilhard Lubin. *In D.J. Juvenalis satyrarum libros Ecphrasis succinta et perspicua*. Rostock: in typographica S. Myliandri, 1602.
One of the editions of Juvenal or one of the joint editions of Juvenal and Persius with commentary by Lubin is possible. *Language(s)*: Latin. Appraised at 2s in c.1650.

164.13 Casi Politica
John Case. *Sphaera civitatis*. Britain or Continent: 1588–1616.
STC 4761 and non-STC. See Shaaber C150–154. *Language(s)*: Latin. Appraised at 1s 4d in c.1650.

164.14 Gulsoni Rhetorica glat.
Aristotle. *Rhetorica*. Edited by Theodore Goulston. London: typis E. Griffini, 1619.
STC 766. *Language(s)*: Greek Latin. Appraised at 1s 4d in c.1650.

164.15 Holyokes Dictionary
Francis Holyoke. *Dictionarium etymologicum latinum*. Britain: 1627–1648.

STC 13619.5 *et seq.* and Wing H2534A. See the annotation to 164.6. *Language(s)*: English Latin. Appraised at 5s in c.1650.

164.16   Brerewood Ethic:

Edward Brerewood. *Tractatus ethici sive commentarii in aliquot Aristotelis libros ad Nichomachum, de moribus.* Oxford: G. Turner, imp. E. Forrest, 1640.

STC 3627. The publication date of this book provides the *terminus a quo* of this book-list. *Language(s)*: Latin. Appraised at 10d in c.1650.

164.17   Buridani Ethica

Joannes Buridanus. [*Aristotle—Ethica: commentary*]. Britain or Continent: date not determined.

STC 4119 and non-STC. Surely the 1637 Oxford edition is more likely than the Paris editions issued between 1489 and 1518. *Language(s)*: Latin. Appraised at 3s in c.1650.

164.18   Conimbrisiensis imperfect

[*Aristotle—Unidentified: commentary*]. (*Coimbra. Collegium Societatis Jesu*). Continent: date not determined.

See Lohr II: 9899. Not appraised. *Language(s)*: Latin Greek (probable).

164.19   Ruvii Logica

Antonio Rubio. [*Aristotle—Organon: commentary*]. Britain or Continent: date not determined.

Wing R2400A and non-STC. *Language(s)*: Latin. Appraised at 1s 6d in 1650c

164.20   Pacii C*ment in Arist. Organon glat. 4° 2 vol.

Julius Pacius. Probably [*Aristotle—Organon: commentary*]. Continent: date not determined.

The difficulty is determining whether this is Pacius's commentary alone or Pacius's edition of Aristotle with commentary. The format designation and number of volumes supplied in the manuscript entry only complicates that determination. The 1597 edition published in England (STC 19083) is a duodecimo single volume in Latin only. *Language(s)*: Greek Latin. Appraised at 3s 6d in c.1650.

164.21   Dictionarium Poeticum

Charles Estienne. [*Dictionarium historicum ac poeticum*]. Continent: date not determined.

Language(s): Latin. Appraised at 1s 8d in c.1650.

164.22   Jewish & Rom: Antiqu:

Unidentified. Place unknown: stationer unknown, date not determined.

STC/non-STC status unknown. Perhaps a combination of Thomas Godwin's works, in English or Latin: see PLRE 165.93:1–2 For a similarly worded entry that specifies Godwin as author. Perhaps two works listed together, one Jewish antiquities (by, e.g., Josephus or Benito Arias Montano), the other on Roman antiquities (by, e.g., Dionysius, *of Halicarnassus*). *Language(s)*: Latin (probable). Appraised at 1s 8d in c.1650.

164.23   Herodianus glat.

Herodian. [*Historiae*]. Britain or Continent: date not determined.

STC 13220 and non-STC. *Language(s)*: Greek Latin. Appraised at 8d in c.1650.

164.24   Senecae Opera 8°

Lucius Annaeus Seneca. [*Works*]. Continent: date not determined.

Editions published in England are folio. *Language(s)*: Latin. Appraised at 1s 8d in c.1650.

164.25   Natalis Comes

Natalis Comes. Unidentified. Continent: date not determined.

The appraisal appears to have been altered from 1s 8d to 1s 6d. *Language(s)*: Latin. Appraised at 1s 6d in c.1650.

164.26   Piccolominei Ethica

Francisco Piccolomini. *Universa philosophia de moribus*. Continent: 1583–1627.

Language(s): Latin. Appraised at 10d in c.1650.

164.27   Pacii Phisica

Julius Pacius. [*Aristotle — Physica: commentary*]. Continent: 1596–1629.

The manuscript entry *Pacii in Arist Phis:* appears earlier in the inventory (between 164.16 and 164.17) and is struck out. *Language(s)*: Greek Latin. Appraised at 1s in c.1650.

164.28   Scoti Gram: Graec.

Alexander Scot. *Universa grammatica graeca*. Continent: 1593–1614.

Shaaber S6470. *Language(s)*: Greek Latin (perhaps). Appraised at 2s in c.1650.

164.29   Rulandi Synonima grae:

Martin Ruland, *the Elder*. *Synonyma*. Continent: date not determined. Not appraised. *Language(s)*: Greek Latin.

164.30:1 2 Greeke Testaments 8°

[*Bible—N.T.*]. Britain or Continent: date not determined.

STC 2795 *et seq.* and non-STC. *Language(s)*: Greek. Appraised with one other at 4s in c.1650.

164.30:2 [See 164.30:1]

[*Bible—N.T.*]. Britain or Continent: date not determined.

STC 2795 *et seq.* and non-STC. *Language(s)*: Greek. Appraised with one other at 4s in c.1650.

164.31   Virgilius

Publius Virgilius Maro. Probably [*Works*]. Britain or Continent: date not determined.

STC 24787 *et seq.*, Wing V599, and non-STC. Not appraised. *Language(s)*: Latin.

164.32   Horacius

Quintus Horatius Flaccus. [*Works*]. Britain or Continent: date not determined.

STC 13784 *et seq.* and non-STC. Not appraised. *Language(s)*: Latin.

164.33   Quintilianus

Marcus Fabius Quintilianus. Unidentified. Place unknown: stationer unknown, date not determined.

STC/non-STC status unknown. Either the *Declamationes* or, perhaps more likely, the *Institutiones oratoriae*, given that the sole work of Quinitilian issued from an English press were two editions of the *Institutiones* (1629 and 1641). The complete works, of course, is also possible. *Language(s)*: Latin. Appraised at 1s 4d in c.1650.

164.34   Clavis l. graec:

Eilhard Lubin. *Clavis graecae linguae*. Britain or Continent: date not determined.

STC 16879 *et seq.*, Wing L3386, and non-STC. *Language(s)*: Greek Latin. Appraised at 2d in c.1650.

164.35   Textoris Epithet:

Joannes Ravisius (Textor). *Epitheta*. Continent (probable): date not determined.

Probably not an STC book, but see STC 20762.5 *et seq.* An epitome was published in England, which this item may be. Not appraised. *Language(s)*: Latin.

164.36 Juvenall
Decimus Junius Juvenalis. [*Works*]. Britain or Continent: date not determined.
STC 14889 *et seq.*, Wing J1282, and non-STC. *Language(s)*: Latin. Appraised at 2d in c.1650.

164.37 Camdeni Gram: graec:
William Camden. *Institutio Graecae grammatices compendiaria, in usum regiae scholae Westmonasteriensis*. Britain or Continent: 1595–1650.
STC 4511 *et seq.*, Wing C365 *et seq.*, and non-STC. See Shaaber C25. *Language(s)*: Greek Latin. Appraised at 2d in c.1650.

164.38 Susenbrotus Rheth:
Joannes Susenbrotus. *Epitome troporum ac schematum*. Britain or Continent: date not determined.
STC 23437 *et seq.* and non-STC. Not appraised. *Language(s)*: Latin.

164.39 Manutii Epistolae
Paolo Manuzio. [*Epistolae*]. Britain or Continent: date not determined.
STC 17286 *et seq.* and non-STC. Not appraised. *Language(s)*: Latin.

164.40 Salustius
Caius Sallustius Crispus. Unidentified. Place unknown: stationer unknown, date not determined.
STC/non-STC status unknown. *Language(s)*: Latin. Appraised at 2d in c.1650.

164.41 AEsopi Fabulae
Aesop. *Fabulae*. Britain or Continent: date not determined.
STC 168 *et seq.*, Wing A711A *et seq.*, and non-STC. Not appraised. *Language(s)*: Latin (probable) Greek (perhaps).

164.42 Sophoclis graec:
Sophocles. [*Works*]. Continent: date not determined.
Language(s): Greek. Appraised at 4d in c.1650.

164.43 Scheibleri Compend:
Christoph Scheibler. *Philosophia compendiosa, seu philosophiae synopsis*. Britain or Continent: 1618–1647.
STC 21814 *et seq.*, Wing S854, and non-STC. *Language(s)*: Latin. Appraised at 3d in c.1650.

164.44 Ovid de tristibus
Publius Ovidius Naso. *Tristia*. Britain or Continent: date not determined. STC 18976.4 *et seq.* and non-STC. Not appraised. *Language(s)*: Latin.

164.45 Pacius in Arist: de Anima gl:
Julius Pacius. [*Aristotle—De anima: commentary*]. Continent: 1596–1621. *Language(s)*: Greek Latin. Appraised at 8d in c.1650.

164.46 Bertii Logica
Pierre Bertius. *Logicae peripateticae libri sex*. Continent: 1604–1636. *Language(s)*: Latin. Appraised at 4d in c.1650.

164.47 Molinaei Logica
Pierre Du Moulin, *the Elder*. *Elementa logica*. Britain or Continent: 1596–1638.
Not appraised. *Language(s)*: Latin.

164.48 Clavis Homerica
Antonius Roberti. *Clavis Homerica, reserans significationes, etymologias, derivationes*. Britain or Continent: 1636–1649.
STC 21072a, Wing R1573, and non-STC. The second edition (1638) was revised by George Perkins, and the 1649 edition bore his name alone. *Language(s)*: Greek Latin. Appraised at 10d in c.1650.

164.49 Silva Synonimorum
Simon Pelegromius. *Synonymorum sylva*. London: (different houses), 1580–1650.
STC 19556 *et seq.* and Wing P1067. Not appraised. *Language(s)*: English Latin.

164.50 Ruseneri Symbolum
Nicolaus Reusner. Probably [*Symbolii imperatorii*]. Britain or Continent: 1588–1650.
STC 20907 *et seq.*, Wing R1188, and non-STC. This work discusses the Roman emperors. A less likely possibility is Reusner's *Symbolorum heroicorum* which treats the iconography of the Holy Roman Emperors and, unlike the work identified here, had limited publication (Jena, 1608). Wing R1188 (1650) carried the unique title *Symbolae heroicae*, and therefore is not likely the item listed here. *Language(s)*: Latin. Appraised at 4d in c.1650.

164.51 Heinsii Orationes
Daniel Heinsius. *Orationes*. Leyden: (different houses), 1612–1642. *Language(s)*: Latin. Appraised at 10d in c.1650.

164.52 Terence
Publius Terentius, *Afer.* [*Works*]. Britain or Continent: date not determined. STC 23885 *et seq.*, Wing T729 *et seq.*, and non-STC. Not appraised. *Language(s)*: Latin.

164.53 Ovids Epistles
Publius Ovidius Naso. [*Heroides*]. London: (different houses), 1567–1639. STC 18939.5 *et seq.* A Latin edition cannot be excluded as a possibility. Not appraised. *Language(s)*: English Latin (perhaps).

164.54 Isocratis 3s [tres] orat.
Isocrates. [*Selected works—Orations*]. Britain or Continent: date not determined.
STC 14274 and non-STC. Not appraised. *Language(s)*: Greek (probable) Latin (probable).

164.55:1 2 Magiri Ethica glat.
John Magirus. [*Aristotle—Ethica: commentary*]. Frankfurt am Main: (different houses), 1601–1628.
The first of two copies. *Language(s)*: Greek Latin. Appraised with one other at 3s in c.1650.

164.55:2 [See 164.55:1]
John Magirus. [*Aristotle—Ethica: commentary*]. Frankfurt am Main: (different houses), 16011628.
The second of two copies. *Language(s)*: Greek Latin. Appraised with one other at 3s in c.1650.

164.56 2 volumes of Tulls Orat:
Marcus Tullius Cicero. [*Selected works—Orations*]. Britain or Continent: date not determined.
STC 5308 *et seq.* and non-STC. Not appraised. *Language(s)*: Latin.

164.57 Casi Logica
John Case. *Summa veterum interpretum in universam dialecticam Aristotelis.* Britain or Continent: 1584–1622.
STC 4762 *et seq.* and non-STC. See Shaaber C155–C157. Not appraised. *Language(s)*: Latin.

164.58 Scaliger de caus: l. lat:
Julius Caesar Scaliger. *De causis linguae latinae libri tredecim.* Continent: date not determined.
Language(s): Latin. Appraised at 10d in c.1650.

164.59 Ovidii Metaphors:
Publius Ovidius Naso. *Metamorphoses*. Britain or Continent: date not determined.
STC 18951 *et seq.*, Wing O680, and non-STC. Not appraised. *Language(s)*: Latin.

164.60 Casi Ethica
John Case. *Speculum moralium quaestionum in universam Ethicen*. Britain or Continent: 1585–1625.
STC 4759 *et seq.* and non-STC. A duplicate of this manuscript entry appears earlier in the inventory (between 164.5 and 164.6), which is struck out. See Shaaber C142–C149. *Language(s)*: Latin. Appraised at 8d in c.1650.

164.61 AEmilius Probus
Cornelius Nepos (Nepotis). *Aemilii Probi vitae excellentium imperatorum*. Continent: date not determined.
Language(s): Latin. Appraised at 3d in c.1650.

164.62 Plinii Eplae [Epistolae]
Pliny, *the Younger. Epistolae*. Continent: date not determined.
Language(s): Latin. Appraised at 4d in c.1650.

164.63 Formulae Orator:
John Clarke, B.D. *Formulae oratoriae, in usum scholarum concinnatae*. London: (different houses), 1630–1647.
STC 5354.7 *et seq.* and Wing C4468bA. Not appraised. *Language(s)*: Latin.

164.64 Tacitus
Publius Cornelius Tacitus. [*Works*]. Continent: date not determined.
See 164.10 for an English edition. *Language(s)*: Latin. Appraised at 1s in c.1650.

164.65 Florus
Lucius Annaeus Florus. [*Epitomae de Tito Livio bellorum omnium annorum*]. Britain or Continent: date not determined.
STC 11101 *et seq.*, Wing F1371, and non-STC. *Language(s)*: Latin. Appraised at 6d in c.1650.

164.66 Suetonius
Caius Suetonius Tranquillus. *De vita Caesarum*. Continent: date not determined.
Language(s): Latin. Appraised at 4d in c.1650.

164.67 Tull: Sentent:

Marcus Tullius Cicero. [*Selections*]. Britain or Continent: date not determined.

STC 5318.3 *et seq.*, Wing C4321, and non-STC. The editions published in England included selections from Terence and Demosthenes as well. Not appraised. *Language(s)*: Latin.

164.68 Claudianus

Claudius Claudianus. Unidentified. Continent (probable): date not determined.

Probably not an STC book, but see STC 5367 *et seq.* The English translation of *The rape of Proserpine* must be considered a possibility. *Language(s)*: Latin (probable). Appraised at 3d in c.1650.

164.69 Val. Maximus

Valerius Maximus. *Facta et dicta memorabilia*. Continent: date not determined.

Language(s): Latin. Appraised at 3d in c.1650.

164.70 Luciani Dialog:

Lucian, *of Samosata*. Probably [*Dialogues — Selected*]. Britain or Continent: date not determined.

STC 16891 *et seq.*, Wing L3427, and non-STC. The seventeenth-century editions published in England make perhaps the selected dialogues more likely than the complete works. *Language(s)*: Greek (probable) Latin (probable). Appraised at 3d in c.1650.

164.71 Smiths Log:

Samuel Smith, *A.M. Aditus ad Logicam*. Britain: 1613–1649.

STC 22825 *et seq.* and Wing S4194. The manuscript entry *Smiths Logick* appears earlier in the inventory (between 164.44 and 164.45), which is struck through. Not appraised. *Language(s)*: Latin.

164.72 Brerew: Elementa Log:

Edward Brerewood. *Elementa logicae*. London: (different houses), 1614–1649.

STC 3613 *et seq.* and Wing B4374. Not appraised. *Language(s)*: Latin.

John Hutton. Scholar (B.A.):
Probate Inventory. 1652

JOHN A. BUTLER

John Hutton was born about 1628 in St. Laurence, Middlesex, matriculating 17 July 1646 from New College "aged 18" and graduating B.A. in 1650. Also admitted a Fellow in 1650 (1648 according to Burrows 1881, 529), he was incorporated at Cambridge in 1652, the year he died (*Alumni Oxonienses*, 2:779).

In May 1648 Hutton ran into trouble with the Parliamentary Visitation under the Chancellorship of the Earl of Pembroke, a Parliamentary nominee, which in its attempts to impose certain standards on the University met with a great deal of opposition. Hutton refused to submit to the Visitation, stating that "Our Colledge Statutes (all of which I have perticulerly sworne to observe) doe expressly forbidd mee to acknowledge any as Visitors which are actuall Members or Students of this Universitie." He did not stop there, but pleaded conscience, writing that "I conceive I cannot (without manifest perjury) acknowledge your power in the Visitinge of mee" (Burrows 1881, 58). When a list was drawn up a few days later listing members of the college to be expelled, Hutton's name was included (Burrows 1881, 93), but the expulsion does not seem to have occurred. Hutton owned a copy of the University statutes (165.112), and seems likely to have been well prepared to argue his case according to the institutional rules as well as by his political conscience.

Apart from the usual books on logic, theology, grammar, and philosophy one would expect in such an inventory, the collection contains an unusual number of literary works. In addition to a solid collection of classical literature (prose, verse, and drama), the poetry included John Gower's *Confessio amantis* (165.12), John Donne's *Poems* (165.54), Abraham Cowley's *Poetical blossoms* (165.29), first published when Cowley was still a schoolboy at Westminster, and collections by John Heywood (165.87), John Owen (165.118), and Thomas Scott (165.130). Hutton had a taste for amorous lyrics, and, in the case of Donne and Cowley, poetry written by young men much like himself. He also owned John Earle's collection of literary characters *Micro-cosmography* (165.101), and satirical prose fiction such as Bishop Joseph Hall's *Mundus alter* (165.115) and French/Scottish Catholic John Barclay's *Euphormionis Lusini satyricon* (165.35), a work based loosely on Petronius's *Satyricon* but merged with an almost picaresque narrative. Continental neo-Latin literary texts include orations by Daniel Heinsius (165.28) and Justus Lipsius (165.72:1) and Friedrich Dedekind's satirical *Grobianus* (165.56), along with works of literary criticism by Famianus Strada (165.32) and Julius Caesar Scaliger (165.22) . Drama was represented by a volume of Ben Jonson's plays in a folio edition.

Hutton seems to have also had some interest in military matters, as his library included *The Art of warre, or Militarie discourses* (165.74) by the rather shadowy Sieur de Praissac, about whom little is known but whose book, lavishly illustrated with woodcuts and diagrams of battles, was very popular, and a work by La Framboisière, a French army surgeon (165.61). He also owned the *Historia navalis* of Sir Thomas Ryves (1583–1652), a distinguished maritime judge who worked for the Admiralty court and fought for Charles I in the Civil War.

Hutton's own evident Royalist and Protestant sympathies are also quite well represented: there is a copy of Sir John Wake's *Rex Platonicus* (1607), a work describing the entertainment given by the University of Oxford before James I in 1605 (165.48), Lancelot Andrewes's *Tortura torti* (165.89:2), a defense of James I's book on the Oath of Allegiance against Cardinal Bellarmine, a psalm translation attributed to James I (165.51), and Charles I's correspondence with Alexander Henderson (c.1583–1646), a Scottish divine who had been the King's chaplain (165.97). Thomas Hobbes' *De cive* (165.81) might be included in this category, though by the time Hutton died Hobbes's reputation among Royalists was mixed.

There are many works on history, not only classical works such as those by Caesar, Herodian, Solinus, and Sallust but also an unidentified English chronicle (165.13), Philippe de Comines' *Memoires* (165.58), and Ludovico Guicciardini's *History of the Low Countries* in Italian (165.11). Finally, he also owned works of alchemy (165.2, 165.117, 165.135), architecture (165.3), and science, including mathematics, astronomy, physics, chemistry, and natural history (165.38, 165.39, 165.84, 165.109, 165.113, 165.122, 165.137).

More than one-quarter of Hutton's books (at least) were published in Britain, an uncommonly high percentage (particularly when compared with earlier collections), and twenty-two were in English (in addition to Latin, French, Italian, and a few each in Greek and Hebrew, perhaps aspirational). Hutton seems to have been a well-rounded and well-read modern young man, abreast with the latest literary developments and interested in what was going on around him.

The one unusual textual feature of this inventory is the form taken by the twenty books not appraised. In nineteen of these cases, instead of the more customary blank appraisal a '0' has been recorded in the 'pounds' column. Possibly these books were appraised as having no value; possibly somebody intended to go back and add values in the shillings and pence columns; possibly this form was adopted for other purposes, now mysterious. The annotation "not appraised" appears in these cases, but that phrase should be understood in the context described above.

Oxford University Archives, Bodleian Library: Hyp.B.14.

§

Burrows, Montagu, ed. 1881. *The Register of the Visitors of the University of Oxford, from A.D. 1647 to A.D. 1658*. [Westminster]: Printed for the Camden Society.

§

165.1	Scheibleri Logica. 4to. Marp: Catt: 1634.
165.2	Lullii opera. 8to. Argent: 1598
165.3	Vitruvius de Architectura. 4to. Lugduni 1552.
165.4	Dictionarium Poeticum. Parisiis .1620.
165.5	Pacius in Aristotelis Organon Aure: Allob: 1605
165.6:A	Herodianus et Zosimus 1581.
165.6:B	[See 165.6:A]
165.7	Erasmi Epistolae in Folio: Basil: 1521.
165.8	Despauterii Commentarii Grammat: Paris: 1537.
165.9	Solini Polyhistor
165.10	Prisciani Gramma: Caesariens: libri omnes. 1528.
165.11	Guicciardines history of the Low Count: in Ital:
165.12	Gower de confessione Amantis. Lon: 1554.
165.13	An Old Englesh Cronicle.
165.14	Ben Johnsons last Tome. 1631.
165.15	Hooker's Ecclesiasticall polities.
165.16:1	Salustius in folio bounde with Valerius Maximus.
165.16:2	[See 165.16:1]
165.17	Plinii Historiae cum Sigismundi Gelenii annotationi:
165.18	Junii Nomenclator. Antwerp: 1583.
165.19	Bellarmini Gramm: Hebraica: 1619.
165.20	Euripides.
165.21	Heliodori Aethiopic: Lugduni .1611.
165.22	Ju: Scaligeri Poetices Libri 7. 1594.
165.23	Varronis opera. 1581.
165.24	Piccolomineus de moribus Franco: 1627.
165.25	Pererii physica. Colon: 1609.
165.26	Melanthoni Philosophia Moral: li: duo. 1556.
165.27	Oppiani Lib: de Venatione et Piscatu

165.28	Hensii orationes
165.29	Cowlys Poems
165.30	Burgerdikii Logica.
165.31	Eustachii Quadripartita Philosophia. Gene: 1634.
165.32	Stradae Prolusiones.
165.33	Plauti Comediae. Francof: 16*0.
165.34	Martialis Epigram: cum Farnibei annot:
165.35	Euphormio.
165.36	Rami Artes.
165.37	Cesaris Comment:
165.38	Goclenii disputatio: physicae. 1598.
165.39	Cardanus de subtilitate. Basil:
165.40	Aristotelis Ethica cum Magi: annota:
165.41	Aristotelis Physica cum comment: Pacii.
165.42	Charron's Wisdome in French. 1607.
165.43	Javelli Metaphy:
165.44	Isocratis orationes et epistolae.
165.45	Amesii medulla.
165.46	Burgersdisii Idea philoso:
165.47	Budaeus de asse. Colon: 1528.
165.48	Rex Platonicus.
165.49:A	Horace Jovenall & Persius.
165.49:B	[See 165.49:A]
165.49:C	[See 165.49:A]
165.50	Virgilius cum notis Farnabii
165.51	King James his psalmes.
165.52	Rithchells metaph:
165.53	Clavis Homerica.
165.54	Don's Poems.
165.55	Sandersoni Logica.
165.56	Fri: Dedekindi Ludus Satyricus.
165.57:1	Pemble de origi: animae et providentia.
165.57:2	[See 165.57:1]
165.58	Cominaei historia Gallica.
165.59	Nowells Catech: Graec: et Lati:
165.60	Panegyricae orat: Gustavi
165.61	Lu: Annae: Florus cum notis El: Vineti, Camertis etc.
165.62	Frambesarii medicina
165.63	Wollaebius
165.64	Catulli Tibulli Propertii nova edit: Lutet: 1577.
165.65	Q. Curtius
165.66	Corne: Agrippa de vanitate omnium scient: etc.
165.67	Virgilii Georgica P: Rami praelecti: illustrata.

165.68	Hesiodus
165.69	Mora: philos: Jo: Casii
165.70	Aristotelis Ethica
165.71	Historiae naval: Rivii.
165.72:1	Lipsii orationes. Carpenters perfect Law of God
165.72:2	[See 165.72:1]
165.73	Terentii Comoed: in quem triplex est Comentatio Antesignani etc.
165.74	The Art of Warr by Jo: Cruso.
165.75	Baronii Philosophia Theolo: ancillans.
165.76	Hyperius de Theologo.
165.77	The Conversions of England by N.D.
165.78	Scheiblerli compendium.
165.79:1	Epitome Sleidani de statu religionis. Musae Sacrae per J: Aylmer
165.79:2	[See 165.79:1]
165.80	Relectiones hyemales de ratione et methodo legendi utrasque Historias, per Deg: Whear
165.81	Hobbs de Cive.
165.82	Busbequius.
165.83	Dounaei praelectiones.
165.84	Clavius in Sphaeram Joha: de S: Bosco.
165.85	Heurnii institutiones medic:
165.86	Buridani Ethica Oxon: 1637.
165.87	The workes of J: Heiwood.
165.88	Orationes Tulli cum Freigii notis.
165.89:1	Bezae quaest: et respon: Christianarum Tortura Torti
165.89:2	[See 165.89:1]
165.90	Breerewoods Ethikes
165.91	A French dictionary by Hollyband
165.92	Clelands Noble man.
165.93:1	Godwins Roman and Jewish Antiquitys
165.93:2	[See 165.93:1]
165.94	Macrobius in Somnium Scipionis et Convivium Saturnaliorum
165.95	The arraignment and conviction of Usury in 6 sermons by Miles Mosse.
165.96	Brerewoods treatise of the Sabbath.
165.97	Papers betweene King Charles and Henderson.
165.98	The touch stone of truth.
165.99	Syntaxis Graeca Jo: Posselii
165.100	Tho: Lydiatt de variis Annorum formis.
165.101	Earles chareckters.
165.102	The Unfortunate Politique
165.103	Faciculus praeceptorum Logicor:
165.104	Javelli physica.

165.105   Sculteti Ethica.
165.106   Rudimenta Relig: Christianae Ebraice explicata. Graece Latine
165.107   Hopton's Concordancy of Yeares.
165.108   Tulli Quaestiones Tusculan:
165.109   Dodonaeus de Sphaera.
165.110   Joh: Setoni Dialectica.
165.111   Contaren de magistratibus et Repub: Venetorum.
165.112   Epitome Statutor: Universitatis Oxon.
165.113   Scribonii physica et sphraerica [sphaerica] doctrina.
165.114   Joh: Buxtorfi Epitome Grammat: Ebraeae.
165.115   Mundus Alter.
165.116   Dictys Cretensis de bello Troiano.
165.117   Magia Naturallis Joh: Baptistae Portae.
165.118   Owen's Epigrams
165.119   Meditationes Sancti Augustini.
165.120   Pub: Papinius Statius.
165.121   Cornelius Tacitus. Amsterodami.
165.122   Gemma Phrisius de princip: Astronomiae etc.
165.123   Joh: Barclaiius ad sectarios.
165.124   Virgilii Bucoloca
165.125   Nonni Panopolitani metaphrasis Evang: secundum Joannem versibus Heroicis.
165.126   Aphoris: Hippocratis. Lugd: Batavo:
165.127   Apolinarius psalmi
165.128   Sleydan de 4or Imperiis
165.129   Epictetus
165.130   Scots poems
165.131:1–8   8 Italian and french
165.132   sparkes vis natura
165.133   Junius Emblems
165.134   Adagia sacra
165.135   Flamells Hiroglificall figures
165.136   Prideaux Hypomnemata
165.137   Franc: Bar: de Verulamis Hist: vitae et Mortis

§

165.1   Scheibleri Logica. 4to. Marp: Catt: 1634.

Christoph Scheibler. *Opus logicum*. Marburg: typis et impensis Casparis Chemlini, 1634.

Language(s): Latin. Appraised at 3s 6d in 1652.

165.2   Lullii opera. 8to. Argent: 1598

Ramón Lull. [*Works*]. Strassburg: sumptibus Lazari Zetzneri, 1598. Not the entire corpus, but conventionally referred to as *opera*. Adams L1694. *Language(s)*: Latin. Appraised at 1s 6d in 1652.

165.3   Vitruvius de Architectura. 4to. Lugduni 1552.

Marcus Vitruvius Pollio. *De architectura libri decem*. Edited by Gulielmus Philander. Lyon: apud Joannem Tornaesium, 1552.
Language(s): Latin. Appraised at 3s in 1652.

165.4   Dictionarium Poeticum. Parisiis.1620.

Charles Estienne. *Lexicon historicum, geographicum, poeticum*. Edited by Federic Morel. Paris: sumptibus Francisci Jacquin, 1620.
An alternate title of *Dictionarium historicum ac poeticum*. *Language(s)*: Latin. Appraised at 3s in 1652.

165.5   Pacius in Aristotelis Organon Aure: Allob: 1605

Julius Pacius. *Aristotelis Stagiritae peripateticorum principiis organum*. Geneva: ex typis Vignonianis, 1605.
The Latin text of the *Organon* by Pacius. *Language(s)*: Greek Latin. Appraised at 1s 6d in 1652.

165.6:A   Herodianus et Zosimus 1581.

Herodian. [*Historiae*]. The Latin version is by Angelus Politianus (Angelo Ambrogini). Geneva: excudebat Henricus Stephanus, 1581 (composite publication).
Language(s): Greek Latin. Appraised [a composite volume] at 2s in 1652.

165.6:B   [See 165.6:A]

Zosimus, *the Historian*. *Historia nova*. The Latin translation by Joannes Leunclavius. [Composite publication].
Language(s): Greek Latin. Appraised [a composite volume] at 2s in 1652.

165.7   Erasmi Epistolae in Folio: Basil: 1521.

Desiderius Erasmus. *Epistolae D. Erasmi Roterodami ad diversos, et aliquot aliorum ad illum*. Basle: apud Jo. Frobenium, 1521.
Language(s): Latin. Appraised at 6d in 1652.

165.8   Despauterii Commentarii Grammat: Paris: 1537.

Jean Despautère. *Commentarii grammatici*. Paris: ex officina Roberti Stephani, 1537.
Language(s): Latin. Appraised at 1s 6d in 1652.

165.9 Solini Polyhistor
Caius Julius Solinus. *Polyhistor.* Continent: date not determined. *Language(s)*: Latin. Appraised at 6d in 1652.

165.10 Prisciani Gramma: Caesariens: libri omnes. 1528.
Priscianus, *Caesariensis. Prisciani grammatici Caesariensis libri omnes.* Cologne: (stationer unknown), 1528.
The stationer is variously supplied as Eucharius Cervicornus and Godefridus Hittorp; conceivably they colloborated on the book's publication as they had with other works. *Language(s)*: Latin. Appraised at 6d in 1652.

165.11 Guicciardines history of the Low Count: in Ital:
Ludovico Guicciardini. *Descrittione di tutti i Paesi Bassi.* Antwerp: (different houses), 1567–1588.
Language(s): Italian. Appraised at 1s in 1652.

165.12 Gower de confessione Amantis. Lon: 1554.
John Gower, *the Poet. De confessione amantis.* London: T. Berthelette, 1554. STC 12144. Not appraised. *Language(s)*: English.

165.13 An Old Englesh Cronicle.
Unidentified. Britain: date not determined.
Not identifiable in the STC. Not appraised. *Language(s)*: English.

165.14 Ben Johnsons last Tome. 1631.
Ben Jonson. [*Works* (part)]. London: J. B[eale] for R. Allot, 1631.
STC 14753.5. This second volume of Jonson's plays (*Bartholomew fair, The devil is an ass,* and *The staple of newes*) was published as a continuation of his *Workes,* the first volume of which was published in 1616. A single octavo edition of *The new inne* is the only other work of Jonson's to appear in 1631. In addition to the compiler's wording indicating that this item is part of a multiple-volumed work, the valuation is more in keeping with a folio than an octavo. *Language(s)*: English. Appraised at 3s in 1652.

165.15 Hooker's Ecclesiasticall polities.
Richard Hooker. *Of the lawes of ecclesiasticall politie.* London: (different houses), 1593–1639.
STC 13712 *et seq. Language(s)*: English. Appraised at 4s in 1652.

165.16:1 Salustius in folio bounde with Valerius Maximus.
Caius Sallustius Crispus. Probably [*Works*]. Continent: date not determined.

Only Sallust's complete *opera* seems to have been published in folio, and nothing of Sallust's was published in England in folio. *Language(s)*: Latin. Appraised with one other at 6d in 1652.

165.16:2 [See 165.16:1]
Valerius Maximus. *Facta et dicta memorabilia*. Continent: date not determined.
Language(s): Latin. Appraised with one other at 6d in 1652.

165.17 Plinii Historiae cum Sigismundi Gelenii annotationi:
Pliny, *the Elder*. *Historia naturalis*. Edited with commentary by Sigmund Gelen. Continent: date not determined.
Language(s): Latin. Appraised at 1s 6d in 1652.

165.18 Junii Nomenclator. Antwerp: 1583.
Adrian Junius. *Nomenclator*. Antwerp: ex off. Christophori Plantini, 1583.
Various vernaculars appear as well. *Language(s)*: Greek Latin. Appraised at 1s in 1652.

165.19 Bellarmini Gramm: Hebraica: 1619.
Roberto Bellarmino, *Cardinal*. *Institutiones linguae hebraicae*. Place not given: apud Franciscum Fabrum, 1619.
The place of publication is variously supplied as Cologne, Geneva, Lyon. *Language(s)*: Hebrew Latin. Appraised at 8d in 1652.

165.20 Euripides.
Euripides. Probably [*Works*]. Continent (probable): date not determined.
Almost certainly not an STC book. At the valuation of three shillings, the 1575 Greek octavo edition of the *Troades* (STC 10567.5), the sole work of Euripides published in England by the date of this inventory, is not likely. *Language(s)*: Greek (probable) Latin (probable). Appraised at 3s in 1652.

165.21 Heliodori Aethiopic: Lugduni .1611.
Heliodorus. *Heliodori Aethiopicorum libri decem*. Lyon: apud viduam Ant. de Harsy, 1611.
Language(s): Latin. Appraised at 1s 4d in 1652.

165.22 Ju: Scaligeri Poetices Libri 7. 1594.
Julius Caesar Scaliger. *Poetices libri septem*. Lyon: apud Petrum Sanctandreanum, 1594.
Language(s): Latin. Appraised at 1s 6d in 1652.

165.23   Varronis opera. 1581.

Marcus Terentius Varro. *Opera quae supersunt.* Edited by Henri Estienne, with notes by Joseph Juste Scaliger. Place not given: [Henricus Stephanus II], 1581.

The place of publication is sometimes supplied as Paris, more often as Geneva. *Language(s)*: Latin. Appraised at 1s in 1652.

165.24   Piccolomineus de moribus Franco: 1627.

Francesco Piccolomini. *Universa philosophia de moribus.* Frankfurt am Main: typis Guolphg. Hofmanni, sumtibus [sic] haeredum Jacobi Fischeri, 1627.

Language(s): Latin. Appraised at 1s in 1652.

165.25   Pererii physica. Colon: 1609.

Benedictus Pererius. *De communibus omnium rerum naturalium principiis et affectionibus libri quindecim.* Cologne: impensis Lazari Zetzneri bibliop., 1609.

Language(s): Latin. Appraised at 1s 6d in 1652.

165.26   Melanthoni Philosophia Moral: li: duo. 1556.

Philipp Melanchthon. *Philosophiae moralis libri duo.* Strassburg: apud B. Fabricium, 1556.

Not appraised. *Language(s)*: Latin.

165.27   Oppiani Lib: de Venatione et Piscatu

Oppianus. [*Aleuticon. Cynegetica*]. Continent: date not determined.

The manuscript entry most closely approximates the 1597 Leyden edition. *Language(s)*: Greek Latin. Appraised at 6d in 1652.

165.28   Hensii orationes

Daniel Heinsius. *Orationes.* Continent: date not determined.

Language(s): Latin. Appraised at 8d in 1652.

165.29   Cowlys Poems

Abraham Cowley. Probably *Poetical blossomes.* London: (different houses) for H. Seile, 1633–1637.

STC 5906 *et seq. Language(s)*: English. Appraised at 6d in 1652.

165.30   Burgerdikii Logica.

Franco Burgersdijck. Unidentified. Place unknown: stationer unknown, date not determined.

STC/non-STC status unknown. Without question, either his *Institutionum logicarum synopsis* or his *Institutionum logicarum libri duo* or a composite edition of both. See Lohr II for the many editions. *Language(s)*: Latin. Appraised at 8d in 1652.

165.31   Eustachii Quadripartita Philosophia. Gene: 1634.
Eustachius, *a Sancto Paulo*. *Summa philosophiae quadripartita*. Geneva: typis J. Stoer, 1634.
Language(s): Latin. Appraised at 8d in 1652.

165.32   Stradae Prolusiones.
Famianus Strada. *Prolusiones academicae*. Britain or Continent: 1617–1644. STC 23351 and non-STC. *Language(s)*: Latin. Appraised at 1s in 1652.

165.33   Plauti Comediae. Francof: 16*0.
Titus Maccius Plautus. *Comoediae*. Frankfurt am Main: (different houses), 1610.
The date in the manuscript entry has been altered and could be either 1600 or 1610, but the only 1600 edition that can be found was published in Lubeck. Several 1610 editions were printed in Frankfurt, by different printers. An "x" appears in the margin next to the appraisal. *Language(s)*: Latin. Appraised at 6d in 1652.

165.34   Martialis Epigram: cum Farnibei annot:
Marcus Valerius Martialis. *Epigrammata*. Edited by Thomas Farnaby. London: (different houses), 1615–1633.
STC 17492 *et seq*. *Language(s)*: Latin. Appraised at 1s in 1652.

165.35   Euphormio.
John Barclay. *Euphormionis lusinini sive Joannis Barclaii satyricon quadripartitum*. Britain or Continent: date not determined.
STC 1396.5 and non-STC. The many editions of this work, in a variety of arrangements, present an extremely complicated printing history. In addition to the two editions appearing in the STC (one with a London imprint when actually published on the Continent), see the scores of editions in Shaaber beginning with B156. *Language(s)*: Latin. Appraised at 1s in 1652.

165.36   Rami Artes.
Pierre de La Ramée. Unidentified. Place unknown: stationer unknown, date not determined.
Whether one of Ramus's works on education (such as the collection *Professio regia, hoc est, septem artes liberales in regia cathedra, per ipsum Parisiis propositiae, the Scholae in liberales artes*, or his *Scholae in tres prima liberales artes*) or on logic (Ramus) and rhetoric (Talon), several English editions of which are titled: *The Artes of Logike and Rhetorike*, cannot be determined. See, for example, Ong, nos. 651, 672, 695, and 697. Not appraised. *Language(s)*: Latin (probable) English (probable)

165.37   Cesaris Comment:
Caius Julius Caesar. *Commentarii*. Britain or Continent: date not determined.
STC 4332 *et seq*. and non-STC. *Language(s)*: Latin. Appraised at 8d in 1652.

165.38 Goclenii disputatio: physicae. 1598.
Rudolphus Goclenius, *the Elder. Physicae disputationes in septem libros distinctae*. Frankfurt am Main: ex officina M. Zachariae Palthenii, 1598.
Language(s): Latin. Appraised at 6d in 1652.

165.39 Cardanus de subtilitate. Basil:
Girolamo Cardano. *De subtilitate*. Basle: (different houses), 1553–1611.
Language(s): Latin. Appraised at 1s in 1652.

165.40 Aristotelis Ethica cum Magi: annota:
John Magirus. [*Aristotle—Ethica*: commentary]. Frankfurt am Main: (different houses), 1601–1628.
With the text. *Language(s)*: Greek Latin. Appraised at 1s 6d in 1652.

165.41 Aristotelis Physica cum comment: Pacii.
Aristotle. *Physica*. Commentary by Julius Pacius. Continent: 1596–1629.
Date range from Lohr II. *Language(s)*: Latin. Appraised at 1s in 1652.

165.42 Charron's Wisdome in French. 1607.
Pierre Charron. *De la sagesse*. Continent: 1607.
There were two French 1607 editions, one from Bordeaux, another from Paris, some sources say in octavo, some duodecimo. *Language(s)*: French. Appraised at 1s in 1652.

165.43 Javelli Metaphy:
Chrysostom Javellus. [*Aristotle—Metaphysica*: commentary]. Continent: 1552–1651.
Not appraised. *Language(s)*: Latin.

165.44 Isocratis orationes et epistolae.
Isocrates. [*Works*]. Continent: date not determined.
Language(s): Greek (probable) Latin (probable). Appraised at 1s in 1652.

165.45 Amesii medulla.
William Ames. *Medulla S.S. theologiae*. Britain or Continent: 1627–1634.
STC 556.5 *et seq.* and non-STC. All Continental editions were published in Amsterdam. See Shaaber A293–A296. STC 14272 and non-STC. The STC book was printed on the Continent *Language(s)*: Latin. Appraised at 6d in 1652.

165.46 Burgersdisii Idea philoso:
Franco Burgersdijck. Unidentified. Place unknown: stationer unknown, date not determined.

STC/non-STC status unknown. Without doubt, either *Idea philosophiae moralis*, *Idea philosophiae naturalis* or both as published in a composite edition at Oxford (STC 4106 *et seq.*). *Language(s)*: Latin. Appraised at 8d in 1652.

165.47 Budaeus de asse. Colon: 1528.

Gulielmus Budaeus. *De asse et partibus eius*. Cologne: opera et impensa Joanis Soteris, 1528.

Not appraised. *Language(s)*: Latin.

165.48 Rex Platonicus.

Sir Isaac Wake. *Rex Platonicus*. Oxford: (different houses), 1607–1636. STC 24939 *et seq. Language(s)*: Latin. Appraised at 6d in 1652.

165.49:A Horace Jovenall & Persius.

Quintus Horatius Flaccus. [*Works*]. Britain or Continent: date not determined (composite publication).

STC 13784 *et seq.* and non-STC. Most of the editions of Horace published in England included the works of Juvenal and Persius, perhaps because of their use as a textbook. Proportionately, fewer of the Continental editions were composite editions of the three classical writers. *Language(s)*: Latin. Appraised [a composite volume] at 1s in 1652.

165.49:B [See 165.49:A]

Decimus Junius Juvenalis. [*Works*]. [Composite publication].

STC 13784 *et seq.* and non-STC. See the annotation to 165.49:A. *Language(s)*: Latin. Appraised [a composite volume] at 1s in 1652.

165.49:C [See 165.49:A]

Aulus Persius Flaccus. [*Works*]. [Composite publication].

STC 13784 *et seq.* and non-STC. See the annotation to 165.49:A. *Language(s)*: Latin. Appraised [a composite volume] at 1s in 1652.

165.50 Virgilius cum notis Farnabii

Publius Virgilius Maro. [*Works*]. Annotated by Thomas Farnaby. London: F. Kyngston, imp. R. Allot, 1634.

STC 24794. *Language(s)*: Latin. Appraised at 6d in 1652.

165.51 King James his psalmes.

The psalmes of king David by king James. (*Bible — O.T.*). Britain: 1631–1637.

STC 2732 *et seq.* Though the translation is attributed to James I, *King of England*, according to the STC, the translation is "largely by W. Alexander, *Earl of Sterling*." *Language(s)*: English. Appraised at 6d in 1652.

165.52 Rithchells metaph:

George Ritschel. *Contemplationes metaphysicae*. Oxford: impensis L. Lichfield academiae typographi et E. Forrest jun. bibliop., 1648.

Wing R1543. *Language(s)*: Latin. Appraised at 6d in 1652.

165.53 Clavis Homerica.

Antonius Roberti. *Clavis Homerica, reserans significationes, etymologias, derivationes*. Revised by George Perkins. Britain or Continent: 1636–1649.

STC 21072a, Wing R1573, and non-STC. The original 1636 edition (Douai) was by Roberti, with later editions revised by George Perkins. By the 1649 edition, the work bore Perkins's name alone. *Language(s)*: Greek Latin. Appraised at 6d in 1652.

165.54 Don's Poems.

John Donne. *Poems, by J.D. With elegies on the authors death*. London: (different houses), 1633–1650.

STC 7045 *et seq.* and Wing D1868 *et seq.* Miles Flesher was involved in the printing of all editions save one, and John Marriot served in different publishing roles in all editions. *Language(s)*: English. Appraised at 8d in 1652.

165.55 Sandersoni Logica.

Unidentified. Place unknown: stationer unknown, date not determined.

Unidentifiable in the STC. Whether Bishop Robert Sanderson's *Logicae artis compendium*, published in the seventeenth century in England, or John Sanderson's *Institutionum dialecticarum libri quatuor*, published on the Continent as early as 1589 as well as in England in the early seventeenth century, cannot be determined despite the similarity of the manuscript entry to the R. Sanderson title. The J. Sanderson work appears in two late sixteenth-century book-lists entered in the same manner as this record (see PLRE 153.7 and PLRE 154.197), the latter exactly as it does here ("Sandersoni Logica"). *Language(s)*: Latin. Appraised at 8d in 1652.

165.56 Fri: Dedekindi Ludus Satyricus.

Friedrich Dedekind. *Ludus satyricus, de morum simplicitate, seu rusticitate*. Continent: 1631–1650.

The three editions of Dedekind's *Grobianus* within the date range are the only editions to carry this title. Not appraised. *Language(s)*: Latin.

165.57:1 Pemble de origi: animae et providentia.

William Pemble. *De formarum origine*. Britain: (different houses) for J.B[artlet], 1629–1650?

STC 19572 *et seq.* and Wing P1114. Following page 49, the running head varies between "De origine Animae in genere" and "De origine Animae Rationalis." *Language(s)*: Latin. Appraised with one other at 6d in 1652.

165.57:2 [See 165.57:1]

William Pemble. *Tractatus de providentia dei*. London: (different houses), 1631–1650?

STC 19588 and Wing P1116b. J. Beale was involved with the publication of both editions. The date range includes Wing P1116b. *Language(s)*: Latin. Appraised with one other at 6d in 1652.

165.58   Cominaei historia Gallica.

Philippe de Comines. [*Memoires*]. Continent: date not determined. *Language(s)*: Latin. Appraised at 2d in 1652.

165.59   Nowells Catech: Graec: et Lati:

Alexander Nowell. *Catechismus*. Greek translation by William Whitaker. London: (different houses), 1573–1638.

STC 18707 *et seq. Language(s)*: Greek Latin. Appraised at 6d in 1652.

165.60   Panegyricae orat: Gustavi

Gustavus Magnus, sive panegyricae orationes. Edited by Andries Cloquius. Leyden: apud Andraeum Cloucquium, 1637.

Authors are variously given as Daniel Heinsius, Andreas Cloquius, Augustus Buchner, and Michael Virdungus among others. A cross appears in the margin next to the appraisal. *Language(s)*: Latin. Appraised at 6d in 1652.

165.61   Lu: Annae: Florus cum notis El: Vineti, Camertis etc.

Lucius Annaeus Florus. [*Epitomae de Tito Livio bellorum omnium annorum*]. Edited, with others, by Joannes Camers. Annotations by Élie Vinet. Place unknown: sumptibus Joannis Vignon, 1606.

The only edition with the editorial participation of Camers and the annotation of Vinet. Place of publication is alternatively given as Lyon and Saint-Gervaise. *Language(s)*: Latin. Appraised at 6d in 1652.

165.62   Frambesarii medicina

Nicolas Abraham de La Framboisière. Unidentified. Continent: date not determined.

Whether the "medicina" in the manuscript entry refers to his *Opera medica*, his *Consultationum medicinalium libri tres*, his *Scholae medicae*, or his *Loix de medecine* cannot be determined. Perhaps the compiler was simply being descriptive. *Language(s)*: Latin (probable) French (perhaps). Appraised at 1s in 1652.

165.63 Wollaebius

Johann Wolleb. Unidentified. Place unknown: stationer unknown, date not determined.

Wing/non-Wing status unknown. None of Wolleb's works was published in England until 1642; all possibilities, therefore, are Wing books. His best known work, published in Latin and translated into English, was *Christianae theologiae compendium*. *Language(s)*: Latin. Appraised at 8d in 1652.

165.64 Catulli Tibulli Propertii nova edit: Lutet: 1577.

Caius Valerius Catullus, Albius Tibullus, and Sextus Propertius. *Catulli Tibulli Propertii nova editio*. Edited by Joseph Juste Scaliger. Paris: apud Mamertum Patissonium, in officina Rob. Stephani, 1577.
Language(s): Latin. Appraised at 8d in 1652.

165.65 Q. Curtius

Quintus Curtius Rufus. *De rebus gestis Alexandri Magni*. Continent: date not determined.

There is no reason to suspect an English translation in this part of the collection. *Language(s)*: Latin. Appraised at 8d in 1652.

165.66 Corne: Agrippa de vanitate omnium scient: etc.

Henricus Cornelius Agrippa. *De incertitudine et vanitate scientiarum*. Continent: date not determined.

Whether the "etc." indicates other books or merely the rest of the long title cannot be determined. Not appraised. *Language(s)*: Latin.

165.67 Virgilii Georgica P: Rami praelecti: illustrata.

Pierre de La Ramée. [*Virgil—Georgics: commentary*]. Continent: 1556–1606.

Ong, nos. 479–483. Not appraised. *Language(s)*: Latin.

165.68 Hesiodus

Hesiod. Probably [*Works*]. Continent: date not determined.
Language(s): Latin (probable) Greek (probable). Appraised at 4d in 1652.

165.69 Mora: philos: Jo: Casii

John Case. Unidentified. Place unknown: stationer unknown, date not determined.

STC/non-STC status unknown. Necessarily, one of his two commentaries on Aristotle's *Ethica*, the *Speculum moralium quaestionum in universam Ethicen Aristotelis* or the *Reflexus speculi moralis qui commentarii vice esse poterit in Magna moralia Aristotelis*, the latter only published Oxford, two times in 1596, one edition with the former. *Language(s)*: Latin. Appraised at 8d in 1652.

165.70   Aristotelis Ethica
Aristotle. *Ethica*. Britain or Continent: date not determined.
STC 752 *et seq.* and non-STC. *Language(s)*: Latin. Appraised at 6d in 1652.

165.71   Historiae naval: Rivii.
Sir Thomas Ryves. [*Historia navalis*]. London: (different houses), 1629–1640.
STC 21474 *et seq.* Book 1 published separately in 1629, Books 1–4 published in 1633 as *Historia navalis antiqua*, and an additional three books published in 1640 as *Historiae navalis mediae*. The manuscript entry could refer to any one of the three publications. *Language(s)*: Latin. Appraised at 6d in 1652.

165.72:1   Lipsii orationes. Carpenters perfect Law of God
Justus Lipsius. *Orationes*. Continent: 1607–c.1630
Language(s): Latin. Appraised with one other at 4d in 1652.

165.72:2   [See 165.72:1]
Richard Carpenter. *The perfect-law of God*. London: printed by F.L., 1652.
Wing C625. This and 165.79:2 are the latest definitely datable books in the collection. *Language(s)*: English. Appraised with one other at 4d in 1652.

165.73   Terentii Comoed: in quem triplex est Comentatio Antesignani etc.
Publius Terentius, *Afer.* [*Works*]. Commentary by Petrus Antesignanus. Lyon: (different houses), 1560.
Two editions, one in quarto, the other in octavo. *Language(s)*: Latin. Appraised at 4d in 1652.

165.74   The Art of Warr by Jo: Cruso.
Sieur Du Praissac. *The art of warre, or Militarie discourses*. Translated by John Cruso. Cambridge: R. Daniel, 1639–1644.
STC 7365.8 *et seq.* One issue (STC 7366) was imprinted as being sold by the London stationer John Williams. *Language(s)*: English. Appraised at 1s in 1652.

165.75   Baronii Philosophia Theolo: ancillans.
Robert Baron. *Philosophia theologiae ancillans*. Britain or Continent: 1621–1649.
STC 1496, Wing B886, and non-STC. *Language(s)*: Latin. Appraised at 8d in 1652.

165.76   Hyperius de Theologo.
Andreas Gerardus, *Hyperius. De theologo, sive De ratione studii theologici*. Continent: date not determined.
Language(s): Latin. Appraised at 6d in 1652.

165.77   The Conversions of England by N.D.
Robert Parsons. *A treatise of three conversions of England.* Saint-Omer: [F. Bellet], 1603.
STC 19416. The several parts of the work were initialled "N.D." *Language(s)*: English. Appraised at 6d in 1652.

165.78   Scheiblerli compendium.
Christoph Scheibler. *Philosophia compendiosa, seu philosophiae synopsis.* Britain or Continent: 1618–1647.
STC 21814 *et seq.*, Wing S854, and non-STC. *Language(s)*: Latin. Appraised at 4d in 1652.

165.79:1   Epitome Sleidani de statu religionis. Musae Sacrae per J: Aylmer
Joannes Philippson, *Sleidanus. De statu religionis et reipublicae, Carolo Quinto, Caesare, commentarii.* Continent: date not determined.
Perhaps bound with the following. *Language(s)*: Latin. Appraised with one other at 1s in 1652.

165.79:2   [See 165.79:1]
John Ailmer. *Musae sacrae, seu Jonas, Jeremiae, Threni, et Daniel graeco redditi carmine.* Oxford: excudebat L. Lichfield Acad. Typog. et veneunt apud Jos. Godwin et Ric. Davis, 1652.
Wing B2739G. May have been bound with the preceding. *Language(s)*: Greek Latin. Appraised with one other at 1s in 1652.

165.80   Relectiones hyemales de ratione et methodo legendi utrasque Historias, per Deg: Whear
Diggory Whear. *Relectiones hymenales, de ratione et methodo legendi utrasque; historias, civiles et ecclesiasticas.* Oxford: L. Lichfield imp. (different houses), 1637.
STC 25328 *et seq. Language(s)*: Latin. Appraised at 6d in 1652.

165.81   Hobbs de Cive.
Thomas Hobbes. *Elementa philosophica de cive.* Continent: 1642–1647.
Not published in Latin in England by the date of this inventory. *Language(s)*: Latin. Appraised at 1s in 1652.

165.82   Busbequius.
Ogier Ghislain de Busbecq. Unidentified. Continent: date not determined.
A cross is in the margin next to the appraisal. *Language(s)*: Latin (probable). Appraised at 4d in 1652.

165.83 Dounaei praelectiones.
Andrew Downes. *Praelectiones in Philippicam de pace Demosthenis.* London: ap. J. Billium, 1621.
STC 7154. *Language(s)*: Greek Latin. Appraised at 4d in 1652.

165.84 Clavius in Sphaeram Joha: de S: Bosco.
Christoph Clavius. *In sphaeram Joannis de Sacro Bosco commentarius.* Continent: date not determined.
Language(s): Latin. Appraised at 2s 6d in 1652.

165.85 Heurnii institutiones medic:
Joannes Heurnius. *Institutiones medicinae.* Continent: 1592–1638.
Not appraised. *Language(s)*: Latin.

165.86 Buridani Ethica Oxon: 1637.
Joannes Buridanus. *Quaestiones in decem libros Ethicorum Aristotelis.* Oxford: L. L[ichfield], imp. W. Cripps, E. Forrest, H. Curteyne & J. Wilmot, 1637.
STC 4119. *Language(s)*: Latin. Appraised at 3s 6d in 1652.

165.87 The workes of J: Heiwood.
John Heywood. *[Works].* London: (different houses), 1562–1598.
STC 13285 *et seq.* Not appraised. *Language(s)*: English.

165.88 Orationes Tulli cum Freigii notis.
Marcus Tullius Cicero. *[Selected works—Orations].* Annotated by Joannes Thomas Freigius. Continent: date not determined.
Language(s): Latin. Appraised at 2s 6d in 1652.

165.89:1 Bezae quaest: et respon: Christianarum Tortura Torti
Théodore de Bèze. *[Quaestiones et responsiones].* Britain or Continent: 1570–1600.
STC 2036 *et seq.* and non-STC. The date range includes both the first and the second parts. Gardy nos. 262–277. *Language(s)*: Latin. Appraised with one other at 1s 6d in 1652.

165.89:2 [See 165.89:1]
Lancelot Andrewes, *Bishop. Tortura Torti: sive, ad Matthaei Torti librum responsio.* Britain or Continent: 1609–1610.
STC 626 *et seq.* and non-STC. This reply of Andrewes to Cardinal Bellarmine (who had written under the pseudonym of Matthaeus Torti) in his attack on James I's book on the oath of allegiance provoked a number of additional works. Many of them carried "Tortura Torti" in their titles, among them works by Martinus Becanus (against Andrewes), Robert Burhill, Samuel Collins, and

Richard Thomson (supporting Andrewes). Conceivably, one of them is intended here. See Shaaber A321. *Language(s)*: Latin. Appraised with one other at 1s 6d in 1652.

165.90   Breerewoods Ethikes

Edward Brerewood. *Tractatus ethici sive commentarii in aliquot Aristotelis libros ad Nichomachum, de moribus*. Oxford: excudebat Guilielmus Turner, impensis Eduardi Forrest, 1640.

STC 3627. *Language(s)*: Latin. Appraised at 1s in 1652.

165.91   A French dictionary by Hollyband

Claude Desainliens (Claude Holyband). *A dictionarie French and English*. London: T. O[rwin] for T. Woodcock, 1593.

STC 6737. Not appraised. *Language(s)*: English French.

165.92   Clelands Noble man.

James Cleland. *Heropaideia, or the institution of a young noble man*. Britain: 1607–1612.

STC 5393 *et seq*. The first word of the title is transliterated from the Greek. *Language(s)*: English. Appraised at 6d in 1652.

165.93:1   Godwins Roman and Jewish Antiquitys

Thomas Godwin. *Romanae historiae anthologia. An English exposition of the Romane antiquities*. Britain: 1614–1648.

STC 11956 *et seq*. and Wing G985 *et seq*. Probably bound with the following; both appeared in quarto format only. Not appraised. *Language(s)*: English.

165.93:2   [See 165.93:1]

Thomas Godwin. *Synopsis antiquitatum Hebraicarum, ad explicationem utriusque testamenti*. Oxford: J. Barnesius, 1616.

STC 11965. Since the manuscript entry is descriptive, it is conceivable that the item listed is, rather, the more widely published *Moses and Aaron. Civil and ecclesiastical rites, used by the Hebrewes* (STC 11951–11955 and Wing G976). Probably bound with the preceding; both appeared in quarto format only. The name form for the author, "Godwin," comes from the STC; most other sources give "Goodwin," sometimes "Godwyn." Not appraised. *Language(s)*: Latin.

165.94   Macrobius in Somnium Scipionis et Convivium Saturnaliorum

Ambrosius Aurelius Theodosius Macrobius. *In somnium Scipionis. Saturnalia*. Continent: date not determined.

Language(s): Latin. Appraised at 2d in 1652.

165.95 The arraignment and conviction of Usury in 6 sermons by Miles Mosse.

Miles Mosse. *The arraignment and conviction of usurie.* London: Widdow Orwin for (different houses), 1595.

STC 18207 *et seq.* The "Widdow Orwin" is Joan Orwin. A variant (STC 18208) has a different imprint. Not appraised. *Language(s)*: English.

165.96 Brerewoods treatise of the Sabbath.

Edward Brerewood. *A learned treatise of the Sabaoth, written to Mr N. Byfield.* Oxford: J. Lichfield for T. Huggins, 1630–1632.

STC 3622 *et seq.* Includes material by Nicholas Byfield. *Language(s)*: English. Appraised at 1s in 1652.

165.97 Papers betweene King Charles and Henderson.

Charles I, *King* and Alexander Henderson. *The papers which passed at New-Castle betwixt His Sacred Majestie and Mr Al: Henderson: concerning the change of church-government.* Britain or Continent: 1649.

Wing C2535 and non-Wing. The edition published at The Hague has a slightly different title. Not appraised. *Language(s)*: English.

165.98 The touch stone of truth.

James Warre. *The touch-stone of truth.* London: (different houses), 1621–1634.

STC 25090 *et seq.* Augustine Mathewes was involved with the publication of all editions. *Language(s)*: English. Appraised at 6d in 1652.

165.99 Syntaxis Graeca Jo: Posselii

Joannes Posselius. *Syntaxis linguae graecae.* Britain or Continent: date not determined.

STC 20138 and non-STC. "Syntaxis" is transliterated from the Greek. *Language(s)*: Greek Latin. Appraised at 3d in 1652.

165.100 Tho: Lydiatt de variis Annorum formis.

Thomas Lydiat. *Tractatus de variis annorum formis.* London: [Eliot's Court Press] ex off. Nortoniana, 1605.

STC 17047. His response to Joseph Scaliger's attack on this work must also be considered (*Defensio tractatus de variis annorum formis contra J. Scaligeri obtrectationem*, STC 17040). *Language(s)*: Latin. Appraised at 6d in 1652.

165.101 Earles chareckters.

John Earle. *Micro-cosmographie.* London: (different houses), 1628–1650.

STC 7439 *et seq.* and Wing E89. *Language(s)*: English. Appraised at 2d in 1652.

165.102 The Unfortunate Politique

Nicolas Caussin. *The unfortunate politique, first written in French by C.N.* Translated by G.P. Oxford: L. Lichfield for J. Godwin, 1638–1639.

STC 4876 *et seq. Language(s)*: English. Appraised at 3d in 1652.

165.103 Faciculus praeceptorum Logicor:

Christopher Airay. *Fasciculus praeceptorum logicorum in gratiam juventutis academicae compositus.* Oxford: G. Turner, 1628–1637.

STC 241 *et seq.* Published anonymously. *Language(s)*: Latin. Appraised at 4d in 1652.

165.104 Javelli physica.

Chrysostomus Javellus. [*Aristotle—Physica: commentary*]. Continent: 1533–1576.

Date range from Lohr II. Not appraised. *Language(s)*: Latin.

165.105 Sculteti Ethica.

Abraham Scultetus. *Ethicorum libri duo.* Continent: 1593–1614.

Not appraised. *Language(s)*: Latin.

165.106 Rudimenta Relig: Christianae Ebraice explicata. Graece Latine

Carel Roorda. *Hinukh hoc est catechesis, sive prima institutio aut rudimenta religionis christianae.* Edited by Joannes Drusius, the Elder. Leyden: Ex off. Plantiniana, apud Franciscum Raphelengium, 1591.

Variously attributed: Adams provides no author or editor (C1036), CLC gives it to Drusius (D863), and most other sources attribute roles as entered here. "Hinukh" is transliterated from the Hebrew. *Language(s)*: Greek Hebrew Latin. Appraised at 4d in 1652.

165.107 Hopton's Concordancy of Yeares.

Arthur Hopton. *A concordancy of yeares.* London: (different houses), 1612–1635.

STC 13778 *et seq. Language(s)*: English. Appraised at 1s in 1652.

165.108 Tulli Quaestiones Tusculan:

Marcus Tullius Cicero. *Quaestiones Tusculanae.* Britain or Continent: date not determined.

STC 5314.5 *et seq.* and non-STC. *Language(s)*: Latin. Appraised at 3d in 1652.

165.109 Dodonaeus de Sphaera.

Rembert Dodoens. *Cosmographica in astronomiam et geographiam isagoge.* Continent: date not determined.

Language(s): Latin. Appraised at 2d in 1652.

165.110   Joh: Setoni Dialectica.

John Seton. *Dialectica*. Britain: 1545–1639.

STC 22250 *et seq.* Of the nearly twenty editions and issues, all but one were published in London. STC 2257 (1631) was issued in Cambridge. Not appraised. *Language(s)*: Latin.

165.111   Contaren de magistratibus et Repub: Venetorum.

Gasparo Contarini, *Cardinal*. *De magistratibus et republica Venetorum*. Continent: date not determined.

Language(s): Latin. Appraised at 8d in 1652.

165.112   Epitome Statutor: Universitatis Oxon.

Statuta selecta è corpore statutorum universitatis Oxon. (*Oxford University — Official Documents*). Compiled by T. Crossfield. Oxford: typis G. Turner pro G. Webb, 1638.

STC 19007. Unlike the item identified here, the title of STC 19006, also relating to the statutes of Oxford, carries the word "epitome" in its title (*Synopsis seu epitome statutorum*), but it is a single-sheet issue, hardly to be valued at 8*d*, and almost certainly would not even be inventoried for probate purposes. There is not one instance of a single-sheet folio appearing in the hundreds of book-lists inventoried for probate at Oxford between 1507 and the date of this document, 1652. The compiler is assumed to have used "epitome" descriptively rather than copying the longer, actual phrase. The rest of his entry matches exactly what is on the title page of STC 19007, a book in octavo format. *Language(s)*: Latin. Appraised at 8d in 1652.

165.113   Scribonii physica et sphraerica [sphaerica] doctrina.

Gulielmus Adolphus Scribonius. *Physica et sphaerica doctrina*. Frankfurt am Main: (different houses), 1593–1600.

The two parts of this work appeared under several different titles, probably accounting for the two editions cited here being described as the third and the fourth despite there being no earlier edition with this title. Contributions by Timothy Bright and Zacharias Palthenius, who served as printer of the 1600 edition, are usually cited. *Language(s)*: Latin. Appraised at 4d in 1652.

165.114   Joh: Buxtorfi Epitome Grammat: Ebraeae.

Johann Buxtorf, *the Elder*. *Epitome grammaticae hebraeae*. Continent: 1613–1652.

Language(s): Hebrew Latin. Appraised at 6d in 1652.

165.115 Mundus Alter.

Joseph Hall, *Bishop. Mundus alter et idem sive terra australis*. Britain or Continent: 1605–1607.

STC 12685 *et seq.* and non-STC. A complicated printing history. Published under the pseudonym Mercurio Britannico. Imprint of both editions is Frankfurt with, however, some quires of the 1607 edition printed in Hanau. Sold by Henry Lownes in London. Marked with a cross in the margin next to the appraisal. *Language(s)*: Latin. Appraised at 6d in 1652.

165.116 Dictys Cretensis de bello Troiano.

Dictys, *Cretensis. De bello troiano*. Continent: date not determined.

Often published with the work of Dares, *the Phrygian*, which may be the case with the item here. *Language(s)*: Latin. Appraised at 6d in 1652.

165.117 Magia Naturallis Joh: Baptistae Portae.

Giovanni Battista della Porta. *Magiae naturalis*. Continent: date not determined.

Not appraised. *Language(s)*: Latin.

165.118 Owen's Epigrams

John Owen. *Epigrammatum libri tres*. Britain or Continent: 1606–1634.

STC 18984.5 *et seq.* and non-STC. Only because of the many editions of the Latin version, as compared to the one English translation of selected epigrams published in 1619, is the original version considered more likely here. The manuscript entry certainly makes the English edition possible. *Language(s)*: Latin (probable) English (perhaps). Appraised at 6d in 1652.

165.119 Meditationes Sancti Augustini.

Augustine, *Saint* (spurious). *Meditationes*. Continent: date not determined. *Language(s)*: Latin. Appraised at 6d in 1652.

165.120 Pub: Papinius Statius.

Publius Papinius Statius. Unidentified. Place unknown: stationer unknown, date not determined.

Wing/non-Wing status unknown. Although nothing of Statius was published in England until 1648, this item could be one of the Wing titles (S5335–5336). *Language(s)*: Latin. Appraised at 6d in 1652.

165.121 Cornelius Tacitus. Amsterodami.

Publius Cornelius Tacitus. Unidentified. Amsterdam: (stationer unknown), date not determined.

Language(s): Latin. Appraised at 8d in 1652.

165.122 Gemma Phrisius de princip: Astronomiae etc.

Reiner Gemma, *Frisius*. *De principiis astronomiae et cosmographiae, deque usu globi*. Continent: date not determined.
Language(s): Latin. Appraised at 2d in 1652.

165.123 Joh: Barclaiius ad sectarios.

John Barclay. *Paraenesis ad sectarios*. Continent: 1617–1638.
Shaaber B204–B206, B208. *Language(s)*: Latin. Appraised at 2d in 1652.

165.124 Virgilii Bucoloca

Publius Virgilius Maro. [*Bucolics*]. Britain or Continent: date not determined.
STC 24813 *et seq.* and non-STC. Not appraised. *Language(s)*: Latin.

165.125 Nonni Panopolitani metaphrasis Evang: secundum Joannem versibus Heroicis.

Nonnus, *Panopolitanus*. *Metaphrasis evangelii secundum Joannem versibus heroicis*. (*Bible—N.T.*). Edited by Friedrich Sylburg. Continent: 1596–1629.
The compiler's manuscript entry is remarkably accurate. Of the numerous editions of this verse paraphrase of John's Gospel, only four editions carry the word "metaphrasis" in the title, all edited by Sylburg. *Language(s)*: Latin. Appraised at 8d in 1652.

165.126 Aphoris: Hippocratis. Lugd: Batavo:

Hippocrates. *Aphorismi*. Leyden: (different houses), date not determined.
Language(s): Greek Latin. Appraised at 4d in 1652.

165.127 Apolinarius psalmi

Apollinarius, *Bishop*. [*Psalms: commentary and text*]. Britain or Continent: date not determined.
STC 2352 and non-STC. The STC book (1590) is in Greek alone. Various Continental editions are Greek-Latin editions. *Language(s)*: Greek (probable) Latin (probable). Appraised at 6d in 1652.

165.128 Sleydan de 4or Imperiis

Joannes Philippson, *Sleidanus*. *De quatuor summis imperiis*. Britain or Continent: date not determined.
STC 19847, Wing S3987, and non-STC. *Language(s)*: Latin. Appraised at 6d in 1652.

165.129 Epictetus

Epictetus. *Enchiridion*. Continent: date not determined.

English versions date from 1567 (STC 10423), but a translation is not likely here. The first Latin edition published in England was in 1655 (Wing E3144), three years after the date of this inventory. *Language(s)*: Latin. Appraised at 6d in 1652.

165.130 Scots poems

Thomas Scott, *Poet*. *Foure paradoxes of arte, of lawe, of warre, of service*. London: (different houses), 1602–1611.
STC 22107 *et seq*. *Language(s)*: English. Appraised at 6d in 1652.

165.131:1–8 8 Italian and french

Unidentified. Places unknown: stationers unknown, dates not determined.
STC/non-STC status unknown. *Language(s)*: French Italian. Appraised as a group at 1s in 1652.

165.132 sparkes vis natura

William Sparke. *Vis naturae et virtus vitae explicatae, comparatae, ad universum doctrinae ordinem constituendum*. London: R. Field, 1612.
STC 23028. *Language(s)*: Latin. Appraised at 2d in 1652.

165.133 Junius Emblems

Adrian Junius. *Emblemata*. Continent: date not determined.
Language(s): Latin. Appraised at 2d in 1652.

165.134 Adagia sacra

Unidentified. Continent (probable): date not determined.
Probably not an STC book. Among those who wrote works that might be entered in this manner are Joachim Zehner, Martin Ruland, *the Elder*, and Andreas Schottus, with the first mentioned being marginally more likely intended here. *Language(s)*: Latin. Appraised at 2d in 1652.

165.135 Flamells Hiroglificall figures

Nicolas Flamel. *Nicholas Flamel, his exposition of the hieroglyphicall figures upon an arch in St. Innocent church-yard in Paris*. Translated by Eirenaeus Orandus. London: T. S[nodham] for T. Walkley, 1624.
STC 11027. Contains translations of works by Artephius and by Joannes Jovius Pontanus. *Language(s)*: English. Appraised at 4d in 1652.

165.136 Prideaux Hypomnemata

John Prideaux, *Bishop*. *Hypomnemata logica, rhetorica, physica, metaphysica, pneumatica, ethica, politica, oeconomica*. Oxford: excudebat impensis suis Leon. Lichfield academiae typographus, 1650?
Wing P3430A. *Language(s)*: Latin. Appraised at 1s in 1652.

165.137   Franc: Bar: de Verulamis Hist: vitae et Mortis

Francis Bacon, *Viscount St. Albans*. *Historia vitae et mortis*. Britain or Continent: 1623–1645.

STC 1156 and non-STC. Only one edition among the four represented in the date range — the *editio princeps* — was published in England. *Language(s)*: Latin. Appraised at 6d in 1652.

Henry Jacob. Scholar (M.A., B.M.):
Inventory against debt. 1653.

RIVES NICHOLSON

Born around 1608 to a puritan family who emigrated to Leiden, probably for its more tolerant religious climate (Jacob's father was a well known semi-Separatist minister who eventually moved to Virginia), Henry Jacob spent his youth and acquired his early education in the Netherlands, studying Arabic under Thomas Erpenius, the renowned Dutch Arabist, and acquiring an exceptional command of Hebrew and other languages. Upon his return to England, Jacob was created Bachelor of Arts at Oxford in January 1629 by virtue of his rigorous language studies in the Netherlands and was later admitted to Merton College as a probationary fellow. Yet the strongly Dutch character of his early education, the prickly oddities of his own nature, and poor health seem to have prevented him from ever acclimating fully to British academic life.

Despite helping various Oxford scholars with instruction in Greek and other languages (and winning praise for his teaching from the educational reformer Samuel Hartlib), Jacob's progress towards his M.A. was slowed by his insufficient training in logic and philosophy, as well as by illness. He completed the degree in 1636 largely thanks to the special intervention of Archbishop William Laud, who secured him a fellowship as a lecturer in philology to junior fellows. His subsequent academic career seems to have followed a downwardly sloping path, despite occasional flashes of promise. Elected superior beadle of divinity in June 1641 and created Bachelor of Medicine in 1642, Jacob acted as amanuensis to the lawyer and linguist John Selden and compiled a catalogue of the growing collection of Hebrew books and manuscripts in the Bodleian. But he appears also to have neglected his duties as lecturer: according to Anthony à Wood, "his head always over busy about critical notions (which made him sometimes a little better than craz'd)" (*Athenae Oxonienses*, 1:330). Suspended at least once, Jacob nonetheless remained at the university until 1648, when he was expelled by the parliamentary visitors, leaving behind him at Oxford a trunk of manuscripts and books that may have been confiscated by the college.

Following his expulsion Jacob lived a hardscrabble existence in London until September of 1652, when — destitute and ill from overmuch study — he moved to Canterbury to be looked after by a physician cousin. He died in November of the same year. (See *ODNB*; *Alumni Oxonienses*, 2:279.) An inventory of his possessions was made on 5 February 1653 at the request of Jacob's friend the Latin poet Henry Birkhead, dean of arts at All Souls and founder of the Oxford poetry professorship (*ODNB*). In a note accompanying the inventory, Birkhead claims that Jacob had owed him forty pounds for a loan in 1648 (presumably to finance Jacob's move to London after his expulsion), as well as additional money for freeing him from prison (presumably for debt) and paying his arrears for lodging in 1652. Birkhead also notes that "the Impression of his booke cost mee neare twenty pounds, of which there be not forty coppy's sold." This debt will be witnessed, he adds, by "Mr Hall the printer" and "Mr Robinson Bookeseller, to whom I payd some part of the money for paper." The book was *Philologiae anakalypterion*, printed in Oxford by Henry Hall in 1652 (Wing J97); a preface by Birkhead offers a short life of Jacob. Another book, *Delphi phoenicizantes* (Oxford, 1655), was attributed to Jacob in the later seventeenth century, but is now thought to be the work of another writer (Wing D1385).

The inventory is vexingly incomplete, identifying only seven out of a sizeable library of some 370 books. It could be that the dishonorable circumstances of Jacob's departure from the college were not thought to merit thoroughness in the compilation of an inventory, being conducted at the request of a creditor rather than at Oxford's behest. A more plausible explanation, however, may be that most of Jacob's books were in Arabic, Greek, or Hebrew script that the compiler could not read and did not bother to describe. Though they cannot reliably suggest the general character of a library as large as Jacob's, the six identified books include works of history, law, medicine, and grammar and etymology. Two are either translated from or in Arabic: Avicenna's *Liber secundus De canone canonis* features an Arabic as well as a Latin title on its title page, and Georgius Elmacinus's *Historia Saracenica* was rendered into Latin from Arabic by Jacob's former teacher Thomas Erpenius. It could be that the library contained an abundance of similar works in non-Roman script that defeated the linguistic capacities and the patience of the compiler. Other identified works in the library include the *Etymologicon magnum*, a book on the etymology of the Greek language originally compiled between 1100 and 1250, and Clenardus's *Institutiones linguae graecae*. The inventory notes that the entire collection was kept in three, presumably large and heavy, trunks.

Oxford University Archives, Bodleian Library: Hyp.B.14.

§

166.1   Diodorus Siculus
166.2   Etymologicon Magnum
166.3   Rabbi Judas Leo.
166.4   Clenardus
166.5:1–60   Threescore bookes in 8vo bound and stitched.
166.6:1–34   Thirty foure quartos bound and stitched
166.7:1   Historia Saracenica
             Mare clausum
             De Canone Canonis
166.7:2   [See 166.7:1]
166.7:3   [See 166.7:1]
166.8:1–9   Nine bookes in folio
166.9:1–5   Five folios
166.10:1–21 Twenty one bookes in 4to
166.11:1–52 Fifty two bookes in 8vo of all sorts
166.12:1–3   Three Folios
166.13:1–7   Paper bookes seven
166.14:1–39 Thirty nine bookes stitched and bound of all sorts
166.15:1–46 Forty six small bookes stitched
166.16:1–74 Threescore and foureteene old and stitched bookes
166.17:1–29 Twenty nine small bookes

§

166.1   Diodorus Siculus

Diodorus, *Siculus. Bibliotheca historia.* Continent: date not determined.

There is no reason to believe that the 1569 selections of Diodorus in English (STC 6893) is represented here, particularly at the valuation. *Language(s)*: Latin. Appraised at 10s in 1653.

166.2   Etymologicon Magnum

Etymologicon magnum. Edited by Friedrich Sylburg. Heidelberg: e typographeio Hieronymi Commelini, 1594.

Founded on 1499 and 1549 works of a similar name, the prefaces of which (by Marcus Marusus and Federico Turrisano) are included in this work. Two editions in the same year. *Language(s)*: Greek Latin. Appraised at 7s in 1653.

166.3   Rabbi Judas Leo.

Leo Juda. Unidentified. Continent: date not determined.

Juda was primarily a translator and editor of the Bible and of theological works by writers such as Erasmus and Zwingli. *Language(s)*: Latin. Appraised at 1s in 1653.

166.4 Clenardus

Nicolaus Clenardus. *Institutiones linguae graecae*. Britain or Continent: date not determined.

STC 5400.5 *et seq.* and non-STC. *Language(s)*: Greek Latin. Appraised at 2s in 1653.

166.5:1–60   Threescore bookes in 8vo bound and stitched.

Unidentified. Places unknown: stationers unknown, dates not determined.

STC/non-STC status unknown. *Language(s)*: Unknown. Appraised as a group at £1 5s in 1653.

166.6:1–34   Thirty foure quartos bound and stitched

Unidentified. Places unknown: stationers unknown, dates not determined.

STC/non-STC status unknown. *Language(s)*: Unknown. Appraised as a group at £1 12s in 1653.

166.7:1   Historia Saracenica Mare clausum De Canone Canonis

Georgius Elmacinus. *Historia Saracenica*. Translated from the Arabic into Latin by Thomas Erpenius. Leyden: ex typographia Erpeniana linguarum orientalium, prostant apud Joannem Maire, et Elzevirios, 1625.

The author's name is usually transliterated as Jirjis ibn al-Amid al-Makin. The customary Latin form is given here. *Language(s)*: Arabic Latin. Appraised with two others at 6s in 1653.

166.7:2   [See 166.7:1]

John Selden. *Mare clausum seu de dominio maris libri duo*. Britain or Continent: 1635–1636.

STC 22175 *et seq.* Two of the STC listed editions were printed on the Continent. *Language(s)*: Latin. Appraised with two others at 6s in 1653.

166.7:3   [See 166.7:1]

Avicenna. *Liber secundus De canone canonis*. Edited and translated by Peter Kirsten. Breslau: Peter Kirsten, 1609.

An Arabic title precedes the Latin form. *Language(s)*: Arabic Latin. Appraised with two others at 6s in 1653.

166.8:1–9   Nine bookes in folio

Unidentified. Places unknown: stationers unknown, dates not determined.

STC/non-STC status unknown. *Language(s)*: Unknown. Appraised as a group at £2 16s in 1653.

166.9:1–5   Five folios

Unidentified. Places unknown: stationers unknown, dates not determined.

STC/non-STC status unknown. *Language(s)*: Unknown. Appraised as a group at £1 10s in 1653.

166.10:1–21   Twenty one bookes in 4to
Unidentified. Places unknown: stationers unknown, dates not determined.
STC/non-STC status unknown. *Language(s)*: Unknown. Appraised as a group at £1 10s in 1653.

166.11:1–52   Fifty two bookes in 8vo of all sorts
Unidentified. Places unknown: stationers unknown, dates not determined.
STC/non-STC status unknown. *Language(s)*: Unknown. Appraised as a group at £1 15s in 1653.

166.12:1–3   Three Folios
Unidentified. Places unknown: stationers unknown, dates not determined.
STC/non-STC status unknown. *Language(s)*: Unknown. Appraised as a group at £1 in 1653.

166.13:1–7   Paper bookes seven
Unidentified. Provenances unknown: dates not determined.
Manuscripts. *Language(s)*: Unknown. Appraised as a group at 5s in 1653.

166.14:1–39   Thirty nine bookes stitched and bound of all sorts
Unidentified. Places unknown: stationers unknown, dates not determined.
STC/non-STC status unknown. *Language(s)*: Unknown. Appraised as a group at 9s in 1653.

166.15:1–46   Forty six small bookes stitched
Unidentified. Places unknown: stationers unknown, dates not determined.
STC/non-STC status unknown. *Language(s)*: Unknown. Appraised as a group at 5s in 1653.

166.16:1–74   Threescore and foureteene old and stitched bookes
Unidentified. Places unknown: stationers unknown, dates not determined.
STC/non-STC status unknown. *Language(s)*: Unknown. Appraised as a group at 6s in 1653.

166.17:1–29   Twenty nine small bookes
Unidentified. Places unknown: stationers unknown, dates not determined.
STC/non-STC status unknown. *Language(s)*: Unknown. Appraised as a group at 5s in 1653.

PLRE Cumulative Catalogue

In the following lists, *entry* refers to a single entry made by a compiler of a manuscript book-list; *record* refers to a single record created from an *entry* by an editor. An *entry* may contain more than one *record*; conversely, a *record* may constitute only part of an *entry*. A *record* always represents at least one book but may represent more, including a multi-volume set. For example, the manuscript entry "Aschames schoolemaster Toxophilus" (PLRE 149.144) constitutes one entry and generates two records: Roger Ascham's *The scholemaster* and his *Toxophilus*.

I. PLRE Database Totals

Book-lists: 196; Entries: 10,382; Records: 11,357
Number of Books Represented: More than 12,997
   (Of the 11,357 records, 142 records specify two or more unidentified books for a determinable total of 1,822 books, adding a net 1,640 books to the record total. In addition, seventy-three records contain an indeterminable number of books, identified in the database as *multiple*. At least 90 manuscript entries may represent the same book [as in the books conveyed from one owner to another, both of whom are listed in the PLRE catalogue, or books that appear in an owner's purchasing list and later are listed in his probate inventory].)

II. Book-list Indices

A. Arrangement and Size of Each PLRE Unit

Volume 1: PLRE 1–4	1,394 records (seven records in Volume 5)
Volume 2: PLRE 5–66	1,151 records
Volume 3: PLRE 67–86	1,365 records
Volume 4: PLRE 87–112	1,673 records
Volume 5: PLRE 113–137	1,815 records
Volume 6: PLRE 138–150	1,632 records
Volume 7: PLRE 151-166	1,442 records
APND Lists: PLRE Ad1–Ad30	885 records

B. Owners of Book-lists Arranged by Owners' Names

Owner and book-list information below is ordered in the following manner:

> Name, degree(s). (Born–died) PLRE number. Profession. Social status. *Date* [of book-list, actual or *terminus ad quem*]: 1631. *Type* [of book-list]: inventory (probate). *Entries*: 25; *Records*: 29.

Allen, Richard, B.A. (c.1547–1569) PLRE 79. Scholar. Professional. *Date:* 1569. *Type:* inventory (probate). *Entries:* 97; *Records:* 98.

Allen, Thomas, B.A. (?–1561) PLRE 69. Scholar. Professional. *Date:* 1561. *Type:* inventory (probate). *Entries:* 34; *Records:* 35.

Anlaby (Aulaby), Edmund, M.A., B.Th. (?–1559) PLRE Ad5. Scholar. Professional. *Date:* 1533, 1559. *Type:* bookseller's accounts, inventory (probate). *Entries:* 28; *Records:* 33.

Anonymous. (?-?) PLRE 164. Scholar (probable). Professional (probable). *Date:* c. 1650. *Type*: inventory. *Entries:* 72; *Records*: 74.

Atkins, Henry, M.A. (?–1560) PLRE 113. Scholar. Professional. *Date:* 1560. *Type:* inventory (probate). *Entries:* 16; *Records:* 16.

Atkinson, John, M.A. (?–1570) PLRE 83. Scholar. Professional. *Date:* 1570. *Type:* inventory (probate). *Entries:* 25; *Records:* 25.

Austin (given name unknown). (?–?) PLRE 98. Scholar (probable). Professional (probable). *Date:* 1572. *Type:* inventory. *Entries:* 20; *Records:* 20.

Badger, John, M.A. (?–1577) PLRE 115. Scholar. Professional. *Date:* 1577. *Type:* inventory (probate). *Entries:* 78; *Records:* 79.

Balborough, William, D.U.L. (?–1514) PLRE 29. Scholar. Professional. *Date:* 1514. *Type:* inventory (probate). *Entries:* 25; *Records:* 29.

Balyn, John, B.A. (?–1513) PLRE 25. Scholar. Professional. *Date:* 1513. *Type:* inventory (probate). *Entries:* 18; *Records:* 18.

Barton, George, B.Th. (?–1602) PLRE 155. Scholar. Professional. *Date*: 1602. *Type*: inventory (probate). *Entries*: 14; *Records*: 15.

Barwyck, Stephen. (?–1547) PLRE Ad29. Butler, Scholar (probable) (student, probable). Retainer, Professional (probable). *Date:* 1547. *Type:* inventory (probate). *Entries:* 35; *Records:* 36.

Batchelor, Robert. (1506–?) PLRE Ad6. Cleric (chaplain), Scholar. Professional. *Date:* 1533. *Type:* bookseller's accounts. *Entries:* 8; *Records:* 10.

Battbrantes, William. (?–1572) PLRE 99. Scholar (student, probable). Professional. *Date:* 1572. *Type:* inventory (probate). *Entries:* 35; *Records:* 35.

Beaumont, Edward, B.A. (1531–1552) PLRE 64. Scholar. Professional. *Date:* 1552. *Type:* inventory (probate). *Entries:* 117; *Records:* 118.

Beddow, John, M.A. (?–c.1577) PLRE 91. Scholar (schoolmaster). Professional. *Dates:* 1571 and 1577. *Type:* inventories. *Entries:* 40; *Records:* 41.

Bidnell, William, M.A. (?–1512) PLRE 23. Scholar. Professional. *Date:* 1512. *Type:* inventory (probate). *Entries:* 9; *Records:* 9.

Bill, Thomas, M.A. (?–1552) PLRE Ad7. Physician, Scholar. Professional. *Date:* 1532. *Type:* bookseller's accounts. *Entries:* 4; *Records:* 4.

Bisley (given name unknown), M.A. (perhaps), B.Th. (perhaps). (?–1543?) PLRE 60. Scholar. Professional. *Date:* 1543. *Type:* inventory (probate). *Entries:* 122; *Records:* 134.

Blomefield, Miles. (1525–1603) PLRE Ad2. Physician, Alchemist. Professional. *Date:* reconstruction. *Type:* reconstruction. *Entries:* 24; *Records:* 25.

Bolt, Thomas. (1557–?) PLRE 132. Scholar (student). Professional. *Date:* 1578. *Type:* inventory. *Entries:* 86; *Records:* 87.

Bonenfant, Thomas, M.A. (?–?) PLRE Ad8. Scholar. Professional. *Date:* 1533. *Type:* bookseller's accounts. *Entries:* 17; *Records:* 18.

Bowerman, John, M.A., B.C.L. (?–1507) PLRE 5. Scholar. Professional. *Date:* 1507. *Type:* will. *Entries:* 3; *Records:* 4.

Bradford, Ralph, M.A. (c.1502?) PLRE Ad9. Scholar. Professional. *Date:* c.1527. *Type:* bookseller's accounts. *Entries:* 13; *Records:* 14.

Brewer, John, M.A. (?–1535) PLRE Ad10. Scholar. Professional. *Date:* 1533. *Type:* bookseller's accounts. *Entries:* 4; *Records:* 4.

Bromsby, John, B.Th. (?–?) PLRE Ad11. Scholar. Professional. *Date:* 1531. *Type:* bookseller's accounts. *Entries:* 4; *Records:* 5.

Brown, Walter, B.Th. (?-1613) PLRE 159. Cleric, Scholar. Professional. *Date*: 1613. *Type*: inventory (probate). *Entries:* 541; *Records*: 548.

Brown, William, M.A. (?–1558) PLRE 67. Scholar. Professional. *Date:* 1558. *Type:* inventory (probate). *Entries:* 223; *Records:* 242.

Bryan, Robert, D.Cn.L. (?–1508) PLRE 11. Scholar. Professional. *Date:* 1508. *Type:* inventory (probate). *Entries:* 19; *Records:* 19.

Buckingham, Edward, B.Cn.L. (?–1568) PLRE Ad12. Scholar. Professional. *Date:* 1533. *Type:* bookseller's accounts. *Entries:* 3; *Records:* 3.

Burton, Edmund, M.A. (?–1529) PLRE 43. Scholar. Professional. *Date:* 1529. *Type:* inventory (probate). *Entries:* 42; *Records:* 46.

Bury, John, B.A. (probable). (?–1567) PLRE 74. Scholar. Professional. *Date:* 1567. *Type:* inventory (probate). *Entries:* 19; *Records:* 19.

Carpenter, Thomas, M.A. (?–1577) PLRE 116. Scholar. Professional. *Date:* 1577. *Type:* inventory (probate). *Entries:* 83; *Records:* 84.

Carter, John, B.C.L. (?–1509) PLRE 17. Scholar. Professional. *Date:* 1509. *Type:* inventory (probate). *Entries:* 3; *Records:* 5.

Cartwright, Thomas, M.A. (?–1532) PLRE 50. Scholar. Professional. *Date:* 1532. *Type:* inventory (probate) and will. *Entries:* 8; *Records:* 11.

Cauthorn, John, B.A. (?–?) PLRE Ad13. Scholar. Professional. *Date:* 1531. *Type:* bookseller's accounts. *Entries:* 12; *Records:* 12.

Chantry, William, B.A. (?–1507) PLRE 6. Scholar. Professional. *Date:* 1507. *Type:* will. *Entries:* 2; *Records:* 3.

Charnock, Roger, M.A. (1549–?) PLRE 117. Scholar. Professional. *Date:* 1577. *Type:* inventory. *Entries:* 80; *Records:* 83.

Chastelain, George. (?–1513) PLRE 26. Stationer. Middle class. *Date:* 1513. *Type:* inventory (probate). *Entries:* 1; *Records:* 1.

Cheke, Agnes. (?–1549) PLRE Ad30. Merchant (vintner). Middle class, Privileged person. *Date:* 1549. *Type:* inventory (probate) *Entries:* 3; *Records:* 4.

Cheyne, Henry, M.A. (?–?) PLRE 138. Scholar. Professional. *Date:* 1581. *Type:* inventory (against debt). *Entries:* 39; *Records:* 43.

Chogan, William. (?–1537) PLRE 56. Scholar (student). Professional. *Date:* 1537. *Type:* will. *Entries:* 1; *Records:* 1.

Cliff, Richard, M.A. (?–1566) PLRE 73. Cleric (chaplain), Scholar. Professional. *Date:* 1566. *Type:* inventory (probate) and will. *Entries:* 261; *Records:* 261.

Cliffley (given name unknown). (?–?) PLRE 118. Cleric (probable). Professional (probable). *Date:* 1577. *Type:* inventory. *Entries:* 22; *Records:* 22.

Coles, John, B.Th. (?–1529) PLRE 44. Scholar. Professional. *Date:* 1529. *Type:* inventory (probate). *Entries:* 5; *Records:* 5.

Collins, Robert. (?–?) PLRE 24. Scholar (student). Professional. *Date:* 1512. *Type:* receipt. *Entries:* 8; *Records:* 8.

Conner, John, B.Th. (c.1490–1569) PLRE 80. Cleric, Scholar. Professional. *Date:* 1569. *Type:* inventory (probate). *Entries:* 46; *Records:* 48.

Cox, Richard, D.Th. (1500–1581) PLRE 1. Cleric (bishop). Gentry. *Date:* 1581. *Type:* inventory. *Entries:* 196; *Records:* 208.

Dalaber, Anthony. (?–1562) PLRE 45. Scholar (student). Professional. *Date:* 1529. *Type:* inventory. *Entries:* 8; *Records:* 8.

Davy, William (perhaps), B.Cn.L. (?–1546) PLRE Ad14. Scholar. Professional. *Date:* 1533. *Type:* bookseller's accounts. *Entries:* 9; *Records:* 9.

Dawson, William, M.A. (?–1577) PLRE 119. Scholar. Professional. *Date:* 1577. *Type:* inventory (probate). *Entries:* 37; *Records:* 37.

Day, Thomas, B.C.L. (?–1570) PLRE 84. Cleric, Scholar. Professional. *Date:* 1570. *Type:* inventory (probate). *Entries:* 137; *Records:* 149.

Dayrell, William, B.A. (?–1577) PLRE 120. Scholar. Professional. *Date:* 1577. *Type:* inventory (probate). *Entries:* 30; *Records:* 30.

Deegen, Peter. (?–1527) PLRE 37. Scholar (student). Professional. *Date:* 1527. *Type:* will. *Entries:* 5; *Records:* 5.

Derbyshire, William. (?–1551) PLRE 61. Scholar (student). Professional. *Date:* 1551. *Type:* inventory (probate). *Entries:* 11; *Records:* 23.

Dering, Sir Edward. (1598–1644) PLRE 4. Member of Parliament. Gentry. *Date:* 1628 and c.1642. *Type:* account book, catalogue, and reconstruction. *Entries:* 638; *Records:* 683. (See Volume 1 and Volume 5.)

Dewer, William, M.A. (probable). (?–1514) PLRE 30. Scholar. Professional. *Date:* 1514. *Type:* inventory (probate). *Entries:* 6; *Records:* 10.

Dewhurst, Giles, M.A. (?–1577) PLRE 121. Scholar. Professional. *Date:* 1577. *Type:* inventory (probate). *Entries:* 45; *Records:* 45.

Dickinson, Thomas (probable), B.A. (?–1558) PLRE Ad15. Scholar. Professional. *Date:* 1533. *Type:* bookseller's accounts. *Entries:* 7; *Records:* 9.

Digby, George and Simon. (?–?) PLRE 81. Scholars (students). Professional. *Date:* 1569. *Type:* inventory. *Entries:* 47; *Records:* 48.

Digby, Simon. (see George Digby).

Dowe, Robert, B.C.L. (1553–1588) PLRE 148. Scholar. Professional. *Date:* 1589. *Type:* inventory (probate). *Entries:* 302; *Records:* 305.

Dunnet, John. (?–1570) PLRE 85. Scholar (student). Professional. *Date:* 1570. *Type:* inventory (probate). *Entries:* 37; *Records:* 37.

Dyllam, Walter. (?–?) PLRE 106. Scholar (student). Professional. *Date:* 1575. *Type:* inventory. *Entries:* 1; *Records:* 3.

Faringdon, Tristram. (?–1577) PLRE 122. Scholar (student). Professional. *Date:* 1577. *Type:* inventory (probate). *Entries:* 17; *Records:* 18.

Ferne, Richard, M.A. (?–1577) PLRE 123. Scholar. Professional. *Date:* 1577. *Type:* inventory (probate). *Entries:* 51; *Records:* 51.

Fisher, Richard, M.A. (?–1602) PLRE 156. Scholar. Professional. *Date*: 1602. *Type*: inventory (probate). *Entries:* 74; *Records*: 79.

Forster, John, B.C.L. (?–1584) PLRE 141. Scholar. Professional. *Date:* 1584. *Type:* inventory (probate). *Entries:* 21; *Records:* 21.

Foster, Thomas. (?–1577) PLRE 124. Unknown. Privileged person (probable). *Date:* 1577. *Type:* inventory (probate). *Entries:* 9; *Records:* 9.

Froster, Roger. (?–1514) PLRE 31. Scholar (student). Professional. *Date:* 1514. *Type:* inventory (probate). *Entries:* 1; *Records:* 1.

Gearing, William, M.A. (?–1607) PLRE 157. Cleric (chaplain), Scholar. Professional. *Date*: 1607. *Type*: inventory (probate). *Entries*: 52; *Records* 54.

Gilbert, John. (?–?) PLRE Ad16. Scholar (student). Professional. *Date:* 1528. *Type:* bookseller's accounts. *Entries:* 2; *Records:* 2.

Gilbert, Nicholas. (see Hilbert, Nicholas).

Glover, John, M.A. (?–1578) PLRE 133. Scholar. Professional. *Date:* 1578. *Type:* inventory (probate). *Entries:* 279; *Records:* 280.

Gofton, William, B.C.L. (?–1507) PLRE 7. Scholar. Professional. *Date:* 1507. *Type:* inventory (probate). *Entries:* 11; *Records:* 12.

Goldsmith, Francis. (?–?) PLRE Ad17. Scholar (student) (probable). Professional (probable). *Date:* 1533. *Type:* bookseller's accounts. *Entries:* 1; *Records:* 1.

Grant, Philip. (?–1560) PLRE 114. Scholar (student). Professional. *Date:* 1560. *Type:* inventory (probate). *Entries:* 26; *Records:* 26.

Gray, John. (?–1577) PLRE 125. Scholar (student). Professional. *Date:* 1577. *Type:* inventory (probate). *Entries:* 18; *Records:* 18.

Griffin, Roger, B.A. (?–1510) PLRE 19. Scholar. Professional. *Date:* 1510. *Type:* inventory (probate). *Entries:* 2; *Records:* 2.

Griffith, Thomas, M.A., B.M. (perhaps). (?–1562) PLRE 70. Scholar, Physician (perhaps). Professional. *Date:* 1562. *Type:* inventory (probate). *Entries:* 92; *Records:* 97.

Gryce, William, D.Th. (?–1528) PLRE 41. Scholar. Professional. *Date:* 1528. *Type:* inventory (probate). *Entries:* 15; *Records:* 15.

Hamlyn, William, M.A. (?–1534) PLRE 51. Scholar. Professional. *Date:* 1534. *Type:* inventory (probate). *Entries:* 10; *Records:* 15.

Hart, Robert, M.A. (?–1571) PLRE 92. Scholar. Professional. *Date:* 1571. *Type:* inventory (probate). *Entries:* 135; *Records:* 137.

Hartburn, John, M.A. (?–1513) PLRE 27. Scholar. Professional. *Date:* 1513. *Type:* inventory (probate). *Entries:* 2; *Records:* 4.

Harwood, Thomas, B.A., D.M. (?–?) PLRE Ad18. Scholar. Professional. *Date:* 1530. *Type:* bookseller's accounts. *Entries:* 14; *Records:* 14.

Hawarden, Robert, M.A. (?–1527) PLRE 38. Scholar. Professional. *Date:* 1527. *Type:* inventory (probate). *Entries:* 6; *Records:* 6.

Haynes, John, M.A. (1562–1585) PLRE 144. Scholar. Professional. *Date:* 1585. *Type:* inventory (probate). *Entries:* 71; *Records:* 72.

Heath, John, M.A. (?–?) PLRE 140. Scholar. Professional. *Date:* 1582. *Type:* inventory (against debt). *Entries:* 5; *Records:* 5.

Heywood, John, B.A. (?–1514) PLRE 32. Scholar. Professional. *Date:* 1514. *Type:* inventory (probate). *Entries:* 13; *Records:* 14.

Higgins, Edward, M.A. (?–1588) PLRE 149. Scholar. Professional. *Date:* 1588. *Type:* inventory (probate). *Entries:* 299; *Records:* 311.

Hilbert, John. (see Gilbert, John).

Hilbert, Nicholas. (c.1509–1561) PLRE Ad19. Scholar (student). Professional. *Date:* 1528. *Type:* bookseller's accounts. *Entries:* 1; *Records:* 1.

Hill, Thomas. (?–1585) PLRE 145. Scholar (probable). Professional (probable). *Date:* 1585. *Type:* inventory (probate). *Entries:* 55; *Records:* 55.

Hodges, Thomas, B.A. (?–1539) PLRE 58. Scholar. Professional. *Date:* 1539. *Type:* inventory (probate). *Entries:* 28; *Records:* 33.

Hogan, Matthias. (?–1508) PLRE 12. Scholar (student). Professional. *Date:* 1508. *Type:* inventory (probate). *Entries:* 2; *Records:* 2.

Homer, Edward, M.A. (?-1614) PLRE 160. Scholar. Professional. *Date*: 1614. *Type*: inventory (probate). *Entries*: 48; *Records*: 50

Hooper, Robert, M.A. (?–c.1571) PLRE 93. Scholar. Professional. *Date:* 1571. *Type:* inventory (probate). *Entries:* 77; *Records:* 77.

Hoppe, Edward, M.A. (?–1538) PLRE 57. Scholar. Professional. *Date:* 1538. *Type:* will. *Entries:* 17; *Records:* 19.

Hornby, Nicholas, B.A., M.A. (perhaps). (?–?) PLRE Ad20. Scholar. Professional. *Date:* c.1532. *Type:* bookseller's accounts. *Entries:* 4; *Records:* 4.

Hornsley, John. (?–1578) PLRE 134. Scholar. Professional. *Date:* 1578. *Type:* inventory (probate). *Entries:* 89; *Records:* 91.

Horsley, Thomas. (?–?) PLRE Ad21. Scholar. Professional. *Date:* 1533. *Type:* bookseller's accounts. *Entries:* 4; *Records:* 4.

Horsman, Leonard, M.A. (?–1551) PLRE Ad22. Scholar. Professional. *Date:* 1531. *Type:* bookseller's account. *Entries:* 24; *Records:* 25.

Horsman, Ralph. (?–?) PLRE Ad23. Scholar (student). Professional. *Date:* 1531. *Type:* bookseller's accounts. *Entries:* 2; *Records:* 2.

Hudson, Thomas, B.A. (?-1618) PLRE 161. Scholar. Professional. *Date:* 1618. *Type*: inventory (probate). *Entries:* 11; *Records*: 12.

Hunt, Robert, D.C.L., D.Th. (c.1499–1536) PLRE 53. Scholar. Professional. *Date:* 1536. *Type:* inventory (probate). *Entries:* 2; *Records:* 5.

Hurde, William. (?–1551) PLRE 62. Scholar (student). Professional. *Date:* 1551. *Type:* inventory (probate). *Entries:* 20; *Records:* 21.

Hutchinson, Henry, B.A. (1550–1573) PLRE 103. Scholar. Professional. *Date:* 1573. *Type:* inventory (probate). *Entries:* 99; *Records:* 99.

Hutton, John, B.A. (?-1652) PLRE 165. Scholar. Professional. *Date*: 1652. *Type*: inventory (probate). *Entries*: 137; *Records*: 146.

Jackson, Lionel, M.A. (?–1514) PLRE 33. Scholar. Professional. *Date:* 1514. *Type:* inventory (probate) and will. *Entries:* 32; *Records:* 33.

Jacob, Henry, M.A., B.M. (1608-1652) PLRE 166. Scholar. Professional. *Date*: 1653. *Type*: inventory (against debt). *Entries*: 17; *Records*: 19.

Jewel, John, D.Th. (1522–1571) PLRE Ad1. Cleric (bishop). Professional. *Date:* reconstruction. *Type:* reconstruction. *Entries:* 74; *Records:* 74.

Johnson, James. (?–1568) PLRE 77. Cleric (chaplain). Professional. *Date:* 1568. *Type:* inventory (probate). *Entries:* 4; *Records:* 4.

Johnson, Philip, B.Th. (?–1576) PLRE 110. Scholar. Professional. *Date:* 1576. *Type:* inventory (probate). *Entries:* 270; *Records:* 274.

Jones, Lewis, B.A. (?–1571) PLRE 94. Scholar. Professional. *Date:* 1571. *Type:* inventory (probate). *Entries:* 41; *Records:* 41.

Jones, Robert. (?–1567) PLRE 75. Sexton. Professional. *Date:* 1567. *Type:* inventory (probate). *Entries:* 23; *Records:* 27.

Kettelby, William, M.A. (?–c.1572) PLRE 104. Scholar. Professional. *Date:* 1573. *Type:* inventory (probate). *Entries:* 93; *Records:* 96.

Kilby, Richard, D.Th. (?-1620) PLRE 162. Scholar. Professional. *Date*: 1620. *Type*: inventory (bequest). *Entries*: 39; *Records*: 42.

Kitley, John, M.A. (?–1531) PLRE 49. Scholar. Professional. *Date:* 1531. *Type:* inventory (probate). *Entries:* 1; *Records:* 2.

Kitson, John, M.A. (?–1536) PLRE 54. Scholar. Professional. *Date:* 1536. *Type:* will. *Entries:* 1; *Records:* 1.

Kyffen, John, B.Cn.L. (?–1514) PLRE 34. Scholar. Professional. *Date:* 1514. *Type:* inventory (probate). *Entries:* 22; *Records:* 24.

Lacy, Dunstan, M.A. (?–1534) PLRE 52. Scholar. Professional. *Date:* 1534. *Type:* will. *Entries:* 27; *Records:* 29.

Lanham, Richard, B.A. (?–?) PLRE 105. Scholar. Professional. *Date:* 1573. *Type:* inventory. *Entries:* 4; *Records:* 4.

Lewis, John. (?–1579) PLRE 137. Manciple, Merchant (white-baker). Middle class, Privileged person. *Date:* 1579. *Type:* inventory (probate). *Entries:* 78; *Records:* 78.

Lewis, Richard. (?-c.1590) PLRE 151. Manciple. Professional, Privileged person. *Date*: c. 1590. *Type*: inventory (probate). *Entries*: 42; *Records*: 47.

Lilbourn, William, M.A. (?–1514) PLRE 35. Scholar. Professional. *Date:* 1514. *Type:* inventory (probate). *Entries:* 9; *Records:* 10.

Lisle (given name unknown). (?–?) PLRE 86. Scholar (student). Professional. *Date:* 1570. *Type:* inventory. *Entries:* 11; *Records:* 11.

Llewellyn, David ap. (?–?) PLRE Ad24. Cleric (friar). Professional. *Date:* 1533. *Type:* bookseller's accounts. *Entries:* 7; *Records:* 7.

Lombard, Nicholas, M.A. (?–1575) PLRE 107. Scholar. Professional. *Date:* 1575. *Type:* inventory (probate) and will. *Entries:* 131; *Records:* 132.

Ludby, Richard. (?–1567) PLRE 76. Cleric. Professional. *Date:* 1567. *Type:* inventory (probate). *Entries:* 25; *Records:* 25.

Lye, Richard. (?–1575) PLRE 108. Manciple. Professional, Privileged person. *Date:* 1575. *Type:* inventory (probate). *Entries:* 94; *Records:* 95.

Marshall, John, M.A. (?–1577) PLRE 126. Scholar. Professional. *Date:* 1577. *Type:* inventory (probate). *Entries:* 30; *Records:* 30.

Mason, Roger, B.Cn.L. (?–1513) PLRE 28. Scholar. Professional. *Date:* 1513. *Type:* inventory (probate). *Entries:* 1; *Records:* 1.

Maudesley, Thomas, B.A. (?–1571) PLRE 95. Scholar (student). Professional. *Date:* 1571. *Type:* inventory (probate). *Entries:* 17; *Records:* 17.

Merven, George, B.A. (?–1529) PLRE 46. Scholar. Professional. *Date:* 1529. *Type:* inventory (probate). *Entries:* 5; *Records:* 5.

Mitchell, John. (?–1572) PLRE 100. Servant. Retainer, Privileged person. *Date:* 1572. *Type:* inventory (probate). *Entries:* 11; *Records:* 11.

Mitchell, William, B.Th. (?–1599) PLRE 154. Scholar. Professional. *Date:* 1599. *Type*: inventory (probate) and bequest. *Entries*: 247; *Records*: 251.

Morcote, John, M.A. (?–1508) PLRE 13. Scholar. Professional. *Date:* 1508. *Type:* inventory (probate). *Entries:* 75; *Records:* 80.

Morrey, Thomas, M.A. (?–1584) PLRE 142. Scholar. Professional. *Date:* 1584. *Type:* inventory (probate) and will. *Entries:* 158; *Records:* 161.

Morgan, Thomas. (?–?) PLRE 87. Scholar (student). Professional. *Date:* 1570. *Type:* inventory. *Entries:* 4; *Records:* 4.

Mychegood, Robert. (?–1508) PLRE 14. Cleric (probable). Professional (probable). *Date:* 1509. *Type:* inventory (probate). *Entries:* 8; *Records:* 8.

Napper, William, B.A. (c.1544–1569) PLRE 82. Scholar. Professional. *Date:* 1569. *Type:* inventory (probate). *Entries:* 118; *Records:* 118.

Neale, Thomas. (1553–1572) PLRE 101. Scholar (student). Professional. *Date:* 1572. *Type:* inventory (probate). *Entries:* 6; *Records:* 6.

Newby, Thomas, M.A. (1561–1587) PLRE 147. Scholar. Professional. *Date:* 1588. *Type:* inventory (probate). *Entries:* 45; *Records:* 45.

Pannell, William, M.A. (?–1537) PLRE Ad25. Scholar. Professional. *Date:* 1533. *Type:* bookseller's accounts. *Entries:* 14; *Records:* 15.

Pantry, John, M.A., D.Th. (?–1541) PLRE 59. Scholar. Professional. *Date:* 1541. *Type:* will and reconstruction. *Entries:* 3; *Records:* 3.

Parkin, Matthew, B.A. (1569–1589) PLRE 150. Scholar. Professional. *Date:* 1589. *Type:* inventory (probate). *Entries:* 80; *Records:* 89.

Payne, Richard, M.A., B.C.L. (?-1597) PLRE 152. Scholar. Professional. *Date*: 1597. *Type*: inventory (probate). *Entries*: 21; *Records*: 32.

Peerpoynt, William. (?–?) PLRE Ad26. Scholar (student). Professional. *Date:* 1531. *Type:* bookseller's accounts. *Entries:* 6; *Records:* 6.

Petcher, Robert, M.A. (?–1507) PLRE 8. Scholar. Professional. *Date:* 1507. *Type:* will. *Entries:* 1; *Records:* 2.

Pope, Thomas, B.A. (?–1578) PLRE 135. Scholar. Professional. *Date:* 1578. *Type:* inventory (probate). *Entries:* 40; *Records:* 41.

Powell, James, M.A. (?–1575) PLRE 109. Scholar. Professional. *Date:* 1575. *Type:* inventory (probate). *Entries:* 42; *Records:* 42.

Price, John, B.Cn.L., B.C.L. (?–1554) PLRE 66. Scholar. Professional. *Date:* 1554. *Type:* inventory (probate). *Entries:* 17; *Records:* 25.

Purfrey, Anthony, B.C.L. (?–1527) PLRE 39. Scholar. Professional. *Date:* 1527. *Type:* inventory (probate). *Entries:* 7; *Records:* 7.

Purviar, Robert, M.A. (?–1536) PLRE 55. Scholar. Professional. *Date:* 1536. *Type:* will and reconstruction. *Entries:* 7; *Records:* 7.

Quarrendon, Thomas, B.C.L. (?–c.1507) PLRE 9. Scholar. Professional. *Date:* 1507. *Type:* inventory (probate). *Entries:* 14; *Records:* 15.

Rawson, Nicholas, B.Th. (?–1511) PLRE 20. Scholar. Professional. *Date:* 1511. *Type:* inventory (probate). *Entries:* 6; *Records:* 6.

Read, Richard. (?-1623). PLRE 163. Manciple. Professional. Privileged person. *Date*: 1623. *Type*: inventory (probate). *Entries*: 1: *Records*: 3.

Reynolds, James, M.A. (?–1577) PLRE 127. Scholar. Professional. *Date:* 1577. *Type:* inventory (probate). *Entries:* 229; *Records:* 231.

Reynolds, Jerome, M.A., B.M. (perhaps). (?–1571) PLRE 96. Scholar, Physician. Professional. *Date:* 1571. *Type:* inventory (probate). *Entries:* 108; *Records:* 108.

Reynolds, John, M.A. (?–1571) PLRE 97. Scholar. Professional. *Date:* 1571. *Type:* inventory (probate). *Entries:* 59; *Records:* 59.

Ringstead, Henry. (?–1561) PLRE Ad27. Appraiser. Privileged person. *Date:* 1533. *Type:* bookseller's acounts. *Entries:* 1; *Records:* 1.

Robinson, John. (?–1508) PLRE 15. Manciple. Professional, Privileged person. *Date:* 1508. *Type:* inventory (probate). *Entries:* 2; *Records:* 2.

Robinson, John, M.A. (?–1511) PLRE 21. Scholar. Professional. *Date:* 1511. *Type:* inventory (probate). *Entries:* 6; *Records:* 6.

Rothley, John, B.Cn.L., B.C.L. (?–1511) PLRE 22. Scholar. Professional. *Date:* 1507. *Type:* inventory. *Entries:* 23; *Records:* 24.

Roxburgh, John, M.A. (?–1509) PLRE 18. Scholar. Professional. *Date:* 1509. *Type:* inventory (probate). *Entries:* 1; *Records:* 1.

Ruckwood, Thomas. (?–1581) PLRE 139. Cleric, Scholar. Professional. *Date:* 1581. *Type:* inventory (probate). *Entries:* 43; *Records:* 43.

Scott, Alan, M.A. (?–1578) PLRE 136. Cleric, Scholar. Professional. *Date:* 1578. *Type:* inventory (probate). *Entries:* 44; *Records:* 44.

Seacole, Richard, B.A. (1550–1577) PLRE 128. Scholar. Professional. *Date:* 1577. *Type:* inventory (probate). *Entries:* 123; *Records:* 125.

Shoesmith, John. (?–1568) PLRE 78. Profession unknown. Privileged person (probable). *Date:* 1568. *Type:* inventory (probate). *Entries:* 11; *Records:* 11.

Sibthorpe, Henry. (?–c.1664) (and Lady Anne Southwell) PLRE Ad3. Soldier, Statesman. Gentry. *Date:* c.1640, c.1650. *Type:* inventory. *Entries:* 110; *Records:* 110.

Simons, Thomas, M.A., B.M. (?–1553) PLRE 65. Scholar. Professional. *Date:* 1553. *Type:* inventory (probate). *Entries:* 131; *Records:* 143.

Simpson, John, M.A. (?–1577) PLRE 129. Scholar. Professional. *Date:* 1577. *Type:* inventory (probate). *Entries:* 130; *Records:* 130.

Singleton, Robert, M.A. (?–1577) PLRE 130. Scholar. Professional. *Date:* 1577. *Type:* inventory (probate). *Entries:* 119; *Records:* 120.

Slatter, Richard, M.A. (?–?) PLRE 111. Scholar. Professional. *Date:* 1576. *Type:* inventory. *Entries:* 12; *Records:* 12.

Smallwood, William, M.A. (?–?) PLRE 102. Scholar. Professional. *Date:* 1572. *Type:* inventory. *Entries:* 17; *Records:* 17.

Southwell, Lady Anne. (?–1636) (see Henry Sibthorpe).

Stanhope, Sir Edward, D.U.L. (c.1546–1608) PLRE 2. Lawyer. Nobility. *Date:* c.1612. *Type:* will and reconstruction. *Entries:* 161; *Records:* 207.

Stanley, Thomas, B.A. (?–1577) PLRE 131. Scholar. Professional. *Date:* 1577. *Type:* inventory (probate). *Entries:* 40; *Records:* 40.

Stocker, William, M.A. (?–?) PLRE 88. Scholar. Professional. *Date:* c.1570. *Type:* inventory. *Entries:* 23; *Records:* 23.

Stonely, Richard. (c.1520–1600) PLRE Ad4. Court official (Teller of the Exchequer). Gentry. *Date:* 1597. *Type:* inventory against debt. *Entries:* 412; *Records:* 418.

Sykes, Nicholas. (?–1562) PLRE 71. Butler. Retainer, Privileged person. *Date:* 1562. *Type:* inventory (probate). *Entries:* 42; *Records:* 42.

Talley, Abbot of. (?–?) PLRE 42. Cleric (monk). Professional. *Date:* 1528. *Type:* inventory. *Entries:* 2; *Records:* 3.

Tatham, John, M.A. (?–1576) PLRE 112. Scholar. Professional. *Date:* 1576. *Type:* inventory (probate). *Entries:* 222; *Records:* 222.

Tatham, Thomas, M.A. (?–1586) PLRE 146. Scholar. Professional. *Date:* 1586. *Type:* inventory (probate). *Entries:* 360; *Records:* 373.

Thixtell, John, B.Th. (?–1541) PLRE Ad28. Scholar. Professional. *Date:* 1528. *Type:* bookseller's accounts. *Entries:* 14; *Records:* 15.

Thomson, Thomas, M.A. (?–1514) PLRE 36. Scholar. Professional. *Date:* 1514. *Type:* will. *Entries:* 14; *Records:* 17.

Thomson, William, M.A. (?–1507) PLRE 10. Scholar. Professional. *Date:* 1507. *Type:* inventory (probate). *Entries:* 30; *Records:* 30.

Thornbury, Thomas. (?–1570) PLRE 89. Scholar (student, perhaps). Professional. *Date:* 1570. *Type:* inventory (probate). *Entries:* 5; *Records:* 5.

Tichborne (given name unknown), B.C.L. (probable). (?–?) PLRE 90. Scholar. Professional. *Date:* 1570. *Type:* inventory. *Entries:* 93; *Records:* 93.

Tillyard, Christopher, B.A. (1575-1598) PLRE 153. Scholar. Professional. *Date*: 1598. *Type*: inventory (probate). *Entries*: 22; *Records*: 25.
Tolley, David, M.A., B.M. (c.1506–1558) PLRE 68. Physician. Professional. *Date:* 1558. *Type:* inventory (probate). *Entries:* 50; *Records:* 50.
Townrow, Henry, B.A. (?–1565) PLRE 72. Scholar. Professional. *Date:* 1565. *Type:* inventory (probate). *Entries:* 18; *Records:* 18.
Townshend, Sir Roger. (1596–1636) PLRE 3. Member of Parliament. Gentry. *Date:* c.1625. *Type:* inventory. *Entries:* 286; *Records:* 296.
Trefry, Abel, M.A. (1577-1610) PLRE 158. Scholar. Professional. *Date*: 1610. *Type*: inventory (probate). *Entries*: 45; *Records*: 45.
Tye, Anthony, M.A. (?–1584) PLRE 143. Scholar. Professional. *Date:* 1584. *Type:* inventory (probate). *Entries:* 106; *Records:* 109.
Upton, William, M.A., B.Th. (perhaps). (?–1527) PLRE 40. Scholar. Professional. *Date:* 1527. *Type:* will. *Entries:* 1; *Records:* 1.
Wicking, John. (?–1551) PLRE 63. Almsman. Retainer. *Date:* 1551. *Type:* inventory (probate) and will. *Entries:* 1; *Records:* 1.
Wood, Richard, M.A. (?–1508) PLRE 16. Scholar. Professional. *Date:* 1508. *Type:* inventory (probate). *Entries:* 13; *Records:* 13.
Woodruff, William, M.A. (?–?) PLRE 47. Scholar. Professional. *Date:* 1529. *Type:* inventory. *Entries:* 35; *Records:* 35.
Yardley, William, B.Cn.L., B.C.L. (?–1530) PLRE 48. Scholar. Professional. *Date:* 1530. *Type:* inventory (probate). *Entries:* 11; *Records:* 11.

C. Owners of Book-lists According to PLRE Number

1. LISTS IN PLRE VOLUMES

PLRE 1: Cox, Richard, D.Th.
PLRE 2: Stanhope, Sir Edward, D.U.L.
PLRE 3: Townshend, Sir Roger
PLRE 4: Dering, Sir Edward
PLRE 5: Bowerman, John, M.A., B.C.L.
PLRE 6: Chantry, William, B.A.
PLRE 7: Gofton, William, B.C.L.
PLRE 8: Petcher, Robert, M.A.
PLRE 9: Quarrendon, Thomas, B.C.L.
PLRE 10: Thomson, William, M.A.
PLRE 11: Bryan, Robert, D.Cn.L.
PLRE 12: Hogan, Matthias
PLRE 13: Morcote, John, M.A.
PLRE 14: Mychegood, Robert
PLRE 15: Robinson, John
PLRE 16: Wood, Richard, M.A.

PLRE 17: Carter, John, B.C.L.
PLRE 18: Roxburgh, John, M.A.
PLRE 19: Griffin, Roger, B.A.
PLRE 20: Rawson, Nicholas, B.Th.
PLRE 21: Robinson, John, M.A.
PLRE 22: Rothley, John, B.Cn.L., B.C.L.
PLRE 23: Bidnell, William, M.A.
PLRE 24: Collins, Robert
PLRE 25: Balyn, John, B.A.
PLRE 26: Chastelain, George
PLRE 27: Hartburn, John, M.A.
PLRE 28: Mason, Roger, B.Cn.L.
PLRE 29: Balborough, William, D.U.L.
PLRE 30: Dewer, William, M.A. (probable)
PLRE 31: Froster, Roger
PLRE 32: Heywood, John, B.A.
PLRE 33: Jackson, Lionel, M.A.
PLRE 34: Kyffen, John, B.Cn.L.
PLRE 35: Lilbourn, William, M.A.
PLRE 36: Thomson, Thomas, M.A.
PLRE 37: Deegen, Peter
PLRE 38: Hawarden, Robert, M.A.
PLRE 39: Purfrey, Anthony, B.C.L.
PLRE 40: Upton, William, M.A., B.Th. (perhaps)
PLRE 41: Gryce, William, D.Th.
PLRE 42: Talley, Abbot of
PLRE 43: Burton, Edmund, M.A.
PLRE 44: Coles, John, B.Th.
PLRE 45: Dalaber, Anthony
PLRE 46: Merven, George, B.A.
PLRE 47: Woodruff, William, M.A.
PLRE 48: Yardley, William, B.Cn.L., B.C.L.
PLRE 49: Kitley, John, M.A.
PLRE 50: Cartwright, Thomas, M.A.
PLRE 51: Hamlyn, William, M.A.
PLRE 52: Lacy, Dunstan, M.A.
PLRE 53: Hunt, Robert, D.C.L., D.Th.
PLRE 54: Kitson, John, M.A.
PLRE 55: Purviar, Robert, M.A.
PLRE 56: Chogan, William
PLRE 57: Hoppe, Edward, M.A.
PLRE 58: Hodges, Thomas, B.A.
PLRE 59: Pantry, John, M.A., D.Th.

PLRE 60: Bisley, M.A. (perhaps), B.Th. (perhaps)
PLRE 61: Derbyshire, William
PLRE 62: Hurde, William
PLRE 63: Wicking, John
PLRE 64: Beaumont, Edward, B.A.
PLRE 65: Simons, Thomas, M.A., B.M.
PLRE 66: Price, John, B.Cn.L., B.C.L.
PLRE 67: Brown, William, M.A.
PLRE 68: Tolley, David, M.A., B.M.
PLRE 69: Allen, Thomas, B.A.
PLRE 70: Griffith, Thomas, M.A., B.M. (perhaps)
PLRE 71: Sykes, Nicholas
PLRE 72: Townrow, Henry, B.A.
PLRE 73: Cliff, Richard, M.A.
PLRE 74: Bury, John, B.A. (probable)
PLRE 75: Jones, Robert
PLRE 76: Ludby, Richard
PLRE 77: Johnson, James
PLRE 78: Shoesmith, John
PLRE 79: Allen, Richard, B.A.
PLRE 80: Conner, John, B.Th.
PLRE 81: Digby, George and Simon
PLRE 82: Napper, William, B.A.
PLRE 83: Atkinson, John, M.A.
PLRE 84: Day, Thomas, B.C.L.
PLRE 85: Dunnet, John
PLRE 86: Lisle
PLRE 87: Morgan, Thomas
PLRE 88: Stocker, William, M.A.
PLRE 89: Thornbury, Thomas
PLRE 90: Tichborne, B.C.L. (probable)
PLRE 91: Beddow, John, M.A.
PLRE 92: Hart, Robert, M.A.
PLRE 93: Hooper, Robert, M.A.
PLRE 94: Jones, Lewis, B.A.
PLRE 95: Maudesley, Thomas, B.A.
PLRE 96: Reynolds, Jerome, B.A., B.M. (perhaps)
PLRE 97: Reynolds, John, M.A.
PLRE 98: Austin
PLRE 99: Battbrantes, William
PLRE 100: Mitchell, John
PLRE 101: Neale, Thomas
PLRE 102: Smallwood, Thomas, M.A.

PLRE 103: Hutchinson, Henry, B.A.
PLRE 104: Kettelby, William, M.A.
PLRE 105: Lanham, Richard, B.A.
PLRE 106: Dyllam, Walter
PLRE 107: Lombard, Nicholas, M.A.
PLRE 108: Lye, Richard
PLRE 109: Powell, James, M.A.
PLRE 110: Johnson, Philip, B.Th.
PLRE 111: Slatter, Richard, M.A.
PLRE 112: Tatham, John, M.A.
PLRE 113: Atkins, Henry, M.A.
PLRE 114: Grant, Philip
PLRE 115: Badger, John, M.A.
PLRE 116: Carpenter, Thomas, M.A.
PLRE 117: Charnock, Roger, M.A.
PLRE 118: Cliffley
PLRE 119: Dawson, William, M.A.
PLRE 120: Dayrell, William, B.A.
PLRE 121: Dewhurst, Giles, M.A.
PLRE 122: Faringdon, Tristram
PLRE 123: Ferne, Richard, M.A.
PLRE 124: Foster, Thomas
PLRE 125: Gray, John
PLRE 126: Marshall, John, M.A.
PLRE 127: Reynolds, James, M.A.
PLRE 128: Seacole, Richard, B.A.
PLRE 129: Simpson, John, M.A.
PLRE 130: Singleton, Robert, M.A.
PLRE 131: Stanley, Thomas, B.A.
PLRE 132: Bolt, Thomas
PLRE 133: Glover, John, M.A.
PLRE 134: Hornsley, John, M.A.
PLRE 135: Pope, Thomas, M.A.
PLRE 136: Scott, Alan, M.A.
PLRE 137: Lewis, John
PLRE 138: Cheyne, Henry, M.A
PLRE 139: Ruckwood, Thomas
PLRE 140: Heath, John, M.A.
PLRE 141: Forster, John, B.C.L.
PLRE 142: Morrey, Thomas, M.A.
PLRE 143: Tye, Anthony, M.A.
PLRE 144: Haynes, John, M.A.
PLRE 145: Hill, Thomas

PLRE 146: Tatham, Thomas, M.A.
PLRE 147: Newby, Thomas, M.A.
PLRE 148: Dowe, Robert, B.C.L.
PLRE 149: Higgins, Edward, M.A.
PLRE 150: Parkin, Matthew, B.A.
PLRE 151: Lewis, Richard
PLRE 152: Payne, Richard, B.C.L..
PLRE 153: Tillyard, Christopher, B.A.
PLRE 154: Mitchell, William, B.Th.
PLRE 155: Barton, George, B.Th.
PLRE 156: Fisher, Richard, M.A.
PLRE 157: Gearing, William, M.A.
PLRE 158: Trefry, Abel
PLRE 159: Brown, Walter, B.Th.
PLRE 160: Homer, Edward, M.A.
PLRE 161: Hudson, Thomas, B.A.
PLRE 162: Kilby, Richard, D.Th.
PLRE 163: Read, Richard
PLRE 164: Anonymous
PLRE 165: Hutton, John, B.A.
PLRE 166: Jacob, Henry, M.A., B.M.

2. APND LISTS

[The source of each book-list follows the name of the owner. In the case of groups of lists from one source, the reference may precede the group.]

PLRE Ad1: Jewel, John, Bishop, D.Th.
  (Neil Ker, "The Library of John Jewel." *Bodleian Library Record* [1977] 9:256–65.)
PLRE Ad2: Blomefield, Miles.
  (Donald Baker and J. L. Murphy, "The Books of Myles Blomefylde," *The Library*, 5th ser. [1976] 31:374–85; John C. Coldewey, "Myles Blomefylde's Library: Another Book." *English Language Notes* [1977] 14:249–50.)
PLRE Ad3: Sibthorpe, Captain Henry (and Lady Anne Southwell).
  (Sister Jean Carmel Cavanaugh, S. L., "The Library of Lady Southwell and Captain Sibthorpe." *Studies in Bibliography* [1967] 20:243–54).
PLRE Ad4: Stonely, Richard.
  (Leslie Hotson, "The Library of Elizabeth's Embezzling Teller." *Studies in Bibliography* [1949] 2:49–61).

APND lists PLRE Ad5–Ad28 are taken from: Elisabeth Leedham-Green, D. E. Rhodes, and F. H. Stubbings. *Garrett Godfrey's Accounts c. 1527–1533*. Cambridge Bibliographical Society, Monograph no. 12. Cambridge: Cambridge University Library, 1992. [*Note:* Degrees assigned are senior degrees that had been earned when books were purchased.]

PLRE Ad5: Anlaby (Aulaby), Edmund (some entries drawn from BCI 1:244–45), M.A. (1533), B.Th. (1559)
PLRE Ad6: Batchelor, Robert
PLRE Ad7: Bill, Thomas, M.A.
PLRE Ad8: Bonenfant, Thomas, M.A.
PLRE Ad9: Bradford, Ralph, M.A.
PLRE Ad10: Brewer, John, M.A.
PLRE Ad11: Bromsby, John, B.Th.
PLRE Ad12: Buckingham, Edward, B.Cn.L.
PLRE Ad13: Cauthorn, John, B.A.
PLRE Ad14: Davy, William (perhaps), B.A.
PLRE Ad15: Dickinson, Thomas (probable), B.A.
PLRE Ad16: Gilbert, John
PLRE Ad17: Goldsmith, Francis
PLRE Ad18: Harwood, Thomas, B.A., D.M.
PLRE Ad19: Hilbert, Nicholas
PLRE Ad20: Hornby, Nicholas, M.A.
PLRE Ad21: Horsley, Thomas
PLRE Ad22: Horsman, Leonard, M.A.
PLRE Ad23: Horsman, Ralph
PLRE Ad24: Llewellyn, David ap
PLRE Ad25: Pannell, William, M.A.
PLRE Ad26: Peerpoynt, William
PLRE Ad27: Ringstead, Henry
PLRE Ad28: Thixtell, John, B.Th.
PLRE Ad29: Barwyck, Stephen (BCI 1:93–94)
PLRE Ad30: Cheke, Agnes (BCI 1:101–2)

D. Dates of Book-lists (actual or terminus ad quem), with PLRE Number

1507:   PLRE 5, 6, 7, 8, 9, 10, 22
1508:   PLRE 11, 12, 13, 15, 16
1509:   PLRE 14, 17, 18
1510:   PLRE 19
1511:   PLRE 20, 21
1512:   PLRE 23, 24
1513:   PLRE 25, 26, 27, 28
1514:   PLRE 29, 30, 31, 32, 33, 34, 35, 36
1527:   PLRE 37, 38, 39
c.1527: PLRE Ad9
1528:   PLRE 40, 41, 42, Ad19, Ad28
1529:   PLRE 43, 44, 45, 46, 47

1530:   PLRE 48, Ad18
1531:   PLRE 49, Ad11, Ad13, Ad22, Ad23, Ad26
1532:   PLRE 50, Ad7
c.1532: PLRE Ad20
1533:   PLRE Ad5 (part), Ad6, Ad8, Ad10, Ad12, Ad14, Ad15, Ad16, Ad17, Ad21, Ad24, Ad25, Ad27
1534:   PLRE 51, 52
1536:   PLRE 53, 54, 55
1537:   PLRE 56
1538:   PLRE 57
1539:   PLRE 58
1541:   PLRE 59
1543:   PLRE 60
1547:   PLRE Ad29
1549:   PLRE Ad30
1551:   PLRE 61, 62, 63
1552:   PLRE 64
1553:   PLRE 65
1554:   PLRE 66
1558:   PLRE 67, 68
1559:   PLRE Ad5 (part)
1560:   PLRE 113, 114
1561:   PLRE 69
1562:   PLRE 70, 71
1565:   PLRE 72
1566:   PLRE 73
1567:   PLRE 74, 75, 76
1568:   PLRE 77, 78
1569:   PLRE 79, 80, 81, 82, 90 (part)
1570:   PLRE 83, 84, 85, 86, 87, 88, 89, 90
1571:   PLRE 91, 92, 93, 94, 95, 96, 97
1572:   PLRE 98, 99, 100, 101, 102
1573:   PLRE 103, 104, 105
1575:   PLRE 106, 107, 108, 109
1576:   PLRE 110, 111, 112
1577:   PLRE 91 (part), 115, 116, 117, 118, 119, 120, 121, 122, 123, 124, 125, 126, 127, 128, 129, 130, 131
1578:   PLRE 132, 133, 134, 135, 136
1579:   PLRE 137
1581:   PLRE 1, 138, 139
1582:   PLRE 140
1584:   PLRE 141, 142, 143
1585:   PLRE 144, 145

1586:   PLRE 146
1587:   PLRE 147
1588:   PLRE 148, 149
1589:   PLRE 150
c.1590: PLRE 151
1597:   PLRE 152, Ad4
1598:   PLRE 153
1599:   PLRE 154
1602:   PLRE 155, 156
1607:   PLRE 157
1610:   PLRE 158
c.1612: PLRE 2
1613:   PLRE 159
1614:   PLRE 160
1618:   PLRE 161
1620:   PLRE 162
1623:   PLRE 163
c.1625: PLRE 3
1628:   PLRE 4 (part)
c.1640: PLRE Ad3 (part)
c.1642: PLRE 4 (part)
c.1650: PLRE 164, Ad3 (part)
1652:   PLRE 165
1653:   PLRE 166
No date (reconstruction):
    PLRE 2 (part), 4 (part), 55 (part), 59 (part), Ad1, Ad2

III. Summaries and Concordances

A. Manuscript Types

1. RECORD TOTALS FROM EACH MANUSCRIPT TYPE

Account book:	177
Bookseller's accounts:	188
Catalogue:	503
Inventory:	1,231
Inventory (against debt):	485
Inventory (probate):	8,017
Inventory (probate) and Will:	86
Memorial book (benefaction):	200
Receipt:	8
Will (or bequest):	100
No manuscript (reconstruction):	112

2. NUMBER OF MANUSCRIPT TYPES PROVIDING BOOK-LISTS
(Some lists derive from more than one manuscript type.)

Account book: 1
Bookseller's accounts: 23
Catalogue: 1
Inventory: 22
Inventory (against debt): 4
Inventory (probate): 124
Inventory (probate) and Will: 7
Memorial book (benefaction): 1
Receipt: 1
Will (or bequest): 17
No manuscript (reconstruction): 4

3. MANUSCRIPT TYPES ACCORDING TO PLRE NUMBERS
(Some lists derive from more than one manuscript type.)

Account book: PLRE 4 (part)

Bequest (not a proved will): PLRE 162

Bookseller's accounts: PLRE Ad5 (part), Ad6, Ad7, Ad8, Ad9, Ad10, Ad11, Ad12, Ad13, Ad14, Ad15, Ad16, Ad17, Ad18, Ad19, Ad20, Ad21, Ad22, Ad23, Ad24, Ad25, Ad26, Ad27, Ad28

Catalogue: PLRE 4 (part)

Inventory: PLRE 1, 3, 22, 42, 45, 47, 81, 86, 87, 88, 90, 91, 98, 102, 105, 106, 111, 117, 118, 132, 140, 162, 164, Ad3

Inventory (against debt): PLRE 138, 140, 166, Ad4

Inventory (probate): PLRE 7, 9, 10, 11, 12, 13 (part), 14, 15, 16, 17, 18, 19, 20, 21, 23, 25, 26, 27, 28, 29, 30 (part), 31, 32, 34, 35, 36 (part), 38, 39, 41, 43, 44, 46, 48, 49, 51, 53, 57 (part), 58, 60, 61, 62, 64 (part), 65, 66, 67, 68, 69, 70, 71, 72, 73 (part), 74, 75, 76, 77, 78, 79, 80, 82, 83, 84, 85, 89, 92, 93, 94, 95, 96, 97, 99, 100, 101, 103, 104, 107 (part), 108, 109, 110, 112, 113, 114, 115, 116, 119, 120, 121, 122, 123, 124, 125, 126, 127, 128, 129, 130, 131, 133, 134, 135, 136, 137, 139, 141, 142, 143, 144, 145, 146, 147, 148, 149, 150, 151, 152, 153, 154, 155, 156, 157, 158, 159, 160, 161, 163, 165, Ad5 (part), Ad30

Inventory (probate) and Will: PLRE 33 (part), 50, 52 (part), 57, 63, 64 (part), 107 (part)

Memorial book (benefaction): PLRE 2 (part)

Receipt: PLRE 24

Will: PLRE 5, 6, 8, 13 (part), 30 (part), 33 (part), 36 (part), 37, 40, 52 (part), 54, 55 (part), 56, 57 (part), 59 (part), 73 (part)

No manuscript (reconstruction): (See also Account book, Catalogue, Memorial book, and Will) PLRE 2 (part), 4 (part), 55 (part), 59 (part), Ad1, Ad2

B. Renaissance Locations of Book-lists

1. RECORD TOTALS FOR EACH LOCATION

Cambridgeshire, Cambridge:	464
Cambridgeshire, Downham:	187
Cambridgeshire, Fenstanton:	21
Kent, Surrenden:	680
London:	418
Middlesex, Acton:	110
Norfolk:	296
Northamptonshire, Brackley:	2
Oxfordshire, Oxford:	9,073
No Renaissance location (reconstruction):	112

2. PLRE NUMBERS OF LISTS IN EACH LOCATION

Cambridgeshire, Cambridge: PLRE 2, Ad5, Ad6, Ad7, Ad8, Ad9, Ad10, Ad11, Ad12, Ad13, Ad14, Ad15, Ad16, Ad17, Ad18, Ad19, Ad20, Ad21, Ad22, Ad23, Ad24, Ad25, Ad26, Ad27, Ad28, Ad29, Ad30

Cambridgeshire, Downham: PLRE 1 (part)

Cambridgeshire, Fenstanton: PLRE 1 (part)

Kent, Surrenden: PLRE 4

London: PLRE Ad4

Middlesex, Acton: PLRE Ad3

Norfolk: PLRE 3

Northamptonshire, Brackley: PLRE 91 (part)

Oxfordshire, Oxford: PLRE 5, 6, 7, 8, 9, 10, 11, 12, 13, 14, 15, 16, 17, 18, 19, 20, 21, 22, 23, 24, 25, 26, 27, 28, 29, 30, 31, 32, 33, 34, 35, 36, 37, 38, 39, 40, 41, 42, 43, 44, 45, 46, 47, 48, 49, 50, 51, 52, 53, 54, 55, 56, 57, 58, 59, 60, 61, 62, 63, 64, 65, 66, 67, 68, 69, 70, 71, 72, 73, 74, 75, 76, 77, 78, 79, 80, 81, 82, 83, 84, 85, 86, 87, 88, 89, 90, 91 (part), 92, 93, 94, 95, 96, 97, 98, 99, 100, 101, 102, 103, 104, 105, 106, 107, 108, 109, 110, 111, 112, 113, 114, 115, 116, 117, 118, 119, 120, 121, 122, 123, 124, 125, 126, 127, 128, 129, 130, 131, 132, 133, 134, 135, 136, 137, 138, 139, 140, 141, 142, 143, 144, 145, 146, 147, 148, 149, 150, 151, 152, 153, 154, 155, 156, 157, 158, 159, 160, 161, 162, 163, 164, 165, 166

No Renaissance location (reconstruction): PLRE 2 (part), 4 (part), 55 (part), 59 (part), Ad1, Ad2

C. Professions of Owners

1. TOTALS OF PROFESSIONS REPRESENTED

Alchemist (see Physician)

Almsman:	1
Appraiser:	1
Butler:	2
Cleric:	1
Cleric (probable):	2
Cleric (bishop):	1
Cleric (chaplain):	4
Cleric (friar):	1
Cleric (monk):	1
Cleric, Scholar:	4
Court Official:	1
Lawyer:	1
Manciple:	5
Merchant (vintner):	1
Merchant (white-baker):	1
Member of Parliament:	2
Physician:	1
Physician, Alchemist:	1
Physician, Scholar:	2
Physician (perhaps), Scholar:	1
Scholar:	113
(see also Cleric, Physician, Schoolmaster)	
Scholar (student):	22
Schoolmaster, Scholar:	1
Servant:	1
Sexton:	1
Soldier, Statesman:	1
Statesman (see Soldier)	
Stationer:	1
Unknown:	3

2. NUMBER OF RECORDS LISTED FOR EACH PROFESSION

Alchemist (see Physician)	
Almsman:	1
Appraiser:	1
Butler:	78
Cleric:	25
Cleric (probable):	30
Cleric (bishop):	282
Cleric (chaplain):	329
Cleric (friar):	7
Cleric (monk):	3

Cleric, Scholar:	789
Court Official:	418
Lawyer:	207
Manciple:	225
Merchant (vintner):	4
Merchant (white-baker):	78
Member of Parliament:	979
Physician:	50
Physician, Alchemist:	25
Physician, Scholar:	112
Physician (perhaps), Scholar:	97
Scholar:	6,950
(see also Cleric, Physician, Schoolmaster)	
Scholar (student):	459
Schoolmaster, Scholar:	41
Servant:	11
Sexton:	27
Soldier, Statesman:	110
Statesman (see Soldier)	
Stationer:	1
Unknown:	85

3. Book-lists by professions, with PLRE numbers

Alchemist (see Physician)
Almsman: PLRE 63
Appraiser: PLRE Ad27
Butler: PLRE 71, Ad29
Cleric: PLRE 76
Cleric (probable): PLRE 14
Cleric (bishop): PLRE 1, Ad1
Cleric (chaplain): PLRE 73, 77, 157, Ad6
Cleric (friar): PLRE Ad24
Cleric (monk): PLRE 42
Cleric, Scholar: PLRE 80, 84, 136, 157
Court Official: PLRE Ad4
Lawyer: PLRE 2
Manciple: PLRE 15, 108, 137, 151, 163
Member of Parliament: PLRE 3, 4
Merchant (vintner): PLRE Ad30
Merchant (white-baker): PLRE 137
Physician: PLRE 50
Physician, Alchemist: PLRE Ad2

Physician, Scholar: PLRE 96, Ad7
Physician (perhaps), Scholar: PLRE 70
Scholar (see also Cleric, Physician, Schoolmaster): PLRE 5, 6, 7, 8, 9, 10, 11, 13, 16, 17, 18, 19, 20, 21, 22, 23, 25, 27, 28, 29, 30, 32, 33, 34, 35, 36, 38, 39, 40, 41, 43, 44, 46, 47, 48, 49, 50, 51, 52, 53, 54, 55, 57, 58, 59, 60, 64, 65, 66, 67, 69, 72, 74, 79, 82, 83, 88, 90, 92, 93, 94, 97, 102, 103, 104, 105, 107, 109, 110, 111, 112, 113, 115, 116, 117, 118, 119, 120, 121, 122, 123, 125, 126, 127, 128, 129, 130, 131, 132, 133, 134, 135, 138, 140, 141, 142, 143, 144, 145, 146, 147, 148, 149, 150, 152, 153, 154, 155, 156, 158, 159, 160, 161, 162, 165, 166, Ad5, Ad8, Ad9, Ad10, Ad11, Ad12, Ad13, Ad14, Ad15, Ad18, Ad20, Ad21, Ad22, Ad23, Ad25, Ad28
Scholar (student): PLRE 12, 24, 31, 37, 45, 56, 61, 62, 83, 85, 86, 87, 89, 95, 98, 99, 101, 106, 114, 139, Ad16, Ad17, Ad19, Ad26
Schoolmaster, Scholar: PLRE 91
Servant: PLRE 100
Sexton: PLRE 75
Soldier, Statesman: PLRE Ad3
Statesman (see Soldier)
Stationer: PLRE 26
Unknown: PLRE 78, 124, 164

D. Social Status of Owners

1. Total of records in PLRE database

Gentry:	1,715
Middle class:	83
Nobility:	207
Privileged person (with others):	250
Privileged person (probable):	20
Professional:	9,067
Professional (probable):	159
Retainer:	90

2. Book-lists by social status, with PLRE numbers

Gentry: PLRE 1, 3, 4, Ad3, Ad4
Middle class: PLRE 26, 137, Ad30
Nobility: PLRE 2
Privileged person (sometimes with others): PLRE 71, 100, 108, 151, 163, Ad27, Ad30
Privileged person (probable): PLRE 78, 124
Professional: PLRE 5, 6, 7, 8, 9, 10, 11, 12, 13, 15, 16, 17, 18, 19, 20, 21, 22, 23, 24, 25, 27, 28, 29, 30, 31, 32, 33, 34, 35, 36, 37, 38, 39, 40, 41, 42, 43, 44, 45,

46, 47, 48, 49, 50, 51, 52, 53, 54, 55, 56, 57, 58, 59, 60, 61, 62, 67, 68, 69, 70, 72, 73, 74, 75, 76, 77, 79, 80, 81, 82, 83, 84, 85, 86, 87, 88, 89, 90, 91, 92, 93, 94, 95, 96, 97, 98, 99, 101, 102, 103, 104, 105, 106, 107, 109, 110, 111, 112, 113, 114, 115, 116, 117, 118, 119, 120, 121, 122, 123, 125, 126, 127, 128, 129, 130, 131, 132, 133, 134, 135, 136, 138, 139, 140, 141, 142, 143, 144, 146, 147, 148, 149, 150, 152, 153, 154, 155, 156, 157, 158, 159, 160, 161, 162, 165, 166, Ad1, Ad2, Ad5, Ad6, Ad7, Ad8, Ad9, Ad10, Ad11, Ad12, Ad13, Ad14, Ad15, Ad16, Ad17, Ad18, Ad19, Ad20, Ad21, Ad22, Ad23, Ad24, Ad25, Ad26, Ad28

Professional (probable): PLRE 14, 118, 145, 164

Retainer: PLRE 63, 71, 100, Ad29

ADDITIONS AND CORRECTIONS

The following entries in Volumes 1-6 have been revised to include additions and corrections, both substantive and accidental, that have been made to the PLRE database since the publication of Volume 6.

1.101　Syntagma de coena dominica authore abdia libertino
Johann Pincier (Abdias Liberinus, *pseudonym*). *Syntagma universae, de sacrosancta Coena Domini*. Place not given: stationer unknown, c.1560.
Language(s): Latin. Appraised at 4d in 1581.

1.174　Diversi volumies of the statutes
Unidentified. [*England—Statutes*]. London: (different houses), date not determined.
STC 9264 *et seq. Language(s)*: English (probable) Latin (probable) Law French (perhaps). Appraised at 6s 8d in 1581.

3.83　Dispensatorium medicum, Melichii phar: in 4°.
Georg Melich (and Franciscus Maria de Tectoriis). *Dispensatorium medicum*. Translated by Samuel Keller. Frankfurt am Main: (different houses), 1601–1624.
Contains both Melich's *De recta medicamentorum* (1586) and Tectoriis' *Compendium medicinae practicae*. The stationers were all of the Plathenius family. *Language(s)*: Latin.

3.143　Comentaires de mont Luc. in 4°.
Blaise de Monluc. *Commentaires*. Continent: 1592–1607.
All editions were published in France. *Language(s)*: French.

3.230　Epicedium Cantabr. — in 4°.
Epicedium Cantabrigiense, in obitum immaturum, semperq; deflendum Henrici, principis Walliae. (*Cambridge University*). Cambridge: ex officina C. Legge, 1612.
STC 4481 *et seq*. Verses by members of the University on the death of Henry, the Prince of Wales. There were several issues in 1612, one of which contains Latin and French verses, another delivering the verses in Latin and English. See H. Forster, "The Rise and Fall of the Cambridge Muses," *Transactions of*

the Cambridge Bibliographical Society (1982) 8:141–72, especially 155. *Language(s)*: Latin English (perhaps) French (perhaps).

4.108:A   14 12 Petrus Galatinus de arcanis Catholicae veritatis. Johannes Reuchlinus de arte cabalistica 1603

Pietro Galatino (Petrus Columna, *Galatinus*). *De arcanis Catholicae veritatis libri XII*. Frankfurt am Main: apud haeredes A. Wecheli, Claudium Marnium & Joannem Aubrium, 1603 (composite publication).

This volume was issued with the work by Johann Reuchlin below. *Language(s)*: Hebrew Latin. Cost [a composite volume] 4s in an unspecified year.

67.208   gasparus de magistratibus et re publica

Gasparo Contarini, *Cardinal*. *De magistratibus et republica Venetorum*. Continent: 1543–1551.

Language(s): Latin.

68.35   fushius in Aphorismos hipocratis

Leonard Fuchs. *In Hippocratis ... septem Aphorismorum libris* [sic] *commentaria*. Translated by Leonard Fuchs, with his explanations of Galen's commentary on the text. Lyon: (different houses), 1558–1559.

Conceivably, the edition of Hippocrates' work that first appeared in 1544 with Fuchs's commentary, but the entry suggests this work. See 68.21 for the same text at the higher valuation of 6*d*. *Language(s)*: Greek Latin. Appraised at 4d in 1558.

73.16   Zwyngli in evang

Ulrich Zwingli. *In evangelicam historiam de Jesu Christo annotationes*. Edited by Leo Juda. Zürich: excud. Christophorus Froschouerus, 1539.

Additions by Caspar Megander. Adams Z236. *Language(s)*: Latin. Appraised at 3s 4d in 1566.

92.117   Casparus Contarenus

Gasparo Contarini, *Cardinal*. Unidentified. Continent: date not determined.

Language(s): Latin. Appraised at 2d in 1571.

93.65   petrus a soto

Pedro de Soto. Unidentified. Continent: date not determined.

Language(s): Latin. Appraised at 6d in 1571.

96.42   opera Petri Galetini

Pietro Galatino (Petrus Columna, *Galatinus*). *Opus de arcanis catholicae veritatis*. Continent: date not determined.

Language(s): Hebrew Latin. Appraised at 5s in 1571.

103.47 **A Comment uppon the 2 epistle of St paule to the corinthians in englishe**

Unidentified. [*Corinthians II: commentary*]. Britain: date not determined. Not found in the STC. *Language(s)*: English. Appraised at 2d in 1573.

103.53 **Questiones Bezae**

Théodore de Bèze. *Quaestionum et responsionum christianarum libellus.* Britain or Continent: 1570–1573.

STC 2036 *et seq.* and non-STC. Gardy, nos. 262–265. *Language(s)*: Latin. Appraised at 2d in 1573.

110.43 **hermonia Calvini**

Jean Calvin. *Harmonia. (Bible—N.T.).* Geneva: (different houses), 1555–1572.

Language(s): Latin. Appraised at 4s in 1576.

110.128 **questiones besi**

Théodore de Bèze. [*Quaestiones et responsiones*]. Britain or Continent: 1570–1576.

STC 2036 and non-STC. The English translation, STC 203738 (1572, 1574), is a remote possibility. The Second Part (*pars altera*) was first issued in 1576, the year of this inventory, and unlike the earlier versions, discussed the sacraments. Gardy, nos. 262–265, 272. *Language(s)*: Latin. Appraised at 2d in 1576.

112.62 **Sermones latemeri**

Hugh Latimer, *Bishop.* [*Sermons*]. London: (different houses), 1549–1575.

STC 15274 *et seq.* Apart from editions of individual sermons, various collections of Latimer's sermons were published. *Language(s)*: English. Appraised with one other at 20d in 1576.

112.83 **flores Aris**

Aristotle. *Flores illustriores Aristotelis.* Probably edited and compiled by Jacques Bouchereau. Continent: 1560–1575.

John Foxall, *Monumentorum,* also known as *Flores e libris Posteriorum Analyticorum Aristotelis,* is a remote possibility. *Language(s)*: Latin. Appraised at 6d in 1576.

116.65 **Vasseus**

Unidentified. Continent (probable): date not determined.

Almost certainly not an STC book. Whether Lodoicus Vassaeus or Joannes Vasseus, whose *De judiciis urinarum* was translated into English in 1553 (STC 24595), cannot be determined. *Language(s)*: Latin (probable). Appraised at 6d in 1577.

117.4:1   Calvinus super 4 evangelistis et Actis

Jean Calvin. *Harmonia.* (*Bible — N.T.*). Continent: 1555–1572.

This and the commentary on Acts were printed separately. This entry must, therefore, refer to two different books. The inventory exists in two manuscripts, the original (A) and a fair copy (B); manuscript A has been adopted as the copy-text. Manuscript B omits *Actis* in this entry. The book includes a commentary on John. *Language(s)*: Latin. Appraised with one other at 6s 8d in 1577.

117.5   Calvini super Epist. pauli

Jean Calvin. [*Epistles — Paul: commentary*]. Continent: 1551–1572.

Perhaps the 1548 edition, but it contains commentary on only four of the Epistles. This entry occurs only in manuscript B. *Language(s)*: Latin. Appraised at 5s in 1577.

129.31   foesii pharmacopeia

Anutius Foesius. *Pharmacopoeia.* Basle: apud Thomam Guerinum, 1561. *Language(s)*: Latin. Appraised at 18d in 1577.

130.26   Calvini Harmonia

Jean Calvin. *Harmonia.* (*Bible — N.T.*). Geneva: (different houses), 1555–1572.

The work was published twice by Stephanus and once by Crispinianus, all three editions in a folio format. A 1563 octavo edition is unlikely to be intended here at the valuation assigned. The book includes a commentary on John. *Language(s)*: Latin. Appraised at 2s 6d in 1577.

134.2   Harmonia Calvini 8°

Jean Calvin. *Harmonia ex tribus evangelistis composita, Matthaeo, Marco, et Luca.* (*Bible — N.T.*). Geneva: excudebant N. Barbirius et T. Courteau, 1563.

The book includes a commentary on John. *Language(s)*: Latin. Appraised at 3s 4d in 1578.

136.44   juels appologi

John Jewel, *Bishop. An apologie or aunswer in defence of the Church of England.* London: R. Wolfe, 1562–1564.

STC 14590 *et seq. Language(s)*: English. Appraised at 4d in 1578.

138.13   Fuchsius in Galene

Leonard Fuchs. Unidentified. Continent: date not determined.

Fuchs edited and translated many of Galen's works. Fuchs's widely published *Institutiones medicinae, sive methodi ad Hippocratis, Galeni* ... might have been referred to in this manner by the compiler. *Language(s)*: Latin. Appraised at 4s in 1581.

142.1   Calvine upon Genesis and th'other 4 bookes of Moses

Jean Calvin. [*Pentateuch: commentary*]. Geneva: (different houses), 1563–1583.

The compiler invariably gives the titles of Calvin's works in English, but only in one case (142.9) is an item described expressly as *anglice*. Calvin's works listed here are, therefore, treated as Latin editions unless otherwise indicated by the compiler. It is assumed that a French edition would also have been designated as such; but there are no other French items in Morrey's list. The 1563 edition of Calvin's commentary on the Pentateuch contains the Biblical text as well. *Language(s)*: Latin. Appraised at 8s in 1584.

142.6   [Calvin] upon the evangelistes

Jean Calvin. *Harmonia.* (*Bible—N.T.*). Geneva: (different houses), 1555–1582.

The book includes a commentary on John. *Language(s)*: Latin. Appraised at 6s in 1584.

142.7   [Calvin] upon the epistles

Jean Calvin. [*Epistles—Paul: commentary*]. Geneva: (different houses), 1551–1580.

Perhaps the 1548 edition, but it contains commentary on only four of the Epistles. *Language(s)*: Latin. Appraised at 5s 6d in 1584.

142.19   [Beza] Questiones

Théodore de Bèze. [*Quaestiones et responsiones*]. Britain or Continent: 1571–1581.

STC 2036 *et seq.* and non-STC. The English translation by Arthur Golding (STC 203740) is possible but unlikely, given the spelling of the entry. The Second Part (*pars altera*), issued in 1576, unlike the earlier versions, discussed the sacraments. Gardy, nos. 262–267, 272–274. *Language(s)*: Latin English (perhaps). Appraised at 6d in 1584.

146.19   methodus lagi

Conradus Lagus (Conrad Haas). *Methodica juris utriusque traditio.* Continent: date not determined.

Language(s): Latin. Appraised at 4d in 1586.

146.131 machivell de principe

Niccolò Macchiavelli. *De principe.* Translated by Sylvester Telius. Continent: date not determined.

The use of the word *de* as opposed to *il* points toward this being a Latin translation from the Italian. *Language(s)*: Latin. Appraised at 3d in 1586.

148.92 Beza Testamentum grae et lat

[*Bible—N.T.*]. Translated and edited by Théodore de Bèze. Continent: 1565–1588.

Language(s): Greek Latin. Appraised at 3s in 1589.

148.139 Lagii Methodus

Conradus Lagus (Conrad Haas). *Methodica juris utriusque traditio.* Continent: 1543–1566.

Language(s): Latin. Appraised at 2s in 1589.

148.188 Ramus in Metaphysicam

Pierre de La Ramée. [*Aristotle—Metaphysica: commentary*]. Continent: 1566–1583.

Language(s): Latin. Appraised at 6d in 1589.

148.195 Exposit. Tit.

Probably Sebastian Brant. [*Expositiones omnium titulorum juris tam civilis quam canonici*]. Continent: date not determined.

Could possibly be Alexander Alesius's *Epistolae ad Titum expositio* (Leipzig, 1552) but given Dowe's interests, the legal work is more likely. *Language(s)*: Latin. Appraised at 2d in 1589.

149.62:2 [See 149.62:1]

Donatus Antonius Altimarus. *De medendis humani corporis malis: ars medica.* Continent: 1558–1575.

Language(s): Latin. Appraised with one other at 3s in 1588.

149.106 machiavelli princeps

Niccolò Machiavelli. [*De principe*]. Continent: date not determined.

The manuscript entry favors the Latin version, but the entry could represent an Italian original. *Language(s)*: Latin. Appraised at 16d in 1588.

149.270 ursinus catechismus englishe

Zacharias Ursinus. *The summe of christian religion.* Translated by Henry Parry, *Bishop.* Oxford and London: J. Barnes [sold by T. Cooke], 1587.

STC 24532. The long title continues "delivered by Zacharias Ursinus, in his lectures upon the catechisme." Ursinus's name does not feature in any of the

English translations of the Heidelberg catechism (STC 13028 *et seq.*) despite his role in the creation of the original. *Language(s)*: English. Appraised with a group at £4 5s 2d in 1588.

149.273   Latimers sermons with others

Hugh Latimer, *Bishop*. [*Sermons*]. London: (different houses), 1562–1584.

STC 15276 *et seq.* STC 15274–15274.7 remain possibilities, but the *with others* in the manuscript entry suggests a larger collection, as the 1562 *27 sermons* ... is, and the phrase may even be an approximation of the long title that reads, in part: "as certayne other commyng to our handes of late." *Language(s)*: English. Appraised with a group at £4 5s 2d in 1588.

150.78   Flores Aristotelis

Aristotle. *Flores illustriores Aristotelis.* Probably edited and compiled by Jacques Bouchereau. Continent: date not determined.

Language(s): Latin. Appraised at 8d in 1589.

ADDRESSES FOR REQUESTING DATA
OR FOR SENDING CORRECTIONS

R. J. Fehrenbach
Department of English
College of William and Mary
Williamsburg, VA 23187–8795 USA
rjfehr@wm.edu

Joseph L. Black
Department of English
University of Massachusetts
Amherst, MA 01003
jblack@english.umass.edu

Index I
Authors and Works

The words *perhaps* and *probable* indicate degrees of doubt about an identification. Names and titles appear in accordance with the methodology described in the introduction to this volume. A search of the database, available upon request, will provide more detailed information, including cross-referencing, than can be offered here.

Acanthius, Georgius. Cicero (spurious). *Rhetorica ad Herennium: commentary*: 159.288
Acciaiolus, Donatus. Aristotle — *Ethica: commentary*: 153.3
Acosta, Joseph de. *Unidentified*: 159.429
Aelianus, Claudius. *Varia historia*: 154.186
Aesop. *Fabulae*: 164.41; 154.187
Agrippa, Henricus Cornelius. *De incertitudine et vanitate scientiarum*: 159.461; 165.66; *De occulta philosophia*: 159.28
Ailmer, John. *Musae sacrae, seu Jonas, Jeremiae, Threni, et Daniel graeco redditi carmine*: 165.79:2
Airay, Christopher. *Fasciculus praeceptorum logicorum in gratiam juventutis academicae compositus*: 165.103
Alabaster, William. *Apparatus in revelationem Jesu Christi*: 159.135
Alberti, Leandro (probable). *Descrittione di tutta Italia* (probable): 159.60
Albertus Magnus. *Compendium theologicae veritatis*: 159.478; *De secretis mulierum et virorum*: 158.28
Alexander, de Ales. *Summa universae theologiae*: 162.33
Alexander, William, *Earl of Sterling*. (See James I, *King*)
Alexandro, Alexander ab. *Geniales dies*: 154.152
Alley, William, *Bishop*. Ptochomouseion. *The poore mans librarie*: 156.4
Althamer, Andreas. *Conciliatio locorum scripturae*: 159.271
Amadis, de Gaule. *tresor des livres, Le* (part) (probable): 159.46
Ames, William. *Medulla S.S. theologiae*: 165.45
Andrewes, Lancelot, *Bishop*. *Concio Latinè habita coram regia majestate*: 159.155; *Responsio ad Apologiam cardinalis Bellarmini, contra praefationem monitoriam Jacobi regis*: 159.106; *Tortura Torti: sive, ad Matthaei Torti librum responsio*: 159.91; 165.89:2; *Unidentified*: 159.188; 159.190
Angelio, Pietro. *Cynegetica*: 156.14:1
Anglerius, Petrus Martyr. *decades of the newe worlde or west India, The*: 159.120
Anonymous. *answere to a sermon preached the 17 of April 1608, by G. Downame,... intituled, A sermon defendinge the honorable function of bishops, An*: 159.181; *book of precedents, A*: 151.27; *death of usury, or the disgrace of usurers, The*: 154.242; *discoverie of the most secret and subtile practises of the Jesuits, A* (probable): 159.515; *remonstrance: or plaine detection of faults in a booke, entituled, a demonstration of discipline, A*: 154.64; *Vocabularius juris utriusque*: 154.119
Anonymous (probable). *Vocabularius juris utriusque* (probable): 152.14

Anti-Coton, or a refutation of Cottons Letter declaratorie: touching the killing of kings: 159.180

Aphthonius, *Sophista*. *Progymnasmata*: 151.35; 153.18:1

Apollinarius, *Bishop*. *Psalms: commentary and text*: 165.127

Appian, *of Alexandria*. *auncient historie and exquisite chronicle of the Romanes warres, An*: 159.119

Aquinas, Thomas, *Saint*. *Epistles—Paul: commentary*: 154.14; *Gospels: commentary*: 154.13; *Job: commentary*: 154.190; *Summa theologica*: 159.16; 164.4

Aretius, Benedictus. *Acts: commentary*: 154.11:2; *Epistles and Revelation: commentary*: 154.12; *Examen theologicum*: 154.87; *Gospels: commentary*: 154.11:1; *Isagoge ad lectionem epistolarum D. Pauli*: 155.13

Argenterius, Joannes. *De urinis liber*: 159.503

Arias Montano, Benito. *Antiquitatum Judaicarum libri IX*: 159.114

Ariosto, Alessandro. *Enchiridion sive interrogatorium perutile pro animabus regendis*: 154.188

Aristophanes. *Works* (probable): 159.402

Aristotle. *Aristotles politiques, or discourses of government*: 158.16; *Ethica*: 153.12; 154.83; 156.59; 165.70; *Metaphysica*: 156.58; 158.13; 160.13; *Organon*: 151.12; 154.45; 159.405; *Physica*: 154.166; 154.39; 158.14; 165.41; *Politica*: 156.61; 158.16; 159.403; *Rhetorica*: 154.165; 156.65; 158.15; 159.358; 164.14; *Selected works—Logica*: 153.14; *Works*: 157.6; 159.7

Aristotle (spurious). *Problemata*: 159.491; *problemes of Aristotle, with other philosophers and phisitions, The*: 159.520

Arminius, Jacobus. *De vero et genuino sensu cap. VII Epistolae ad Romanos dissertatio*: 159.323; *Examen modestum libelli*: 159.325; *Orationes, itemque tractatus insigniores aliquot*: 159.401; Unidentified: 159.321

Ascham, Roger. *Familiarium epistolarum libri tres*: 154.170; *scholemaster or plaine and perfite way of teachyng children, the Latin tong, The*: 159.302

Athanasius, *Saint*. *Works*: 162.30

Augustine, *Saint*. *De consensu evangelistarum*: 160.14; *De fide et operibus*: 160.37; *De haeresibus*: 159.379; 154.112; *Enchiridion*: 159.260; *Works*: 159.1

Augustine, *Saint* (spurious). *Meditationes*: 165.119

Ausonius, Decimus Magnus. *Works*: 156.53; 159.311

Avicenna. *Liber secundus De canone canonis*: 166.7:3

Avila, Luis de. *Commentariorum de bello Germanico libri duo*: 151.28

Azor, Juan. *Institutiones morales*: 162.16; *Institutiones morales (part)* 159.79

Bèze, Théodore de. *Ad tractationem De ministrorum evangelii gradibus, ab Hadriano Saravia Bela editam*: 154.235; *Apologia pro justificatione per unius Christi viva fide apprehensi justitiam gratis imputatam*: 154.236; *Confessio christianae fidei*: 157.30; *De controversiis in coena Domini*: 154.86; *Homiliae in historiam Domini resurrectione*: 154.77; *In historiam passionis et sepulturae Domini nostri Jesu Christi*: 154.78; *Job: commentary and paraphrase*: 154.189; *Psalms: paraphrase*: 155.11; *Quaestiones et responsiones*: 165.89:1; *Sermons upon the three first chapters of the Canticle of Canticles*: 152.4:2; 154.51

Babington, Gervase, *Bishop*. *briefe conference betwixt mans frailtie and faith, A*: 154.93; *profitable exposition of the Lord's prayer, by way of questions and answers, A*: 154.92;

very fruitfull exposition of the commaundements by way of questions and answeres, A: 154.91
Bacon, Francis, *Viscount St. Albans. Essayes*: 159.381; 159.502; *Historia vitae et mortis*: 165.137
Baker, Humphrey. *well sprynge of sciences, The*: 154.174
Baldwin, William. *myrroure for magistrates, A*: 159.122
Bales, Peter. *arte of brachygraphie, The*: 158.41
Bancroft, Richard, *Archbishop. sermon preached at Paules Crosse the 9. of Februarie, 1588, A*: 159.182; *survay of the pretended holy discipline, A*: 159.179
Bandello, Matteo (probable). *Certaine tragicall discourses* (probable): 159.140
Barclay, John. *Euphormionis lusinini sive Joannis Barclaii satyricon quadripartitum*: 165.35; *Paraenesis ad sectarios*: 165.123
Barclay, William, *Professor of Civil Law. De potestate papae*: 159.324
Barlow, William, *Bishop of Rochester and of Lincoln. One of the foure sermons preached before the kings majestie, at Hampton Court*: 159.152
Barlow, William, *Archdeacon of Salisbury. navigators supply, The. Conteining many things belonging to navigation*: 159.209
Barnaud, Nicolaus. *Dialogi ab Eusebio Philadelpho cosmopolita in Gallorum et caeterarum nationum gratiam compositi*: 159.238
Baron, Robert. *Philosophia theologiae ancillans*: 165.75
Baronius, Cesare, *Cardinal. Annales ecclesiastici*: 159.2; *Annales ecclesiastici* (part): 159.38; *Tractatus de monarchia Siciliae*: 159.360
Baronius, Justus. *Praescriptionum adversus haereticos perpetuarum ex SS. Orthodoxis potissimum patribus tractatus VI*: 159.332
Barradas, Sebastianus. *Commentariorum in concordiam et historiam evangelicam*: 159.10
Barrough, Philip. *methode of phisicke, The*: 154.43
Barth, Caspar von. *Amabilium libri IV*: 159.350
Basil, *Saint, the Great. Works* (probable): 159.15
Bastingius, Jeremias. *catechisme of christian religion, taught in the Low Countries, and dominions of the countie Palatine, A*: 154.97
Beard, Thomas. *theatre of Gods judgements, The*: 155.8
Becanus, Martinus. *De triplici sacrificio, naturae, legis, gratiae*: 159.531; *Disputatio theologica de triplici coena: Calvinistica, Lutherana, Catholica*: 159.261; *Enchiridion variarum disputationum*: 159.223; *Opuscula theologica (part)*: 159.337; *Tractatus de Deo attributis divinis (perhaps)*: 159.340; *Unidentified*: 159.161; 159.280
Beda, *the Venerable. Historia ecclesiastica gentis anglorum*: 159.447
Bell, Thomas. *downefall of poperie: proposed by way of a new challenge to English jesuits, The*: 159.191; *Thomas Bels motives: concerning romish faith*: 154.57
Bellarmino, Roberto, *Cardinal. Disputationes de controversiis christianae fidei, adversus nostri temporis haereticos*: 154.5; 159.3; *Institutiones linguae hebraicae*: 159.217; 165.19; *Recognitio librorum omnium*: 159.395; *Unidentified*: 159.45
Bencius, Franciscus. *Unidentified*: 158.22; 159.242
Benefield, Sebastian. *Doctrinae christianae sex capita, totidem praelectionibus in Schola Theologica Oxoniae*: 159.111; *sermon preached in St Maries Oxford, March xxiv. MDCX. at the inauguration of king James, A*: 159.183
Beni, Paolo. *Qua tandem ratione dirimi possit controversia quae inpraesens de efficaci Dei auxilio et libero arbitrio inter nonnullos catholicos agitatur*: 159.117

Bernard, *Saint. Works*: 159.33
Bertius, Pierre. *Logicae peripateticae libri sex*: 164.46
Bertram, Bonaventure Corneille. *De politia judaica*: 157.32
Besse, Pierre de. *Democritus christianus, id est, Contemptus vanitatum mundi*: 161.5
Bible, The: 152.1:1; 152.1:2; 152.1:3; 152.1:4; 154.4; 154.23; 154.99; 154.100; 154.247; 155.1; 156.16; 157.24; 158.1; 158.2; 159.5; 159.19; 159.21; 159.32; 159.118; 159.246; 159.248; 160.3; 161.1; 162.1; 162.15; 162.27; 163.1:1
  Old Testament: 157.40; 159.456; 162.2; 165.79.2
  Ecclesiastes: 154.107
  Genesis: 154.72; 154.243; 159.229
  Job: 154.189
  Lamentations: 154.49; 157.19
  Proverbs: 154.193; *Proverbs* (part): 157.13
  Proverbs, Ecclesiastes: 154.16
  Psalms: 151.40; 154.56; 154.108; 155.11; 159.244; 159.471; 159.481; 159.536; 160.32:2; 160.36; 162.11:1; 165.51
  New Testament: 151.17; 151.20; 153.8; 154.10; 154.15; 154.21; 154.34; 154.76; 154.155; 154.246; 156.35; 156.72; 157.1; 159.237; 159.390; 159.414; 159.439:1; 159.439:2; 159.474; 160.10; 160.43; 164.30:1; 164.30:2
  Epistles—Corinthians: 159.299
  Epistles—Paul: 159.307
  Gospels: 160.5
  Gospels—John: 165.125
  Gospels—Matthew, Mark, and Luke: 152.7
Biblical concordance (unidentified): 159.61
Bilson, Thomas, Bishop. *De perpetua ecclesiae christi gubernatione*: 159.216; *perpetual governement of Christes church, The*: 154.65; 159.175; *true difference betweene christian subjection and unchristian rebellion, The*: 159.78; 154.90; 157.8; *Unidentified*: 152.3:1–2
Bishop, John. *Beautifull blossomes, gathered. . .from the best trees of all kyndes, divine, philosophicall, astronomicall*: 159.137
Blackwell, George. *large examination taken at Lambeth, of M. G. Blakwell, A* (probable): 159.396
Blagrave, John (probable). *art of dyalling in two parts, The* (probable): 159.208
Blebelius, Thomas. *Grammaticae hebraeae sanctae linguae institutiones*: 157.41; 159.251
Boaistuau, Pierre. *theatre du monde, Le*: 159.459
Boccaccio, Giovanni. *Filocopo, Il*: 156.31; *Unidentified*: 159.47; 156.46; 158.37; 159.492
Bodin, Jean, *Bishop. De republica*: 154.122; *Methodus ad facilem historiarum cognitionem*: 159.455
Bosendorf, Hermann. *Apodixes, sive demonstrationes tres horrendarum blasphemiarum ecclesiae a Calvino reformatae*: 159.498
Bosquier, Philippe. *Unidentified*: 159.431
Botero, Giovanni. *Amphitheatridion*: 159.113; *Unidentified*: 159.104
Boys, John. *exposition of al the principall scriptures used in our English liturgie, An* (probable): 159.500; *exposition of al the principall scriptures used in our English liturgie, An*: 160.15; *exposition of the dominical epistles and gospels used in our English liturgie, An* (probable): 160.31

Brachylogus juris civilis, sive Corpus legum: 159.272
Brant, Sebastian. *Expositiones omnium titulorum juris tam civilis quam canonici*: 159.300
Brerewood, Edward. *Elementa logicae*: 164.72; *learned treatise of the Sabaoth, written to Mr N. Byfield, A*: 165.96; *Tractatus ethici sive commentarii in aliquot Aristotelis libros ad Nichomachum, de moribus*: 164.16; 165.90
breviat cronicle contaynynge all the kinges from brute to this daye, A: 159.425
Bricot, Thomas. *Aristotle—Physica: commentary*: 156.48
Broughton, Hugh. *concent of scripture, A*: 159.110; *Responsum ad epistolam Judaei sitienter expetentis cognitionem fidei christianorum*: 159.157
Brucioli, Antonio (probable). *commentary upon the canticle of canticles, A* (probable): 159.158
Bruno, Vincenzo. *Unidentified*: 159.470
Buchanan, George. *Psalms: paraphrase*: 160.36; *Rerum Scoticarum historia*: 159.256; *Selected works*: 159.336
Buchler, Joannes. *Thesaurus poeticus*: 159.359
Budaeus, Gulielmus. *De asse et partibus eius*: 165.47
Bulkeley, Edward. *apologie for religion, or an answere to an unlearned pamphlet intituled: Certain articles, or forcible reasons, An*: 159.176
Bullinger, Heinrich. *Sermonum decades*: 157.25
Bullinger, Heinrich (perhaps). *briefe and compendiose table in a manner of a concordaunce of the whole Bible, A* (perhaps): 154.211
Buratelli, Gabriele. *Praecipuarum controversiarum Arist. et Platonis conciliatio*: 156.67
Burgersdijck, Franco. *Unidentified*: 165.30; 165.46
Burhill, Robert. *Contra Martini Becani, jesuitae Moguntini, Controversiam Anglicanam* (probable): 159.351
Buridanus, Joannes. *Aristotle—Ethica: commentary*: 164.17; *Quaestiones in decem libros Ethicorum Aristotelis*: 165.86
Busbecq, Ogier Ghislain de. *Unidentified*: 154.218; 165.82
Buteo, Joannes, *pseudonym*. *De quadratura circuli libri duo*: 159.294
Butler, Charles. *Rameae rhetoricae libri duo*: 154.228
Buxtorf, Johann, the Elder. *Epitome grammaticae hebraeae*: 165.114; *Epitome radicum hebraicarum*: 159.443

C, H. *forrest of fancy. Wherein is conteined very prety apothegmes, and pleasaunt histories, both in meeter and prose, The*: 159.163
Cabasilas, Nilus, *Archbishop*. *De primatu papae Romani libri duo*: 154.240
Caesar, Caius Julius. *Commentarii*: 154.139; 165.37
Caesarius, Joannes, *Juliacensis*. *Dialectica*: 151.21
Cajetan de Vio, Thomas, *Cardinal*. *Epistles—Paul: commentary and text*: 159.307; *Proverbs, Ecclesiastes, Isaiah: commentary*: 159.236
Calepino, Ambrogio. *Dictionarium*: 154.9
Calvin, Jean. *Aphorismi doctrinae christianae*: 159.484; *Catechism*: 154.94; 159.489; *Commentarii in Acta Apostolorum*: 157.23:2; *Commentarii in epistolas Pauli atque in ep. ad Hebraeos et omnes epistolas canonicas*: 157.22; *Harmonia ex tribus evangelistis, adjuncto Joanne*: 157.23:1; *harmonie upon the three evangelists, Matthew, Mark and Luke, A*: 152.7; *In librum Psalmorum commentarius*: 157.21; *Institutio Christianae religionis*: 157.20; 158.3; 159.146; *Institutio Christianae religionis—epitome*: 154.84;

Institution de la religion chrestienne: 152.8; *Minor prophets: commentary*: 152.2:2; *Unidentified*: 152.2:1; 154.24

Cambridge University. *Epicedium Cantabrigiense, in obitum...Henrici, principis Walliae*: 159.112:2

Camden, William. *Britannia sive florentissimorum regnorum, Angliae, Scotiae, Hiberniae chorographica descriptio*: 154.40; 158.34; *Institutio Graecae grammatices compendiaria, in usum regiae scholae Westmonasteriensis*: 160.21; 164.37

Camerarius, Joachim, *the Elder. Cicero—Quaestiones Tusculanae: commentary*: 153.15

Campensis, Joannes. *Grammatica hebraica*: 159.293

Campian, Edmund. *Rationes decem*: 158.21; 160.23

Caninius, Angelus. *De locis s. scripturae hebraicis*: 159.254; *Hellenismos*: 154.220

Caninius, Angelus (perhaps). *Hellenismos* (perhaps): 159.257

Canisius, Petrus, *Saint. Summa doctrina Christianae*: 154.178

Cano, Francisco Melchor, *Bishop. De locis theologicis*: 154.116; 159.385

Cardano, Girolamo. *Cardanus comforte translated into Englishe*: 159.172; *De subtilitate*: 165.39

Carew, Richard. *survey of Cornwall, The*: 158.38

Carion, Johann. *Chronica*: 159.490

Carpenter, Richard. *perfect law of God, The*: 165.72:2

Carranza, Bartholome, *Archbishop. Summa conciliorum*: 154.176; 159.466

Casaubon, Isaac. *Isaaci Casauboni ad epistolam illustr. cardinalis Perronii responsio*: 159.156

Case, John. *Aristotle—Physica: commentary*: 160.2; *Speculum moralium quaestionum in universam Ethicen*: 164.60; *Sphaera civitatis*: 164.13; *Summa veterum interpretum in universam dialecticam Aristotelis*: 161.11; 164.57; *Unidentified*: 165.69

Cassander, Georgius. *Consultatio de articulis religionis inter catholicos et protestantes controversis*: 159.354

Castiglione, Baldassare, *Count. De curiali sive aulico libri quatuor ex Italico sermone in Latinum conversi*: 158.24; *El cortesano*: 159.304

Catechisms (unidentified): 151.39; 154.95

Catullus, Caius Valerius. *Catulli Tibulli Propertii nova editio*: 165.64; *Works*: 159.420; 160.34

Caussin, Nicolas. *unfortunate politique, first written in French by C.N., The*: 165.102

Ceporinus, Jacobus. *Compendium grammaticae graecae*: 151.14; 154.138

Chappuys, Gabriel. *L'Histoire du royaume de Navarre*: 156.45

Charles, I, *King* and Alexander Henderson. *papers which passed at New Castle betwixt His Sacred Majestie and Mr Al: Henderson: concerning the change of church government, The*: 165.97

Charron, Pierre. *De la sagesse*: 165.42

Chaucer, Geoffrey. *workes, The*: 159.57

Chemnitius, Martinus. *Examen concilii Tridentini*: 152.5; 154.6; 157.26; *Harmonia evangelica*: 154.55; *Loci theologici*: 154.56

Cheyne, James, *Canon of Tournai. Aristotle—Metaphysica: commentary*: 160.8

Chytraeus, David. *Chronicon Saxoniae*: 159.392; *De studio theologiae recte inchoando*: 159.276

Chytraeus, Nathan. *Ethe kai pathe, seu de affectibus movendis, Aristotelis ex II. rhetoricorum doctrina explicat*: 159.268

Cicero, Marcus Tullius. *De officiis*: 154.71; *De oratore*: 151.41; 153.9; 157.46; 158.32; *Epistolae ad Atticum*: 156.24; 157.45:1; *Epistolae ad familiares*: 151.19; 156.19; 157.45:2; *Pro lege Manilia*: 151.34:1; *Pro Marcello*: 151.34:2; *Pro Sestio*: 151.38; *Quaestiones Tusculanae*: 165.108; *Selected works — Epistolae*: 159.219; 160.38; *Selected Works — Orations*: 151.8; 153.2; 156.18; 156.64; 164.54; 165.88; *Selected works — Philosophica*: 156.21; 157.44; *Selected works — Philosophica* (part): 160.19; *Selected works — Rhetorica* (probable): 160.33; *Selections*: 164.67; *Selections — Fragmenta*: 156.13; *Works*: 154.36; 158.10; 159.18
Cicero, Marcus Tullius (spurious). *Rhetorica ad Herennium*: 154.149
Clapham, Henoch. *Antidoton: or a soveraigne remedie against schisme and heresie: from that parable of tares*: 159.509; *briefe of the Bible, drawne first into English poësy, and then illustrated by apte annotations, A*: 158.40
Clarke, John, BD. *Formulae oratoriae, in usum scholarum concinnatae*: 164.63
Claudianus, Claudius. *Unidentified*: 164.68
Clavius, Christoph. *In sphaeram Joannis de Sacro Bosco commentarius*: 165.84
Cleland, James. *Heropaideia, or the institution of a young noble man*: 165.92
Clenardus, Nicolaus. *Institutiones linguae graecae*: 154.46; 157.43; 161.8; 166.4; *Unidentified*: 159.232
Clenardus, Nicolaus (perhaps). *Institutiones linguae graecae* (perhaps): 153.18:2
Clichtoveus, Jodocus. *Antilutherus*: 159.31; *Fundamentum logicae*: 160.44; *Homiliae*: 156.39
Cloquius, Andries (editor). *Gustavus Magnus, sive Panegyricae orationes*: 165.60
Coimbra. Collegium Societis Jesu. *Aristotle — Logica: commentary*: 159.72; *Aristotle — Physica: commentary*: 159.67; *Aristotle — Unidentified: commentary*: 164.18
Coke, Sir Edward. *lord Coke his speech and charge (at the assises of Norwich), The. With a discoverie and the abuses and corruption of officers*: 161.10:1
Colerus, Jacobus (probable). *De animarum immortalitate* (probable): 159.64
Columbus, Realdus. *De re anatomica*: 159.486
Comes, Natalis. *Unidentified*: 153.1; 164.25
Comines, Philippe de. *Memoires*: 165.58; *Memoires* (probable): 159.48; 159.519
Comino, Ventura (probable). *Thesaurus politicus* (probable): 159.387
Contarini, Gasparo, Cardinal. *De magistratibus et republica Venetorum*: 159.363; 165.111
Cooke, James. *Juridica trium quaestionum ad majestatem pertinentium determinatio; opposita praecipue epistolae cuidam dedicatoriae*: 159.166
Cooper, Thomas, Bishop. *Thesaurus linguae Romanae et Britannicae*: 154.31
Copley, Anthony. *answere to a letter of a jesuited gentleman, An*: 159.508
Coqueau, Léonard. *Examen praefationis monitoriae Jacobi I praemissae apologiae suae pro juramento fidelitatis*: 159.39
Cordus, Valerius. *Dispensatorium*: 154.181
Corpus juris canonici: 152.13
Corpus juris civilis: 151.6; 152.11; 152.12; 154.168; 154.169; 156.8; 156.44; 159.66; *Corpus juris civilis — Digesta*: 152.10:1
Cosin, Richard. *answer to the two first and principall treatises of a certeine factious libell, An abstract of certeine acts of Parlement, An*: 159.98; *apologie: of, and for sundrie proceedings by jurisdiction ecclesiasticall, An*: 152.19; 159.138
Costerus, Franciscus. *Enchiridion controversiarum de religione*: 159.228
Cotton [Coton], Pierre. *Responsio apologetica adversus Anticotini, et sociorum criminationes*: 159.343

Councils of the Church: *Concilia omnia tam generalia quam particularia*: 162.22
Councils—Trent: 152.5; 154.6; 157.26; *Acta Concilii Tridentini* (probable): 154.194; 159.344; *Catechismus ex decreto Concilii Tridentini*: 154.114; *Concilii Tridentii restitutioni opposita gravamina*: 154.196
Covarruvias a Leyva, Diego, *Bishop of Segovia*. Unidentified: 159.430
Cowley, Abraham. *Poetical blossomes* (probable): 165.29
Crespin, Jean. *Lexicon graecolatinum*: 164.5
Cudsemius, Petrus. *De desperata Calvini causa tractatus brevis*: 159.352
Curio, Caelius Secundus. *Cicero—De partitione oratoria: commentary* [and other works]: 156.69
Curtius Rufus, Quintus. *De rebus gestis Alexandri Magni*: 154.132; 159.445; 165.65
Cyprian, *Saint*. *Works*: 159.355
Cyril, *of Alexandria, Saint*. *Works* (probable): 162.24

D, G. (probable). *A briefe discoverie of doctor Allens seditious drifts, contrived in a pamphlet* (probable): 159.131
Daneau, Lambert. *Ad R. Bellarmini disputationes theologicas responsio*: 154.154; *Christianae isagoges*: 159.366; *Commentariorum in Prophetas minores tomus pr.-sec*: 154.73; *Elenchi haereticorum*: 157.38; *Orationis dominicae explicatio*: 154.102; *Politicorum aphorismorum silva*: 159.482
Daniel, Samuel. *first part of the historie of England, The*: 159.177
Daniel, Samuel (probable). *tragedie of Philotas, The* (probable): 159.313
Dedekind, Friedrich. *Ludus satyricus, de morum simplicitate, seu rusticitate*: 165.56
Delrio, Martin Antonio. *Disquisitionum magicarum libri sex*: 159.262; *Vindiciae areopagiticae contra Josephum Scaligerum*: 159.353
Demosthenes. *Works*: 154.2; 159.11
De polonica electione, in comitiis Warsauiensibus, anni 1587 acta: et quae secuta sunt, usque ad coronationem Sigismundi III et captum Maximilianum: 159.169
Dering, Edward. *Hebrews: commentary*: 154.50
Desainliens, Claude. *Frenche schoolemaister, wherin is shewed, the pronouncing of the Frenche tongue*: 159.283; *A dictionarie French and English*: 165.91
Despautère, Jean. *Commentarii grammatici*: 165.8
Dictionaries (unidentified): 151.42:2; 154.8; 156.23; 159.43; 159.303; 162.5; 162.12; 162.31
Dictys, *Cretensis*. *De bello troiano*: 165.116
Digges, Thomas. *briefe report of the militarie services done in the Low Countries, by the erle of Leicester: written by one that served in good place there, A*: 159.194
Diodorus, *Siculus*. *Bibliotheca historia*: 166.1
Dionysius, *Cisterciensis*. *Liber in quatuor sententiarum*: 159.34
Dionysius, *of Halicarnassus*. *Antiquitates sive origines Romanae*: 159.13; *Delle cose antiche della Citta di Roma*: 156.11
Dod, John. *plaine and familiar exposition of the Ten commandements, with a methodicall short catechisme, A*: 157.12; *plaine and familiar exposition of the ninth and tenth chapters of the Proverbs of Salomon, A*: 157.13
Dodoens, Rembert. *Cosmographica in astronomiam et geographiam isagoge*: 165.109
Donne, John. *Poems, by J.D. With elegies on the authors death*: 165.54
Downes, Andrew. *Praelectiones in Philippicam de pace Demosthenis*: 165.83
Drayton, Michael. *Poly-Olbion*: 159.55

Drusius, Joannes. *Observationes*: 159.419
Du Jon, François, *the Elder*. *De politiae Mosis observatione*: 154.202; *De theologia vera*: 154.82; *Ecclesiastici sive de natura et administrationibus ecclesiae Dei*: 159.258; *Eirenicum de pace ecclesiae catholicae*: 154.231; *Expositio prophetae Danielis*: 154.68:2; *Grammatica hebraeae linguae*: 159.308; *Jude: commentary*: 154.232; *Libri Geneseos analysis*: 154.68:1; *Libri II. Mosis, qui Exodus vulgo inscribitur, analytica explicatio*: 154.69
Du Jon, François, *the Elder* (editor). *Unidentified*: 154.238
Du Moulin, Pierre, *the Elder*. *Elementa logica*: 164.47
Du Praissac, *Sieur*. *art of warre, or Militarie discourses, The*: 165.74
Duprat, Pardoux. *Lexicon juris civilis et canonici*: 156.52
Du Preau, Gabriel. *Elenchus haereticorum omnium*: 159.263; *Narratio historica conciliorum omnium ecclesiae christianae*: 159.269
Duns, John, *Scotus*. *Aristotle—Metaphysica: commentary*: 159.37; 159.84

Earle, John. *Microcosmographie*: 165.101
Eedes, Richard. *Six learned and godly sermons*: 159.314
Elias, *Levita*. *Grammatica hebraica*: 159.82; *Unidentified*: 159.160
Eliot, John. *Orthoepia Gallica. Eliots fruits for the French: which teacheth to speake the French tongue*: 159.108
Elmacinus, Georgius. *Historia Saracenica*: 166.7:1
Elyot, Sir Thomas. *boke named the governour, The*: 159.282; *image of governance compiled of the actes of Alexander Severus, The*: 159.469; 159.534
England, Church of.
  Articles: 159.285
  Constitutions and Canons: 157.14; 159.184
  Injunctions, General, 1559: 159.168
England—Statutes: 152.9:1; 156.5:1–4; 159.73; 159.103
  General Collections: 159.328; 159.535
Epictetus. *Enchiridion*: 159.287; 165.129
Epiphanius, *Bishop of Constantia*. *Contra octoginta haereses* (probable): 159.42
Erasmus, Desiderius. *Adagia*: 151.42:1; 154.175; 164.3; *Apophthegmata*: 156.32; *Colloquia*: 151.37; 159.507; *De duplici copia verborum ac rerum*: 151.4; 151.9; 156.40; *Epistolae D. Erasmi Roterodami ad diversos, et aliquot aliorum ad illum*: 165.7; *Parabolae sive similia*: 159.528
Erythraeus, Valentinus. *De ratione legendi, explicandi et scribendi epistolas libri tres*: 156.71
Estella, Diego de. *De contemnendis mundi vanitatibus*: 155.12; 160.24
Estienne, Charles. *Dictionarium historicum ac poeticum*: 164.21; *Lexicon historicum, geographicum, poeticum*: 165.4; *Pratum, lacus, arundinetum*: 159.516
Estienne, Henri. *Ad Senecae lectionem proodopoeia*: 159.279; *L'introduction au traité de la conformité des merveilles anciennes avec les modernes: ou, traité préparatif à l'apologie pour Hérodote*: 159.427; *Schediasmatum variorum*: 156.25
Euclid. *Elementa*: 159.391
Euripides. *Works*: 159.423; *Works* (probable): 159.418; 165.20
Eusebius, *Pamphili, Bishop*. *Historia ecclesiastica*: 157.3; *Works* (probable): 154.1
Eustachius, *a Sancto Paulo*. *Summa philosophiae quadripartita*: 165.31
Eustratius, *Archbishop of Nicaea*. *Aristotle—Ethica: commentary and text*: 156.57

Faber, Jacobus, *Stapulensis*. *Aristotle—Physica: commentary and paraphrase*: 154.27; 156.56; *Aristotle—Selected Works—Logica: commentary*: 154.26
Feguernekinus, Isaacus. *Enchiridion locorum communium theologicorum*: 154.101; 159.259
Felicius, Constantius. *conspiracie of Lucius Catiline, The*: 159.125
Fenton, Roger. *treatise of usury, divided into three bookes, A*: 159.139
Fernelius, Joannes. *Unidentified*: 154.121
Ferrarius, Joannes. *woorke of Joannes Ferrarius Montanus, touchynge the good orderynge of a common weale, A*: 159.124
Ferronus, Arnoldus. *De rebus gestis Gallorum*: 159.368
Ferus, Joannes. *Exodus, Numbers, Deuteronomy, Joshua, Judges: commentary*: 154.157; 159.342; *In totam Genesim enarrationes*: 159.229; *Jobi historiae explicatio in CXIIII conciones distributa*: 154.205; *John: commentary*: 159.382; *Matthew: commentary*: 159.322; 160.1
Field, Richard. *Of the church, five bookes*: 159.90
Fioravanti, Leonardo. *Capricci medicinali*: 156.26
Fisher, John, *Saint and Cardinal*. *treatise concernynge the fruytfull saynges of Davyd in the seven penytencyall psalmes, This*: 154.230
Flacius, Matthias, *Illyricus*. *Catalogus testium veritatis*: 162.21; *Unidentified*: 159.145
Flacius, Matthias, *Illyricus* (editor). *Ecclesiastica historia*: 162.14
Flamel, Nicolas. *Nicholas Flamel, his exposition of the hieroglyphicall figures upon an arch in St. Innocent churchyard in Paris*: 165.135
Floccus, Andreas Dominicus. *De magistratibus sacerdotiisque Romanorum*: 158.33; 159.460
Florio, John. *Florios second frutes,. . .to which is annexed his Gardine of recreation* (probable): 158.19
Florus, Lucius Annaeus. *Epitomae de Tito Livio bellorum omnium annorum*: 158.36; 159.222; 164.62; 164.65
Fonseca, Petrus. *Institutionum dialecticarum libri octo*: 154.151
Fornerius, Gulielmus. *Selectiones*: 159.142
Fox Morzillo, Sebastiano. *Ethices philosophiae compendium*: 151.16
Fraunce, Abraham. *Abrahami Fransi insignium, armorum, emblematum, hieroglyphicorum, et symbolorum explicatio*: 159.205
Freigius, Joannes Thomas. *Quaestiones geometricae et steriometricae*: 154.191; *Unidentified*: 154.160
Frischlin, Nicodemus. *Facetiae selectiores*: 159.449
Fuchs, Leonard. *Hippocrates—Aphorismi: commentary and text*: 159.297; *Institutionum medicinae*: 159.255
Fulgentius, *Bishop of Ruspa* (probable). *Works* (probable): 159.386
Fulke, William. *defense of the sincere and true translations of the holie scriptures into the English tong, against G. Martin, A*: 159.227; *retentive, to stay good christians, against the motives of R. Bristow, A* (probable): 159.495; *text of the New Testament translated by the papists, The*: 157.1; *New Testament—commentary*: 154.15
Fuller, Nicholas, *Prebendary*. *Miscellaneorum theologicorum libri III*: 159.329
Fullonius, Gulielmus. *Acolastus de filio prodigo*: 151.33

Galatino, Pietro. *Opus de arcanis catholicae veritatis*: 162.37
Galen. *De simplicium medicamentorum facultatibus*: 156.17
Garnet, Henry. *treatise of christian renunciation, A*: 158.39

Gascoigne, George. *steele glas, The. A satyre*: 159.133; *Works*: 159.127
Gelli, Giovanni Battista. *Circes of John Baptista Gello, Florentyne*: 159.296
Gellius, Aulus. *Noctes Atticae*: 159.462
Gemma, Reiner, *Frisius*. *Arithmetica practicae methodus facilis*: 156.37; *De principiis astronomiae et cosmographiae, deque usu globi*: 165.122
Genebrardus, Gilbertus, *Archbishop* (translator). *Chronologia hebraeorum major (Seder 'Olam)*: 162.20
Gentilis, Albericus. *De legationibus, libri tres*: 159.415; *Regales disputationes tres: id est, De potestate regis absoluta, De unione regnorum Britanniae, De vi civium in regem semper injusta*: 159.202
Gentillet, Innocent (probable). *Commentariorum de regno aut quovis principatu recte administrando libri tres. Adversus N. Machiavellum* (probable): 159.454
Gerardus, Andreas, *Hyperius*. *Aristotle — Physica: paraphrase*: 153.19:1; *De theologo, sive De ratione studii theologici*: 157.31; 154.109; 165.76
Gifford, George. *Fifteene sermons, upon the Song of Salomon*: 157.51; *Sermons upon the whole booke of the Revelation*: 157.16
Gildas. *Liber querulus de excidio Britanniae*: 159.476
Giovio, Paolo, *Bishop*. *Ragionamento sopra i motti e disegni d'arme e d'amore*: 156.29; *Unidentified*: 162.19
Goclenius, Rudolphus, *the Elder*. *Exercitationes ethicae*: 154.161; *Physicae disputationes in septem libros distinctae*: 165.38; *Scholae, seu Disputationes physicae*: 154.162
Godwin, Francis, *Bishop*. *catalogue of the bishops of England, with a briefe history of their lives and actions, A*: 159.178
Godwin, Thomas. *Romanae historiae anthologia. An English exposition of the Romane antiquities*: 165.93:1; *Synopsis antiquitatum Hebraicarum, ad explicationem utriusque testamenti*: 165.93:2
Gouveaus, Antonius de. *Histoire orientale des grans progres de l'eglise Cathol. apost. et Rom*: 159.218
Gower, John, *the Poet*. *De confessione amantis*: 165.12
Grammar (unidentified): 156.14:2
Grange, John, *Student in the Common Law*. *golden Aphroditis: a pleasant discourse, The*: 159.148
Grassaille, Charles de. *Regalium Franciae libri duo*: 159.273
Gregory I, *Saint, Pope*. *Works* (probable): 162.34
Gretser, Jacob. *Lixivium pro abluendo male sano capite anonymi cuiusdam fabulatoris, et, ut vocant novellantis, qui caedem christianissimi Galliae et Navarrae Regis Henrici IV. in Jesuitas, partim aperte partem tacite confert*: 159.210
Guevara, Antonio de, *Bishop*. *diall of princes, The*: 159.50
Guicciardini, Francesco. *historie of Guicciardin, conteining the warres of Italie, The*: 159.54; *Hypomneses politicae*: 159.525; *description of the Low countreys gathered into an epitome, The*: 159.389; *Descrittione di tutti i Paesi Bassi*: 165.11
Gulielmus, *Parisiensis, Professor*. *Gospels and Epistles (liturgical): commentary and text*: 162.32; *Unidentified*: 154.42
Gustavus Magnus, sive Panegyricae orationes: 165.60
Gwinne, Matthew. *Orationes duae Londini habitae in aedibus Greshamiis, 1598*: 159.468
Gwinne, Matthew (probable). *Nero tragaedia nova* (probable): 159.159

Habermann, Johann. *Liber radicum seu lexicon ebraicum*: 157.5
Haddon, Walter. *Contra Hieron. Osorium,. . .responsio apologetica*: 152.4:1; *Lucubrationes passim collectae, et editae*: 159.141
Hall, Joseph, Bishop. *discovery of a new world, or a description of the South Indies, by an English Mercury, The*: 159.305; *Mundus alter et idem sive terra australis*: 165.115
Happellius, Wigandus. *Linguae sanctae canones grammatici*: 154.135
Harpsfield, Nicholas. *Dialogi sex contra summi pontificatus, monasticae vitae, sanctorum, sacrarum imaginum oppugnatores, et pseudomartyres*: 159.81
Harris, Richard. *Concordia Anglicana de primatu ecclesiae regio; adversus Becanum De dissidio Anglicano*: 159.505
Haymo, *Bishop of Halberstadt*. *Homiliae*: 160.35
Hayne, Thomas (erroneously attributed). *briefe discourse of the scriptures: declaring the severall stories, lives, and deaths of the fathers, from Adam, unto Joseph, A* (probable): 159.253
Heidelberg catechism: 154.97; 154.98
Heidfeld, Johann. *Sphinx philosophica*: 159.357
Heinsius, Daniel. *Orationes*: 164.51; 165.28
Heliodorus. *Heliodori Aethiopicorum libri decem*: 165.21; *Historia Aethiopica*: 159.424
Hemmingsen, Niels. *Catechismi quaestiones concinnatae*: 154.118
Henderson, Alexander (See Charles I, *King*).
Henry VIII, *King of England*. *Assertio septem sacramentorum adversus M. Lutherum*: 159.451
Hermanni, Philippus. *first part of the key of philosophie, The*: 154.204
Hermes, Trismegistus. *Ars chemica, quod sit licita recte exercentibus*: 159.452
Herodian. *Historiae*: 154.124; 158.31; 159.22; 159.63; 159.133; 164.23; 165.6:A; *Historiarum liber primus, Clio*: 156.54:1
Herolt, Joannes. *Sermones discipuli*: 154.47
Heshusius, Tilemannus, *Bishop*. *Psalms: commentary*: 154.25
Hesiod. *Works* (probable): 165.68
Heurnius, Joannes. *Institutiones medicinae*: 165.85
Heyns, Peeter. *miroir du monde, Le*: 159.537
Heywood, John. *Works*: 165.87
Heywood, Thomas. *first and second partes of king Edward the fourth, The*: 159.206
Hippocrates. *Aphorismi*: 165.126
Hobbes, Thomas. *Elementa philosophica de cive*: 165.81
Hoby, Sir Edward. *countersnarle for Ishmael Rabshacheh, A*: 161.10:2
Holyoke, Francis. *Dictionarium etymologicum latinum*: 164.15
Homer. *Iliad*: 154.147; 159.416; 160.20; *Odyssey*: 154.146; 159.233
Hooker, Richard. *Of the lawes of ecclesiasticall politie*: 159.53; 165.15
Hopton, Arthur. *concordancy of yeares, A*: 165.107
Horatius Flaccus, Quintus. *Epistolarum libri duo et in eas praelectiones methodicae per C. Minoem*: 153.20; *Works*: 154.37; 159.426; 164.32; 165.49:A; *Works* (probable): 154.140:1; 156.47:1; 156.47:2; 159.432; *Works* (perhaps): 154.140:2
Horne, Robert, *Bishop* (probable). *answeare made by Rob. bishoppe of Wynchester, to a booke entituled, The declaration of suche scruples, touchinge the othe of supremacy, as J. Fekenham, by wrytinge did deliver, An*, probably: 153.16

Hotman, François. *P. Sixti fulmen brutum in Henricum sereniss. Regem Navarrae et illustrissimum Henricum Borbonium, Principem Condaeum*: 159.301
Hotman, Jean. *Antichoppinus*: 154.222
Howard, Henry, *Earl of Surrey. Songes and sonettes, written by Henry Haward late earle of Surrey, and other*: 159.274
Howson, John, *Bishop. second sermon, preached at Paules Crosse, the 21. of May, 1598, A. Concluding a former sermon*: 159.193:2; *sermon preached at Paules Crosse the 4. of December. 1597. [Showing] that all buying and selling of spirituall promotion is unlawfull, A*: 159.193:1; *Uxore dimissa propter fornicationem aliam non licet superinducere...Accessit eiusdem theseos defensio contra reprehensiones T. Pyi*: 159.96
Hozyusz, Stanislaus, *Cardinal. Works*: 162.26
Huarte, Juan. *Examen de ingenios. The examination of mens wits*: 159.154
Hues, Robert. *Tractatus de globis et eorum usu*: 159.483
Hugo, de Sancto Caro. *Postilla*: 162.15
Hugo, de Sancto Victore. *Works*: 162.25
Hull, John. *Saint Peters prophesie of these last dayes*: 160.6
Hull, William. *The third worke of mercy*: 160.30
Humphrey, Laurence. *Joannis Juelli Angli, episcopi Sarisburiensis vita et mors; verae doctrinae defensio*: 152.4:4; 154.209
Hunnius, Aegidius. *Calvinus Judaizans*: 159.494
Hutton, Thomas. *Reasons for refusal of subscription to the booke of common praier, under the hands of certaine ministers of Devon, and Cornwall*: 159.77

Indagine, Joannes ab. *Chiromantia*: 159.365
Index librorum prohibitorum: 159.320
Isocrates. *Ad Demonicum*: 151.10:1; 151.10:2; *Selected works—Orations*: 164.54; *Works*: 165.44; *Works* (probable): 154.123

Jackson, Thomas, *Dean of Peterborough. eternall truth of scriptures, The*: 159.100
Jaffe, Samuel, *ben Isaac Ashkenazy. Yepheh mareh*: 162.8
James I, *King of England. apologie for the oath of allegiance: first set forth without a name, now acknowledged by James, King, An*: 159.189; *psalmes of king David by king James, The*: 165.51
James, Thomas, *D.D. Catalogus librorum bibliothecae publicae quam Thomas Bodleius in academia Oxoniensi nuper instituit*: 159.89; *treatise of the corruption of scripture, councels, and fathers, by the prelats, of the Church of Rome, A*: 159.95
Javellus, Chrysostom. *Aristotle—Metaphysica: commentary*: 165.43; *Aristotle—Physica: commentary*: 165.104
Jerome, *Saint. Works* (part): 159.35
Jewel, John, *Bishop. Apologia ecclesiae anglicanae*: 159.440; *apologie, or aunswer in defence of the Church of England, An*: 152.4:5; 153.4; *Joannis Juelli...adversus Thomam Hardingum, volumen*: 154.58; *Thessalonians: commentary and text*: 154.76
John XXI, *Pope. Summulae logicales*: 164.8
John, *Chrysostom, Saint. Homiliae*: 159.523; *Works*: 162.39
John, *of Damascus, Saint* (probable). *Unidentified*: 159.58
John, *of Salisbury, Bishop of Chartres. Policraticus de nugis curialium*: 159.225
Jonson, Benjamin. *Sejanus his fall*: 158.45; 159.171; *Works* (part): 165.14

Josephus, Flavius. *Works* (probable): 159.473
Juda, Leo. *Unidentified*: 166.3
Junctinus, Franciscus. *Tabulae resolutae astronomicae*: 159.69
Junius, Adrian. *Emblemata*: 165.133; *Nomenclator*: 156.30; 165.18
Junius, Balduinus. *Conciones super evangelia*: 159.361
Jurgiewicius, Andreas. *Quinti evangelii professores antiquissimi et celeberrimi Nullus et Nemo*: 159.511
Justinian I. *Corpus Juris Civilis*: 152.11; 159.66; *Codex*: 151.6; 154.169; *Institutiones*: 152.12; 154.168; 156.8; 156.44
Justinus, *the Historian*: (See Trogus Poempeius)
Juvenalis, Decimus Junius. *Works*: 159.407:A; 159.499:A; 164.36; 165.49:B

Keckermann, Bartholomaeus. *Systema S.S. theologiae, tribus libris adornatum*: 159.346; 160.17; *Unidentified*: 159.334; 159.378
Kimchi, David. *Sefer hash-shorashim*: 162.11:2
Kimchi, David (editor). *Psalms*: 162.11:1

La Framboisière, Nicolas Abraham de. *Unidentified*: 165.62
La Place, Pierre de (perhaps). *Politique discourses, treating of the differences and inequalities of vocations* (perhaps): 159.132
La Primaudaye, Pierre de. *French academie, The*: 159.102
La Ramée, Pierre de. *Ciceronianus*: 156.68:2; *Dialectica*: 154.215; 154.217; *Grammatica*: 154.139; 158.25; *Unidentified*: 165.36; *Virgil — Georgics: commentary*: 165.67
La Roche de Chandieu, Antoine. *Works*: 154.7
Lancelotto, Giovanni Paolo (perhaps). *Institutiones juris canonici* (perhaps): 156.9
Languet, Hubert. *Vindiciae contra tyrannos*: 159.284
Latimer, Hugh. *Sermons*: 159.76
Lavater, Ludwig. *Proverbs, Ecclesiastes: commentary and text*: 154.16
Lemnius, Levinus. *sanctuarie of salvation, helmet of health, and mirrour of modestie, The*: 154.229; *Unidentified*: 154.183; 156.27
Lentulo, Scipio. *Italicae grammatices*: 159.510
Lessius, Leonardus. *De gratia efficaci decretis divinis libertate arbitrii et praescientia Dei conditionata*: 159.92; *Quae fides et religio sit capessenda, consultatio*: 159.373
Levi ben Gershon. *Perush 'al hat-Torah*: 162.6
Lily, William. *Institutio compendiaria totius grammaticae*: 154.153
Linacre, Thomas. *De emendata structura Latini sermonis libri sex*: 156.41
Lipsius, Justus. *Electa*: 159.105; *Orationes*: 165.72:1; *Politicorum sive civilis doctrinae libri sex*: 159.388; *Saturnalium sermonum libri duo*: 159.74; *Unidentified*: 159.376
Littleton, Sir Thomas. *Tenures*: 152.9:2; 158.44; 159.538
Liturgies — Latin Rite.
  Breviaries: 159.488
  Psalters: 160.32:1
Liturgy (unidentified): 160.40
Lively, Edward. *Annotationes in quinq; priores ex minoribus prophetis*: 154.241
Livius, Titus. *Historiae Romanae decades*: 159.411; 154.3
Lorme, Charles de. *Pteleinodaphneiai. Hoc est, laureae apollinares a prima ad supremam, sive enneas quaestionum medicinum*: 159.527

Loyseleur, Pierre (attributed). *apologie or defence, of the most noble prince William, The*: 159.150

Lubbertus, Sibrandus. *De Papa Romano libri decem*: 157.28; *Epistolica disceptatio de fide justificante*: 159.215

Lubin, Eilhard. *Clavis graecae linguae*: 164.34; *In D.J. Juvenalis satyrarum libros Ecphrasis succincta et perspicua*: 164.12

Lucanus, Marcus Annaeus. *Pharsalia*: 159.234

Lucian, of Samosata. *Dialogues—Selected* (probable): 159.267; 159.306; 164.70; *Unidentified*: 151.13; *Works* (perhaps): 159.477

Luis, de Granada. *De doctrina sive disciplina vitae spiritualis libellus*: 160.47; *Ecclesiasticae rhetoricae, sive de ratione concionandi libri VI*: 159.383; *Unidentified*: 160.42:1–3

Lull, Ramón. *Unidentified*: 158.29; *Works*: 159.312; 165.2

Luther, Martin. *Galatians: commentary*: 154.54; 160.26; *Works*: 162.13

Lychetus, Franciscus. *Duns, Scotus—Sentences: commentary* (probable): 159.14

Lycosthenes, Conrad. *Apophthegmata*: 154.148; *Prodigiorum ac ostentorum chronicon*: 159.51

Lydiat, Thomas. *Tractatus de variis annorum formis*: 165.100

Müller, Philipp. *Miracula chymica et misteria medica*: 159.530

Macarius, *Aegyptius*. *Homiliae spirituales quinquaginta*: 159.339

Macchiavelli, Niccolò. *arte of warre, The*: 159.94; *De principe*: 154.158; 159.291; *Discorsi*: 159.265; *Disputationum de republica libri iii*: 154.159; 159.226

Macrobius, Ambrosius Aurelius Theodosius. *In somnium Scipionis. Saturnalia*: 165.94

Macropedius, Georgius. *Unidentified*: 154.214

Maffeius, Raphael, *Volaterranus*. *Commentariorum urbanorum octo et triginta libri* (probable): 162.35;

Magdeburg centuriators: 162.14

Magirus, John. *Aristotle—Ethica: commentary*: 159.235; 164.55:1; 164.55:2; 165.40; *Physiologiae peripateticae libri sex*: 161.4

Magna Carta cum statutis: 159.535

Maldonatus, Joannes. *Gospels: commentary and text*: 159.9

Mancinus, Dominicus (probable). *De quatuor virtutibus* (probable): 159.315

Manuzio, Paolo. *Antiquitatum Romanarum liber de legibus*: 159.286; *Epistolae*: 154.164; 156.66; 164.39

Maranta, Robertus. *Speculum aureum, et lumen advocatorum*: 156.33

Marlorat, Augustine. *Genesis: commentary and text*: 154.72; *Novi testamenti catholica expositio ecclesiastica*: 154.10

Marnix van Sant Aldegonde, Philips van (attributed). *tragicall historie of the troubles and civile warres of the lowe countries, otherwise called Flanders, A*: 159.134

Marot, Clément. *Works*: 159.444

Martialis, Marcus Valerius. *Epigrammata*: 159.480; 165.34

Martinius, Petrus. *Grammatica hebraica*: 159.514; 154.137; *Mafteah leshon hakodesh*: 152.18; *Mafteah leshon hakodesh, that is the key of the holy tongue*: 154.136

Marulic, Marko. *Unidentified*: 160.41

Mascarenhas, Fernando Martins. *Tractatus de auxiliis divinae gratiae ad actus supernaturales*: 159.317

Mattioli, Pietro Andrea (perhaps). *Unidentified*: 156.70

Mela, Pomponius. *De situ orbis*: 154.126
Melanchthon, Philipp. *Argumentorum et objectionum de praecipuis articulis doctrinae Christianae*: 155.10; *Loci communes theologici*: 154.81; 157.29; *Philosophiae moralis libri duo*: 165.26; *Examen theologicum*: 160.7
Menezes, Aleixo de. *messe des anciens chrestiens dicts de S. Thomas, en l'Evesche d'Angamal, es Indes Orientales, Le*: 159.218:B
Mercerus, Joannes, *Professor of Hebrew*. *Tabulae in Chaldaeam grammaticen*: 159.80
Mercklin, Joannes. *Quaestionum rhetoricarum*: 154.213
Meredeth, Richard. *Two sermons preached before his majestie*: 159.197
Mexia, Pedro. *Historia imperial y caesarea*: 156.6
Middleton, Thomas. *trick to catch the old-one, A*: 159.173
Molanus, Joannes. *Pontificii et regii librorum censoris, libri quinque*: 159.464
Molina, Ludovicus, *Jesuit*. *Concordia liberi arbitrii cum gratia donis*: 159.68
Mollerus, Henricus. *Psalms: commentary*: 154.17
Monardes, Nicolas. *Unidentified*: 159.126
Moncaeus, Franciscus. *Aaron purgatus sive de vitulo aureo libri duo*: 159.496; 159.521
Montaigne, Michel de. *essais, Les*: 159.250
Montluc, Jean de, *Bishop*. *Epistola de Andium Duce in regnum Polonicorum allegendo*: 151.18
More, Sir Thomas. *Utopia*: 161.9; *workes of Sir T. More. . .wrytten by him in the Englysh tongue, The*: 159.40
Morelius, Gulielmus. *Verborum latinorum cum graecis gallicisque conjunctorum, commentarii*: 157.9
Morison, Sir Richard. *Apomaxis calumniarum, convitiorumque, quibus Joannes Cocleus,. . . Henrici octavi, famam impetere,. . .studuit*: 159.107
Mornay, Philippe de. *De veritate religionis christianae liber*: 154.85; *treatise of the church, A*: 157.11
Morton, Thomas, *Bishop*. *Apologiae catholicae, in qua paradoxa, haereses, blasphemiae, scelera, quae Jesuitae impingunt, diluuntur*: 159.93; 159.433; *De notis ecclesiae*: 159.347; *full satisfaction concerning a double Romish iniquitie; hainous rebellion, and more then heathenish aequivocation, A*: 159.143
Moses ben Maimon. *Mishneh Torah* (probable): 162.3
Mosse, Miles. *arraignment and conviction of usurie, The*: 165.95
Muffet, Peter. *Proverbs: commentary and text*: 154.193
Multiple. *answere of the vicechancelour, the doctors, both the proctors, and other the heads of houses in the universitie of Oxford. To the humble petition of the ministers of the Church of England, desiring reformation of certaine ceremonies and abuses, The*: 159.186; *Justa Oxoniensium. (Lachrymae Oxoniensis stillantes in tumulum principis Henrici)*: 159.112:1; *Midrash Rabbah*: 162.7:1
Musculus, Wolfgang. *Loci communes*: 157.27

Nachmanides, Moses. *Pentateuch: commentary*: 162.7:2
Nathan ben Jehiel. *Lexicon Talmudico-Rabbinico*: 162.4
Nepos, Cornelius. *Aemilii Probi vitae excellentium imperatorum*: 164.61
Nonnus, *Panopolitanus*. *Metaphrasis evangelii secundum Joannem versibus heroicis*: 165.125
Norden, John. *Unidentified*: 159.165
Nowell, Alexander. *Catechismus*: 151.22; 165.59; *true report of the disputation or rather private conference had in the Tower of London, with E. Campion, Jesuite, A*: 159.149

Oecumenius, *Bishop of Tricca. Epistles — Paul: commentary*: 154.74
Olevian, Caspar. *Galatians: commentary*: 152.4:3
Omphalius, Jacobus. *Unidentified*: 156.68:1; 159.278
Oppianus. *Aleuticon. Cynegetica*: 165.27
Oriano, Lanfrancus de. *Practica Lanfranci*: 159.394
Origen. *Works*: 162.23; *Works* (part): 159.23
Ormerod, Oliver. *picture of a papist: or, a relation of the damnable heresies, The*: 159.130; *picture of a puritane: or, a relation of the opinions, and practises of the Anabaptists in Germanie, and of the puritanes in England, The*: 159.214
Orsini, Fulvio. *Illustrium imagines*: 158.26
Ortelius, Abraham. *Theatrum orbis terrarum* (probable): 155.4
Osiander, Andreas, *the Younger. Papa non papa*: 159.529
Osiander, Lucas, *the Elder. Epitomes historiae ecclesiasticae*: 159.86
Osiander, Lucas, *the Elder* (probable). *Unidentified*: 155.5
Osiander, Lucas, *the Younger. Enchiridion controversiarum, quas Augustanae confessionis theologi habent cum Calvinianis*: 159.290
Osorio da Fonseca, Jeronimo, *Bishop. five bookes. . .contayninge a discourse of civill, and christian nobilitie, The*: 159.128; *In Gualterum Haddonum magistrum libellorum supplicum libri tres*: 159.275; *learned and very eloquent treatie, writen in Latin by H. Osorius, wherein he confuteth a certayne aunswere made by M. W. Haddon, A*: 153.11
Ovidius Naso, Publius. *Heroides*: 151.29:1; 154.144; 164.53; *Metamorphoses*: 151.7:1; 151.7:2; 151.29:2; 153.10; 154.143; 159.338; 164.59; *Tristia*: 164.44
Owen, John. *Epigrammatum libri tres*: 159.524; 165.118
Oxford University.
  Official Documents: 159.186; 165.112
  Verses, Addresses:
    Justa Oxoniensium: 159.112:1
    Oxoniensis Academiae funebre officium in memoriam Elisabethae reginae: 160.16

P, T. (probable). *Of the knowledge and conducte of warrres, two bookes* (probable): 159.151
Pacius, Julius. *Aristotelis Stagiritae peripateticorum principiis organum*: 165.5; *Aristotle — De anima: commentary*: 164.45; *Aristotle — Physica: commentary*: 164.27; *Juris quo utimur epitome secundum ordinem Institutionum Imperialium digesta*: 154.198; *Aristotle — Organon: commentary* (probable): 164.20
Pagninus, Sanctes. *Thesauri linguae sanctae epitome*: 154.134; 155.9; 159.12; 159.243
Painter, William. *second tome of the palace of pleasure, The*: 159.121
Palingenius, Marcellus. *Zodiacus vitae*: 153.13:1; 153.13:2; 154.177
Paracelsus. *Unidentified*: 159.428
Paradin, Claude. *Devises heroiques*: 159.501
Pareus, David. *In genesin Mosis commentarius* (probable): 159.62; *Quaestiones controversae theologicae, de jure regum et principum contra papam romanum*: 159.512
Parry, Henry, *Bishop. De regno Dei, et victoria christiana, conciones duae*: 159.211
Parsons, Robert. *book of Christian exercise, A*: 154.96; *treatise of three conversions of England, A*: 165.77
Peckham, John, *Archbishop of Canterbury. Perspectiva communis*: 154.245; 159.116:1
Pelegromius, Simon. *Synonymorum sylva*: 153.17; 164.49
Pellicanus, Conradus. *Gospels, Acts: commentary*: 154.18

Pemble, William. *De formarum origine*: 165.57:1; *Tractatus de providentia dei*: 165.57:2
Peraldus, Gulielmus. *Homeliae sive sermones eximii, praestantesque super Evangelia Dominicalia totius anni*: 159.245
Peraldus, Gulielmus (probable). *Summa virtutum ac vitiorum* (probable): 159.240
Pererius, Benedictus. *De communibus omnium rerum naturalium principiis et affectionibus, libri quindecim*: 165.25; *Genesis: commentary*: 159.8
Perez de Hita, Ginés. *Historia de los vandos de los Zegries y Abencerrajes cavalleros morso de Granada, de las civiles guerras*: 156.42
Perkins, William. *De praedestinationis modo et ordine*: 154.224; *direction for the government of the tongue, A*: 154.226; *exposition of the Lords prayer, in the way of catechising, An*: 153.6; *exposition of the symbole or creed of the apostles, An*: 154.208; *Problema de Romanae fidei ementito catholicismo*: 157.15; *Prophetica, sive de sacra et unica ratione concionandi tractatus*: 154.225; *reformed catholike: or, a declaration shewing how neere we may come to the present church of Rome, A*: 154.192; *Two treatises. I. Of. . .repentance. II. Of the combat of the flesh and spirit*: 154.227; *works of that famous and worthie minister of Christ, in the universitie of Cambridge, M. W. Perkins: gathered into one volume, and newly corrected according to his owne copies, The*: 157.7
Perkins, William (probable). *golden chaine, or the description of theologie, containing the order of the causes of salvation and damnation according to Gods woord, A* (probable): 153.19:2
Perottus, Nicolaus. *Cornucopia*: 164.1
Persius Flaccus, Aulus. *Works*: 159.407:B; 159.499:B; 165.49:C
Peter Chrysologus. *Sermones*: 159.264
Peter Lombard. *Sententiarum libri IIII*: 159.377; *Sententiarum libri IIII* (probable): 154.115
Petrarca, Francesco. *Phisicke against fortune, as well prosperous, as adverse*: 159.97; *Works*: 159.44
Petronius Arbiter. *Satyricon*: 158.30
Petrus, Comestor. *Historia scholastica*: 160.4
Peucer, Kaspar. *Commentarius de praecipuis divinationum generibus*: 156.15
Pflacher, Moses. *Analysis typica omnium cum veteris tum novi Testamenti librorum historicorum*: 154.70
Philippson, Joannes, Sleidanus. *De quatuor summis imperiis*: 154.129; 159.266; 165.128; *De statu religionis et reipublicae, Carolo Quinto, Caesare, commentarii*: 159.239; 165.79:1
Piccolomini, Francesco. *Universa philosophia de moribus*: 164.26; 165.24
Pie, Thomas. *Epistola ad ornatissimum virum D. Johannem Housonum qua dogma eius novum et admirabile de Judaeorum divortiis refutatur*: 157.17
Pilotus, Joannes. *Gallicae linguae institutio*: 159.362
Pindar. *Works*: 159.417; *Works* (probable): 154.184
Piscator, Johann. *Acts: commentary*: 154.195; *Antidromus ad prodromum Andreae Schaafmanni*: 154.239; *Epistles—Paul: commentary*: 154.105; *Epistles: commentary*: 154.106; *Matthew: commentary and text*: 154.103; *Gospels—Unidentified: commentary*: 154.104; *Unidentified*: 157.36
Piscator, Johann (probable). *Disputatio theologica de praedestinatione* (probable): 159.504
Platea, Franciscus de. *Opus restitutionum, usurarum, et excommunicationum*: 159.115
Plato (probable). *Unidentified*: 151.30
Plautus, Titus Maccius. *Comoediae*: 151.2; 154.38; 157.47; 159.310; 165.33

Pliny, *the Elder. Historia naturalis*: 165.17
Pliny, *the Younger. Epistolae*: 159.465; 164.62
Plutarch. *De non irascendo*: 159.281; *lives of the noble Grecians and Romanes, The*: 154.30; 155.3; *Moralia*: 157.49; 158.11; 159.375; *Vitae parallelae*: 157.48; 158.12; 159.412; *Works* (perhaps): 152.17
Polanus, Amandus. *De verbo Dei didascalia in sex disputationes tributa*: 158.6; *Partitiones theologicae juxta naturalis methodi leges conformatae duobus libris*: 157.39; *Unidentified*: 154.111
Politianus, Angelus. *Silva cui titulus Nutricia*: 159.167
Pollux, Julius. *Onomasticon*: 164.11
Polybius. *Historiae*: 159.436
Porta, Giovanni Battista della. *De furtivis literarum notis*: 159.88; *Magiae naturalis*: 159.399; 165.117
Posselius, Joannes. *Syntaxis linguae graecae*: 151.25; 165.99
Price, Daniel. *Spirituall odours to the memory of prince Henry, in foure of the last sermons* (probable): 160.11
Prideaux, John, *Bishop. Hypomnemata logica, rhetorica, physica, metaphysica, pneumatica, ethica, politica, oeconomica*: 165.136
Priscianus, *Caesariensis. Prisciani grammatici Caesariensis libri omnes*: 165.10
Proclus, *Diadochus. Sphaera*: 154.173
Ptolemy, Claudius. *Geographia*: 159.75
Pulton, Ferdinand (editor). *abstract of all the penall statutes, An*: 159.103
Purbach, Georg. *Novae theoricarum planetarum*: 154.171

Quintilianus, Marcus Fabius. *Unidentified*: 154.150; 157.42; 164.33

Raemond, Florimond de. *Fabula Joannae quae pontificis Romani sedem occupasse falso credita est*: 159.345
Rainerius, *de Pisis. Pantheologia, sive Summa universae theologiae*: 159.30
Rainolds, John. *De romanae ecclesiae idolatria* [sic], *in cultu sanctorum, reliquiarum... libri duo*: 154.62; *Sex theses de sacra scriptura, et ecclesia*: 157.52; *summe of the conference betwene J. Rainoldes and J. Hart, The*: 154.63; *Unidentified*: 154.233
Rainolds, John (probable). *Unidentified*: 152.3:3
Raleigh, Sir Walter. *discoverie of the large, rich, and bewtiful empire of Guiana, The*: 159.204
Rampegollis, Antonius de. *Figurae Bibliae*: 159.472
Ransovius, Henricus. *De conservanda valetudine liber*: 159.463
Rastell, John, *Barrister and Printer. exposicions of the termes of the lawes of England, with divers rules, The*: 159.333
Rastell, William (editor). *Registrum omnium brevium tam originalium quam judicialium*: 156.1:4
Ravisius, Joannes. *Epistolae*: 159.435; *Epitheta*: 154.60; 164.35; *Epitheta—Epitome*: 151.1; *Officina*: 159.408
Rawlinson, John. *Romish Judas, The. A sermon*: 159.198
Regimen sanitatis Salernitatum: 154.182
Remus, Georgius (probable). *In Solomonis ecclesiasten, qui de vanitate rerum, et adipiscendo summo bono, spicilegium alterum* (probable): 154.89:2; *Vir pius et sapiens. Hoc est, in Solomonis regis Paroimion librum, post aliorum messes spicilegium primum [alterum]* (probable): 154.89:1

Rennecherus, Herman. *Unidentified*: 154.237
Reuchlin, Johann (editor) (probable): *Clarorum virorum epistolae* (probable): 159.295
Reusner, Nicolaus. *Symboli imperatorii*: 159.421; *Symbolii imperatorii* (probable): 164.50
Rhodolphus, Caspar (probable). *Dialectica*: 154.167
Ribadeneira, Pedro de. *Princeps christianus adversus Nicolaum Machiavellum*: 159.331
Riccoboni, Antonio. *Aristotle — Rhetorica: commentary and paraphrase*: 159.249
Rider, John, *Bishop*. *Bibliotheca scholastica*: 164.6
Ridolfi, Pietro. *Dictionarium concionatorum pauperum*: 159.220
Rispolis, Joannes Matthaeus de. *Status controversiae praedefinitionum et praedeterminationum cum libero arbitrio*: 159.341
Ritschel, George. *Contemplationes metaphysicae*: 165.52
Roberti, Antonius. *Clavis Homerica, reserans significationes, etymologias, derivationes*: 165.53; 164.48
Rollock, Robert. *Romans: commentary*: 154.75
Roorda, Carel. *Hinukh hoc est catechesis, sive prima institutio aut rudimenta religionis christianae*: 165.106
Rosinus, Joannes. *Romanarum antiquitatum corpus absolutissimum*: 154.29
Rous, Francis, *the Younger*. *Archaeologiae Atticae libri tres. Three bookes of the Attick antiquities*: 164.7
Roussel, Michel. *L'Antimariana, ou réfutation des propositions de Mariana*: 159.318
Royardus, Joannes. *Homiliae*: 160.18
Rubio, Antonio. *Aristotle — Organon: commentary*: 164.19
Ruland, Martin, *the Elder*. *De inferno, seu, Cacodaemonum, damnatorumq; domicilio: tractatus*: 154.221; *Synonyma*: 164.29
Ryff, Walther Hermann. *Enchiridion remediorum*: 159.349
Ryves, Sir Thomas. *Historia navalis*: 165.71

Saba, Abraham ben Jacob. *Pentateuch: commentary*: 162.10:1
Saint German, Christopher. *Doctor and student*: 159.384
Salignacus, Bernardus. *Unidentified*: 159.116:2
Sallustius Crispus, Caius. *Works* (probable): 159.410; 165.16:1; *Unidentified*: 151.15; 154.185; 164.40
Salmeron, Alfonsus. *Commentarii in Evangelicam historiam, et in Acta Apostolorum*: 162.17
Saluste du Bartas, Guillaume de. *Weekes*: 152.20
Salvart, Jean-François (editor). *Harmonia Confessionum fidei orthodoxarum et reformatarum ecclesiarum*: 154.207
Sanchez, Gaspar, *de Granada*. *Conciones in Dominicis, et feriis quadragesimae*: 159.241
Sanderson, John. *Institutionum dialecticarum libri quatuor*: 153.7; 154.197; 159.506
Sandys, Sir Edwin. *relation of the state of religion: and with what hopes and pollicies it hath beene framed, and is maintained in the severall states of these westerne parts of the world, A*: 159.185
Saravia, Hadrianus. *Defensio tractationis de diversis ministrorum evangelii gradibus, contra Responsionem T. Bezae*: 154.66
Saravia, Hadrianus (probable). *De diversis ministrorum evangelii gradibus* (probable): 154.67
Sardi, Alessandro. *Liber de nummis: in quo antiqua pecunia romana et graeca metitur precio eius, quae nunc est in usu*: 159.201

Savage, Francis. *conference betwixt a mother a devout recusant, and her sonne a zealous protestant, seeking by humble and dutifull satisfaction to winne her unto the trueth, A*: 159.393

Scaliger, Julius Caesar. *De causis linguae latinae libri tredecim*: 159.367; 164.58; *Exotericarum exercitationum liber XV*: 154.120; 159.309; *Poetices libri septem*: 165.22

Scapula, Joannes. *Lexicon graecolatinum novum*: 155.2; 157.4; 159.59

Schönborn, Bartholomaeus. *Computus vel calendarium astronomicum*: 154.172

Scharpius, Joannes. *Tractatus de justificatione hominis coram Deo*: 161.7

Scheibler, Christoph. *Opus logicum*: 165.1; *Philosophia compendiosa, seu philosophiae synopsis*: 164.43; 165.78

Schindler, Valentin. *Institutiones hebraicae*: 159.292

Schreckenfuchs, Erasmus Oswald. *Commentaria in Sphaeram Joannis de Sacrobusto*: 151.3

Schroeder, Johann. *Opusculum theologicum*: 161.6

Scot, Alexander. *Universa grammatica graeca:* 164.28

Scott, Thomas, *Poet*. *Foure paradoxes of arte, of lawe, of warre, of service*: 165.130

Scribonius, Gulielmus Adolphus. *Physica et sphaerica doctrina*: 165.113; *Triumphus logicae Rameae* (probable): 154.216

Scultetus, Abraham. *Ethicorum libri duo*: 159.298; 165.105; *Medulla theologiae patrum* (part 1): 159.87

Seder 'Olam: 162.20

Selden, John. *duello or single combat, The*: 159.196; *Jani Anglorum facies altera*: 159.441; 159.493; *Mare clausum seu de dominio maris libri duo*: 166.7:2

Seneca, Lucius Annaeus. *Tragoediae*: 159.413; *Unidentified*: 160.45; *Works*: 164.24

Serarius, Nicolaus. *Rabbini et Herodes, seu De tota rabbinorum gente*: 159.289

Sermon (unidentified): 154.234

Serres, Jean de. *De fide catholica*: 159.518; *Ecclesiastes: commentary and text*: 154.107

Seton, John. *Dialectica*: 165.110; *Dialectica* (probable): 151.32

Sextus, Empiricus. *Works*: 159.29

Shakespeare, William (probable). *Hystorie, of Henrie the fourth, The* (probable): 159.200

Sigonio, Carlo. *De republica Hebraeorum libri VII*: 159.372; *Unidentified*: 159.20

Sisto, *da Siena*. *Bibliotheca sancta*: 159.17

Smith, Samuel, *A.M. Aditus ad Logicam*: 164.71

Smith, Sir Thomas, *Doctor of Civil Laws*. *common-welth of England, and maner of government thereof, The*: 159.174

Smyth, William. *Gemma Fabri*: 154.200

Solinus, Caius Julius. *Polyhistor*: 165.9

Sophocles. *Works*: 154.145; 164.42

Soto, Domingo de. *De justitia et jure libri decem*: 162.36

Spagnuoli, Baptista. *Unidentified*: 154.163

Spangenberg, Johann. *Epistles (liturgical): commentary and text*: 154.155

Sparke, William. *Vis naturae et virtus vitae explicatae, comparatae, ad universum doctrinae ordinem constituendum*: 165.132

Spenser, Edmund (perhaps). *shepheardes calendar conteyning twelve aeglogues proportionable to the twelve monethes, The* (perhaps): 159.207

Sprenger, Jacob. *Malleus maleficarum*: 159.434

Stapleton, Thomas. *Gospels (liturgical): commentary*: 159.327; *Promptuarium catholicum*: 159.330

Statius, Publius Papinius. *Unidentified*: 165.120
Stow, John. *Chronicles and annals*: 154.41
Strada, Famianus. *Prolusiones academicae*: 165.32
Strebaeus, Jacobus Lodovicus. *Cicero—De partitione oratoria: commentary and text*: 156.63
Stubbs, John. *discoverie of a gaping gulf whereinto England is like to be swallowed by an other French mariage, The*: 159.522
Suarez, Francisco. *Aristotle—Metaphysica: commentary*: 159.4; *Varia opuscula theologica*: 159.65
Suetonius Tranquillus, Caius. *De vita Caesarum*: 154.125; 159.442; 164.66
Susenbrotus, Joannes. *Epitome troporum ac schematum*: 164.38
Sylburg, Friedrich (editor). *Etymologicon magnum*: 166.2

Tacitus, Publius Cornelius. *Works*: 158.17; 164.10; 164.64; *Unidentified*: 159.56; 159.371; 165.121
Taegius, Franciscus. *siege de Pavie ensemble les assaulx: sailliez: Escarmouchex et battailes, Le*: 159.123
Talaeus, Audomarus. *Academia*: 156.62; *Rhetorica*: 158.35; 154.212
Talmud (part): 162.8; dictionary: 162.4; 162.5; index: 162.38
Tasso, Torquato. *Godfrey of Bulloigne, or the recoverie of Hierusalem*: 159.532
Terentius, Publius, *Afer. Works*: 154.142; 156.50; 158.27; 164.9; 164.52; 165.73; *Works* (probable): 151.23; 159.437
Tertullianus, Quintus. *Works*: 162.28
Theodoret, *Bishop. Works*: 162.29
Theodorus, *Gaza. Institutiones grammaticae*: 156.54:2
Theodosius II, *Emperor of the East. Codex Theodosianus*: 151.5
Theophylact, *Archbishop of Achrida. Gospels: commentary and text*: 160.5
Thomas, Thomas. *Dictionarium linguae Latinae et Anglicanae*: 158.5; 159.221; *Dictionarium linguae Latinae et Anglicanae...cum Graecarum dictionum adjectione auctior*: 159.129
Thucydides. *De bello peloponnesiaco*: 154.131; 159.406
Titelmann, Franz. *Aristotle—Selected works—Philosophia naturalis: commentary*: 159.370
Toletus, Franciscus, *Cardinal. Aristotle—De anima: commentary*: 156.60; *Aristotle— Physica: commentary*: 161.3; *Aristotle—Selected works—Logic: commentary*: 159.83
Topsell, Edward. *reward of religion, The*: 154.206; 157.33
Torrella, Gaspar. *Pro regimine seu preservatione sanitatis. De esculentis et poculentis dialogus*: 154.219
Toxites, Michael. *Cicero (spurious)—Rhetorica ad Herennium: commentary and text*: 156.28
Travers, Walter. *Ecclesiastica disciplina*: 154.201
Trelcatius, Lucas, *the Younger. Scholastica et methodica locorum communium s. theologiae institutio, didactice et elenctice in epitome explicata*: 157.35; 160.12:A
Tritheim, Johann von. *Catalogus scriptorum ecclesiasticorum*: 159.71
Trogus Pompeius and *Justinus, the Historian. Epitomae in Trogi Pompeii historias*: 154.128; 156.36; 156.38; 158.20
Truxillo, Thomas de. *Sermones*: 159.374
Twyne, Brian. *Antiquitatis academiae Oxoniensis apologia*: 159.99

Udall, John. *commentarie upon the Lamentations of Jeremy, A*: 157.19; *Lamentations: commentary and paraphrase*: 154.49
Ulstadius, Philippus. *Coelum philosophorum*: 159.479
Unidentified (author). *Acts: commentary* (probable): 159.277; *Aristotle — Parva naturalia: commentary*: 156.55; *Comoediae: commentary*: 159.422; *Seneca — Unidentified: commentary*: 160.25
Unidentified (author and work): 151.26; 151.36; 151.39; 151.42:2; 152.6; 152.15; 152.16; 152.21; 153.21; 153.22:1–5; 154.8; 154.14:1–80; 154.48; 154.95; 154.113; 154.179; 154.180; 154.199; 154.210; 155.6:1:1–2; 155.6:2:1–6; 156.1:1–3; 156.5:1–4; 156.7; 156.10; 156.3; 156.12; 156.14:2; 156.20; 156.22; 156.23; 156.34; 156.43; 156.49:1–2; 156.73; 156.74:1–14; 158.23 158.42:1–2; 158.43; 159.36; 159.41:1–4; 159.43; 159.49; 159.61; 159.70; 159.101; 159.109; 159.147; 159.153; 159.162; 159.164; 159.187; 159.199; 159.203; 159.212; 159.213; 159.247; 159.270; 159.303; 159.316; 159.319; 159.335; 159.348; 159.369; 159.380; 159.400; 159.409; 159.446; 159.448; 159.457; 159.467; 159.475; 159.487; 159.497; 159.517; 159.526; 159.533:1–24; 159.539:1–18; 159.540; 159.541; 160.28:1–12; 160.29; 160.40; 160.48:1–5; 162.5; 162.9; 162.10:2; 162.12; 162.18; 162.31; 163.1:2; 163.1:3; 164.22; 165.13; 165.131:1–8; 165.134; 165.55; 166.5:160; 166.6:1–34; 166.8:1–9; 166.9:1–5; 166.10:1–21; 166.11:152; 166.12:1–3; 166.13:1–7; 166.14:1–39; 166.15:1–46; 166.16:1–74; 166.17:1–29
Ursinus, Zacharias. *Doctrinae christiana compendium*: 154.98; *Enchiridion catecheticum*: 154.203; *summe of christian religion, The*: 151.39; 157.10; *summe of christian religion, The* (probable): 158.4

Vadianus, Joachim (perhaps). *Epitome trium terrae partium* (perhaps): 159.356
Valentia, Gregorius de. *Aquinas — Summa theologica: commentary*: 159.6
Valerius Maximus. *Facta et dicta memorabilia*: 153.5; 154.127; 159.453; 164.69; 165.16:2
Valla, Laurentius. *Unidentified*: 154.244
Varro, Marcus Terentius. *De re rustica*: 159.230; *Opera quae supersunt*: 165.23
Vassaeus, Lodoicus. *In anatomen corporis humani tabulae quatuor*: 159.364
Velleius Paterculus, Caius. *Historia Romana duo volumina*: 158.18; 159.404
Vergilius, Polydorus. *Anglica historia* (probable): 159.25; *Unidentified*: 156.2; 159.438
Vermigli, Pietro Martire. *Judges: commentary*: 154.22; *Sainctes prieres recueillies des pseaumes de David*: 159.458;
Verro, Sebastian. *Physicorum libri x*: 154.223; 159.398
Vigelius, Nicolaus. *Dialectices juris civilis libri III*: 152.10:2; *Digestorum pars prima (septima)*: 152.10:1
Virgilius Maro, Publius. *Bucolics*: 151.31; 165.124; *Works*: 154.28; 159.231; 165.50; *Works* (probable): 151.24; 154.141; 160.39; 160.46; 164.2; 164.31
Vitruvius Pollio, Marcus. *De architectura libri decem*: 165.3
Vivaldus, Joannes Ludovicus. *Aureum opus de veritate contritionis*: 160.22
Vives, Joannes Ludovicus. *Unidentified*: 159.252
Voellus, Joannes. *Generale artificium orationis cuiuscunque componendae*: 159.450
Voragine, Jacobus de. *Legenda aurea sanctorum*: 159.52
Vorstius, Conrad. *Enchiridion controversiarum: seu index errorum ecclesiae Romanae, una cum antidoto*: 157.34; 160.12:B

Wake, Sir Isaac. *Rex Platonicus*: 165.48
Walsingham, Thomas. *Historia brevis Thomae Walsingham, ab Edwardo primo, ad Henricum quintum*: 159.26
Warre, James. *touchstone of truth, The*: 165.98
Waser, Caspar. *Institutio linguae Syrae*: 159.144; 159.247
Wecker, Hanss Jacob. *Unidentified*: 154.44
Wesenbecius, Matthaeus. *Digesta: commentary*: 156.51
Whear, Diggory. *Relectiones hymenales, de ratione et methodo legendi utrasque; historias, civiles et ecclesiasticas*: 165.80
Whitaker, William. *Ad Nicolai Sanderi demonstrationes quadraginta, in octavo visibilis Monarchiae positas, responsio*: 157.37; 159.136; *Praelectiones. . .in quibus tractatur controversia de ecclesia*: 157.18; *Unidentified*: 159.85
Whitgift, John, *Archbishop. defense of the aunswere to the Admonition, against the Replie, The*: 154.20
Wiclif, John. *Two short treatises, against the orders of the begging friars*: 159.397
Widdrington, Roger, *pseudonym. Apologia cardinalis Bellarmini pro jure principum* (probable): 159.326
Widley, George. *doctrine of the sabbath, handled in foure treatises, The*: 160.9
Wier, Johann. *De praestigiis daemonum*: 155.7
Wilcox, Thomas. *exposition uppon the booke of the Canticles, An*: 154.117; *Psalms: commentary*: 154.53; *short, yet sound commentarie; written on the Proverbes of Salomon, A*: 154.52
Wildenbergius, Hieronymus. *Totius philosophiae humanae digestio* (probable): 159.485
Wilkes, William. *Obedience or ecclesiasticall union*: 159.192
Willet, Andrew. *catholicon, that is, a generall preservative or remedie against the pseudocatholike religion, gathered out of the epistle of S. Jude, A*: 157.50; *Limbomastix: that is, a canvise of Limbus patrum, shewing that Christ descended not in soule to hell*: 159.513; *Synopsis papismi, that is, a generall viewe of papistry*: 154.59; *Tractatus de Salomonis nuptiis*: 160.27
William, *of Newburgh. Rerum anglicarum libri quinque*: 159.224
Willich, Jodocus. *Commentaria in utramque ad Timotheum Pauli epistolam*: 151.11
Wolleb, Johann. *Unidentified*: 165.63
Worthington, Thomas. *Unidentified*: 159.170.
Wright, Thomas, *Priest. passions of the minde, The*: 159.195

Xenophon. *Works*: 159.27

Zanchius, Hieronymus. *Compendium praecipuorum capitum doctrinae Christianae*: 158.9; *De incarnatione Filii Dei*: 154.80; *De natura Dei, seu de divinis attributis, libri V*: 158.7; *De operibus Dei intra spacium sex dierum creatis opus*: 154.35; 161.2; *De redemptione*: 154.32; *De religione christiana fides*: 154.61; 158.8; *De scriptura sacra*: 154.79; *De tribus Elohim*: 154.33; *In D. Pauli epistolam ad Ephesios, commentarius*: 154.34; *Tractationum theologicarum volumen*: 154.32; *Unidentified*: 154.88
Zepper, Wilhelm. *Unidentified*: 154.110
Zerbus, Gabriel. *Liber anathomie corporis humani*: 159.24
Zosimus, *the Historian. Historia nova*: 165.6:B
Zwingli, Ulrich. *In evangelicam historiam de Jesu Christo annotationes*: 157.2; *New Testament: commentary*: 154.19

Index II
Editors and Compilers

Allenson, John: 157.18
Antesignanus, Petrus: 165.73
Arias Montano, Benito: 159.5; 162.1
Artopoeus, Petrus: 159.244
Ascham, Margaret: 159.302
Barclay, John (probable): 159.324
Beard, Thomas: 155.8
Bellerus, Gaspar: 159.254
Bersmanus, Gregorius: 159.234; 159.338
Bèze, Théodore de: 152.4:3; 156.35; 159.237
Bond, John: 159.426
Bunny, Edmund: 154.84
Camers, Joannes: 165.61
Cloquius, Andries: 165.60
Cope, Alan: 159.81
Crosse, Richard: 157.10
Crossfield, Thomas: 165.112
Daneau, Lambert: 154.112; 159.379
Danett, Thomas: 159.389
Drusius, Joannes, *the Elder*: 165.106
Du Jon, François, *the Elder*: 154.238; 159.299
Estienne, Henri, *the Younger*: 165.23
Farnaby, Thomas: 165.34; 165.50
Fell, Samuel (probable): 159.112:1
Flacius, Matthias, *Illyricus*: 162.14
Freigius, Joannes Thomas: 156.64; 165.88
Fuchs, Leonard: 159.297
Fulke, William: 154.15; 157.1
Galen: 159.297
Garlandius, Joannes: 159.452
Gelen, Sigmund: 165.17
Goulston, Theodore: 164.14
Grant, Edward: 154.170
Hatcher, Thomas: 159.141
Hester, John: 154.204
Humphrey, Laurence: 154.200
James, Thomas: 159.397
Juda, Leo: 157.2
Kimchi, David: 162.11:1
Kirsten, Peter: 166.7:3
Lambinus, Dionysius: 154.37

Lawne, William: 154.84
Leyser, Polykarp: 154.55
Lipsius, Justus: 158.17
Maceriensis, Joannes: 159.34
Magini, Giovanni Antonio: 159.75
Magirus, John: 165.40
Meyen, Joannes a: 159.231
Morel, Federic: 165.4
Pacius, Julius: 154.45; 159.405; 165.41
Pareus, David: 154.98
Pareus, Johann Philipp: 159.310
Parker, Matthew, *Archbishop*: 159.26
Perkins, George: 165.53
Perkins, George (perhaps): 164.48
Pezel, Christoph: 155.10
Philander, Gulielmus: 165.3
Piscator, Johann: 159.484
Pricket, Robert: 161.10:1
Pulton, Ferdinand: 159.103
Rastell, William: 156.1:4; 159.40
Reuchlin, Johann (probable): 159.295
Sabinus, Georgius: 154.143
Salvart, Jean-François: 154.207
Scaliger, Joseph Juste: 165.23; 165.64
Servius Maurus Honoratus: 154.28
Sylburg, Friedrich: 165.125; 166.2
Sylvius, Dethlerus: 159.463
Vatablus, Franciscus: 162.27
Vinet, Élie: 165.61
Ward, Samuel, *of Cambridge*: 157.15

Index III
Translators

Alexander, William, *Earl of Sterling*: 165.51
Amyot, Jacques, *Bishop*: 152.17
Arias Montano, Benito: 159.5

Barker, William (perhaps): 159.119
Bavande, William: 159.124
Beard, Thomas: 155.8
Bedingfield, Thomas: 159.172
Bèze, Théodore de: 154.21; 156.35; 159.237
Blandy, William: 159.128
Boscán, Juan: 159.304
Bowes, Thomas: 159.102

Carew, Richard (probable): 159.532
Clerke, Bartholomew: 158.24
Cruso, John: 165.74

Danett, Thomas: 159.389
Dee, John (perhaps): 158.16
Du Jon, François, *the Elder*: 158.1; 159.19; 159.299; 159.536
Dulcken, Antonius: 160.47

Eden, Richard: 159.120
Elyot, Sir Thomas: 159.469
Ens, Gaspar: 159.387
Eobanus, Helius, *Hessus*: 154.156
Erasmus, Desiderius: 151.20
Erpenius, Thomas: 166.7:1
Estienne, Henri, *the Younger*: 159.29

Fen, John: 153.11
Fenton, Sir Geoffrey: 159.54
Fenton, Sir Geoffrey (probable): 159.140
Fetherstone, Christopher: 152.7
Fuchs, Leonard: 159.297

Genebrardus, Gilbertus, *Archbishop*: 162.20

Hakewill, George (perhaps): 159.180
Harmar, John, *the Elder*: 152.4:2; 154.51
Healey, John: 159.305

Hervet, Gentian: 159.29
Hester, John: 154.204
Hill, Robert: 153.19:2

Iden, Henry: 159.296

James I, *King*: 165.51
Jerome, *Saint*: 154.100; 159.32; 159.246
Junius, Franciscus, *the Elder*: 154.4

Kinder, Henry: 154.229
Kirsten, Peter: 166.7:3

Leunclavius, Joannes: 165.6:B
Lok, Michael (perhaps): 159.120
Lynne, Walter (perhaps): 154.211

Malineus, Gulielmus: 151.28
Martin, Gregory: 154.15
Martinez van Waucquier, Matthias: 161.5
Molle, John: 157.11

North, Sir Thomas: 154.30; 155.3; 159.50

Orandus, Eirenaeus: 165.135
Oranus, Joannes: 159.331

P, G: 165.102
Pacius, Julius: 164.45; 165.5
Pagit, Eusebius: 152.7
Pagninus, Sanctes: 159.5
Pareus, David: 157.10
Parry, Henry, *Bishop*: 157.10
Paynell, Thomas: 159.125
Perpezatius, Joannes: 159.343
Politianus, Angelus: 165.6:A

Raemond, Jean-Charles de: 159.345
Ratcliffe, Aegremont (perhaps): 159.132

Stocker, Thomas: 159.134
Stupanus, Johann Niklaus: 154.159; 159.226

Telius, Sylvester: 154.158
Telius, Sylvester (probable): 159.291
Tremellius, Joannes Immanuel: 154.4; 158.1; 159.19; 159.536
Tuppius, Laurentius: 154.196

Twyne, Thomas: 159.97

Udall, John: 152.18; 154.136

Venturi, Francesco: 156.11
Vulcanius, Bonaventura: 154.240

Whitaker, William: 154.58; 165.59
Whitehorne, Peter: 159.94

Index IV
Stationers
(Publishers, Printers, Booksellers)

The stationers' names in the annotated book–lists are drawn either from imprints and colophons, which offer the names in a variety of forms, or from bibliographical sources, none of which consistently agree with another on those forms. For indexing purposes and for searching the database, PLRE has, therefore, constructed a uniform stationers' name list. English stationers' names, with a few exceptions, are derived from the STC, Volume 3; the forms of Continental names drive from a number of sources, including the STC, but most especially Adams. Accordingly, the names below do not always duplicate forms that appear in the annotated book–lists.

Adams, Thomas: 159.193:1; 159.193:2
Aggas, Edward (perhaps): 159.132
Albinus, Bernardus: 154.198
Albinus, Joannes: 159.223; 159.261; 159.332; 159.340; 159.337; 159.531
Allde, Edward (probable): 159.214
Allott, Robert: 165.14; 165.50
Andreae, Joannes: 159.215
Antonius, Wilhelm: 159.202
Aspley, William: 159.139; 159.500; 160.15; 160.31

Barbirius, Nicolaus: 157.21; 157.23:1; 157.23:2;
Barker, Christopher: 159.149
Barker, Christopher, Deputies of: 152.19; 154.15; 154.65; 154.66; 159.138
Barker, Robert: 159.106; 159.155; 159.189; 159.190; 159.209; 159.396
Barker, Robert (probable): 159.188
Barnes, John: 159.111; 160.11
Barnes, Joseph: 152.4:2; 154.51; 157.8; 157.10; 157.34; 157.35; 159.77; 159.89; 159.96; 159.99; 159.166; 159.183; 159.186; 159.397; 160.11; 160.16; 165.93:2
Barret, William: 159.305
Bartlet, John: 165.57:1
Bascarinis, Nicolaus de: 156.11
Bassaeus, Nicolaus: 159.339
Basson, Govert: 159.323; 159.325
Beale, John: 165.14; 165.57:2
Behem, Caspar: 159.201
Behem, Franciscus (perhaps): 159.342
Bellet, François (probable): 165.77
Bene-natus, Joannes: 154.220
Berthelet, Thomas: 159.107; 165.12

Besicken, Joannes: 154.219
Beys, Adrien: 159.360; 159.527
Beys, Gilles: 153.20
Bill, John: 159.112:1; 159.216; 165.83
Bindoni, Francesco, *the Younger*: 156.67
Bindoni, Gaspar, et fratres: 156.67
Birckman, Arnold, Heirs of: 159.342
Bishop, Edward: 159.314
Bishop, George: 152.7; 154.40; 154.63; 154.64; 154.67; 159.178; 159.209; 159.227; 159.241; 159.495
Blount, Edward: 159.159; 159.305; 159.313;
Blower, Ralph: 158.41
Bollifant, Edmund: 154.90
Bolton, Robert: 159.515
Bomberg, Daniel: 162.2
Bomberg, Daniel (probable): 162.6
Boyle, Richard: 159.180
Bradock, Richard (probable): 159.130
Bradwood, Melchisidec: 159.313
Bragadini, Alvise (probable): 162.3
Broome, Joan: 157.10
Browne, John 1: 159.55
Burby, Cuthbert: 159.211
Burre, Walter: 159.195
Butter, Nathaniel: 159.351; 161.10:2
Bynneman, Henry: 159.20; 159.26; 159.119; 159.133; 159.148; 159.227

Cardon, Horatius: 159.317; 159.343
Cartier, Gabriel: 154.68:2
Cawood, John: 159.40; 159.296
Chard, Thomas: 154.58; 154.91; 154.92; 154.93; 157.37; 158.41; 159.98; 159.136; 159.389
Chaudiere, Regnaud: 159.341
Chemlin, Kaspar: 161.6; 165.1
Cloquius, Andries: 165.60
Cockyn, Henry: 159.137
Coldock, Francis: 154.170; 159.131
Colinaeus, Simon: 159.31; 159.516
Commelinus, Heironymus: 162.27; 166.2
Conincx, Arnout: 159.135
Cooke, Toby: 152.4:2; 154.51
Corvinus, Christoph: 154.89:1; 154.89:2; 154.239; 159.268; 159.504
Courteau, Thomas: 157.21; 157.22; 157.23:1; 157.23:2
Crato, Johann, Heirs of: 157.41; 159.251
Cripps, Henry: 165.86
Crith, Johann: 160.47

Daniel, Roger: 165.74
Davis, Richard: 165.79:2
Dawson, Thomas: 152.7
Dawson, Thomas (probable): 159.97
Dawson, Thomas (perhaps): 159.132; 159.134
Day, John 1: 152.4:1; 152.4:4; 154.209; 156.4; 159.184
Day, John 1 (probable): 159.285
Denham, Henry: 159.98
Dexter, Robert: 154.193
Durerius, Ivo: 151.18
Duval, Denys: 153.20

Egelnolph, Paul: 154.161
Eld, George: 158.45; 159.171; 159.173; 159.192; 159.197; 159.515; 160.11
Eld, George (probable): 159.196; 159.305; 159.515; 161.10:2
Eliot's Court Press: 154.40; 154.66; 165.100
Eliot's Court Press (probable): 159.178
Eliot's Court Press (perhaps): 159.156
Elzevir, House of: 166.7:1
Emmelius, Samuel: 159.452
Erpenius, House of: 166.7:1

Faber, Franciscus: 165.19
Fabricius, Blasius: 165.26
Father Garnet's First Press: 158.39
Field, Richard: 159.43; 159.143; 159.468; 165.132
Field, Richard (probable): 159.108; 159.158; 159.216
Fischer, Jakob, Heirs of: 165.24
Foillet, Jacob: 154.159
Forrest, Edward: 164.16; 165.52; 165.86; 165.90
Forster, Michael: 154.203
Forsteriano, ex typographia: 159.87
Fosbrooke, Nathaniel: 159.130; 159.214; 160.6
Fouler, Joannes: 153.11
Froben, Johann: 165.7
Froschouer, Christoph: 154.16; 154.18; 154.19; 157.2

Gilles, Nicolas: 156.45
Giustiniani, Marcantonio: 162.11:2
Godwin, Joseph: 165.79:2; 165.102
Grevenbruch, Gerard: 159.387
Griffin, Edward 1: 159.351; 164.14
Griffin, Edward 1 (probable): 159.112:1
Gross, Henning: 159.234
Gryphius, Sebastian, Heirs of: 156.14:1

Guarinus, Thomas: 154.135
Gubbin, Thomas: 159.205
Gymnicus, Joannes 2: 162.17

Haestens, Hendrik Lodowijcxsoon van: 159.269
Hall, William: 159.198; 159.505
Harnisch, Josua: 154.32; 154.80
Harnisch, Mattheaus: 154.34; 154.35; 154.61
Harnisch, Wilhelm: 154.32
Harnisch, Wilhelm, Widow of : 158.9
Harsy, Antonius de, Widow of: 165.21
Hatfield, Arnold: 157.17; 159.193:2; 159.194
Helme, John: 159.196; 159.441; 159.493
Henricpetri, Sebastian: 154.191
Henricpetrina, House of: 151.3
Hierat, Antonius: 162.17
Hodgets, John: 159.198
Hoffman, Wilhelm: 159.349
Hoffman, Wolfgang: 165.24
Hondius, Jodocus: 159.181
Huggins, Thomas: 165.96

Islip, Adam: 155.8; 158.16; 159.314

Jackson, Hugh: 157.25
Jackson, John 1: 154.90
Jackson, Roger: 159.192
Jacquin, François: 165.4
Jaggard, John: 158.38
James, Jacob, *pseudonym*: 159.238
Jobin, Bernhard: 156.71
Johnson, Arthur: 159.176
Juvenis, Martin: 159.29

Kempensis, Godefridus: 159.464
Kinckius, Johann: 161.5
Kingston, Felix: 159.124; 159.134; 159.139; 159.200; 159.211; 159.500; 160.9; 160.15; 165.50
Kingston, Felix (probable): 159.508; 159.509; 159.513; 160.31;
Kirsten, Peter: 166.7:3
Kitson, Abraham: 154.57

L, F: 165.72:2
Lancellotus, Joannes: 159.62
Law, Matthew: 159.152
Legat, John 1: 154.57; 154.192; 154.208; 154.225; 154.227; 154.242; 157.7; 157.15; 157.18; 157.50; 159.393

Legge, Cantrell: 159.112:2
Le Preux, Franciscus: 154.17
Le Preux, Joannes: 154.77; 154.78; 154.86; 154.154; 154.235; 154.236
Le Preux, Ponset: 159.34
Lichfield, John: 165.96
Lichfield, Leonard: 165.52; 165.79.2;165.80; 165.86; 165.96; 165.136
Lippius, Balthasar: 159.289
Locatellus, Bonetus: 159.24
Lownes, Matthew: 159.55; 159.95
Lownes, Humphrey 1: 159.95
Lownes, Humphrey 1 (probable): 159.55
Lucius, Jacob: 154.25

Maire, Jean: 166.7:1
Man, Thomas 1: 154.49; 154.52; 154.53; 154.59; 154.117; 157.12; 157.13; 157.19; 157.51; 159.158; 159.513; 160.9
Mareschall, Joannes: 159.299
Marriot, John: 165.54
Marsh, Thomas: 154.230; 159.50; 159.128; 159.140; 159.172
Mathewes, Augustine: 165.98
Middleton, Henry: 157.25
Middleton, Henry (probable): 159.137
Millangius, Simon: 159.345
Moretus, Joannes: 159.353
Myliander, Stephan: 164.12
Mylius, Crato: 151.11

Newbery, Ralph: 154.41; 154.64; 154.67; 154.76; 159.209
Newbery, Ralph (perhaps): 159.119
Newman, Thomas: 159.205
Norton, House of: 165.100
Norton, John: 159.156
Nutius, Martin, Heirs of: 159.361

Okes, Nicholas: 160.30
Okes, Nicholas (probable): 159.208; 161.10:1
Oporinus, House of: 152.10:1
Oporinus, Joannes: 156.28; 162.14
Orwin, Joan: 154.59; 165.95
Orwin, Thomas: 154.52; 154.59; 154.92; 158.19; 159.205; 165.91

Page, William (probable): 159.522
Palthenius, Zacharias: 159.235; 165.38
Pasquatus, Laurentius: 159.117
Patisson, Mamert: 165.64
Pesnot, Carolus: 159.245
Petri, Henricus: 159.51

Plantin, Christopher: 153.7; 154.197; 159.81; 159.105; 162.1; 165.18
Plantin, House of: 154.69; 154.202; 154.231; 154.240; 159.82; 159.114; 159.144; 159.353; 165.106
Porter, John: 154.200
Potter, George: 157.11
Purfoote, Thomas 1: 159.163

Quentel, Arnold: 159.263
Quentel, Peter: 159.71

Rade, Gilles van den: 157.28
Rand, Samuel: 160.30
Raphelengius, Franciscus: 152.18; 154.69; 154.82; 154.136; 154.202; 154.231; 154.240; 159.114; 159.144; 165.106
Rassfeldt, Lambertus: 159.498
Raworth, Robert (probable): 161.10:1
Read, Richard (probable): 159.159
Redmer, Richard: 159.505
Rhodius, Jona: 159.62; 159.310
Riverius, Gulielmus: 159.496; 159.521
Robinson, Robert: 159.204
Rocket, Henry (perhaps): 159.173
Rouille, Guillaume: 159.294

Sanctandreanus, House of: 154.68:1; 159.503
Sanctandreanus, Petrus: 154.207; 154.107; 165.22
Sartorius, Adam: 159.210; 159.395
Schirat, Michael: 154.201
Schleich, Clemens: 159.64
Schönfeld, Johann: 159.512
Scotus, Octavianus, Heirs of (probable): 159.24
Seile, Henry: 165.29
Selden, John: 159.441; 159.493
Seton, Gregory: 159.182; 159.194
Shaw, George: 158.41
Short, Peter: 159.389
Simmes, Valentine: 159.195
Singleton, Hugh: 154.229
Singleton, Hugh (probable): 159.522
Smith, Toby: 159.134
Smith, Ralph: 159.133
Snodham, Thomas: 159.441; 159.493; 165.135
Snodham, Thomas (probable): 159.180; 161.10:2
Snowdon, Lionel: 157.11
Soter, Joannes: 165.47
Spies, Johann: 154.55; 154.56
Stafford, Simon: 158.38

Stansby, William: 159.100
Stansby, William (probable): 160.6
Steelsius, Joannes: 151.28
Steinman, Johann: 159.234
Stephanus, Franciscus: 159.516
Stephanus, Henricus 2: 156.25; 159.279; 165.6:A; 165.6:B
Stephanus, Henricus 2 (probable): 165.23
Stephanus, Robertus 1: 165.8
Stephanus, Robertus 2: 165.64
Stoer, Jacobus: 165.31
Strasser, Johann: 159.39

Thorp, Giles: 159.181
Thorpe, Thomas: 158.45; 159.171
Tottel, Richard: 159.40; 159.151
Tournes, Jean de: 165.3
Toy, Humphrey: 154.20
Tramezino, Michele: 156.11
Turner, William: 164.16; 165.90; 165.103. 165.112

Vautrollier, Thomas 1: 154.54; 154.58; 154.84; 157.37; 159.136; 159.495
Vautrollier, Thomas 2: 159.202
Vignon, Eustathius: 152.4:3; 154.73; 154.102; 154.112; 157.32; 157.38
Vignon, Eustathius (probable): 159.366
Vignon, House of: 165.5
Vignon, Jean: 165.61

Waldegrave, Robert: 154.97; 154.117
Waldkirch, Konrad von: 158.6; 159.443
Walkley, Thomas: 165.135
Walley, John: 159.40
Waterson, Simon: 157.15; 157.50; 159.77; 159.90; 159.96; 159.185; 159.197; 159.208
Waterson, Simon (perhaps): 157.7; 159.186
Watkins, Richard: 159.97
Weaver, Edmund: 159.143; 159.211
Webb, William 1: 165.112
Wechel, Andreas: 154.139; 159.258
Wechel, Johann, Widow of: 159.339
White, William: 159.253
White, William (perhaps): 159.110
Wight, John: 159.124
Willer, Georg: 159.350
Williams, John (perhaps): 165.74
Windet, John: 154.206; 157.33; 159.152; 159.532
Wolfe, Reyner: 152.4:5; 153.4
Wolfe, John: 159.108; 159.179; 159.509
Wolfe, John (probable): 159.131

Wolff, Johann: 159.349
Woodcock, Thomas: 158.19; 165.91
Wykes, Henry: 153.16

Zetzner, Lazarus: 159.312; 159.329;165.2; 165.25
Ziletti, Giordano: 156.29

Index V
Places of Publication

Amberg: 154.203; 159.87; 159.512
Amsterdam: 159.157; 159.181; 165.121
Antwerp: 153.7; 154.197; 159.105; 159.135; 159.353; 159.361; 165.11; 165.18; 151.28; 162.1; 159.81
Arras: 159.496; 159.521

Basle: 151.3; 152.10:1; 152.10:2; 154.8; 154.44; 154.135; 154.191; 156.28; 158.6; 159.51; 159.443; 165.7; 165.39; 159.244; 162.14
Bordeaux: 159.345
Breslau: 166.7:3
Britain: 152.3:1–2; 152.4:2; 153.6; 153.19:2; 154.199; 154.226; 154.233; 154.234; 156.5:1–4; 158.4; 158.5; 158.40; 159.73; 159.78; 159.129; 159.221; 159.328; 159.384; 159.425; 159.520; 164.6; 164.7; 164.9; 164.10; 164.15; 164.71; 165.13; 165.51; 165.57:1; 165.92; 165.93:1; 165.110
Britain (probable): 156.5:1–4; 159.187; 159.199;
Britain (perhaps): 159.47
Britain or Continent: 151.1; 151.4; 151.7:1; 151.7:2; 151.8; 151.9; 151.12; 151.14; 151.17; 151.19; 151.20; 151.23; 151.24; 151.31;151.33; 151.35; 151.37; 151.41; 152.1:1; 152.1:2; 152.1:3; 152.1:4; 152.9:2; 153.2; 153.8; 153.9; 153.10; 153.12; 153.13:1; 153.13:2; 153.17; 153.18:1; 153.18:2; 153.19:1; 154.4; 154.23; 154.47; 154.62; 154.70; 154.75; 154.94; 154.96; 154.99; 154.101; 154.103; 154.104; 154.105; 154.106; 154.125; 154.128; 154.129; 154.138; 154.140:1; 154.140:2; 154.141; 154.142; 154.143; 154.148; 154.149; 154.153; 154.164; 154.166; 154.173; 154.177; 154.182; 154.189; 154.195; 154.215; 154.216; 154.217; 154.223; 154.224; 154.246; 154.247; 155.1; 155.11; 156.18; 156.19; 156.31; 156.36; 156.38; 156.40; 156.41; 156.47:1; 156.47:2; 156.50; 156.54:1; 156.66; 156.72; 157.20; 157.24; 157.30; 157.31; 157.39; 157.43; 157.45:2; 157.46; 157.52; 158.1; 158.2; 158.8; 158.20; 158.24; 158.25; 158.27; 158.28; 158.32; 158.34; 158.35; 158.37; 158.44; 159.19; 159.85; 159.88; 159.91; 159.146; 159.150; 159.156; 159.202; 159.239; 159.256; 159.257; 159.259; 159.260; 159.265; 159.266; 159.267; 159.275; 159.306; 159.324; 159.326; 159.347; 159.388; 159.390; 159.398; 159.407:A; 159.410; 159.411; 159.413; 159.415; 159.416; 159.432; 159.435; 159.437; 159.439:1; 159.439:2; 159.440; 159.451; 159.459; 159.474; 159.476; 159.483; 159.484; 159.488; 159.489; 159.491; 159.499:A; 159.506; 159.507; 159.510; 159.523; 159.524; 159.528; 159.538; 160.2; 160.3; 160.10; 160.12:A; 160.12:B; 160.20; 160.23; 160.26; 160.27; 160.32:1; 160.32:2; 160.36; 160.39; 160.43; 160.45; 160.46; 161.1; 161.8; 161.11; 163.1:1; 164.2; 164.3; 164.5; 164.13; 164.17; 164.19; 164.23; 164.30:1; 164.30:2; 164.31; 164.32; 164.34; 164.36; 164.37; 164.38; 164.39; 164.41; 164.43; 164.44; 164.47; 164.48; 164.50; 164.52; 164.54; 164.56; 164.57; 164.59; 164.60; 164.65; 164.67; 164.70; 165.32; 165.35; 165.37; 165.45; 165.49:A; 165.53; 165.70; 165.75; 165.78; 165.89:1;

165.89:2; 165.97; 165.99; 165.108; 165.115; 165.118; 165.124; 165.127; 165.128; 165.137; 166.4; 166.7:2

Cambridge: 157.7; 157.18; 159.112:2; 159.393; 165.74
Cambridge and London: 157.15; 157.50
Cologne: 154.157; 154.205; 155.12; 159.71; 159.263; 159.342; 159.387; 159.464; 160.24; 162.17; 165.10; 165.25; 160.47; 161.5; 165.47

Continent: 151.2; 151.5; 151.6; 151.16; 151.21; 151.25; 151.29:1; 151.30; 151.34:1; 151.34:2; 151.38; 151.40; 151.42:1; 151.42:2; 152.5; 152.8; 152.11; 152.12; 152.13; 152.14; 153.1; 153.3; 153.5; 153.14; 153.15; 154.1; 154.2; 154.3; 154.5; 154.7; 154.9; 154.11:1; 154.11:2; 154.12; 154.13; 154.14; 154.21; 154.22; 154.26; 154.27; 154.28; 154.29; 154.33; 154.36; 154.37; 154.38; 154.39; 154.45; 154.46; 154.60; 154.71; 154.74; 154.79; 154.81; 154.83; 154.85; 154.87; 154.88; 154.98; 154.100; 154.109; 154.110; 154.114; 154.115; 154.116; 154.118; 154.119; 154.120; 154.121; 154.122; 154.123; 154.124; 154.126; 154.127; 154.130; 154.131; 154.132; 154.133; 154.134; 154.137; 154.139; 154.144; 154.145; 154.146; 154.147; 154.150; 154.151; 154.152; 154.155; 154.158; 154.160; 154.162; 154.165; 154.167; 154.168; 154.169; 154.171; 154.175; 154.176; 154.178; 154.181; 154.183; 154.184; 154.186; 154.187; 154.188; 154.190; 154.194; 154.196; 154.212; 154.213; 154.218; 154.221; 154.222; 154.232; 154.237; 154.243; 154.244; 154.245; 155.2; 155.4; 155.5; 155.7; 155.9; 155.10; 155.13; 156.2; 156.6; 156.7; 156.8; 156.9; 156.12; 156.13; 156.15; 156.16; 156.17; 156.21; 156.23; 156.24; 156.25; 156.27; 156.30; 156.32; 156.33; 156.35; 156.37; 156.39; 156.42; 156.43; 156.44; 156.46; 156.48; 156.51; 156.52; 156.53; 156.54:2; 156.55; 156.56; 156.57; 156.58; 156.59; 156.60; 156.61; 156.63; 156.64; 156.65; 156.68:1; 156.68:2; 156.69; 156.70; 157.3; 157.4; 157.6; 157.9; 157.26; 157.27; 157.29; 157.40; 157.42; 157.44; 157.45:1; 157.47; 157.48; 157.49; 158.7; 158.10; 158.11; 158.12; 158.13; 158.14; 158.15; 158.17; 158.18; 158.21; 158.22; 158.23; 158.26; 158.29; 158.30; 158.31; 158.33; 158.36; 159.1; 159.2; 159.3; 159.4; 159.5; 159.6; 159.7; 159.8; 159.9; 159.10; 159.11; 159.12; 159.13; 159.14; 159.15; 159.16; 159.17; 159.18; 159.20; 159.21; 159.22; 159.23; 159.25; 159.27; 159.30; 159.32; 159.33; 159.35; 159.36; 159.37; 159.38; 159.42; 159.43; 159.44; 159.45; 159.46; 159.48; 159.58; 159.59; 159.60; 159.61; 159.63; 159.65; 159.66; 159.67; 159.68; 159.72; 159.74; 159.75; 159.80; 159.82; 159.83; 159.84; 159.86; 159.92; 159.101; 159.104; 159.109; 159.113; 159.115; 159.116:1; 159.116:2; 159.142; 159.145; 159.153; 159.160; 159.161; 159.164; 159.167; 159.217; 159.218:A; 159.219; 159.220; 159.222; 159.224; 159.225; 159.226; 159.228; 159.229; 159.230; 159.231; 159.232; 159.233; 159.236; 159.237; 159.240; 159.241; 159.242; 159.243; 159.246; 159.248; 159.249; 159.250; 159.254; 159.255; 159.262; 159.264; 159.271; 159.272; 159.273; 159.276; 159.278; 159.280; 159.281; 159.284; 159.286; 159.287; 159.288; 159.290; 159.293; 159.295; 159.297; 159.298; 159.300; 159.301; 159.303; 159.304; 159.307; 159.308; 159.309; 159.311; 159.318; 159.319; 159.320; 159.321; 159.322; 159.327; 159.330; 159.331; 159.334; 159.336; 159.338; 159.344; 159.346; 159.352; 159.354; 159.355; 159.356; 159.358; 159.359; 159.362; 159.363; 159.364; 159.367; 159.370; 159.371; 159.372; 159.373; 159.374; 159.375; 159.377; 159.382; 159.383; 159.385;

159.386; 159.391; 159.392; 159.394; 159.399; 159.402; 159.403; 159.404;
159.405; 159.406; 159.408; 159.412; 159.414; 159.417; 159.418; 159.419; 159.420;
159.421; 159.423; 159.429; 159.430; 159.431; 159.434; 159.436; 159.442; 159.444;
159.447; 159.449; 159.450; 159.453; 159.454; 159.455; 159.458; 159.460; 159.461;
159.462; 159.463; 159.465; 159.466; 159.471; 159.472; 159.477; 159.478; 159.479;
159.480; 159.481; 159.482; 159.485; 159.486; 159.497; 159.501; 159.511; 159.514;
159.519; 159.525; 159.529; 159.530; 159.537; 160.1; 160.4; 160.5; 160.8; 160.13;
160.14; 160.17; 160.18; 160.19; 160.22; 160.33; 160.34; 160.35; 160.37; 160.38;
160.41; 160.42:1–3; 160.44; 161.2; 161.3; 161.4; 161.9; 162.4; 162.5; 162.7:1;
162.7:2; 162.8; 162.9; 162.10:1; 162.10:2; 162.12; 162.13; 162.15; 162.16; 162.18;
162.19; 162.20; 162.21; 162.22; 162.23; 162.24; 162.25; 162.26; 162.28; 162.29;
162.30; 162.31; 162.32; 162.33; 162.34; 162.35; 162.36; 162.37; 162.38; 162.39;
164.1; 164.4; 164.8; 164.11; 164.18; 164.20; 164.21; 164.24; 164.25; 164.26;
164.27; 164.28; 164.29; 164.42; 164.45; 164.46; 164.58; 164.61; 164.62; 164.64;
164.66; 164.69; 165.9; 165.16:1; 165.16:2; 165.17; 165.27; 165.28; 165.36; 165.41;
165.42; 165.43; 165.44; 165.56; 165.58; 165.62; 165.65; 165.66; 165.67; 165.68;
165.72:1; 165.76; 165.79:1; 165.81; 165.82; 165.84; 165.88; 165.94; 165.104;
165.105; 165.109; 165.111; 165.114; 165.116; 165.117; 165.119; 165.122; 165.123;
165.125; 165.129; 165.133; 166.1; 166.3

Continent (probable): 151.10:1; 151.10:2; 151.26; 151.29:2; 151.36; 154.24; 154.113;
154.156;; 156.10; 156.14:2; 156.22; 156.34; 156.49:1–2; 158.3; 159.49; 159.52;
159.70; 159.162; 159.170; 159.270; 159.277; 159.291; 159.348; 159.365; 159.376;
159.400; 159.422; 159.424; 159.427; 159.428; 159.445; 159.448; 159.457; 159.467;
159.470; 159.473; 159.490; 159.492; 164.35; 164.68; 165.20; 165.134

Delft: 159.215

Edinburgh: 154.97; 159.238

Franeker: 157.28
Frankfurt am Main: 154.6; 154.55; 154.56; 159.62; 159.235; 159.258; 159.310; 159.339;
159.349; 164.55:1; 164.55:2; 165.24; 165.33; 165.38; 165.40; 165.113
Freiburg: 159.39

Geneva: 152.2:2; 154.10; 154.17; 154.73; 154.77; 154.78; 154.86; 154.102; 154.107;
154.112; 154.154; 154.207; 154.236; 157.21; 157.22; 157.23:1; 157.23:2; 157.32;
157.38; 159.366; 161.7; 165.31; 165.5; 165.6:A; 152.4:3; 159.379
Geneva (probable): 154.235; 159.279

Hanau: 159.350
Heidelberg: 154.68:1; 154.201; 159.329; 159.503; 162.27; 166.2
Helmstadt: 154.25
Herborn: 159.268; 159.357; 159.504

Ingolstadt: 159.210; 159.395
Isny: 162.11:1

Leipzig: 159.234
Leyden: 154.69; 154.82; 154.202; 154.231; 154.238; 159.114; 159.144; 159.269;
    159.323; 159.325; 159.401; 164.51; 165.126; 166.7:1; 152.18; 154.136; 154.240;
    165.60; 165.106
London: 151.22; 151.27; 152.4:1; 152.4:4; 152.4:5; 152.7; 152.9:1; 152.19; 152.20;
    153.4; 153.16; 154.15; 154.20; 154.30; 154.31; 154.40; 154.41; 154.43; 154.49;
    154.50; 154.52; 154.53; 154.54; 154.57; 154.58; 154.59; 154.63; 154.64; 154.65;
    154.66; 154.67; 154.76; 154.84; 154.90; 154.91; 154.92; 154.93; 154.117;
    154.170; 154.174; 154.192; 154.193; 154.200; 154.204; 154.206; 154.208;
    154.209; 154.211; 154.225; 154.227; 154.229; 154.230; 154.241; 154.242;
    155.3; 155.8; 156.1:4; 156.4; 157.1; 157.11; 157.12; 157.13; 157.14; 157.16; 157.17;
    157.19; 157.25; 157.33; 157.37; 157.51; 158.16;158.19; 158.38; 158.39; 158.41;
    158.45; 159.26; 159.40; 159.50; 159.53; 159.54; 159.55; 159.57; 159.76; 159.90;
    159.93; 159.94; 159.95; 159.97; 159.98; 159.100; 159.102; 159.103; 159.106;
    159.107; 159.108; 159.110; 159.119; 159.120; 159.121; 159.122; 159.124; 159.125;
    159.127; 159.128; 159.130; 159.131; 159.132; 159.133; 159.134; 159.136; 159.137;
    159.138; 159.139; 159.140; 159.141; 159.143; 159.148; 159.149; 159.151; 159.152;
    159.154; 159.155; 159.158; 159.159; 159.163; 159.165; 159.168; 159.171; 159.172;
    159.173; 159.174; 159.175; 159.176; 159.177; 159.178; 159.179; 159.180; 159.182;
    159.184; 159.185; 159.188; 159.189; 159.190; 159.191; 159.192; 159.193:2;
    159.194; 159.195; 159.196; 159.197; 159.198; 159.200; 159.204; 159.205; 159.206;
    159.207; 159.208; 159.209; 159.211; 159.214; 159.216; 159.227; 159.253; 159.274;
    159.282; 159.283; 159.285; 159.296; 159.302; 159.305; 159.313; 159.314;
    159.315; 159.333; 159.351; 159.381; 159.389; 159.396; 159.426; 159.433; 159.441;
    159.468; 159.469; 159.493; 159.495; 159.500; 159.502; 159.505; 159.508;
    159.509; 159.513; 159.515; 159.522; 159.532; 159.534; 159.535; 159.536; 160.6;
    160.9; 160.15; 160.21; 160.29; 160.30; 160.31; 161.10:1; 161.10:2; 164.14; 164.49;
    164.53; 164.63; 164.72; 165.12; 165.14; 165.15; 165.29; 165.34; 165.50; 165.54;
    165.57:2; 165.59; 165.71; 165.72:2; 165.83; 165.87; 165.91; 165.95; 165.98;
    165.100; 165.101; 165.107; 165.130; 165.132; 165.135
London (probable): 151.32; 156.1:1–3; 159.203
London and Cambridge: 157.15; 157.50
London and Oxford: 157.10
Louvain: 153.11
Lusignan: 151.18
Lyon: 156.14:1; 159.69; 159.245; 159.294; 159.317; 159.343; 165.3; 165.21; 165.22;
    165.73

Münster: 159.498
Mainz: 159.201; 159.223; 159.261; 159.289; 159.332; 159.337; 159.340; 159.531
Marburg: 154.161; 165.1
Montbeliard: 154.159
Morges: 154.72

Neustadt an der Haardt: 154.32; 154.34; 154.35; 154.61; 154.79; 154.80; 158.9; 160.7

Oxford: 154.51; 154.228; 157.8; 157.34; 157.35; 159.77; 159.89; 159.96; 159.99; 159.111; 150.112:1; 159.166; 159.183; 159.186; 159.193:1; 159.397; 160.11; 160.16; 164.16; 165.48; 165.52; 165.79:2; 165.80; 165.86; 165.90; 165.93:2; 165.96; 165.102; 165.103; 165.112; 165.136
Oxford and London: 157.10

Padua: 159.117
Paris: 153.20; 154.220; 156.45; 156.62; 159.31; 159.341; 159.360; 159.368; 159.516; 159.518; 159.527; 165.8; 152.17; 159.29; 159.34; 165.4; 165.64
Place not given: 159.28; 159.169; 159.299; 165.19; 165.23
Place unknown: 151.13; 151.15; 151.39; 152.2:1; 152.3:3; 152.6; 152.15; 152.16; 152.21; 153.21; 153.22:1–5; 154.42; 154.68:2; 154.95; 154.108; 154.111; 154.163; 154.180; 154.185; 154.214; 155.14:1–80; 156.3; 156.20; 156.73; 156.74:1–14; 157.36; 159.56; 159.118; 159.123; 159.126; 159.170; 159.212; 159.213; 159.247; 159.252; 159.316; 159.335; 159.369; 159.378; 159.380; 159.409; 159.438; 159.446; 159.456; 159.475; 159.487; 159.517; 159.526; 159.533:1–24; 159.539:1–18; 159.540; 159.541; 160.25; 160.28:1–12; 160.40; 160.48:1–5; 163.1:2; 163.1:3; 164.22; 164.33; 164.40; 165.30; 165.46; 165.55; 165.61; 165.63; 165.69; 165.120; 165.131:1–8; 166.5:1–60; 166.6:1–34; 166.8:1–9; 166.9:1–5; 166.10:1–21; 166.11:1–52; 166.12:1–3; 166.14:1–39; 166.15:1–46; 166.16:1–74; 166.17:1–29
Provenance unknown: 154.48; 154.179; 154.210; 155.6:1:1–2; 155.6:2:1–6; 158.42:1–2; 158.43; 159.41:1–4; 159.79; 159.147; 166.13:1–7

Rome: 154.219
Rostock: 164.12

Saint-Omer: 165.77
Schweinfurt: 161.6
Siegen: 154.89:1; 154.89:2; 154.239
Speier: 154.198
Strassburg: 151.11; 156.71; 159.312; 159.452; 165.2; 165.26

Venice: 156.11; 156.26; 156.29; 156.67; 159.24; 162.2; 162.3; 162.6; 162.11:2

Wittenberg: 154.172; 157.5; 157.41; 159.64; 159.251; 159.292; 159.494

Zürich: 154.16; 154.18; 154.19; 157.2

Index VI
Dates of Publication

Date ranges are not included. The abbreviation *c.* derives from the bibliographical source consulted. The word *probable* is a PLRE qualification.

1491: 159.167
c.1505: 159.34
1506: 154.219
1521: 165.7
1524: 159.31
1525: 159.123
1528: 165.10; 165.47
1531: 159.71
1533: 159.28
1537: 159.107; 165.8
1539: 157.2
1542: 151.11; 162.11:1
1543: 159.516
1545: 156.11
1546: 162.11:2
1547: 162.6
1550: 151.28
1552: 165.3
1554: 165.12
1555: 154.230
1556: 165.26
1557: 159.40; 159.51
1559: 159.124; 159.294
1560: 165.73
1561: 154.135; 156.14:1
1564: 157.21; 157.23:2
1565: 157.22
1566: 153.16; 159.452
1568: 153.11
1569: 151.3; 159.29
1571 (probable): 159.184
1573: 152.4:4; 154.209; 156.67
1574: 154.20; 154.201; 159.26; 159.238
1576: 159.128; 159.133; 159.245
1577: 152.4:1; 154.213; 159.137; 159.148; 165.64
1578: 154.220; 159.119; 159.132; 159.151; 159.299
1579: 159.163
1579: 159.201; 159.522
1580: 159.495; 159.536
1581: 154.207; 159.258; 165.23; 165.6:A; 165.6:B
1583: 154.191; 157.37; 159.136; 159.149; 159.227; 165.18
1583 (probable): 159.134; 152.7; 153.20; 154.72; 159.98; 159.464
1585: 154.117; 157.8
1585 (probable): 154.61
1586: 154.16; 154.73; 154.90; 159.268; 159.279
1587: 152.4:2; 154.51; 154.241; 157.25; 157.41; 159.64; 159.194; 159.251
1588: 154.15; 154.92; 159.131; 159.169; 159.182; 159.205
1589: 153.7; 154.52; 154.197; 159.234
1590: 154.64; 154.67
1591: 154.17; 154.35; 154.97; 158.19; 159.503; 165.106
1592: 154.225; 154.229; 154.236
1593: 152.18; 154.55; 154.57; 154.65; 154.77; 154.80; 154.136; 154.202; 154.226; 154.231; 158.6; 158.39; 159.108; 159.114; 159.179; 159.389; 165.91
1594: 154.34; 154.40; 154.66; 154.68:1; 154.68:2; 154.82; 154.221; 154.242; 159.339; 159.532; 165.22; 166.2
1595: 154.240; 165.95
1596: 154.62; 154.89:1; 154.89:2; 154.203; 154.239; 156.45; 159.204
1597: 154.32; 154.69; 154.195; 154.208; 155.8; 158.41; 159.193:1; 159.209
1598: 154.200; 158.9; 158.16; 159.87; 159.158; 159.193:2; 165.2; 165.38

1599: 157.18
1600: 159.254; 159.393; 159.443; 159.509
1601: 157.10; 159.178; 159.508
1602: 157.50; 158.38; 164.12
1603: 157.17; 159.117; 159.159; 160.16; 165.77
1604: 157.15; 159.314; 159.513; 160.9
1605: 158.45; 159.77; 159.89; 159.171; 159.185; 159.192; 159.202; 159.214; 159.263; 159.317; 159.468; 161.6; 165.5; 165.100
1606: 157.11; 157.13; 157.34; 157.35; 159.90; 159.96; 159.130; 159.143; 159.157; 159.197; 159.211; 159.223; 165.61
1607: 159.135; 159.289; 159.313; 159.353; 159.396; 160.47; 161.10:1; 165.42
1608: 159.99; 159.166; 159.173; 159.261; 159.395; 159.397; 159.498; 159.527
1609: 159.62; 159.181; 159.189; 159.208; 159.341; 159.360; 165.25; 166.7:3; 159.218:A, 159.218:B
1609?: 159.305
1610: 159.92; 159.106; 159.111; 159.155; 159.196; 159.210; 159.269; 159.310;
 159.318; 159.337; 159.349; 159.441; 159.493; 159.515; 159.531; 165.33
1611: 159.180; 159.198; 159.216; 159.326; 159.340; 159.343; 165.21
1612: 159.112:1; 159.112:2; 159.156; 159.215; 159.323; 159.325; 159.329; 159.350; 159.505; 159.512; 165.132
1613: 159.100; 159.351; 160.11; 161.10:2
1614: 159.253
1616: 165.93:2
1619: 164.14; 165.19
1620: 165.4
1621: 165.83
1624: 165.135
1625: 166.7:1
1627: 165.24
1631: 165.14
1634: 165.1; 165.31; 165.50
1637: 165.60; 165.80; 165.86
1638: 165.112
1640: 164.16; 165.90
1648: 165.52
1649: 165.97
1650?: 165.136
1652: 165.72:2; 165.79:2

R. J. Fehrenbach is Professor of English, Emeritus, at the College of William and Mary.

❦

Joseph L. Black is Associate Professor of English at the University of Massachusetts Amherst.